THE OF
MUHA
JURIS

THE ORIGINS OF MUHAMMADAN JURISPRUDENCE

By

JOSEPH SCHACHT

OXFORD
AT THE CLARENDON PRESS

Oxford University Press, Walton Street, Oxford OX2 6DP

OXFORD LONDON GLASGOW

NEW YORK TORONTO MELBOURNE WELLINGTON

KUALA LUMPUR SINGAPORE JAKARTA HONG KONG TOKYO

DELHI BOMBAY CALCUTTA MADRAS KARACHI

NAIROBI DAR ES SALAAM CAPE TOWN

First published 1950
Reprinted 1953, 1959, 1967, and 1975
First published in Paperback 1979

British Library Cataloguing in Publication Data

Schacht, Joseph
The Origins of Muhammadan jurisprudence.
1. Islamic law
I. Title
340.5′9 (Law) 79–40261
ISBN 0–19–825357–5

Printed in Great Britain
at the University Press, Oxford
by Eric Buckley
Printer to the University

PREFACE

THIS book is concerned with the origins of Muhammadan jurisprudence. I shall, of course, often have occasion to refer to examples taken from Muhammadan law, which is the material of Muhammadan jurisprudence. But the history of positive law in Islam as such, and the relationship between the ideals of legal doctrine and the practical administration of justice fall outside the scope of the present inquiry.

The sacred law of Islam is an all-embracing body of religious duties rather than a legal system proper; it comprises on an equal footing ordinances regarding cult and ritual, as well as political and (in the narrow sense) legal rules. In choosing the examples I shall concentrate as much as possible on the (properly speaking) legal sphere. This course not only recommends itself for practical reasons; it is also historically legitimate. For the legal subject-matter in early Islam did not primarily derive from the Koran or from other purely Islamic sources; law lay to a great extent outside the sphere of religion, was only incompletely assimilated to the body of religious duties, and retained part of its own distinctive quality. No clear distinction, however, can be made, and whenever I use the term Muhammadan law, it is meant to comprise all those subjects which come within the sacred law of Islam.

I feel myself under a deep obligation to the masters of Islamic studies in the last generation. The name of Snouck Hurgronje appears seldom in this book; yet if we now understand the character of Muhammadan law it is due to him. Goldziher I shall have occasion to quote often; I cannot hope for more than that this book may be considered a not unworthy continuation of the studies he inaugurated. Margoliouth was the first and foremost among my predecessors to make more than perfunctory use of the then recently printed works of Shāfiʿī; in reviewing the field which is surveyed here in detail he came nearest, both in his general attitude to the sources and in several important details, to my conclusions. Lammens, though his writings rarely touch Muhammadan law and jurisprudence directly, must be mentioned in the preface to a book which is to a great part concerned with the historical appreciation of Islamic 'traditions'; my investigation of legal traditions has brought me to respect and admire his critical insight whenever his *ira et studium* were not engaged. In the present generation, Bergsträsser, with penetrating insight, formulated the main problems posed by the formative period of Muhammadan law and offered a tentative solution. Although my results are rather different from those which he might have expected, I must pay homage to the memory of my late teacher who guided my first steps in Muhammadan jurisprudence.

All my previous studies in Muhammadan law have led, in a way, to the writing of this book. But, when I came to write it, the refusal of the Egyptian authorities to allow me to return to my work and home in Cairo in 1939 deprived me of the use of my library at the time I needed it most. I particularly regret that I was thereby prevented from consulting the *Kitāb al-Ḥujaj* by Shaibānī, the *Kitāb al-Sunan* by Shāfiʿī, the *Kitāb al-Diyāt* by Abū ʿĀṣim Nabīl, the *Muntaqā min Akhbār al-Aṣmaʿī*, and the materials for my own editions, in varying stages of preparation, of the *History of the Judges* by Wakīʿ, of the *Kitāb al-Aṣl* by Shaibānī, and of the *Kitāb al-Masāʾil* by Ibn Ḥanbal. That I was able, notwithstanding this handicap, to use all essential texts, I owe mainly to the British Museum and to the Griffith Institute in Oxford, and to the unfailing courtesy and helpfulness of their staffs.

I wish to express my deepfelt gratitude to the Governing Body of St. John's College, Oxford, and to Mr. K. Sisam, formerly Secretary to the Delegates of the Clarendon Press, for the active interest they took in my studies in general and in this book in particular, and for the assistance they gave me. Professor F. de Zulueta has accompanied my studies in Muhammadan law and jurisprudence with sympathy and interest since the invitation given by him and by the late H. Kantorowicz to contribute to the projected *Oxford History of Legal Science* which unfortunately had to be abandoned. Dr. D.

Daube, of Gonville and Caius College, Cambridge, kindly enlightened me on points of Roman law, and Dr. S. Weinstock of Oxford most obligingly translated for me from the Hungarian a paper by Goldziher. Without the unfailing encouragement and help of Professor H. A. R. Gibb this book would hardly have been completed. Lastly, I wish to thank my wife for her truly invaluable aid in preparing the manuscript; to her I dedicate this book as a *δόσις ὀλίγη τε φίλη τε*.

I cannot do better than address the reader in the words of Shāfi'ī (*Risāla*, 59): 'I lost some of my books but have verified what I remembered from what is known to scholars; I have aimed at conciseness, so as not to make my work too long, and have given only what will be sufficient, without exhausting all that can be known on the subject.'

J. S.

OXFORD
April 1948

PREFACE TO THE FOURTH IMPRESSION

I HAVE made only a few small changes and additions, incorporating some of my more recent conclusions, but have not attempted to add to the book substantially. It remains a work of research that does not aim at giving a comprehensive account of legal science in the first few centuries of Islam. For a general picture of the development of Muhammadan jurisprudence as a whole, from its beginnings to modern times, I may refer the reader to my *Introduction to Islamic Law*, second impression, Oxford, 1966.

January 1967

J. S.

CONTENTS

PART I

THE DEVELOPMENT OF LEGAL THEORY

CHAPTER 1. THE CLASSICAL THEORY OF MUHAMMADAN LAW. THE FUNCTION OF TRADITIONS . 1

CHAPTER 2. THE ANCIENT SCHOOLS OF LAW. SHĀFI'Ī'S ATTITUDE TO THEM . . . 6

CHAPTER 3. SHĀFI'Ī AND LEGAL TRADITIONS . . 11

CHAPTER 4. TRADITIONS IN THE ANCIENT SCHOOLS OF LAW 21

A. The Medinese 22

B. The Iraqians 27

C. The Syrians 34

CHAPTER 5. TECHNICAL CRITICISM OF TRADITIONS BY SHĀFI'Ī AND HIS PREDECESSORS . . 36

CHAPTER 6. ARGUMENTS FOR AND AGAINST TRADITIONS 40

A. Adversaries of traditions in general . . 40

B. Arguments against traditions from the Prophet . 44

C. Arguments in favour of traditions from the Prophet 53

D. Conclusions 57

CHAPTER 7. *SUNNA*, 'PRACTICE', AND 'LIVING TRADITION' 58

A. General 58

B. The Medinese 61

C. The Syrians 70

D. The Iraqians 73

E. Shāfi'ī 77

F. Conclusions 80

CHAPTER 8. CONSENSUS AND DISAGREEMENT . . 82
A. The old idea of consensus . . . 82
B. The Medinese and consensus . . . 83
C. The Iraqians and consensus . . . 85
D. The Muʿtazila and consensus . . . 88
E. Shāfiʿī and consensus . . . 88
F. The later doctrine of consensus . . . 94
G. Disagreement 95

CHAPTER 9. ANALOGY, SYSTEMATIC REASONING, AND PERSONAL OPINION . . . 98
A. The Umaiyad period 100
B. The Iraqians 103
C. The Medinese 113
D. The Syrians 119
E. Shāfiʿī 120
F. The Muʿtazila 128
G. The traditionists 128
H. Traditions against human reasoning in law . 129

CHAPTER 10. FINAL REMARKS ON LEGAL THEORY . 133

PART II

THE GROWTH OF LEGAL TRADITIONS

CHAPTER 1. PRELIMINARY REMARKS . . . 138

CHAPTER 2. THE GROWTH OF LEGAL TRADITIONS IN THE LITERARY PERIOD. CONCLUSIONS ON THE PRE-LITERARY PERIOD . . . 140

CHAPTER 3. THE CONFLICT OF DOCTRINES AS REFLECTED IN THE GROWTH OF TRADITIONS . . 152

CHAPTER 4. THE EVIDENCE OF *ISNĀDS* . . . 163

CHAPTER 5. THE ORIGIN OF LEGAL TRADITIONS IN THE FIRST HALF OF THE SECOND CENTURY A.H. 176

CHAPTER 6. LEGAL MAXIMS IN TRADITIONS . . 180

PART III

THE TRANSMISSION OF LEGAL DOCTRINE

CHAPTER 1. UMAIYAD PRACTICE AS THE STARTING-POINT OF MUHAMMADAN JURISPRUDENCE . . 190
A. Preliminary remarks 190
B. Umaiyad popular practice . . . 192
C. Umaiyad administrative practice . . 198
D. The attitude of the ancient schools of law to Umaiyad practice 213

CHAPTER 2. COMMON ANCIENT DOCTRINE AND CROSS-INFLUENCES 214
A. The common ancient doctrine . . 214
B. Early cross-references and cross-influences . 218
C. Later polemics and influences . . 222
D. Conclusions 222

CHAPTER 3. THE KORANIC ELEMENT IN EARLY MUHAMMADAN LAW 224

CHAPTER 4. THE IRAQIANS 228
A. Shuraiḥ 228
B. Ḥasan Baṣrī 229
C. Sha'bī 230
D. Ibn Mas'ūd and his Companions . . 231
E. Ibrāhīm Nakha'ī 233
F. Ḥammād 237
G. The Iraqian opposition . . . 240
H. Sufyān Thaurī 242

CHAPTER 5. THE MEDINESE AND MECCANS . . 243
A. The 'seven lawyers of Medina' . . . 243
B. Zuhrī 246
C. Rabī'a 247

D. Yaḥyā b. Saʿīd 248
E. The Medinese opposition . . . 248
F. The Meccans 249
CHAPTER 6. THE TRADITIONISTS . . . 253
CHAPTER 7. THE MUʿTAZILA 258
CHAPTER 8. KHĀRIJĪ LAW 260
CHAPTER 9. SHĪʿA LAW 262

PART IV

THE DEVELOPMENT OF TECHNICAL LEGAL THOUGHT

CHAPTER 1. THE DEVELOPMENT OF LEGAL REASONING IN GENERAL 269
CHAPTER 2. SYSTEMATIZING AND ISLAMICIZING . . 283
CHAPTER 3. AUZĀʿĪ'S REASONING . . . 288
CHAPTER 4. THE REASONING OF INDIVIDUAL IRAQIANS. 290
A. Ibn Abī Lailā 290
B. Abū Ḥanīfa 294
C. Abū Yūsuf 301
D. Shaibānī 306
CHAPTER 5. MĀLIK'S REASONING . . . 311
CHAPTER 6. SHĀFIʿĪ'S REASONING . . . 315
EPILOGUE 329
APPENDIX I. CHRONOLOGY OF SHĀFIʿĪ'S WRITINGS . 330
APPENDIX II. LIST OF PARAGRAPHS IN SHĀFIʿĪ'S TREATISES 331
BIBLIOGRAPHY AND LIST OF ABBREVIATIONS . . 336
Arabic 336
European 339
INDEX OF LEGAL PROBLEMS 341
GENERAL INDEX 344
ADDENDA 349

PART I

THE DEVELOPMENT OF LEGAL THEORY

CHAPTER 1

THE CLASSICAL THEORY OF MUHAMMADAN LAW. THE FUNCTION OF TRADITIONS

THE classical theory of Muhammadan law, as developed by the Muhammadan jurisprudents, traces the whole of the legal system to four principles or sources: the Koran, the *sunna* of the Prophet, that is, his model behaviour, the consensus of the orthodox community, and the method of analogy.[1] The essentials of this theory were created by Shāfiʿī, and the first part of this book, which is concerned with the development of legal theory, centres in a study of Shāfiʿī's achievement.[2] Closely connected with and not second to his material contribution to Muhammadan jurisprudence, is the part Shāfiʿī played in the formation of technical legal thought: he carried it to a degree of competence and mastery which had not been achieved before and was hardly equalled and never surpassed after him. The fourth part of this book, therefore, is devoted to a study of technical legal thought in Shāfiʿī and his predecessors. The second part starts from the conclusions which can be drawn from Shāfiʿī's attitude to the second of the principles of law, the *sunna* of the Prophet as laid down in traditions, and aims at working out a method by which these legal traditions may be used for following the development of legal doctrine step by step through the still largely uncharted period before Shāfiʿī. The results so gained will enable us to realize that the starting-point of Muhammadan jurisprudence lies in the practice of the late Umaiyad period, and the third part of this book accordingly tries to trace the transmission of legal doctrine from its start down to the beginnings of the literary period.

Though Shāfiʿī laid down the essentials of the classical theory

[1] See Snouck Hurgronje, *Verspr. Geschr.* ii. 286–315: *Le droit musulman* (1898); Margoliouth, *Early Development*, 65 ff.; Schacht, in *E.I.* iv, s.v. *Uṣūl*.

[2] On Shāfiʿī, see Bergsträsser, in *Islam*, xiv. 76 ff.; Heffening, in *E.I.* iv, s.v.

of Muhammadan law, he did not say the last word with regard either to consensus or to analogy. Analogy was the last of the four principles to gain explicit recognition, and even after Shāfi'ī's time had to overcome much negative resistance and positive disapproval; the history of this process has been studied by Goldziher in one of his fundamental works which also contains an analysis of Shāfi'ī's contribution to legal theory.[1] As regards consensus, Snouck Hurgronje has made clear its all-important function as the ultimate mainstay of legal theory and of positive law in their final form:[2] the consensus guarantees the authenticity and correct interpretation of the Koran, the faithful transmission of the *sunna* of the Prophet, the legitimate use of analogy and its results; it covers, in short, every detail of the law, including the recognized differences of the several schools. Whatever is sanctioned by consensus is right and cannot be invalidated by reference to the other principles. Thus the classical doctrine, but we shall find that for Shāfi'ī consensus played a much more modest part. It is easy to see that the element of retrospective guarantee embodied in the classical doctrine of consensus is hardly compatible with the free movement and violent conflict of opinions, such as we witness in the creative period of Muhammadan law to which Shāfi'ī belongs.

We are therefore left, as far as Shāfi'ī and his predecessors and contemporaries are concerned, with two recognized material sources, the Koran and the *sunna*. We may take the importance of the Koranic element in Muhammadan law for granted, though we shall have to qualify this for the earliest period;[3] but for Shāfi'ī the *sunna* takes a place comparable to that filled by the consensus in the later system. It is one of the main results of the first part of this book, that Shāfi'ī was the first lawyer to define *sunna* as the model behaviour of the Prophet, in contrast with his predecessors for whom it was not necessarily connected with the Prophet, but represented the traditional, albeit ideal, usage of the community, forming their 'living tradition' on an equal footing with customary or generally agreed practice. For Shāfi'ī, therefore, only the actions of the Prophet carry authority, and he admits on principle only traditions from the Prophet

[1] *Zâhiriten*; p. 20 ff. on Shāfi'ī.
[2] *Verspr. Geschr.* ii, loc. cit. and *passim*; *Mohammedanism*, 77–92.
[3] See below, p. 224 ff.

himself, although he still shows traces of the earlier doctrine by admitting traditions from the Companions of the Prophet, and opinions of their Successors and even later authorities as subsidiary arguments.

His predecessors and contemporaries, on the other hand, while certainly already adducing traditions from the Prophet, use them on the same level as they use traditions from the Companions and Successors, interpret them in the light of their own 'living tradition' and allow them to be superseded by it. Two generations before Shāfiʿī reference to traditions from Companions and Successors was the rule, to traditions from the Prophet himself the exception, and it was left to Shāfiʿī to make the exception his principle. We shall have to conclude that, generally and broadly speaking, traditions from Companions and Successors are earlier than those from the Prophet.

In the preceding paragraphs I have referred repeatedly to traditions from the Prophet and others. They are not identical with the *sunna* but provide its documentation, whether we take *sunna* with Shāfiʿī and the later theory as the model behaviour of the Prophet, or in its older meaning as the traditional usage of the community which is to be verified by reference to ancient authorities. All alleged information from the Prophet and others is couched in the form of single statements generally short, each preceded by a chain of transmitters (*isnād*) which is intended to guarantee its authenticity.[1] To serve this purpose the *isnād* must be uninterrupted and must lead to an original eye- or ear-witness, and all transmitters must be absolutely trustworthy. The criticism of traditions as practised by Muhammadan scholars was almost invariably restricted to a purely formal criticism of *isnāds* on these lines.

The traditions, mainly from the Prophet, that passed the more or less severe tests of this kind applied to them, were collected in the third century A.H. in a number of works, six of which were later invested with particular authority and form together the classical corpus of orthodox Muhammadan tradition. They are the works of Bukhārī, Muslim, Abū Dāwūd,

[1] The *isnād* always begins with the lowest authority and traces the transmission backwards, e.g. 'Shāfiʿī relates from [i.e. on the authority of] Mālik from Nāfiʿ from Ibn ʿUmar that the Prophet . . . .' This is abbreviated in this book as 'Shāfiʿī—Mālik—Nāfiʿ—Ibn ʿUmar—Prophet'.

Tirmidhī, Ibn Māja, and Nasā'ī. Other well-known collections of traditions, to which we shall have occasion to refer, are by Ibn Ḥanbal, Dārimī, Dāraquṭnī, and Baihaqī. This concentration of interest on traditions from the Prophet, and the almost complete neglect of traditions from Companions, not to mention Successors and later authorities, reflects the success of Shāfi'ī's systematic insistence that only traditions going back to the Prophet carry authority.

It is generally conceded that the criticism of traditions as practised by the Muhammadan scholars is inadequate and that, however many forgeries may have been eliminated by it, even the classical corpus contains a great many traditions which cannot possibly be authentic. All efforts to extract from this often self-contradictory mass an authentic core by 'historic intuition', as it has been called, have failed. Goldziher, in another of his fundamental works,[1] has not only voiced his 'sceptical reserve' with regard to the traditions contained even in the classical collections,[2] but shown positively that the great majority of traditions from the Prophet are documents not of the time to which they claim to belong, but of the successive stages of development of doctrines during the first centuries of Islam. This brilliant discovery became the corner-stone of all serious investigation of early Muhammadan law and jurisprudence,[3] even if some later authors, while accepting Goldziher's method in principle, in their natural desire for positive results were inclined to minimize it in practice.

The importance of a critical study of legal traditions for our research into the origins of Muhammadan jurisprudence is therefore obvious. This book will be found to confirm Goldziher's results, and to go beyond them in the following respects: a great many traditions in the classical and other collections were put into circulation only after Shāfi'ī's time; the first considerable body of legal traditions from the Prophet originated towards the middle of the second century, in opposition to slightly earlier traditions from Companions and other autho-

[1] *Muh. St.* ii. 1–274: 'Ueber die Entwickelung des Ḥadīth'; see p. 5 for a general statement of his thesis.

[2] Or, as Goldziher expresses it in *Principles*, 302: 'Judged by a scientific criterion, only a very small part, if any, of the contents of these canonical compilations can be confidently referred to the early period from which they profess to date.'

[3] Snouck Hurgronje, *Verspr. Geschr.* ii. 315.

rities, and to the 'living tradition' of the ancient schools of law; traditions from Companions and other authorities underwent the same process of growth, and are to be considered in the same light, as traditions from the Prophet; the study of *isnāds* often enables us to date traditions; the *isnāds* show a tendency to grow backwards and to claim higher and higher authority until they arrive at the Prophet; the evidence of legal traditions carries us back to about the year 100 A.H. only; at that time Islamic legal thought started from late Umaiyad administrative and popular practice, which is still reflected in a number of traditions.

CHAPTER 2

THE ANCIENT SCHOOLS OF LAW. SHĀFI'Ī'S ATTITUDE TO THEM

SHĀFI'Ī is known as the founder of one of the four surviving orthodox schools of law. It was not his intention to found such a school, and Muzanī, the author of the earliest handbook of the Shāfi'ite school, declares at the beginning of his work:[1] 'I made this book an extract from the doctrine of Shāfi'ī and from the implications of his opinions, for the benefit of those who may desire it, although Shāfi'ī forbade anyone to follow him or anyone else.' Shāfi'ī devotes a considerable part of his writings to discussions with and polemics against his opponents, but always with a view to making them acknowledge and follow the *sunna* of the Prophet, and he speaks repeatedly against the unquestioning acceptance of the opinion of men.[2]

The older schools of law to which Shāfi'ī is opposed, know a certain degree of personal allegiance to a master and his doctrine.[3] Amongst the Iraqians, we find Abū Yūsuf refer to Abū Ḥanīfa as 'the prominent lawyer', and Shaibānī to 'the companions of Abū Ḥanīfa'; Shāfi'ī refers to those 'who follow the doctrine of Abū Ḥanīfa', or to his 'companions', and calls him 'their master'; but also Abū Yūsuf has followers of his own. The most outspoken passage is one in which an Iraqian opponent, presumably Shaibānī, acknowledges Shāfi'ī's doctrine as good, but Shāfi'ī retorts that, as far as he knew, neither the opponent had adopted it nor another of his ilk who lorded it over them, presumably Abū Ḥanīfa.[4]

Some of the Medinese rely on Mālik for their knowledge of traditions, and consider Mālik's *Muwaṭṭa'* as their authoritative

[1] *Mukhtaṣar*, i. 2.

[2] *Tr. III*, 71, 148 (p. 246); *Tr. IV*, 250; *Tr. VII*, 274; *Ikh.* 148 f. In the time of Shāfi'ī, the word *taqlīd*, though occasionally used of the adherence to the doctrine of a master, was not yet the technical term for it which it became later. Cf. below, p. 18, n. 5, 79 (on *Tr. III*, 65), 122 (on *Tr. IV*, 253), 131, 136, n. 4.

[3] Ash'arī, *Maqālāt*, ii. 479 f. opposes the adherents of the old schools (*ahl al-ijtihād*) who admit *taqlīd*, to some followers of Shāfi'ī (*ba'ḍ ahl al-qiyās*) who do not admit it. Ibn Ḥazm deplored that the followers of Shāfi'ī accepted the principle of *taqlīd*, first introduced by the adherents of the old schools. See his *Iḥkām*, ii, 120, and Goldziher, *Ẓâhiriten*, 212.

[4] *Ikh.* 122.

book 'which they prefer to all others and which they are accustomed to follow'; they are the 'followers' of Mālik and he is their 'master'; they regard his opinion as if it were the consensus, and there is no consensus for them besides Mālik in Medina. But they are only a fraction of the Medinese, just as the followers of Abū Ḥanīfa are only part of the Iraqians.

The real distinguishing feature between the ancient schools of law is neither the personal allegiance to a master nor, as we shall see later, any essential difference of doctrine, but simply their geographical distribution. Shāfi'ī is explicit about it: 'Every capital of the Muslims is a seat of learning whose people follow the opinion of one of their countrymen in most of his teachings.'[1] Shāfi'ī goes on to mention the local authorities of the people of Mecca, Basra, Kufa, Syria; elsewhere, he refers to the Iraqians and Medinese, the Basrians and Kufians, the scholars of each place where knowledge of traditions is to be found, the people of the different countries, and he gives detailed lists of these local authorities.

One of these lists shows the variety of doctrines within the great geographical divisions: 'In Mecca there were some who hardly differed from 'Aṭā', and others who preferred a different opinion to his; then came Zanjī b. Khālid and gave legal opinions, and some preferred his doctrine, whereas others inclined towards the doctrine of Sa'īd b. Sālim, and the adherents of both exaggerated. In Medina people preferred Sa'īd b. Musaiyib, then they abandoned some of his opinions, then in our own time Mālik came forward and many preferred him, whereas others attacked his opinions extravagantly. I saw Ibn Abil-Zinād exaggerate his opposition to him, and Mughīra, Ibn Ḥāzim and Darāwardī follow some of his opinions, whereas others attacked them [for it]. In Kufa I saw people incline towards Ibn Abī Lailā and attack the doctrines of Abū Yūsuf, whereas others followed Abū Yūsuf and disagreed with Ibn Abī Lailā and with his divergences from Abū Yūsuf, and others again inclined towards the doctrine of Sufyān Thaurī and that of Ḥasan b. Ṣāliḥ. I have also heard of other instances of this kind, similar to those which I have observed and described. Some Meccans even think of 'Aṭā' more highly than of the Successors, and some of their opponents place Ibrāhīm Nakha'ī

[1] *Tr. III*, 148 (p. 246).

[of Kufa] at the top. Perhaps all these adherents of different masters exaggerate.'[1]

Shāfi'ī insists on the fact that the reputation of all these authorities varies much, and that they hardly agree on a single point of law or a general principle. If Shāfi'ī denies here the existence of reasoned agreement even between the several prominent scholars in each centre, he does not, on the other hand, imply the existence of any clear-cut, fundamental differences in legal theory between the local schools; it was exactly their common reliance on 'living tradition' and their free exercise of personal opinion, in other words, their lack of strict rules such as were elaborated only by Shāfi'ī,. that led to wide divergences in doctrine.

There was as yet no trace of the particular reputation of Medina as the 'true home of the *sunna*',[2] a reputation incompatible with Shāfi'ī's terse statement: 'We follow this [tradition from the Prophet], and so do all scholars in all countries except Medina, and so do the great authorities',[3] and with his sustained polemics against the Medinese.

The three great geographical divisions that appear in the ancient texts are Iraq, Hijaz, and Syria. Within Iraq, there is a further division into Kufians and Basrians. Although occasional references to the Basrians are not lacking,[4] little is known about their doctrine in detail,[5] and our knowledge of the ancient Iraqians is mainly confined to the Kufians. In Hijaz there are also two centres, Medina and Mecca,[6] and again our infor-

[1] *Tr. IV*, 257.

[2] This reputation appears implicitly in the tradition in praise of the 'scholar of Medina' (first in Ibn Ḥanbal, see below, p. 174, s.v. Ibn 'Uyaina), and explicitly in Ibn Qutaiba, 332. The traditions in praise of Medina in *Muw.* iv. 59 f. and in *Muw. Shaib.* 376, are still silent on this particular claim. *Tr. III*, 148 (p. 242) is concerned with the Medinese 'living tradition' as opposed to traditions from the Prophet.

[3] *Tr. III*, 41. In *Tr. III*, 34, he invokes the legal opinion of 'all people outside Medina, those from Mecca, the East and Yemen' against the Medinese doctrine.

[4] See, e.g., *Tr. I*, 49 (see below, p. 219); *Tr. III*, 143, 148 (p. 243; a discussion with a Basrian); *Tr. VIII*, 11 (Shaibānī does not belong to the Basrians); *Tr. IX*, 22; *Ikh.* 36, 62, 181, 264; *Ris.* 43 (and *ed. Shākir*, p. 305), 62 (ancient authorities of Basra); Ibn Sa'd, vii. 158, l. 15. See also below, p. 229.

[5] Already Shāfi'ī's Iraqian opponent in *Ikh.* 337 did not know the opinion of the muftis in Basra.

[6] See, e.g., *Tr. III*, 15 (cf. *Muw.* iii. 183), 26 (cf. Zurqānī, i. 263: presumably a Meccan opinion and tradition), 34, 53, 87 ('Aṭā' and his companions); *Ikh.* 338 (the same); *Ris.* 62 (ancient authorities of Mecca); *Umm*, vi. 185 (cf. *Tr. III*, 57). See also below, pp. 249 ff.

mation on Medina is incomparably more detailed. The Syrian school is mentioned rarely,[1] but we have some authentic documentation on its main representative Auzā'ī.

Egypt did not develop a school of law of its own, but fell under the influence of the other schools. There were followers of the Iraqian doctrine in Egypt, but most of the scholars there belonged to the Medinese school of which they formed a branch. Shāfi'ī refers to them in the writings of his later, Egyptian, period as 'Egyptians' or as 'some of the people of our country'.[2]

Shāfi'ī considers himself a member of the Medinese school, and references to the Medinese or Hijazis as 'our companions', and to Mālik as 'our master' or 'our and your master' occur over the whole range of his writings, from his early to his late period. Also his Iraqian opponents regard him as one of the Medinese, or a follower of Mālik, or one of the Hijazis in general. But Shāfi'ī does not identify himself with the particular adherents of Mālik within the school of Medina, although he is eager to defend Mālik against an undeserved attack. In other contexts, Shāfi'ī keeps his distance from the Medinese in general and denies responsibility for those of their opinions which he does not share.

No compromise was possible between Shāfi'ī and the Medinese, nor indeed any other ancient school of law, on their essential point of difference in legal theory, concerning the overriding authority of traditions from the Prophet, as opposed to the 'living tradition' of the school. When he comes to this subject Shāfi'ī attacks the Medinese with the strongest possible words. The whole of *Tr. III* is a sustained attack on the Medinese for their failure to follow the traditions from the Prophet which they relate themselves (and, failing that, their own traditions from Companions and Successors), and an effort to convert them to his own point of view. In this connexion Shāfi'ī even uses arguments which do less than justice to the Medinese.[3]

[1] *Tr. III*, 65 (cf. Ṭabarī, 81); *Tr. VIII*, 11; *Ris.* 62; *Āthār Shaib.* 37. Shaibānī (*Tr. VIII*, 1) speaks of 'the Muslims without exception, all Hijazis and Iraqians together', as if the Syrians did not count, and Abū Yūsuf (*Tr. IX*, 1) throws the Syrian Auzā'ī together with the Hijazis.

[2] *Tr. III*, 148 (p. 240); *Ikh.* 32 f., 91 f., 122, 132, 217 f., 289; *Umm*, vi. 185. In several of these contexts they are explicitly identified with the Medinese; *Ikh.* 34, Shāfi'ī calls them 'our companions', which is his usual reference to the Medinese, and p. 35, 'our Hijazi companions'.

[3] See below, p. 321.

Shāfiʿī attacks the Iraqians just as vigorously as he does the Medinese. Even where he has to agree with the Iraqians and to disagree with the Medinese, he is inclined to dissociate himself from the former and identify himself with the latter. Often he shows himself one-sided by sparing or excusing the Medinese and directing his full attack against the Iraqians. He shows the same sympathy for Auzāʿī as against the Iraqians. He attacks the Iraqians repeatedly with unjustified arguments and distorts their doctrine.[1] A strong personal prejudice against Shaibānī appears in several places, most clearly in *Tr. VIII*, 3, where Shāfiʿī calls Mālik 'a greater than he'.

Only in *Ikh.*, a treatise of late composition, we find several very polite references to the Iraqians; Shāfiʿī hopes that the argument which he is going to give will enable his Kufian interlocutor to convince all his companions who, after all, know the several doctrines and logical reasoning (p. 38); Shāfiʿī acknowledges that his interlocutor has shown himself objective throughout, and now, knowing where the truth lies, he has to draw the consequences (p. 53); Shāfiʿī refers to 'a prominent scholar belonging to those who disagree with us most persistently', that is, the Iraqians (p. 328).

Apart from his sentimental attachment to the Medinese, and notwithstanding his vigorous polemics, Shāfiʿī shows himself on the whole remarkably free from school bias. He started as a follower of the school of Medina. Having developed his legal theory and put the whole of the law on a new basis, he turned against his erstwhile companions and tried to convert them to his doctrine. Finally he also tried to convince the Iraqians, whom in his earlier period he had treated with scorn.

Soon after the time of Shāfiʿī the geographical character of the ancient schools of law disappeared more and more, and the personal allegiance to a master became preponderant.

[1] See below, pp. 321 ff..

CHAPTER 3

SHĀFI'Ī AND LEGAL TRADITIONS

THE main theme of Shāfi'ī's discussion with his opponents is the function of the traditions from the Prophet. Shāfi'ī insists time after time that nothing can override the authority of the Prophet, even if it be attested only by an isolated tradition, and that every well-authenticated tradition going back to the Prophet has precedence over the opinions of his Companions, their Successors, and later authorities. This is a truism for the classical theory of Muhammadan law, but Shāfi'ī's continual insistence on this point shows that it could not yet have been so in his time.

Shāfi'ī, it is true, claims that his opponents agree with his essential thesis: '*Q.*: Is there a *sunna* of the Prophet, established by a tradition with an uninterrupted chain of transmitters (*isnād*), to which the scholars in general refuse assent? *A.*: No; sometimes we find that they disagree among themselves, some accepting it and others not; but we never find a well-authenticated *sunna* which they are unanimous in contradicting.'[1] But Shāfi'ī's introduction of the element of unanimity into the discussion and, even more so, the actual doctrines of the ancient schools of law which provide him with the subject-matter for his sustained polemics, show that his claim of a general agreement is only a clever debating point made by him. With their own legal theory much less developed, and forced by Shāfi'ī to confront a problem of which they had not been consciously aware, the ancient schools of law had no answer, and Shāfi'ī made the most of his opportunity. This explains the influence that his doctrine was to have on the legal theory of all schools.

Shāfi'ī prides himself on having always held this attitude towards traditions from the Prophet, and he declares: 'I have unwaveringly held, thanks be to Allah, that if something is reliably related from the Prophet, I do not venture to neglect it, whether we have a great or a small opposition of Companions and Successors against us.'[2] We find, nevertheless, traces of an attitude corresponding to that of the ancient schools in some of

[1] *Ris.* 65 and, with more details, *Ikh.* 338 f.

[2] *Tr. III*, 148 (p. 247).

his early treatises, and in other instances it can be inferred from later information. But these are exceptions, and on the whole Shāfi'ī's doctrine on this point is as consistent as he claims it to be. His development from a natural acceptance of the Medinese doctrine in which he grew up, to the systematic acceptance of the traditions from the Prophet, is reflected in *Ris.* 38 where he tells how he learned a certain formula in his youth from his masters, later heard the *isnād* which belonged to it and which carried it back to the Caliph 'Umar, and finally heard his companions [that is, the traditionists] relate different forms on the authority of the Prophet.

The main text, in which Shāfi'ī puts forward his theory of traditions, is *Tr. III*, directed against the Medinese. He begins by stating his case: 'Every tradition related by reliable persons as going back to the Prophet, is authoritative and can be rejected only if another authoritative tradition from the Prophet contradicts it; if it is a case of repeal of a former ordinance by a later, the later is accepted; if nothing is known about a repeal, the more reliable of the two traditions is to be followed; if both are equally reliable, the one more in keeping with the Koran and the remaining undisputed parts of the *sunna* of the Prophet is to be chosen; traditions from other persons are of no account in the face of a tradition from the Prophet, whether they confirm or contradict it; if the other persons had been aware of the tradition from the Prophet, they would have followed it' (*Tr. III*, Introd.). Shāfi'ī repeats and elaborates this statement, the second half of which is particularly important, with tedious monotony.

It is significant that Shāfi'ī insists on these repeated statements of a principle which was to become a commonplace later, when discussing problems on which he and the Medinese follow the same traditions from the Prophet. The battle is joined in earnest when Shāfi'ī comes to those numerous cases where the Medinese set aside traditions from the Prophet in favour of traditions from other persons. He confesses that he has tried hard to find an excuse which would justify this procedure in his own eyes or in the eyes of any other scholar, but has been unable to find it. This, he says, applies only to traditions transmitted by reliable persons, but these must be accepted unquestioningly, and no tradition from the Prophet can be set aside for anything but another tradition from him; men need the guidance of the Prophet because Allah has obliged them to follow him. What Shāfi'ī has said ought to convince his interlocutor Rabī' that he must never reject a tradition from the Prophet except for another tradition from him, if both disagree.[1]

The Medinese, then, and the ancient schools of law in general, had already used traditions from the Prophet as the basis of many decisions, but had often neglected them in favour of the reported practice or opinions of his Companions, not to mention their own established practice. Shāfi'ī realized that this gave no consistent and convincing basis for legal decisions, and the only certain authority he could find was that of the Prophet. So he made the traditions from the Prophet, to the exclusion of everything else, the basis of his doctrine. This simple solution enabled him to find a way through the maze of conflicting traditions from the Prophet, the Companions, and other authorities.[2] But by restricting himself to traditions from the Prophet, which were in his time a purely accidental group, Shāfi'ī cut himself off from the natural and continuous development of doctrine in the ancient schools of law.

According to Shāfi'ī the traditions from the Prophet have to be accepted without questioning and reasoning: 'If a tradition is authenticated as coming from the Prophet, we have to resign ourselves to it, and your talk and the talk of others about why and how is a mistake. . . . The question of how can only be applied to human opinions which are derivative and devoid of authority; if obligatory orders, by asking why, could be subjected to analogy or to the scrutiny of reason, there would be no end to arguing, and analogy itself would break down' (*Ikh.* 339).

When confronted with two or more traditions from the Prophet which contradict one another Shāfi'ī uses harmonizing interpretation. His *Kitāb Ikhtilāf al-Ḥadīth* is particularly devoted to this subject. If one knows two seemingly contradictory traditions and finds that they can be harmonized by distinguishing between their respective circumstances, one must do so (p. 271). Shāfi'ī never considers two traditions from the Prophet contradictory, if there is a way of accepting them both; he does not invalidate a single one, because all are equally bind-

[1] *Tr. III*, 18. Similar passages *Ris.* 47, *Ikh.* 19, and often.
[2] This consideration is obvious from *Tr. III*, 6, and from *Ikh.* 133.

ing; he considers them contradictory only when one cannot possibly be applied without rejecting the other (p. 330). He gives a detailed statement on his method of interpreting traditions in *Ris.* 30 f.

When conflicting traditions cannot be harmonized Shāfi'ī's declared intention, as we have seen, is to choose the one more in keeping with the Koran and the remaining undisputed parts of the *sunna* of the Prophet. He elaborates this rule in several passages, such as *Ris.* 40 f., where he says: 'If two traditions are contradictory, the choice between them must be made for a valid reason; for instance, one chooses the one which is more consistent with the Koran. If there is no relevant text in the Koran, one chooses the more reliable tradition, the one related by men who occur in a better-known *isnād*, who have a greater reputation for knowledge, or better memory, or else one chooses the one related by two or more authorities in preference to a single authority, or the one which is more consistent with the general tendency of the Koran or with the other *sunnas* of the Prophet or more in keeping with the doctrine of the scholars or easier with respect to analogy, and finally the one followed by the majority of the Companions.'[1] But Shāfi'ī often has to fall back on the artificial expedient of counting the traditions and letting the greater number prevail, an expedient which was already used before him.[2] The affirmative statement prevails over the negative one because it implies a better memory, and the fuller statement which contains additional matter, is to be preferred to the shorter one.[3] But Shāfi'ī himself acts against this last rule in *Ikh.* 364 f., and even gives theoretical reasons for doing so.[4] All these considerations do not afford him a sure guidance, and he is reduced to affirming, in the manner customary in the ancient schools of law, that those traditions and variants which he does not accept, are unreliable.[5]

[1] See for the application of this method, *Ikh.* 208, 219 f. (below, p. 319), 222 f., 234, 267, &c.

[2] For its use by Shāfi'ī, see *Tr. III*, 89; *Ikh.* 165, 206 f., 212, 230 f., 290; for its use before Shāfi'ī, see *Ikh.* 243.

[3] The affirmative statement is preferred: *Ikh.* 212, 215; the fuller statement is preferred: *Ikh.* 228, 409.

[4] *Tr. I*, 49; *Ikh.* 379. The ancient schools of law, particularly the Iraqians, are inclined to prefer the negative and the shorter statement, and to argue *e silentio*: *Tr. III*, 10, 17; *Ikh.* 48, 50.

[5] *Tr. III*, 17. Further on Shāfi'ī's method of interpretation, see below, pp. 47, 56.

'The assumption of repeal is not resorted to, unless it can be established by a tradition from the Prophet, or by a chronological indication showing that one tradition comes after the other, or by a statement coming from those who have heard the tradition from the Prophet, or from the generality of the scholars, or by another method through which the repealing text and the repealed one become clear' (*Ikh.* 57). But Shāfi'ī is not always able to apply his own method. In *Ikh.* 88 ff., in face of the settled opinion on a major point of ritual, he assumes repeal and neglects an otherwise well-authenticated tradition, basing himself on traditions from persons other than the Prophet, and making assumptions of a kind which he rejects indignantly when they come from his opponents.[1]

As regards the repeal of traditions or, technically, the *sunna* of the Prophet by the Koran and vice versa, Shāfi'ī holds that the Koran can be repealed only by the Koran, and not by the *sunna* which is supplementary to it; the *sunna*, on the other hand, can be repealed only by another *sunna*. Whenever Allah changes His decision on a matter on which there is a *sunna* the Prophet invariably introduces another *sunna*, repealing the former. Otherwise it would be possible to reject any tradition from the Prophet which did not agree with the Koran, and every *sunna* could be abandoned if it stood beside a Koranic passage which was couched in general terms even though the *sunna* could be made to agree with it.[2] This theory seems to balance Koran and *sunna* evenly, but it makes the *sunna* as expressed in traditions from the Prophet prevail over the Koran because, as we shall see, the Koran is to be interpreted in the light of the traditions. Shāfi'ī's theory of repeal breaks down over the problem of punishments for adultery and fornication.[3]

'The Koran does not contradict the traditions, but the traditions from the Prophet explain the Koran' (*Tr. IX*, 5). 'The *sunna* of the Prophet is never contradictory to the Koran, but explanatory; no tradition from the Prophet can possibly be regarded as contradicting the obvious meaning of the Koran; no *sunna* ever contradicts the Koran, it specifies its meaning' (*Ris.* 33). 'The best interpretation of the Koran is that to which

[1] *al-aghlab* 'I prefer to think', *yashbah* 'presumably'. See also *Ikh.* 245 f., 258.
[2] *Ris.* 17 f. (to be corrected after *ed. Shākir*, p. 112), 30 ff.; *Ikh.* 41 f., 48.
[3] *Ris.* 20 ff.; *Ikh.* 44, 249 ff.

the *sunna* of the Prophet points, and the best way of interpreting traditions is not to make them contradictory, because we must accept the information of trustworthy persons as much as possible' (*Ikh.* 296). Shāfiʿī repeats and elaborates these statements in other passages.[1] He speaks contemptuously of those who dare to criticize traditions because they seem to contradict the Koran: 'If it were permissible to abandon a *sunna* for the opinions of those who are ignorant of the place which is assigned to it in the Koran itself, one might as well regard a number of fundamental doctrines, all of which are based on enactments of the Prophet, as repealed by the Koran. Whoever holds this, spirits away the majority of the *sunnas* of the Prophet, and that is ignorance' (*Ris.* 33 f.).

Shāfiʿī bases his unquestioning acceptance of traditions from the Prophet on the Koranic passages which make it a duty to obey the Prophet.[2] He interprets the term *ḥikma* 'wisdom', which is used in the Koran together with 'book' as a name for the divine revelation, as referring to the *sunna* of the Prophet expressed in traditions (*Tr. IV*, 251). On the question whether the *sunna* of the Prophet is to be regarded, like the Koran, as divinely inspired (*waḥy*), Shāfiʿī shows himself non-committal.[3] But, in any case, 'the enactments of the Prophet are accepted as coming from Allah in the same way as the explicit orders of the Koran, because Allah has made obedience to the Prophet obligatory' (*Tr. VII*, 271), and 'everything legally relevant that the Prophet has allowed or forbidden, has in fact been allowed or forbidden by Allah, because Allah has ordered the Prophet to allow or forbid it' (*Tr. IX*, 5).

All this applies to traditions from the Prophet only. Shāfiʿī distinguishes sharply between them and traditions from Companions and others; even in his terminology he generally reserves the term *athar* for the latter. Traditions from Companions carry no authority when they conflict with information from the Prophet; they are not of the same standing, and are irrelevant beside them. One of the most detailed statements to this effect occurs in *Ikh.* 138 ff.:

[1] This is the doctrine of the traditionists; see Ibn Qutaiba, 312: 'The traditions from the Prophet explain the Koran and make its meaning clear.'

[2] *Ris.* 17; *Tr. V*, 262; *Ikh.* 41, and often.

[3] *Tr. VII*, 271; *Ris.* 16. See also Ibn Qutaiba, 246 ff., for a later harmonizing opinion.

'The only criterion for the reliability of a tradition is its transmission from the Prophet by reliable men, and the fact that some Companions have agreed with it does not strengthen it, nor does the fact that some Companions have acted against it warrant its rejection, because they are themselves, together with all Muslims, dependent on the orders of the Prophet, and not qualified to confirm them or to detract from them by their concurring or dissenting opinions. If it is objected that a tradition from the Prophet becomes suspect if some Companions act differently, the tradition [regarding the action] of those Companions may as well be suspected for the same reason, or both be suspected equally, but what is transmitted from the Prophet deserves more consideration. As to opinions which are not transmitted from the Prophet, nobody may regard them as going implicitly back to him, because some Companions were unaware of the orders of the Prophet, and they must be quoted only as their private opinions, as long as the Companion does not relate them from the Prophet. If one pretends that the opinion of a Companion cannot have originated but with the Prophet, one ought never to disagree with the opinions of the Companion in question; yet there is no man, after the Prophet, whose opinions are not partly accepted and partly rejected in favour of those of another Companion. Only the words of the Prophet cannot be rejected on account of the opinions of another.'

As he did with his doctrine on traditions from the Prophet, Shāfi'ī claims that this supplement to it is common ground for him and his opponents, particularly the Iraqians,[1] but again it is obvious from Shāfi'ī's sustained polemics and from passages such as *Tr. VIII*, 40, that he forces his point of view on them, rejects their rudimentary theory, and puts them in a position which leaves them without justification for their different attitude.

In Shāfi'ī's view it is ignorance to interpret a *sunna* of the Prophet in the light of a tradition from a Companion, as if it would be confirmed thereby; traditions from others than the Prophet ought rather to be interpreted in the light of what is related from the Prophet (*Tr. I*, 51); he even goes so far as to say that the words of the Prophet are a better indication of what the Prophet meant than the statement of another person, and that no conclusions on what the Prophet meant can be drawn

[1] *Tr. III*, 148 (p. 244).

except from his own words (*Ikh.* 325). The tradition of a Companion from the Prophet must prevail over the differing action of the same Companion (*Tr. II*, 3 (*t*)).

Shāfi'ī's own reasoning does not always reach this standard. But no sacrifice of principle is involved when he argues *ad hominem* from traditions from Companions against the representatives of the ancient schools.[1]

On the other hand, Shāfi'ī does not hesitate to use traditions from Companions as additional evidence besides information from the Prophet on his *sunna*. This is sometimes meant also as an argument *ad hominem*, but mostly not, and it plays indeed a considerable part in Shāfi'ī's reasoning in *Tr. I*, *Tr. II*, *Tr. III*, and elsewhere. Occasionally Shāfi'ī uses traditions from the first four Caliphs, or from Companions and from later authorities, in order to show, in the style of the ancient schools of law, the continuity of doctrine from the time the Prophet gave his ruling or performed his model action. Apart from this Shāfi'ī often uses traditions from Companions as authorities in cases where no traditions from the Prophet are available.[2] He says explicitly: 'As long as there exists a ruling in Koran and *sunna*, those who are aware of it have but to follow them; if it does not exist, we turn to the opinion of the Companions of the Prophet or of one of them, and we prefer the opinion of the Caliphs: Abū Bakr, 'Umar or 'Uthmān. . . .[3] If no opinion is available from the Caliphs, the other Companions of the Prophet have a sufficient status in religion to justify us in following their opinion, and we ought rather to follow them than those who come after them.'[4]

This reference to the opinions of the Companions is called *taqlīd*.[5] It was common to Shāfi'ī and to the ancient schools of law, and while Shāfi'ī, as a matter of principle, subordinated

[1] *Tr. III*, 68, 72, and often.

[2] See, e.g., *Tr. I*, 59, 86, 89, 130, 139, 216, 234; *Tr. II*, 10 (*e*), 10 (*j*), 12 (*i*), 21 (*g*); *Tr. III*, 140, 141 (subsidiary to the Koran); *Tr. VIII*, 1; *Tr. IX*, 6, 7 (the tradition from the Prophet is not well authenticated), 11, 29; *Umm*, iv. 11. In *Tr. III*, 68 Shāfi'ī says: 'It is awkward to disagree with 'Umar alone, and still more awkward if 'Umar is supported by the *sunna*' (i.e. a tradition from the Prophet).

[3] Other lists include 'Alī, and Shāfi'ī says in *Tr. II*, 5 (*f*): 'If we considered this tradition from 'Alī well authenticated, we should follow it.'

[4] *Tr. III*, 148 (p. 246).

[5] *Tr. I*, 10, 184; *Tr. III*, 85, 87, 128, 148 (p. 246); *Tr. VIII*, 10. On the later meaning of *taqlīd*, see above, p. 6, n. 2.

traditions from Companions to traditions from the Prophet and to his *sunna*, he nevertheless attacked both the Iraqians and the Medinese for not following the traditions from the Companions consistently enough.[1]

Notwithstanding his reference to the position of authority occupied by the Companions of the Prophet, Shāfi'ī is unable to produce a stringent argument in favour of accepting their opinions: '*Q.*: What do you say of the opinions of the Companions of the Prophet, if they disagree? *A.*: We adopt those which agree with the Koran or the *sunna* or the consensus, or are more correct from the point of view of analogy. *Q.*: What of the opinions of a single Companion, on which neither agreement nor disagreement of the others is known: is an argument in favour of adopting them to be found in the Koran or the *sunna* or the consensus? *A.*: There is no argument in the Koran or in the *sunna*, and the scholars sometimes adopt the opinion of a single Companion and sometimes discard it, and differ concerning some of those opinions which they adopt.' Shāfi'ī's own attitude is to follow them if there is no ruling in the Koran or the *sunna* or the consensus, nor anything that can be deduced from these sources by analogy, but it is rare to find an opinion of an isolated Companion which is not contradicted by another (*Ris.* 82). So Shāfi'ī is reduced to repeating the argument of the ancient schools: 'The Companions knew the meaning of the Koran best and their opinion, we trust, does not disagree with the Koran' (*Umm*, vii. 20). But this is inconsistent because he refuses, as a matter of principle, to assign to the Companions the same role with regard to the *sunna* of the Prophet. In so far as the Companions act as transmitters of traditions from the Prophet, Shāfi'ī claims that 'all are reliable, thanks to Allah's grace' (*Ikh.* 360), but he does not yet know the tradition from the Prophet which was to be used later to justify reference to them as authorities: 'My Companions are like lodestars.'

Traditions from Companions are superseded not only by explicit traditions from the Prophet, but by analogical and other conclusions drawn from these last.[2] They are not superseded by later authorities or by personal opinion (*ra'y*).[3] In his earliest

[1] *Tr. I*, 183; *Tr. III*, 29, 69, 137.
[2] *Tr. III*, 16, 76 f., 83 f.; *Tr. IX*, 40; *Ris.* 75.
[3] *Tr. III*, 57, 148 (p. 248).—*Tr. III*, 73, 77.

treatises Shāfi'ī followed traditions from Companions even if they went against systematic analogy, but later, though still in his early period, he let analogy prevail.[1] He interprets traditions from Companions in the same harmonizing way as he does traditions from the Prophet, but shows his reserved attitude to them by his frequent doubts as to whether they are well authenticated.

Traditions from the Successors, the generation following that of the Companions of the Prophet, enjoy still less authority: 'traditions from Companions are preferable to those from Successors, or at least equal to them' (*Ikh.* 51); opinions of Successors are not a decisive argument.[2] But although every systematic justification is lacking, Shāfi'ī uses them from time to time as subsidiary arguments or when higher authorities are not available.

Shāfi'ī had to fight in order to secure for the traditions from the Prophet the overriding authority which he claimed for them, and in particular to make them prevail over the traditions from Companions. He still recognized these last in a subordinate position, but was unable to find a conclusive systematic justification for their use. The same applies even more to traditions from Successors. We must conclude that his opponents, the adherents of the ancient schools of law, did not as yet acknowledge the absolute precedence of the traditions from the Prophet, and argued mainly from traditions from Companions and Successors. The authority that Shāfi'ī still leaves to these, is an unsystematic survival from the earlier period, and his preference, as a matter of principle, for the traditions from the Prophet is his great systematic innovation.

[1] See for his earlier doctrine *Tr. VIII*, 15 and *Tr. I*, 195, for his later doctrine *Tr. VII*, 275 (middle); these three passages refer to the same problem.

[2] *Tr. III*, 148 (p. 246); *Tr. VIII*, 10; *Ris.* 74.

CHAPTER 4

TRADITIONS IN THE ANCIENT SCHOOLS OF LAW

THE attitude of the Iraqians and of the Medinese to legal traditions is essentially the same, and differs fundamentally from that of Shāfi'ī. *Ikh.* 30 ff. shows that both the Iraqians and the Medinese neglect traditions from the Prophet in favour of systematic conclusions from general rules, or of opinions of the Companions; Shāfi'ī argues first (pp. 30 ff.) against the Medinese from the point of view of the Iraqians, and then (pp. 34 ff.) in turn against these; he says: 'these same arguments apply to you when you follow the same method with regard to other traditions from the Prophet'; he states that both groups of opponents use the same arguments, and that his own arguments against both are the same, and he uses each party in order to refute the other. There are several other passages to the same effect.

Shāfi'ī finds their attitude a mass of inconsistencies: 'You diverge from what you yourselves relate from Ibn 'Umar, and from what others relate from the Prophet, without following the opinion of any Companion or Successor from whom you might transmit it, as far as I know. I do not know why you transmit traditions: if you transmit them in order to show that you know them and diverge from them in full knowledge, you have achieved your purpose and shown that you diverge from the doctrine of our forebears; if you transmit them in order to follow them, you are mistaken when you neglect them, and you neglect much of the little that you transmit; but if the proof, in your opinion, does not lie in traditions, why do you go to the trouble of transmitting them at all, using that part of them with which you agree as an argument against those who disagree?' (*Tr. III*, 146).

Even if this and other passages were not part of Shāfi'ī's polemics, it would be obvious from the sources other than his writings, that they give no complete picture of the attitude of the ancient schools of law to tradition,[1] and we shall investigate

[1] Compare Shāfi'ī's caricature in *Tr. III*, 65, with Mālik's statement of his doctrine in Ṭabarī, 81.

the unifying idea behind this seeming inconsistency in Chapter 7; for the moment, we are concerned with the actual treatment of traditions from the Prophet and others in the ancient schools.

The first striking fact is that the traditions from the Prophet are greatly outnumbered by those from Companions and Successors. As regards the Medinese, Mālik's *Muwaṭṭa'* contains, according to one of the lists quoted by Zurqānī (i. 8), 822 traditions from the Prophet as against 898 from others, that is, 613 from Companions and 285 from Successors. The edition of the *Muwaṭṭa'* by Shaibānī contains, according to the Commentary (pp. 36 ff.), 429 traditions from the Prophet as against 750 from others, that is, 628 from Companions, 112 from Successors, and 10 from later authorities. In *Tr. III*, where Shāfi'ī discusses the points on which the Egyptian Medinese diverge from traditions transmitted by themselves, §§ 1–61 deal with traditions from the Prophet, §§ 63–147 with traditions from others, mostly from Companions (§§ 101 and 105–8 deal with traditions from Successors and later authorities). As regards the Iraqians, the references of Ibn Abī Lailā, Abū Ḥanīfa, and Abū Yūsuf to the Prophet in *Tr. I*, where Shāfi'ī discusses the inter-Iraqian differences of doctrine, are much less numerous than those to Companions and Successors. The *Kitāb al-Āthār* of Abū Yūsuf contains 189 traditions from the Prophet, 372 from Companions, 549 from Successors. In the (incomplete) *Kitāb al-Āthār* of Shaibānī we find 131 traditions from the Prophet, 284 from Companions, 550 from Successors, and 6 from later authorities. Only the Syrian Auzā'ī, in the fragments which are preserved in *Tr. IX* and in Ṭabarī, refers to the Prophet much more frequently than to Companions, but mostly in general terms and without a proper *isnād*; also the subject-matter sets these historical traditions apart from the legal traditions proper.

A. The Medinese

Mālik enjoins that traditions be followed (Ṭabarī, 81); the details of his doctrine show that he harmonizes an old-established tradition from the Caliph Abū Bakr with historical traditions from the Prophet (*Mud.* iii. 7 f.). The Egyptian Medinese 'reproach others immoderately with diverging from traditions from the Prophet, blame them for rejecting them or interpreting them arbitrarily', but, Shāfi'ī adds, they do the same themselves (*Ikh.* 124). Shāfi'ī boasts that he has better traditions than the Medinese (*Tr. III*, 53); but Ibn Wahb collects an imposing array of them on the problem in question (*Mud.* iv. 28). For Shāfi'ī, however, the Medinese are not serious in the respect they pay to traditions; he calls them 'self-professed followers of traditions', and says of one of them: 'He only affected respect for the traditions in general, and then diverged from their meaning' (*Ikh.* 323).

Mālik and the Medinese in general anticipate Shāfi'ī's harmonizing interpretation of traditions, both from the Prophet and from Companions. But, compared with Shāfi'ī, they use this method sparingly, and they generally seem to make an arbitrary choice between conflicting traditions. Mālik sometimes expresses this by the words 'I prefer' (*aḥabb ilaiya*).[1]

Whereas Shāfi'ī professes to follow the traditions from the Prophet and to disregard everything else in all circumstances, the Medinese choose freely among the traditions from the Prophet and from others, and even reject both kinds altogether. Rabī' says explicitly: 'Our doctrine is to authenticate only those traditions that are agreed upon by the people of Medina, to the exclusion of other places' (*Tr. III*, 148, p. 242). In the opinion of the Medinese, sound reason and analogy supersede traditions (*Tr. III*, 145 (*a*)). Mālik considers it necessary to justify his doctrine not only by a harmonizing interpretation of traditions, but also by legal and moral reasoning,[2] and he declares himself ignorant of what a particular tradition from the Prophet may mean, in view of the practical difficulties of its application.[3]

Traditions from the Prophet are often superseded by traditions from Companions, or even disregarded without any apparent reason. They are regularly interpreted in the light of traditions from Companions, on the assumption that the Companions know the *sunna* of the Prophet best.[4] Mālik therefore reasons: 'There is no evidence that the Prophet gave the command in question after the battle of Ḥunain;[5] that he gave it

[1] But Mālik's expression 'the best that I have heard' (*aḥsan mā sami't*) does not usually refer to traditions; see below, p. 101, n. 1.

[2] Compare *Tr. III*, 13 with *Muw.* iii. 103 and *Mud.* x. 91.

[3] Compare *Tr. III*, 31 with *Muw.* i. 67 and *Mud.* i. 5.

[4] Zurqānī, *passim*, goes as far as to suppose that traditions from Companions go back to the Prophet merely because their contents seem to warrant it.

[5] This was corrected in the parallel text *Muw.* ii. 305 into 'except on the day of

then is an established fact which is not disputed, but there is no evidence that he ordered it or acted upon it afterwards; and although Abū Bakr sent out many military expeditions, there is no evidence that he did so either, nor did 'Umar' (Ṭabarī, 87). And the Medinese interpret a tradition from the Prophet in the light of a judgment of 'Umar, 'because 'Umar would not be unaware of, and would not act against, the orders of the Prophet'.[1] Opinions of a Companion prevail over what the same Companion may relate from the Prophet.[2] We also find traditions from the Prophet minimized or interpreted restrictively without the justification of traditions from Companions.[3] On the whole we can say that the Medinese give preference to traditions from Companions over traditions from the Prophet. This attitude, which is reflected in an anecdote on Zuhrī and Ṣāliḥ b. Kaisān in Ibn Sa'd (ii_2. 135), is of course inacceptable to Shāfi'ī.

In his polemics against the Medinese, Shāfi'ī repeatedly attacks the idea that the practice of the first Caliphs Abū Bakr, 'Umar and 'Uthmān, to whom he sometimes adds Ibn 'Umar and even the later Umaiyad Caliph 'Umar b. 'Abdal'azīz who is technically a Successor, might either confirm or weaken the authority of a tradition from the Prophet (*Tr. III*, 2 and often). We must not conclude from this that the Medinese doctrine was based consciously or to any considerable extent on a group of traditions from the first Caliphs as such. This is already disproved by the contents of *Tr. III* which contains traditions from Abū Bakr only in §§ 63–5 and from 'Uthmān only in § 89, as opposed to traditions from 'Umar in §§ 66–88 and from Ibn 'Umar in §§ 111–47. Shāfi'ī himself, within the limits which he assigned to traditions from Companions, considered the decisions of the first Caliphs more authoritative than traditions from other Companions,[4] and he forced this concept of the practice of Abū Bakr, 'Umar, and 'Uthmān, a concept which was narrower than the corresponding idea of the Syrians,[5] on the Medinese as a rationalization of their attitude to traditions from Companions, only in order

Ḥunain'. Mālik had overlooked the fact that the day of Ḥunain was the last relevant battle during the life of the Prophet.

[1] *Ikh.* 325. See also *Tr. III*, 26 (*Muw.* i. 263), 27 (*Muw.* i. 246; *Muw. Shaib.* 133), 83, 119.

[2] This doctrine is ascribed to Qāsim b. Muḥammad: *Tr. III*, 148 (p. 246 f.).

[3] Mālik, quoted in Zurqānī, i. 184, says: 'Not everything that occurs in a tradition is to be taken literally' (compare this with *Ikh.* 177 ff.). See also *Tr. III*, 38 (*Muw.* ii. 348), 48, 67 (*Mud.* xv. 195).

[4] See above, p. 18.

[5] See below, pp. 70 ff.

to refute it.[1] In later times, however, the idea took root in the Mālikī school; Khaṭṭābī (quoted in Zurqānī, ii. 169) makes the continuous practice of the first three Caliphs a criterion for choosing between conflicting traditions, and 'Iyāḍ (quoted ibid. i. 248) gives an argument *e silentio* from the first four Caliphs, in order to show that a certain tradition from the Prophet does not contain a general ruling but refers to a personal privilege of his.

The two particular authorities of the Medinese among the Companions are 'Umar and Ibn 'Umar. The role of 'Umar as a main authority of the Medinese is explicitly stated in many passages in *Tr. III*, for instance in § 87: 'You reply: If something is related from 'Umar, one does not ask why and how, and one does not counter it by interpreting the Koran differently.' The doctrine that a decision of 'Umar ought to prevail over a tradition from the Prophet, is expressed in a Medinese tradition which reflects the discussions in the generation before Mālik: Shāfi'ī—Mālik—Zuhrī—Muḥammad b. 'Abdallāh b. Ḥārith b. Naufal—Sa'd b. Abī Waqqāṣ and Ḍaḥḥāk b. Qais differed on the practice of *tamattu'* at the pilgrimage; Ḍaḥḥāk disapproved of it, and Sa'd blamed him; Ḍaḥḥāk referred to 'Umar's prohibition, Sa'd to the example of the Prophet. Mālik prefers the opinion of Ḍaḥḥāk, because 'Umar would be better informed about the Prophet than Sa'd. Shāfi'ī tries to minimize and to explain away 'Umar's order (*Tr. III*, 39).[2]

Ibn 'Umar is still known to Maqrīzī (ii. 332) as the main authority of the Medinese. His role appears from numerous polemical passages in *Tr. III*, such as: 'You neglect the tradition from the Prophet on the strength of an analogy based on the opinion of Ibn 'Umar, and say: 'Ibn 'Umar cannot be ignorant of the doctrine of the Prophet'' (§ 119); 'we find that you are indignant at the thought of ever differing from Ibn 'Umar' (§ 145 (*a*)).[3]

[1] This is obvious from *Tr. III*, 148 (p. 242). See also below, p. 26.—The tradition in which the Prophet enjoins observance of his *sunna* and of the *sunna* of the well-guided Caliphs (Abū Dāwūd, *Bāb fī luzūm al-sunna*; Tirmidhī, *Abwāb al-'ilm, Bāb mā jā' fil-akhdh bil-sunna*; Ibn Māja, *Bāb ittibā' sunnat al-khulafā' al-rāshidīn*), bears the hall-mark of the early 'Abbāsid period. See its prototype below, p. 62 n. 2.

[2] Wensinck in *Acta Orientalia*, ii. 178, 197 ff., has shown, with particular reference to Tirmidhī's collection of traditions, how an ideal picture of 'Umar, created partly after that of St. Peter, was made the half-inspired basis of a great part of religious law.

[3] On 'Umar b. 'Abdal'azīz as an auxiliary authority of the Medinese see below, p. 192.

The references in Shāfiʿī to ʿUmar and Ibn ʿUmar as the main authorities of the Medinese are invariably accompanied by the charge of inconsistency which he levels against them, because they often disagree with their own authorities. We shall have to draw the conclusions from this in Chapter 7, and are concerned for the moment only with establishing the fact that the Medinese at the time of Mālik thought themselves free to reject traditions from Companions.[1] Shāfiʿī declares that they do so for no good reason: 'You contradict Ibn ʿUmar and ʿUrwa [a Successor]'. Rabīʿ replies: 'But you also hold this opinion'. Shāfiʿī explains: 'Yes, because the Prophet did it, and then Abū Bakr, ʿUmar and ʿUthmān'. Rabīʿ concludes: 'So we agree with you'. Shāfiʿī retorts: 'Yes, but without knowing why' (*Tr. III*, 119). This passage, incidentally, confirms that reference to the practice of the first Caliphs is not an argument of the Medinese but peculiar to Shāfiʿī.

In Shāfiʿī's time the Medinese had not yet gained the reputation for a particular interest in traditions with which they were credited later. In *Tr. III*, 146, Shāfiʿī charges them with neglecting much of the little that they transmit, and in § 85 he says: 'If you abandon the tradition from the Prophet on . . . [here Shāfiʿī mentions a particular case] for the doctrine of ʿUmar, and the doctrine of ʿUmar on . . . [here Shāfiʿī mentions another case] for that of Ibn ʿUmar, and Ibn ʿUmar's doctrine in countless cases for your own opinion, your alleged traditional knowledge is only what you think yourselves.'

Traditions from Successors play a considerable part in the doctrine of the Medinese (see the statistics at the beginning of this chapter). They are carefully transmitted as relevant and often supersede traditions from Companions, for instance in *Tr. III*, 121, where Shāfiʿī says: 'If it is permissible to disagree with Ibn ʿUmar on the strength of the opinion of some Successor, may then others also disagree with him for the same reason, or do you forbid others what you allow yourselves? Then you would not be acting fairly, for you may not disregard Ibn ʿUmar on account of some Successor and on account of the opinion of your master [Mālik], and in another case consider the opinion of Ibn ʿUmar as an argument against the *sunna*

[1] The Medinese say: 'This does not look like a decision of ʿUmar' (*Tr. III*, 82; see also *Muw.* iii. 66).

[that is, a tradition from the Prophet].' The Medinese presume that when the Successor Ibn Musaiyib gave an opinion, 'he would not have done so unless it were based on his knowledge of an authority for his doctrine' (*Tr. III*, 77). But traditions from Successors are not followed automatically. The main Medinese authorities in the generation of the Successors will be discussed later.[1]

B. The Iraqians

The Iraqians were alleged by their opponents to care little for traditions, or at least less than the Medinese, and a slightly modified form of this view has remained part of the present common opinion. But the contemporary texts show that this is not so. We have seen that it is not the Iraqians but the Medinese that Shāfiʿī charges with neglecting much of the little that they transmit[2]. In more than one passage, the Iraqians show themselves more knowledgeable on traditions than the Medinese or the Syrians, and Abū Ḥanīfa and Abū Yūsuf are both ahead of Mālik in the systematic collection of traditions.[3] Against this, it is without importance that Shāfiʿī in an isolated passage taunts the Iraqians with deriving their knowledge of traditions from remote sources and possessing nothing like the knowledge of his companions the Medinese.[4]

The argument that the opinions of their opponents are not based on traditions from the Prophet, is common to the Iraqians and the Medinese in their polemics against one another.[5] We shall see from the following analysis that the attitude of the Iraqians to traditions is essentially the same as that of the Medinese, but that their theory is more developed.

According to Shāfiʿī, it is Shaibānī's principle that no opinion on law is valid unless it is based on binding information[6] or analogy (*Tr. VIII*, 3); a binding tradition, one from a Companion in the case in question, has precedence over analogy (*Ikh.* 117 f.); it is equally inexcusable to contradict the text of a tradition or to make a mistake in applying it (*Ikh.* 282).

[1] Below, p. 243 ff.
[2] Above, pp. 21, 23.
[3] See below, p. 33 f.
[4] *Tr. VIII*, 13. This argument hardly plays a role elsewhere.
[5] *Tr. III*, 24, 26.
[6] *Khabar lāzim*; on the meaning of this term, see below, p. 136, n. 2.

The Iraqian opponent repeatedly agrees with Shāfiʿī that no one has any authority beside the Prophet. We have seen[1] that these statements must be taken with a certain reserve, but a passage such as *Muw. Shaib.* 357, where Shaibānī insists on the decisive role of a decision of the Prophet, shows that the Iraqians had indeed anticipated and explicitly formulated this essential thesis, and applied it occasionally. They are, however, still far from Shāfiʿī's unquestioning reliance on traditions from the Prophet alone.

Abū Yūsuf says in *Tr. IX*, 5: 'Take the traditions that are generally known, and beware of those that are irregular (*shādhdh*)'; he quotes a tradition that the Prophet declared in the pulpit: 'Traditions from me will spread; those that agree with the Koran are really from me, but what is related from me and contradicts the Koran is not from me'; further a tradition from ʿAlī (with an Iraqian *isnād*): 'Traditions from the Prophet are to be interpreted in the most righteous and godfearing way', and a tradition from ʿUmar (also with an Iraqian *isnād*), that he warned a group of Companions who were setting out for Kufa, to relate traditions from the Prophet only sparingly, because the people there were humming with the Koran like bees. ʿUmar accepted a tradition from the Prophet only on the evidence of two witnesses, and ʿAlī refused to accept traditions from the Prophet unless he had them confirmed by oath.

'The wider the spread of transmission', Abū Yūsuf says, 'the easier it is to eliminate those traditions which are not recognized, or are not recognized by the specialists on law, or do not agree with Koran and *sunna*. Beware of irregular traditions and keep to those which are accepted by the community, recognized by the specialists on law, and in agreement with Koran and *sunna*; measure things by that standard; what differs from the Koran does not come from the Prophet, even if it is related from him'. Abū Yūsuf adds a tradition that the Prophet said in his last illness: 'I allow only what Allah allows, and forbid only what Allah forbids; they ought not to shelter behind my authority',[2] and concludes: 'Make the Koran and the *sunna* which you know, your leader and guide; follow that and measure by it those problems which are not clear to you from Koran and *sunna*.'

[1] Above, p. 11.
[2] The wording of this tradition is derived from Koran xliii. 43.

This is the opposite of Shāfiʿī's interpretation of the Koran in the light of the traditions from the Prophet.

Apart from these restrictions to its application, the Iraqian thesis of the overruling authority of traditions from the Prophet is definitely relegated to a subordinate place by the importance which the Iraqians attach, in theory and practice, to traditions from Companions. We find this principle explicitly formulated in many places, for instance, *Tr. I*, 89: 'They pretend that they differ from no one among the Companions of the Prophet'; § 183: 'Abū Ḥanīfa pretends that he never diverges from the opinions of the Companions'; *Tr. VIII*, 9, where Shāfiʿī addresses Shaibānī: 'It is your avowed principle not to disagree with the decisions of any of the Companions, when no other Companion is known to have differed'. It is certainly on account of their explicit formulation of this principle, that Shāfiʿī acknowledges repeatedly that the Iraqians have got a better excuse than the Medinese for diverging from traditions from the Prophet.[1]

The argument of the Iraqians for attaching this importance to the opinions of the Companions is the same as that of the Medinese, that the Companions would not have been unaware of the practice and the decisions of the Prophet,[2] and it was claimed that their opinions were likely to coincide with the decisions of the Prophet: 'Ibn Masʿūd was asked about a problem; he replied: "I am not aware of any decision of the Prophet on this"; asked to give his own opinion (*ra'y*), he gave it; thereupon one of the men in his circle declared that the Prophet had given the same decision, and Ibn Masʿūd was exceedingly glad that his opinion coincided with the decision of the Prophet.'[3] It is therefore not surprising that traditions from Companions supersede traditions from the Prophet, that both kinds of traditions are mentioned on the same level, and that traditions from the Prophet are interpreted in the light of traditions from Companions.[4]

[1] *Tr. III*, 61, and often.

[2] *Tr. IX*, 40, and elsewhere.

[3] *Āthār A.Y.* 607; *Āthār Shaib.* 22; *Muw. Shaib.* 244, all through Abū Ḥanīfa—Ḥammād—Ibrāhīm Nakhaʿī; the parallel version in Shaibānī's *K. al-Ḥujaj* (quoted in *Comm. Āthār A.Y.*) has it through Shaʿbī; it is not earlier than the period of Shaʿbī and Ḥammād. Another version, in which the respect for traditions is even more strongly expressed, is in Ibn Ḥanbal and some of the classical collections; see *Comm. Muw. Shaib.* 244. For a counter-tradition against this, see below, p. 50.

[4] The doctrine of the decisive character of traditions from Companions persisted in the school of Abū Ḥanīfa.

We must conclude that the reference to traditions from Companions is the older procedure, and the theory of the over-ruling authority of traditions from the Prophet an innovation, which was as yet imperfectly adopted by the Iraqians and consistently applied only by Shāfiʿī.

Whereas the method of harmonizing interpretation of traditions is not unknown to the Iraqians, and when no harmonizing is possible, the majority of the Companions is occasionally considered as decisive, they usually choose seemingly arbitrarily one out of several contradictory traditions, even if they could be brought into agreement. Shāfiʿī states in *Tr. III*, 13, that they choose 'that one which they find more in keeping with the *sunna*', and we shall see later[1] what the Iraqians mean by it. This acceptance or rejection of traditions, according to whether they agree or disagree with the previously established doctrine of the school, was later developed into a fine art by Ṭaḥāwī whose efforts at harmonizing are overshadowed by his tendency to find contradictions, so that he can eliminate those traditions which do not agree with the doctrine of the Ḥanafī school, by assuming their repeal. The interpretation by the ancient Iraqians of those traditions which they accept, confirms that their decisive criterion is the previously established doctrine.

The Iraqians reject traditions from the Prophet, because the tradition in question disagrees with the Koran (*Ikh.* 345 ff.); or because the rule expressed in it is not mentioned in the Koran[2] or in parallel traditions from the Prophet, and nothing similar to it is related from the four Caliphs who carried out the divine commands after the Prophet (*Tr. III*, 10); or because 'everyone has abandoned it' (*Ikh.* 336); or because the general opinion is different, and the traditions from the Prophet to the contrary can be explained away or considered as repealed (*Muw. Shaib.* 142); or simply for systematic reasons, because the tradition in question would make the doctrine inconsistent. Shāfiʿī is justified in charging the Iraqians with accepting traditions more easily from Companions than from the Prophet (*Ikh.* 345 ff.). They had, of course, often to disagree with traditions from Companions too, particularly as many mutually contradictory traditions are related from their two main authorities

[1] Below, pp. 73 ff.

[2] Mālik argues against this reasoning of the Iraqians in *Muw.* iii. 183.

ʿAlī and Ibn Masʿūd. Shāfiʿī collects the points on which the Iraqians diverge from ʿAlī and Ibn Masʿūd, in *Tr. II*.

The role of ʿAlī and Ibn Masʿūd as Iraqian authorities is discussed in *Ikh.* 215 f., a passage which contains a rather one-sided, but from Shāfiʿī's point of view logical, summary of the attitude of the ancient schools of law to their eponyms. The Iraqian opponent states that Ibrāhīm Nakhaʿī disapproved of a tradition from the Prophet and said: 'Should Wā'il [the transmitter] be more knowledgeable than ʿAlī and Ibn Masʿūd?'[1] He then acknowledges that Ibrāhīm did not relate from ʿAlī and Ibn Masʿūd that they saw the Prophet act differently from what Wā'il related, but Ibrāhīm supposed that had they seen him act as related by Wā'il, they would have transmitted it or acted upon it. He is forced to admit that Ibrāhīm transmitted no explicit statement from ʿAlī and Ibn Masʿūd, and concedes that Ibrāhīm could not have been aware of all their traditions and actions. He also concedes that not all decisions of Ibrāhīm went back to ʿAlī and Ibn Masʿūd. Therefore, Shāfiʿī concludes, the opponent has no right to draw conclusions from Ibrāhīm's general reference to ʿAlī and Ibn Masʿūd, because Ibrāhīm and others sometimes followed other authorities on points on which these two were silent. Even if Ibrāhīm related something from ʿAlī and Ibn Masʿūd, it would not be acceptable because he was not in direct contact with them, and now, Shāfiʿī says, the opponent wants to invalidate Wā'il's tradition from the Prophet on the ground that Ibrāhīm did not know the opinion of ʿAlī and Ibn Masʿūd on that point. If the opponent, as he does, claims that Ibrāhīm may have had positive information, this does not better his argument because, in fact, he did not transmit it. And if he means that Ibrāhīm's hearers presumed that he transmitted it from ʿAlī and Ibn Masʿūd without saying so, we might as well presume on all points on which nothing is related from him, that he knew [and therefore shared] the correct decision although he did not express it; and if in this case something different were related from ʿAlī and Ibn Masʿūd, the opponent could not use it as an argument.

[1] Cf. *Āthār A.Y.* 105; *Muw. Shaib.* 87; *Mud.* i. 68. It is significant that the original text in these three versions refers to Ibn Masʿūd and his Companions (see below, pp. 231 ff.); Shāfiʿī, who does not recognize this basis of the Iraqian doctrine, replaces it by "ʿAlī and Ibn Masʿūd'.

Beside 'Alī and Ibn Mas'ūd stands 'Umar as an Iraqian authority, and this triad was still known to Khwārizmī who says (ii. 41): 'Abū Ḥanīfa learned law from Ḥammād, Ḥammād from Ibrāhīm Nakha'ī, Ibrāhīm from the Companions of Ibn Mas'ūd, and they in their turn from the specialists on law among the Companions of the Prophet, Ibn Mas'ūd, 'Alī, and 'Umar.'

'Alī as an authority of the Iraqians is opposed to 'Umar as an authority of the Medinese in *Tr.* iii, 87. Ibn Mas'ūd is the authority of the Kufians, as opposed to the Basrians (*Ikh.* 62), and he is still known as such to Maqrīzī (ii. 332). There are traditions opposing his opinion to that of 'Umar, or showing 'Umar as asking for his decision and agreeing with him, and his personal authority is claimed for the doctrine of the school which goes under his name. We have seen that the opinion of Ibn Mas'ūd was supposed to coincide with the decision of the Prophet; but this is only a justification *ex post facto*, and the two *Kitāb al-Āthār* of Abū Yūsuf and Shaibānī, which give the traditional basis of the Iraqian doctrine, contain hardly any traditions through Ibn Mas'ūd from the Prophet. As to 'Umar as an Iraqian authority, Shāfi'ī states that Abū Ḥanīfa often follows 'Umar (by *taqlīd*) and makes him his only authority (*Tr. I*, 184). The few cases where Ibn 'Umar appears as an Iraqian authority seem all copied from the Medinese model.

Traditions from Successors are often adduced by the Iraqians on the same level as traditions from Companions, and even more frequently by themselves alone. In the time of Shaibānī and Shāfi'ī, however, it was recognized that the opinions of Successors as such were not authoritative; this theoretical position contrasts strangely with the extensive use that had been, and still was being, made of them. In *Tr. VIII*, 13, the Iraqian opponent calls Sa'īd b. Jubair 'a certain Successor whose opinion carries no weight'; in § 6 Shaibānī objects to Shāfi'ī (who in this early treatise still uses the old-fashioned argument from authorities other than the Prophet) that the opinions of Ibn Musaiyib, Ḥasan Baṣrī, and Ibrāhīm Nakha'ī are not authoritative; Shāfi'ī replies that Shaibānī himself sometimes falls into error by following their opinions, and in § 15 he says: 'If Shaibānī's argument is that Ibrāhīm Nakha'ī has said so, then he says himself that Ibrāhīm and other Successors are no authority.'

But the main authority for the Kufian Iraqian doctrine is this very Ibrāhīm Nakha'ī. Out of the 549 traditions from Successors in the *Kitāb al-Āthār* of Abū Yūsuf, and the 550 in the *Kitāb al-Āthār* of Shaibānī, not less than 443 and 472 respectively are those of Ibrāhīm himself, and a further 15 and 11 respectively are related through Ibrāhīm from other Successors. Ibrāhīm is also the transmitter of a considerable proportion of traditions from the Prophet and from Companions in these two works, namely 53 out of 189 from the Prophet and 147 out of 372 from Companions in *Āthār A.Y.*, and 26 out of 131 from the Prophet and 104 out of 284 from Companions in *Āthār Shaib.* The passage *Ikh.* 215 f. which we have summarized before,[1] shows how the name of Ibrāhīm was used in order to involve higher authorities. The two *Kitāb al-Āthār* and *Tr. II* show that Ibrāhīm is the main transmitter from Ibn Mas'ūd and nevertheless diverges from him frequently, and that Ibrāhīm's doctrine almost invariably prevails with the Kufians.

This relationship between traditions from a Successor and a Companion corresponds to that between traditions from Companions and from the Prophet, and a parallel conclusion imposes itself: the reference to the Successor preceded the reference to the Companion, and it was only as a consequence of theoretical considerations that the authority was transferred backwards from the Successor to the Companion, just as it was later, and for a similar reason, transferred backwards from the Companions to the Prophet. The Medinese doctrine is not concentrated in one Successor as the Kufian is, but the attitude of the Medinese to Successors and Companions is the same as that of the Iraqians, and the same conclusion must be drawn.

As to individual Iraqians, we find Abū Ḥanīfa already technically interested in traditions. He collects identical traditions with different *isnāds*, and Medinese traditions in addition to Iraqian ones. Abū Yūsuf continues the systematic collection of traditions and shows himself interested and knowledgeable in traditions (*Tr. IX*, 2). Being later, he is subject to a stronger influence from traditions going back to the Prophet and Companions than Abū Ḥanīfa, and compared with the few cases in which Abū Ḥanīfa introduces a tradition into the discussion for the first time or changes the doctrine on account of it, the cases in which Abū Yūsuf does so are more numerous.[2] Shaibānī's

[1] Above, p. 31.

[2] See below, p. 301 f.

technical interest in traditions is attested by his edition of Mālik's *Muwaṭṭa'*, and his habitual formula 'We follow this' shows the degree to which he is, at least formally, under the influence of traditions. Again we find that he changes the doctrine on account of traditions, particularly those from the Prophet.[1] This does not prevent his being inconsistent and eclectic, thereby laying himself open to Shāfi'ī's constant criticism of the representatives of the ancient schools. As Abū Ḥanīfa before him, Shaibānī takes the doctrine of Medinese Successors into account.

C. The Syrians

Auzā'ī is the only representative of the Syrians on whom we have authentic information in *Tr. IX* and in Ṭabarī, and his attitude to traditions is essentially the same as that of the Medinese and the Iraqians. Practically all his statements of doctrine are concerned with the law of war, for which narratives on the expeditions of the Prophet of primarily historical import and usually lacking an *isnād* provide a background of precedents sensibly different in character from the legal traditions proper. If, therefore, references to the action of the Prophet occur frequently in Auzā'ī, similar references are not less frequent in Iraqian texts on the same subject. (It happens that the law of war is only very succinctly treated in *Muw.* and *Muw. Shaib.*).

Auzā'ī states, quoting Koran xxxiii. 21, that 'the Prophet is a good example' (*Tr. IX.* 23), and that 'the Prophet deserves most to be followed and to have his *sunna* observed' (§ 50), but in order to establish the practice of the Prophet he refers to 'what happened at the time of the Prophet and afterwards' (§ 26 and elsewhere). He refers to Ibn 'Umar beside the Prophet (§ 31), and to Abū Bakr, 'Umar, and the Umaiyad Caliph 'Umar b. 'Abdal'azīz by themselves.[2] The usual argument of the ancient schools in favour of the authority of the Companions occurs in Ṭabarī, 103: Auzā'ī cannot imagine that anyone could be so bold as to doubt that Abū Bakr and his companions knew the interpretation of the Koran better than Abū Ḥanīfa. In *Tr. IX*, 15, Auzā'ī refers to 'the scholars our predecessors', and in Ṭabarī, 70, he regards the opinion of the

[1] See below, p. 306 f.

[2] *Tr. IX*, 22, 25, 28; Ṭabarī, 82, 87.

scholars as pertinent to the question of whether to accept or to reject a tradition from the Prophet.[1] Ibn Qutaiba, 63, relates that Auzāʿī used to blame Abū Ḥanīfa not because he followed his personal opinion (*ra'y*)—since, he said, all of us do so—but because, when confronted with a tradition from the Prophet, he diverged from it; if this is authentic, it does not go beyond the usual polemics between the schools and does not prove for Auzāʿī an attitude to traditions different from that of the other ancient schools of law. Auzāʿī appears as the authority of Abū Ḥanīfa for several traditions from the Prophet in *Āthār Shaib.*, and he himself knows a Basrian tradition from ʿUmar.[2]

[1] Abū Yūsuf directs the same reasoning against Auzāʿī: *Tr. IX*, 10.
[2] *Tr. IX*, 22 (cf. *Kharāj*, 126 f.).

CHAPTER 5

TECHNICAL CRITICISM OF TRADITIONS BY SHĀFI'Ī AND HIS PREDECESSORS

THE use of traditions in the ancient schools of law took little account of the standards of criticism which in the time of Shāfi'ī had been developed by the specialists on traditions (*Tr. III*, 62). Their technical terms *thābit* 'well-authenticated', *mashhūr* 'well-known', *mauṣūl* or *muttaṣil* 'with an uninterrupted *isnād*', *maqṭū'* or *munqaṭi'* 'with an interrupted *isnād*', *mursal* 'lacking [the mention of] the first transmitter', *ḍa'īf* 'weak', *majhūl* 'unknown, not identified', *munkar* 'objectionable', were known to Shāfi'ī and his opponents, the adherents of the ancient schools, alike,[1] but it was left to Shāfi'ī to introduce as much of the specialized criticism of traditions as existed in his time into legal science.

Shāfi'ī tries to follow a middle course between two opposite tendencies: some do not pay sufficient attention to traditions, 'others aspire to a thorough traditional foundation of their doctrine, so much so that they accept traditions from transmitters from whom it would be better not to accept them, ... provided only their traditions agree with their opinions, and reject traditions from reliable people if they happen to contradict their opinions. He who scrutinizes the traditional foundations of legal doctrines with competence and accuracy, is staggered by the *mursal* traditions of all who are not prominent Successors' (*Ris.* 64). It is Shāfi'ī's rule that only well-authenticated traditions are to be accepted (*Ikh.* 58), that is to say, the criterion of their reliability or lack of it is the *isnād*.

It is stated on the authority of the Successor Ibn Sīrīn that the demand for and the interest in *isnāds* started from the civil war (*fitna*), when people could no longer be presumed to be reliable without scrutiny;[2] we shall see later[3] that the civil war which

[1] The technical criticism of traditions as known to Shāfi'ī and his opponents, represents an earlier stage than the fully developed 'science of traditions', for which see Marçais, *Taqrīb*. In particular, the systematization of the degrees of reliability by the categories *ṣaḥīḥ, ḥasan, gharīb* did not yet exist.

[2] Muslim, introduction: *Bāb bayān ann al-isnād min al-dīn;* Tirmidhī, at the end. Without mention of the period in Dārimī, introduction: *Bāb fil-ḥadīth 'an al-thiqāt*.

[3] Below, p. 71 f.

began with the killing of the Umaiyad Caliph Walīd b. Yazīd (A.H. 126), towards the end of the Umaiyad dynasty, was a conventional date for the end of the good old time during which the *sunna* of the Prophet was still prevailing; as the usual date for the death of Ibn Sīrīn is A.H. 110, we must conclude that the attribution of this statement to him is spurious. In any case, there is no reason to suppose that the regular practice of using *isnāds* is older than the beginning of the second century A.H.[1]

Shāfi'ī resigns himself to assuming the good faith of the transmitters, notwithstanding the existence of many errors of which he is aware. 'We are not much embarrassed', he says, 'by the fact that well-authenticated traditions disagree or are thought to disagree, and the specialists on traditions are not embarrassed by traditions that are likely to be erroneous and the like of which are not well authenticated' (*Ikh.* 365 f.). He is loath to face the fact of *tadlīs*, which consists in dissembling or eliminating the names of discreditable transmitters from *isnāds* (*Ris.* 53); but he knows that Mālik and Ibn 'Uyaina, two of his most highly esteemed authorities, practised *tadlīs*.[2] Shāfi'ī's lenient standards appear in *Tr. III*, 56, where Rabī' asks him: 'Did Ibn Zubair hear this from the Prophet?', and he replies: 'Yes, he remembered it from him; he was 9 years old when the Prophet died.'

Criticism of traditions on material grounds is not quite as exceptional in Shāfi'ī's writings as one would expect in view of *Tr. III*, 148 (p. 241), where Rabī' asks: 'Is it possible to throw doubt on any tradition?', and Shāfi'ī replies: 'Only if two contradictory traditions are related from the same man, then we follow one of them.' But Shāfi'ī recognizes such criticism cautiously in *Ris.* 55 where he says: 'In most cases the truthfulness or lack of truthfulness of a tradition can only be known through the truthfulness or lack of truthfulness of the trans-

[1] Horovitz (in *Islam*, viii. 44 and in *Islamic Culture*, i. 550) has pointed out that the *isnād* was already established in the generation of Zuhrī (d. A.H. 123 or later), but to project its origin backwards into 'the last third of the first century A.H. at the latest' or 'well before the year A.H. 75', is unwarranted. Caetani (*Annali*, i. Introduction, § 11) has shown that the *isnād* was not yet customary in the time of 'Abdalmalik (A.H. 65–86). Sa'īd b. Jubair (d. 95) is represented as rebuking a hearer who asks him his *isnād* (Dārimī, *Bāb fi tauqīr al-'ulamā'*), but Ibn Mubārak (d. 181) already considers it 'part of the religion' (Muslim, *Bāb al-nahy 'an al-riwāya 'an al-ḍu'afā'*).

[2] For Mālik: *Tr. III*, 97; for Ibn 'Uyaina: *Tr. IX*, 9; *Umm*, iv. 69.

mitter, except in a few special cases when he relates what cannot possibly be the case, or what is contradicted by better-authenticated information.'[1]

Shāfiʿī is rather careless about his *isnāds*, and often refers to his immediate authority simply as 'a reliable man'; but 'reliable' means nothing and is put in only for convenience, as appears from *Tr. III*, 148 (p. 249) where the *isnād* runs: Shāfiʿī—a reliable man—ʿAbdallāh b. Ḥārith (unless, Shāfiʿī is not sure, he has heard it from ʿAbdallāh b. Ḥārith directly) —Mālik, or from *Tr. IX*, 38, where Shāfiʿī says: 'a reliable man, I think Ibn ʿUlaiya'. In *Ikh.* 88 Shāfiʿī relates a tradition from 'more than one scholar', and still calls it 'a very reliable *isnād*'. In *Tr. IX*, 9, he says: 'I remember having heard from one of our companions whom I met personally'; this shows that Shāfiʿī did not have all his traditions from his authorities personally, and in *Ikh.* 359 he refers to a written record.

Shāfiʿī agrees with the Iraqians and the specialists that *munqaṭiʿ* traditions, that is, traditions with an interrupted *isnād* from which a link is missing, are not to be recognized if they stand by themselves (*Ikh.* 53); Shāfiʿī never recognizes them if their transmitters are *majhūl*, that is, not well known (*Ris.* 32). But this theoretical position had been gained only recently and was not yet consistently applied in actual reasoning. The gap between theory and practice could not be illustrated better than by *Tr. VIII*, 1, where Shaibānī and Shāfiʿī confront each other with objections to their respective traditions because they are *maqṭūʿ*, which means the same as *munqaṭiʿ*.

Mursal is a special case of *munqaṭiʿ*, where the mention of the first transmitter is lacking. In later terminology its use is restricted to traditions from the Prophet which are related without the authority of a Companion who was present; but in Shāfiʿī's time it was still used in a wider sense, including traditions from Companions without the authority of a Successor who was in immediate touch with them. The numerous traditions of Ibrāhīm Nakhaʿī from Ibn Masʿūd are *mursal* in this sense because Ibrāhīm was not in direct touch with Ibn Masʿūd. Shāfiʿī and the representatives of the ancient schools treat the *mursal* in the same way in which they treat the *munqaṭiʿ*; these

[1] For individual cases, see *Tr. I*, 194; *Tr. III*, 30 (compared with *Muw.* iii. 11); *Tr. VIII*, 13 (p. 293); *Ikh.* 195 ff., 301, 318.

last in particular use *mursal* traditions from the Prophet and from Companions freely in favour of their own doctrine, but are inclined to reject reference to them on the part of their opponents as inconclusive. It is obvious that the actual reasoning represents the older and the emerging theoretical doctrine the later stage, and also that *mursal* traditions are, generally speaking, older than traditions with full *isnāds*. The *mursal*, which forms the most important group of *munqaṭi'*, reflects the interval between the real origins of Muhammadan law and the much earlier period in which its fictitious authorities were being sought.

Shāfi'ī disregards the *mursal* in theory and in his actual reasoning.[1] On the other hand, he does not hesitate to use the *mursal* from the Prophet and from Companions as a subsidiary argument, or when he has forgotten the relevant traditions with full *isnāds*, or even by itself. He states explicitly in *Ris.* 63 f. that the *munqaṭi'*, that is, the *mursal*, of the prominent Successors is to be accepted under safeguards, although it has not the same authority as traditions with full *isnāds* (*muttaṣil*); this is followed by a denunciation of the *mursal* of others.

The use of *mursal* traditions from the Prophet and from Companions by Mālik is well known. On the other hand, Mālik disregards *mursal* traditions which disagree with his doctrine, even if he relates them himself (*Tr. III*, 34), and the Medinese suspect those traditions which do not agree with their doctrine (*Tr. VIII*, 14).

The Iraqians show the same inconsistency with regard to the *mursal*. They use *mursal* traditions as arguments, and even consider a tradition with a full *isnād* as repealed by a *mursal* (*Muw. Shaib.* 113), but at the same time do not consider the *mursal* as well authenticated.[2] In particular, they recognize the *mursal* traditions of Ibrāhīm Nakha'ī from Ibn Mas'ūd, and justify this even theoretically by making Ibrāhīm say: 'Whenever I say: "Ibn Mas'ūd has said so-and-so", this has been related to me by more than one of his companions.'[3]

On 'isolated' traditions (*khabar al-wāḥid*) see below, pp. 50 ff.

[1] *Tr. VIII*, 1, 13; *Ikh.* 195, 360.

[2] *Ikh.* 360, 375, 390.

[3] *Tr. II*, 11 (*b*); Tirmidhī, at the end; with more details in Ṭaḥāwī, i. 133; this last version emphasizes that Ibrāhīm's *mursal* from Ibn Mas'ūd, implying the existence of several parallel reports, is even more reliable than his traditions from him through one individually named intermediary.

CHAPTER 6

ARGUMENTS FOR AND AGAINST TRADITIONS

A. Adversaries of Traditions in General

IN the time of Shāfiʿī, traditions from the Prophet were already recognized as one of the material bases of Muhammadan law. Their position in the ancient schools of law was, as we have seen, much less certain. The early sources give ample evidence of the process by which traditions from the Prophet gained recognition, and of the opposition which their claims provoked. Some of this evidence has been collected by Goldziher and need not be duplicated here.[1] The new evidence, with which this chapter is concerned, shows that the hostility towards traditions came not only or even mainly from unorthodox circles, from 'philosophers, sceptics and heretics', but rather that it was the natural reaction of the early specialists on law against the introduction of a new element, a reaction traces of which survive in the attitude of the ancient schools of law. It follows that the traditions from the Prophet do not form, together with the Koran, the original basis of Muhammadan law, but an innovation begun at a time when some of its foundations already existed.

Shāfiʿī knows two groups of anti-traditionists: those who reject the traditions altogether, and those who reject the *khabar al-khāṣṣa*. We shall see[2] that the latter are simply the followers of the ancient schools of law. As regards the former, *Tr. IV*, 250–4, contains a discussion with a learned representative of them. Their arguments are that the Koran 'explains everything' (Koran, xvi. 89) and must not be interpreted in the light of traditions; no individual authority for the traditions is quite reliable, and a man may challenge traditions without becoming an unbeliever; how then can they serve as a guide to the uniformly plain meaning of the Koran and be put on the same footing as the Koran? 'Why do you', they ask Shāfiʿī, 'accept

[1] *Muh. St.* ii. 135 f.; further in *Z.D.M.G.* lxi. 860 ff.; and in *Islam*, iii. 230 ff.
[2] Below, p. 41 ff

traditions of this doubtful quality, whereas we only accept something that is beyond doubt, as the Koran is?' The interlocutor, who has become converted by Shāfiʿī's arguments, explains that there are two schools of thought amongst his former companions: some confine themselves strictly to the Koran, others accept only explanatory traditions on subjects mentioned in the Koran. On the other hand, the anti-traditionists acknowledge the consensus on the ground that the Muslims, Allah willing, would not agree on any given doctrine unless they were right, and so their majority (*ʿāmmatuhum*) could not be mistaken as to the meaning of the Koran, even if individuals might be.[1]

Those who reject the traditions altogether are the same as the *ahl al-kalām*, which is Shāfiʿī's term for the Muʿtazila.[2] This is made certain by *Ikh.* 29 ff., where the relevant point is that the *ahl al-kalām*, in rejecting the traditions altogether, are more consistent than the adherents of the ancient schools; an Iraqian opponent uses this argument against the Medinese (p. 33 f.), and Shāfiʿī has heard some of the *ahl al-kalām* use it against the Iraqians (p. 37). This identification is confirmed by the general attitude and the detailed arguments of the *ahl al-kalām* as they appear in the whole of Ibn Qutaiba's *Taʾwīl Mukhtalif al-Ḥadīth*. The *ahl al-kalām* are the extreme wing of the anti-traditionists.

The moderate wing is represented by those who reject the *khabar al-khāṣṣa*, that is, traditions based on the authority of individual transmitters only.[3] It was Shāfiʿī who, for polemic reasons, applied this name to them,[4] and they do not, in fact, reject the *khabar al-khāṣṣa* on principle. Shāfiʿī discusses their doctrine in detail in *Tr. IV*, 254–62; the whole passage shows that they are identical with the followers of the ancient schools of law, who prefer the 'living tradition' of the school to individual traditions from the Prophet.[5] The actual attitude of the ancient schools to 'isolated' traditions, which will be considered

[1] See also *Tr. III*, 148 (p. 242): 'They say: "We acknowledge only the consensus".'

[2] See below, p. 258.

[3] This term is slightly wider than, although it largely coincides with, those commonly used for 'isolated' traditions (*khabar al-wāḥid, khabar al-infirād*; see below, p. 50).

[4] See particularly *Tr. IV*, 256 (towards the end).

[5] The actual opponents in this passage are Iraqians, but the Medinese hold the same opinion (p. 257).

later,[1] is the same as that ascribed by Shāfiʿī to those who reject the *khabar al-khāṣṣa*.[2]

According to Shāfiʿī, their doctrine rests on the following bases:

(*a*) what is related by many from many (*mā naqalat-hu ʿāmma ʿan ʿāmma*), such as the main duties on which one can be absolutely certain of the orders of Allah and of the Prophet;

(*b*) the Koran, in cases where several interpretations are possible, that is, in so far as it does not fall under (*a*). In these cases the Koran should be taken in its literal (*ẓāhir*) and general (*ʿāmm*) meaning, unless there is a consensus to the contrary;[3]

(*c*) the consensus of the Muslims (including the consensus related from the preceding generations), even if it is not based on the Koran or a *sunna* [that is, a tradition from the Prophet]. The consensus is as good as a generally accepted *sunna*, and it is never an arbitrary opinion (*ra'y*) because this last is subject to divergencies;[4]

(*d*) traditions based on the authority of individual transmitters. But these may serve as an argument only if they are transmitted in a way which makes them safe from error;

(*e*) analogy. But a conclusion by analogy may only be drawn if the two problems in question are exactly parallel.

The consensus is the final argument on all subjects, and not subject to error, but (*c*) is different from (*a*); (*a*) comprises the scholars and the people, that is, all Muslims, and (*c*) is the consensus of the scholars who have the requisite knowledge. The consensus of the scholars or the lack of it, is an indication of the state of agreement or disagreement in the preceding generation, whether the scholars quote a tradition or not; their agreement is only feasible on the basis of an authoritative

[1] Below, p. 51.

[2] Or the *khabar al-infirād* (pp. 257, 258).

[3] That is, it must not be interpreted restrictively in the light of traditions from the Prophet which are not supported by the consensus.

[4] *Sunna* is used here in the meaning given to it by Shāfiʿī, and Shāfiʿī states in fact that he has edited this discussion. The reference to *ra'y* answers Shāfiʿī's standing objection that the 'living tradition' of the ancient schools is only a mass of arbitrary opinions.

tradition, and a tradition is authoritative only if they accept it unanimously as such.[1] Shāfiʿī draws the, to him, obvious conclusion that this means depriving the traditions of their authority, and substituting the consensus for them.

To us, if we may anticipate part of the results of Chapter 8 below, Shāfiʿī's doctrine expresses the reaction of a traditionist against the principle of consensus as embodying the 'living tradition'; this principle had found natural recognition in the ancient schools of law and was to come into its own again in the doctrine of consensus of the classical theory of Muhammadan law, a theory which had to take into account, however, the status which had meanwhile been won by Shāfiʿī for the traditions from the Prophet.

This seemingly simple picture of what Shāfiʿī regards as the anti-traditionist attitude of the ancient schools has to be qualified in two respects. Firstly, at the time when Shāfiʿī appeared, the ancient schools were already on the defensive against the mounting tide of traditions from the Prophet. We find a trace of this in the preceding extract. It becomes clearer still from a passage in the same context (p. 256) where Shāfiʿī claims that the opponents regard as the best authorities on law those who are most knowledgeable on traditions. But the list of ancient authorities on law which Shāfiʿī gives in this connexion and which has been translated before,[2] contains the names of lawyers and not of traditionists, and the farther we go back, the more we find the lawyers independent of traditions.

Secondly, the ancient schools of law make an exception in favour of traditions from individual Companions of the Prophet. This is only another aspect of the independent authority which they ascribe to certain Companions and which we have discussed in Chapter 4. From the point of view of the traditionists a single Companion, whether he transmits explicitly from the Prophet or gives his own doctrine which can be presumed to agree with a decision of the Prophet, is only a single transmitter. The adherents of the ancient schools had therefore to justify their apparent inconsistency in relying on the authority of single

[1] The assumption that the consensus was necessarily based on traditions, was forced on the ancient schools of law either by Shāfiʿī himself or by the traditionists. See the parallel passage in *Ris.* 65 (below, p. 90 and n. 2). The authentic reasoning of the ancient schools shows no trace of this assumption.

[2] Above, p. 7 f.

Companions. This is the background of a passage (pp. 258 ff.) which, on the face of it, seems rather surprising in a context which treats of the anti-traditionist attitude of the ancient schools.

The Iraqian opponent, speaking for the ancient schools in general, explains that a *sunna* of the Prophet can be established in the ways (*a*) and (*d*) above, and further, if one Companion relates something from the Prophet and no other Companion contradicts him. Then one must conclude that he related it in the midst of the Companions and that they did not contradict him because they knew that he was right. So it can be considered as a tradition from the Companions in general. The same applies to their silence on a decision given by one of them.

This passage makes sense only if we regard the last words as operative, and take it as intended to justify the reliance on the opinions of individual Companions, as practised in the ancient schools of law. The kind of argument which the followers of the ancient schools use here in favour of traditions related by individual Companions from the Prophet, they use elsewhere in favour of Companions' opinions as against traditions from the Prophet.[1] At the stage of discussion which Shāfi'ī has preserved, the followers of the ancient schools used the existence of traditions related by single Companions from the Prophet as an argument in order to justify their reliance on the opinions of the Companions themselves. But Shāfi'ī, in stating the case of the ancient schools polemically, shifted the emphasis to their implicit recognition of 'isolated' traditions from the Prophet.[2]

B. Arguments against Traditions from the Prophet

We now turn to the individual arguments that were brought forward against traditions from the Prophet.

The most sweeping argument occurs in *Ikh.* 366 ff. Here the representative of one of the two groups opposed to traditions addresses Shāfi'ī: 'You regard two things as grounds for the rejection of a tradition: the ignorance of an unreliable trans-

[1] See below, p. 50.

[2] The term '*sunna* of the Prophet' meant for Shāfi'ī a formal tradition from the Prophet, but it was used by the others, the Iraqians in particular, in order to claim for their 'living tradition' the general authority of the Prophet; see below, p. 73 f.

mitter, and the existence of another tradition to the contrary. Our thesis is that what is possible with one tradition is possible with all of them'—in other words, that the recognized traditions are no more reliable than the rejected ones. Shāfi'ī justifies his attitude by the parallel of a judge who will accept the evidence of a witness whom he knows to be reliable, will reject that of one whose character has been challenged, and will reserve his judgment on the evidence of a third whose status he does not know. Shāfi'ī denies his opponents the right of rejecting traditions to which no direct objection can be made. The same argument recurs in Ibn Qutaiba, 10 f., in the mouth of the *ahl al-kalām*.

Criticism of traditions on material grounds, which is not unknown even to Shāfi'ī,[1] is pushed to the extreme by the *ahl al-kalām*. They point out that many traditions are contrary to reason (*naẓar*) and observation (*'iyān*), absurd and ridiculous.[2] It is worth noticing that this kind of reasoning which occurs continuously in Ibn Qutaiba, is not discussed by Shāfi'ī.[3]

An argument frequently used by the adversaries of traditions from the Prophet, is that they contradict the Koran which ought to be the main object of study in preference to traditions, and the standard by which traditions are accepted or rejected. Shāfi'ī calls this 'rejecting the traditions by comparing them with the Koran' (*Tr. IX*, 5). This reasoning is put into the mouth of Companions such as 'Ā'isha, 'Alī, Ibn 'Abbās, 'Umar, and even, illogically enough, of the Prophet himself. In *Ris.* 32, the opponent refers to a tradition which makes the Prophet say: 'Compare what is related on my authority, with the Koran; if it agrees with it, I have said it, and if it does not agree, I have not said it.'[4] Shāfi'ī, however, does not consider this tradition well authenticated. Another tradition to the same effect makes the Prophet say: 'People ought not to shelter behind my authority (*lā yamsikann al-nās 'alaiya bi-shai'*); I allow only what Allah allows, and forbid only what Allah forbids.'[5] Shāfi'ī

[1] See above, p. 37 f.

[2] Ibn Qutaiba, 147, 151, 234, 324, and often; Mas'ūdī, i. 270 f.; iv. 26. See also the caricature of a legal discussion in Jāḥiẓ, *Ḥayawān*, i. 141 ff., 180.

[3] The reason is probably that many of the more extravagant of these traditions came into circulation only after the time of Shāfi'ī; see below, p. 256.

[4] For parallel versions see above, p. 28, and below, p. 253 f.

[5] For a parallel version, see above, p. 28.

discusses this tradition in *Tr. V*, 264, and explains it away as referring to personal privileges of the Prophet.

The same anti-traditionist reasoning is supposed but refuted in a tradition which makes the Prophet say: 'Let me find no one of you reclining on his couch, and, when confronted with an order or a prohibition from me, saying: I do not know [whether this is authentic or not], we follow [only] what we find in the Koran.'[1] Shāfi'ī quotes this tradition in *Tr. V*, 264, and in *Ris.* 15 on the authority of Ibn 'Uyaina with a full *isnād* back to the Prophet, but in *Ris.* 15 also on the authority of Ibn 'Uyaina from Muhammad b. Munkadir as a *mursal* from the Prophet. This latter form of the *isnād* is certainly the original one and shows that the polemics of the traditionists and anti-traditionists, which are reflected in this tradition, took place in the generation before Ibn 'Uyaina, that is, in the first third of the second century A.H.

This kind of argument drawn from the Koran against traditions from the Prophet is particularly familiar to the Iraqians;[2] but it is also used by the *ahl al-kalām*.[3] As the latter go much farther in their anti-traditionist attitude, we find Shāfi'ī and the Iraqians on common ground against 'those who follow the outward meaning of the Koran and disregard the traditions' (*Umm*, vi. 115).

A secondary stage of this anti-traditionist argument is represented by the assumption that the Koran repeals traditions. In *Ris.* 32 where the opponent uses this argument, Shāfi'ī replies that no scholar will say that. But *Ikh.* 48 shows that an opinion based on this reasoning was held 'to this very day', and *Tr. III*, 60, identifies the holders of this opinion as the Medinese.[4] Shāfi'ī's final argument in favour of the traditions, here and in other cases, is the truism that to reason in this way would mean whittling away the majority of the *sunnas* of the Prophet (*Ris.* 33 f.).

The followers of traditions went a step farther and formulated the principle that the *sunna* prevails over the Koran, but the Koran does not prevail over the *sunna*,[5] or that the Koran may

[1] The text contains several expressions typical of the discussions in the second century A.H.

[2] See above, pp. 28, 30.

[3] Ibn Qutaiba, 53, 112, 256.

[4] For the details, see below, p. 263.

[5] Dārimī, *Bāb al-sunna qāḍiya 'alā kitāb Allāh*.

be repealed by the *sunna* of the Prophet.[1] As Shāfi'ī identifies himself with the traditionists and shares their other arguments against the adherents of the ancient schools and the *ahl al-kalām*,[2] it is safe to assume that this extreme position of which I find no trace in Shāfi'ī's writings or before him, was taken or at least gained prominence only after his time.

The anti-traditionist attitude showed itself further in unwillingness to relate traditions from the Prophet, insistence on their small number, warnings against careless attribution of traditions to the Prophet, and similar considerations which were especially popular in Iraq.[3] Statements to this effect voiced originally the opposition of the ancient Iraqians to the growing number of traditions from the Prophet and attempted to justify the Iraqians' customary reliance on later authorities. By an easy transition, this kind of reasoning could be adopted by the moderate traditionists and used by them as a proof of the care with which, they claimed, traditions from the Prophet had been transmitted.

Such arguments, however, could not prevent the growth of traditions from the Prophet, and the followers of the ancient schools had to explain away traditions which contradicted their own established doctrine. We have already given details of the interpretation of traditions from the Prophet as practised by Shāfi'ī and by the followers of the ancient schools,[4] and are concerned here only with one particular aspect of their interpretative reasoning. This is the fact that the method of interpreting traditions, practised in the ancient schools, tended to disparage and reject traditions from the Prophet,[5] whereas Shāfi'ī, by harmonizing interpretation, did his utmost to acknowledge and maintain them.[6]

According to *Ikh.* 328 ff., the Iraqians are inclined to look for contradictions in the traditions, and where two are contradictory to reject one.[7] Shāfi'ī, who applies harmonizing interpreta-

[1] Ibn Qutaiba, 243 ff., 250, 260.
[2] See below, section C.
[3] Dārimī, *Bāb man hāb al-futyā*.
[4] Above, pp. 13 f., 23, 30.
[5] This tendency prevailed, too, among the *ahl al-kalām* who used considerations familiar to the Iraqians in particular, with an extreme anti-traditionist bias: Ibn Qutaiba, 182, 195 ff., 241 ff., 256, 343.
[6] See below, p. 56 f.
[7] Also the *ahl al-kalām* point out contradictions in traditions: Ibn Qutaiba, 153, 268 ff. and often.

tion, considers their destructive criticism of traditions as a 'perversion of straightforward interpretation' and a 'screen in front of those who are not perspicacious enough' (p. 331 f.). The Iraqians go so far as to suppose that two contradictory traditions cancel each other out, thus leaving the way free for the use of analogy (*Ris.* 81). Ṭaḥāwī often reasons in the same way; as do the Mālikīs, except that they substitute practice (*ʿamal*) for analogy (e.g. Zurqānī, iii. 36).

An easy method of explaining away traditions from the Prophet was the gratuitous assumption of repeal. We find this assumption made by the Iraqians (e.g. *Muw. Shaib.* 142), by the Medinese, who refer to the different practice of Medina (e.g. *Ikh.* 217 f.), and by Auzāʿī, who refers to the different practice of Abū Bakr (*Tr. IX*, 29). Shāfiʿī refused to recognize this method, since its use would enable all traditions to be whittled away (*Ris.* 17).

Another easy method of disposing of traditions from the Prophet by interpretation was to represent them as particular commands, applicable only to the occasion on which they were given. This argument is exemplified by a tradition on the artificial creation of foster-parentship between adults (*Muw.* iii. 89). According to it, ʿĀ'isha made a habit of this practice, but the other wives of the Prophet regarded his ruling as a special one for the benefit of the individual in question. The argument is meant to invalidate the tradition related from ʿĀ'isha in favour of the practice. The anti-traditionist argument in its turn was met by two counter-arguments. According to one ʿĀ'isha referred, against her fellow wife Umm Salama, to the example of the Prophet (Muslim, quoted in Zurqānī, *ad loc.*). According to the second the other wives of the Prophet were engaged in the same practice.[1] In Shāfiʿī's time, the ancient schools had systematized the anti-traditionist argument by regarding particular commands of the Prophet as based on the exercise of his discretion (*ijtihād*), and concluding that the imam, the head of the state, was authorized to do the same.[2] The examples adduced here are Medinese, but Iraqians also used this argument.

[1] Two traditions to this effect are related by Nāfiʿ: *Muw.* iii. 87 f.; *Muw. Shaib.* 272.

[2] *Tr. III*, 61 (cf. Zurqānī, iii. 204). To the pair *ḥukm* and *ijtihād* in *Tr. III* corresponds the pair *fatwā* and *ḥukm* in Zurqānī.

A further method of invalidating traditions by interpretation was to regard them as referring to personal privileges of the Prophet. This method, which is a special case of the one discussed in the preceding paragraph, is refuted, and therefore supposed to exist, in two traditions. In one of them (*Muw.* ii. 89; *Muw. Shaib.* 178) the Prophet declares explicitly that a certain practice is no special privilege of his and says: 'I hope that I am the most god-fearing and the most learned among you.' According to the other (*Muw.* ii. 92; *Muw. Shaib.* 180), a man sends his wife to consult Umm Salama, a wife of the Prophet, on a certain practice; Umm Salama replies that the Prophet has this practice, but the man is all the more dejected because the Prophet has special privileges, and sends his wife again; the Prophet declares angrily that he is more mindful of Allah's orders than anyone. There is a further tradition about this particular case (*Muw.* ii. 94) which presents the anti-traditionist tendency directly. In this version 'Ā'isha declares that the Prophet had indeed the practice in question, but adds: 'The Prophet kept himself more under control than all of you.'

Both Iraqians and Medinese used this method of assuming a personal privilege on the part of the Prophet, and the traditionists themselves adopted it when they wanted to invalidate a tradition which contradicted their own. Shāfi'ī's reply is always the same: 'If one started that line of reasoning, there would be no end to it ... and the *sunnas* would be whittled away' (*Tr. IX*, 39).

There is further the assumption that actions of the Prophet as reported in traditions represent only his personal taste or preference.[1] The idea that one ought to follow the Prophet even in his personal tastes was as yet unknown to Shāfi'ī, though it had already found expression before him.[2]

These examples are not meant to be exhaustive, but are sufficient to show the importance of anti-traditionist interpretations in the period before Shāfi'ī.

We have seen in Chapter 4 that the ancient schools of law based their doctrines, generally speaking, on traditions going

[1] *Muw.* iv. 204 and *Ikh.* 149. This example is Medinese; the Iraqians minimize the effect of the tradition in question by interpretation, see *Muw. Shaib.* 280.

[2] See *Muw.* iii. 32. Ibn Qutaiba (58 f.) still rejected the idea although it was voiced in Mu'tazila circles. In Ṭaḥāwī, ii. 314, it has become part of the accepted doctrine.

back to Companions rather than on those going back to the Prophet. Their common thesis that the Companions could not be unaware of the *sunna* of the Prophet and would know it best, takes its place beside the other arguments put forward against traditions from the Prophet. The extreme group of anti-traditionists use the same reasoning as that used by the adherents of the ancient schools of law.[1] They point out that other Companions are more knowledgeable than a certain Abū Tha'laba, whose tradition from the Prophet is to be rejected.[2] And in direct opposition to the Iraqian tradition which claims for the doctrine of Ibn Mas'ūd, by implication, the authority of the Prophet,[3] a counter-tradition makes 'Alī say: 'The word of a bedouin from the tribe Ashja' cannot prevail over the Koran' (*Comm. Muw. Shaib.* 245, n. 1). Here, an originally anti-traditionist argument is used in the polemics of the ancient schools.[4]

Finally, there is the argument based on the lack of documentation of traditions from the Prophet. In its simplest form, common to all types of anti-traditionist, it says that an 'isolated' tradition, that is, a tradition transmitted by a single individual (*khabar al-wāḥid, khabar al-infirād*), cannot be accepted as well authenticated. The simplest variant of the argument maintains that a tradition, to be accepted, must be transmitted by at least two reliable witnesses, as is the case with legal evidence. This conclusion is expressed in a tradition by which 'Umar is shown as not content with the information of a single individual on a decision of the Prophet, but asking for confirmation by another person.[5] But a tradition based on the statement of one person can, as is the case with legal evidence, be accepted if it is confirmed by oath.[6]

This parallel between traditions and legal evidence is drawn explicitly by the representative of the ancient schools in the detailed discussion in *Ris.* 52 f., and it is indeed so obvious that

[1] See above, pp. 25, 31.

[2] *Ikh.* 46. Further reasoning of the *ahl al-kalām* against the Companions: Ibn Qutaiba, 24 ff.

[3] See above, p. 29, n. 3.

[4] See below, p. 227 f.

[5] *Ris.* 59 f.; *Muw.* iv. 200. Parallel traditions, also on 'Umar, are in Bukhārī, *Kitāb al-i'tiṣām bil-kitāb wal-sunna*, and in Zurqānī, iv. 44. See also Ibn Qutaiba, 48.

[6] See the tradition on 'Alī referred to, together with the tradition on 'Umar, by Abū Yūsuf in *Tr. IX*, 5: above, p. 28.

even Shāfi'ī, who argues strongly for the acceptance of traditions even if they are transmitted by single individuals only, has to acknowledge it to a certain extent.[1] He points out, among other things, that the number of witnesses demanded for legal evidence is not always two. This fact is used in favour of the *khabar al-wāḥid* in two traditions which make 'Uthmān and Zaid b. Thābit respectively accept the information of one woman on certain decisions of the Prophet (*Ris.* 60). For these decisions concern feminine matters, and a widely held doctrine admitted the evidence of one woman on such subjects.

The disparagement of the *khabar al-wāḥid* was, in fact, so typical of the ancient schools of law that Shāfi'ī, using a synonym, could refer to them as 'those who reject the *khabar al-khāṣṣa*'.[2] According to them, it is ignorance to accept the *khabar al-infirād* (*Tr. IV*, 256, at the end). Abū Yūsuf warns against isolated traditions[3] and says: 'We consider an isolated tradition irregular, and do not follow it' (*Tr. IX*, 9). Shaibānī points out that a certain tradition is isolated, and states that the majority of scholars do not follow it (*Muw. Shaib.* 148). According to Ṭaḥāwī, ii. 280, an isolated tradition cannot serve to establish matter additional to the Koran and to generally recognized traditions, or prove their repeal. The Medinese reject isolated traditions from the Prophet (*Tr. III*, 148, p. 242), and hold that their own consensus takes precedence over them (*Ris.* 73). They are not consistent, however, and Shāfi'ī can say to them: 'If Mālik objects that this is an isolated tradition,[4] then what does he think of all those cases where he relates isolated traditions and relies on them? Either the isolated tradition is a reliable argument . . . or it is not; and if not, you must discard all those cases in which you rely on isolated traditions' (*Tr. III*, 148, p. 249). The same applies to the Iraqians.

The *ahl al-kalām* go farther and demand that a tradition, to be accepted, must be transmitted by many from many (*mā rawāh al-kāffa 'an al-kāffa*) or widely spread (*khabar al-tawātur*).[5] In defining this condition they disagree: 'They disagree as to how a tradition becomes certain. Some say: through one

[1] See *Ikh.* 3 f., 35, 366 ff., and elsewhere.
[2] See above, pp. 41 ff.
[3] See above, p. 28.
[4] In this case not from the Prophet, but from a Companion.
[5] On another term see above, p. 42.

veracious transmitter; others say: through two, because Allah demands two trustworthy witnesses; others say: through three, because the Koran says (ix. 122): "a troop of every division of them", and the smallest number to which the term troop can be applied, is three; others say: through four, because Allah demands four witnesses [in the case of adultery]; others: through twelve, because the Koran says (v. 12): "We raised up of them twelve wardens"; others: through twenty, because the Koran says (viii. 65): "If there be of you twenty patient men"; others: through seventy, because the Koran says (vii. 154): "And Moses chose from his people seventy men"' (Ibn Qutaiba, 78 f.). The most commonly held opinion demanded twenty transmitters in each generation.[1]

According to Shāfiʿī, the *khabar al-wāḥid*, if related by a trustworthy transmitter, is sufficient to establish the *sunna* of the Prophet; it cannot be refuted by conclusions drawn from the Koran or from another tradition which is capable of several interpretations; and it does not matter that it is transmitted by only one person (*Tr. III*, 10). It can be invalidated only by a greater number of traditions to the contrary (*Ikh.* 165; *Ris.* 40). Shāfiʿī devotes three long passages to a detailed argument for the *khabar al-wāḥid*.[2] He even claims a consensus of the scholars, past and present, in its favour;[3] but this claim is belied by the strength of the opposition. His only concession is that the *khabar al-wāḥid* is weaker than a unanimously recognized *sunna* and does not produce absolute knowledge, although it must serve as a basis for action.[4]

The later theory on the *khabar al-wāḥid* did not go as far as Shāfiʿī's doctrine.[5] Among the authors of collections of traditions, Bukhārī (*Kitāb akhbār al-āḥād*) repeats Shāfiʿī's essential arguments, Muslim (*Bāb ṣiḥḥat al-iḥtijāj bil-ḥadīth al-muʿanʿan*) takes the acceptance of the *khabar al-wāḥid* as common ground, Tirmidhī (at the end) includes it in his category of *gharīb* ('strange') traditions, thus setting it apart, and Dāraquṭnī (p. 361) accepts it only with certain qualifications.

[1] See Nyberg, in *E.I.*, s.v. Muʿtazila.
[2] *Tr. IV*, 258 ff.; *Ikh.* 4 ff.; *Ris.* 51 ff.
[3] See particularly *Ikh.* 25 f.
[4] *Ris.* 82 (quoted below, p. 135); *Ikh.* 5.
[5] See Marçais, *Taqrīb* (in *J.A.*, 9th ser., xviii. 113, n. 1).

C. Arguments in favour of Traditions from the Prophet

We have had to review in section B, in connexion with the arguments brought forward against the traditions from the Prophet, a number of those adduced in their favour. The present section is, therefore, confined to those arguments of the traditionists which have not been already discussed.

The argument that the Koran is more authoritative than traditions from the Prophet is countered by the assertion that the Prophet to whom the Koran was revealed, knew best how to interpret it, and that he acted as Allah ordered him to act (*Ikh.* 404). This reasoning is put into the mouth of Sa'īd b. Jubair and of 'Umar himself.[1] The fear is expressed that unsound doctrine will follow a widespread knowledge of the Koran,[2] and the Prophet is made to declare that the Koran alone is no guarantee against error.[3] One decision of the Prophet is put in a pointed manner under the aegis of the Koran, although it does not occur there.[4] A tradition related by Muṭṭalib b. Ḥanṭab from the Prophet claims that the *sunna*, as embodied in traditions from the Prophet, contains all orders and prohibitions in the same way as the Koran; it makes the Prophet say: 'I have left nothing on which Allah has given you an order, without giving you that order, and nothing on which Allah has given you a prohibition, without giving you that prohibition' (*Ris.* 15). This Muṭṭalib b. Ḥanṭab, who is mentioned also elsewhere in Shāfi'ī, is ostensibly a Companion of

[1] Dārimī, *Bāb al-sunna qāḍiya 'alā kitāb Allāh*; *Bāb ittibā' al-sunna.*

[2] Abū Dāwūd, *Bāb fī luzūm al-sunna.*

[3] Tirmidhī, *Bāb mā jā' fī dhahāb al-'ilm*: the Prophet predicts the disappearance of knowledge; Ziyād b. Labīd remarks: 'But we have got the Koran'; the Prophet replies: 'Surely you are not one of the scholars of Medina; consider what happened to the Jews and Christians although they had the Torah and the Gospel.' Jubair b. Nufair has it confirmed by 'Ubāda b. Ṣāmit that Abul-Dardā' relates this tradition correctly.—The tradition presupposes the claim of Medina to be the home of the true *sunna*, and is, therefore, later than Shāfi'ī (see above, p. 8). The names of the two Companions on whose authority it is related are taken from the two versions of the tradition on Mu'āwiya which expresses a similar tendency in favour of traditions from the Prophet (see below, p. 55).

[4] *Muw.* iv. 7; *Muw. Shaib.* 305: the Prophet is asked to give judgment according to the Koran, on a married woman and an unmarried man who have committed adultery; he has the woman lapidated and the man flogged and banished. This is obviously later than the Iraqian traditions on the problem of banishment (see below, p. 209).

the Prophet; but the biographical works know him only as a late Successor; a Companion of that name, known to later biographical works only, does not occur in *isnāds*; this shows how carelessly the *isnāds* were sometimes put together.[1]

The traditionists defended themselves against the reproach of ignorance of law by quoting the words attributed to the Prophet: 'Luck to the man who hears my words, remembers them, guards them and hands them on; many a transmitter of legal knowledge is no lawyer himself, and many a one transmits legal knowledge to persons who are more learned in it than he is' (*Ris.* 55, 65).[2]

The practice, prevalent in the ancient schools, of referring to Companions and Successors is countered by numerous traditions which represent, with an obvious polemical tendency, Companions and later authorities as deferring to traditions from the Prophet. Shāfi'ī has collected a number of these traditions in *Ris.* 59 and 61 f. The following examples are typical. 'Umar changes his customary decision on hearing that the Prophet has decided differently. 'Umar inquires whether anyone knows of a decision of the Prophet on a problem; when informed of it, he gives judgment accordingly and says: 'Had we not heard this, we should have given another judgment', or: 'We should almost have given judgment according to our own opinion (*ra'y*).' Ibn 'Umar relates: 'We used to conclude the agricultural contract of *mukhābara* and thought it unexceptionable, but we stopped doing it when we heard that the Prophet had forbidden it.'

These traditions, and others, reflect the struggle of the traditionists for the mastery over law. The following two traditions take us directly into the time of this struggle.

(*a*) Shāfi'ī—anonymous—Ibn Abī Dhi'b—Sa'd b. Ibrāhīm gave a judgment according to the opinion of Rabī'a b. Abī 'Abdalraḥmān, and Ibn Abī Dhi'b informed him of a tradition from the Prophet to the contrary; when Sa'd referred his

[1] Sheikh Shākir concludes painstakingly in a note extending from p. 97 to p. 103 of his edition of *Ris.*, that the person in Shāfi'ī's *isnād* is another Companion of the same name.

[2] The *isnād* runs: Ibn 'Uyaina (a main representative of the traditionists)—'Abdalmalik b. 'Umair—'Abdalraḥmān—his father Ibn Mas'ūd—Prophet; the name and authority of Ibn Mas'ūd are borrowed from the Iraqians against whom this tradition is directed.

dilemma to Rabī'a, mentioning that Ibn Abī Dhi'b was reliable, Rabī'a replied: 'You have used your discretion (*ijtihād*) and your judgment is given for good'; but Sa'd said: 'Am I to execute my judgment and reverse the judgment of the Prophet? I will rather reverse my judgment and execute the judgment of the Prophet'; he called for the written document, tore it up, and gave judgment to the contrary.

(*b*) Shāfi'ī—Abū Ḥanīfa b. Simāk Shihābī—Ibn Abī Dhi'b—Maqburī—Abū Shuraiḥ Ka'bī—the Prophet in the year of the conquest of Mecca declared that the avenger of a murdered man can choose between weregeld and retaliation; Abū Ḥanīfa Shihābī asked Ibn Abī Dhi'b: 'Do you accept this?' Thereupon Ibn Abī Dhi'b 'pushed my breast, shouted loudly, abused me and said: "I relate to you a tradition from the Prophet and you ask whether I accept it! Yes, I accept it, and this is my duty and the duty of whosoever hears it; Allah has chosen Muhammad from all mankind and guided mankind through him and by him, and has decreed for it what he decreed for him and through him; men have only to follow him with good or bad grace, and no Muslim can escape from that." And he did not cease until I implored him to be silent.' This Ibn Abī Dhi'b is a prominent traditionist. It is obvious that Shāfi'ī has taken over the traditionists' argument.

The blame which Ibn Abī Dhi'b and Shāfi'ī attached to those who did not subordinate their legal doctrine to traditions from the Prophet was projected back into the early period. For example, a tradition informs us that Mu'āwiya concluded a certain contract, and that Abul-Dardā' informed him that the Prophet had forbidden this kind of contract. Mu'āwiya replied that he considered his transaction unexceptionable, but Abul-Dardā' said: 'I give him information from the Prophet, and he informs me of what he thinks (*ra'y*); I will not live together with you in the same country.' Abul-Dardā' then informed 'Umar, and 'Umar forbade Mu'āwiya to conclude this kind of contract.[1] A similar story on the same contract about Mu'āwiya and 'Ubāda b. Ṣāmit is reported in the classical collections of traditions.[2]

Information coming from the Prophet is opposed to informa-

[1] *Muw.* iii. 112; *Muw. Shaib.* 350; *Ris.* 61, &c.

[2] e.g. Ibn Māja, *Bāb ta'ẓīm ḥadīth rasūl Allāh.*

tion derived from other persons in a tradition related by Muʿtamir on the authority of his father, Sulaimān, from Ibn ʿAbbās, who is reported to have said: 'Are you not afraid to say: "The Prophet said so-and-so, and N.N. said so-and-so"? '[1] Muʿtamir is the person in whom the *isnāds* of several other traditions of a traditionist bias converge. He or someone using his name must therefore be considered responsible for them. We need not go into the numerous other traditions of the same tendency, couched in more general terms, in the classical collections.[2]

Finally, to counter the more or less arbitrary interpretations by which the ancient schools of law tended to eliminate traditions, Shāfiʿī employed a consistent method of interpretation which he applied both to Koran and traditions and which he opposed explicitly to that used by his predecessors.[3] It is based on the distinction between general (*ʿāmm*, *jumla*, *mujmal*) and particular or explanatory (*khāṣṣ*, *mufassir*) statements, a distinction which enables him to harmonize rulings apparently contradictory. A general ruling stated in general terms (*jumla makhrajuhā ʿāmm*) may still envisage a special case (*yurād biha l-khāṣṣ*).[4] But every ruling must be taken in its obvious or literal (*ẓāhir*) and unrestricted meaning unless there is an indication to the contrary on the authority of the Prophet or in the consensus of the scholars.[5] In practice, both considerations work invariably in favour of the acceptance of traditions.[6] Shāfiʿī devotes a considerable part of the *Risāla* and many passages in the *Ikhtilāf al-Ḥadīth* to the development of this theory of interpretation, and he co-ordinates it with his acceptance of traditions from single individuals. It must be considered as his personal achievement, although considerations of *ʿāmm*, *jumla*, *khāṣṣ*, and *ẓāhir* were not unknown to the ancient schools of law.

Shāfiʿī's disciple Muzanī, in his *Kitāb al-Amr wal-Nahy*, takes up the theory of his master and applies it to the question of how far a command, or imperative, may be taken to express a per-

[1] Dārimī, *Bāb mā yuttaqā min tafsīr ḥadīth al-nabī*.

[2] See particularly Muslim, introductory chapters; Abū Dāwūd, *Kitāb al-sunna*; Tirmidhī, *Abwāb al-ʿilm*; Ibn Māja and Dārimī, introductory chapters.

[3] *Ikh.* 37 f., 47, 306, 328 ff.

[4] *Ris.* 9 f.; *Ikh.* 321.

[5] *Ris.* 46; *Ikh.* 56, 150 ff.

[6] See, e.g., *Ris.* 29; *Ikh.* 23 ff., 297, 401.

mission, and whether a prohibition may convey not a total but only a partial interdiction.

Shāfiʿī does not go as far as some extreme followers of traditions of whom he says: 'Another party is simply ignorant, clings to its ignorance and refuses to learn, and therefore becomes embarrassed. These are the people who say: "You reject one tradition and accept another"' (*Ikh.* 367 f.). Shāfiʿī answers them with the same reasoning he uses in his reply to the parallel thesis of their direct adversaries, the extreme anti-traditionists.[1] This is the only important case in which Shāfiʿī does not identify himself with the traditionists.

D. Conclusions

Most arguments against traditions transmitted from the Prophet are common to the ancient schools of law; the Medinese are in no way more enthusiastic about them than the Iraqians. The arguments in favour of traditions from the Prophet are often derived from, or secondary to, arguments against them; the unwillingness to accept them came first. It is not the case, as has often been supposed *a priori*, that it was the most natural thing, from the first generation after the Prophet onwards, to refer to his real or alleged rulings in all doubtful cases. Traditions from the Prophet had to overcome a strong opposition on the part of the ancient schools of law, let alone the *ahl al-kalām*, before they gained general acceptance. Shāfiʿī still had to fight hard to secure the recognition of their overriding authority. At the same time it is obvious that once this thesis had been consciously formulated, it was certain of success, and the ancient schools had no real defence against the rising tide of traditions from the Prophet. But this relatively late development, which we may call natural, must not blind us to the essentially different situation in the early period.

[1] Above, p. 45. Shāfiʿī's mention of 'those who aspire to a thorough traditional foundation of their doctrine' (above, p. 36) possibly refers to the same group of uncritical traditionists.

CHAPTER 7

SUNNA, 'PRACTICE' AND 'LIVING TRADITION'

THE classical theory of Muhammadan law defines *sunna* as the model behaviour of the Prophet.[1] This is the meaning in which Shāfiʿī uses the word; for him, '*sunna*' and '*sunna* of the Prophet' are synonymous. But *sunna* means, strictly speaking, nothing more than 'precedent', 'way of life'. Goldziher has shown that this originally pagan term was taken over and adapted by Islam,[2] and Margoliouth has concluded that *sunna* as a principle of law meant originally the ideal or normative usage of the community, and only later acquired the restricted meaning of precedents set by the Prophet.[3] The aim of the present chapter is to analyse in detail the meaning in which *sunna* is used by Shāfiʿī and in the ancient schools of law—an analysis which will be found to confirm the conclusion of Margoliouth—and beyond this, to investigate the concepts which in the ancient schools occupied the place filled in the later system by the '*sunna* of the Prophet'. The foremost of these concepts, which on one side are closely connected with the ancient meaning of *sunna*, and on the other merge into consensus, is the customary or 'generally agreed practice' (*ʿamal, al-amr al-mujtamaʿ ʿalaih*). Lacking an indigenous term for this group of concepts, we shall call them the 'living tradition' of the ancient schools, not by way of projecting a category of the later system, under another name, back into the early period, but in recognition of the fact that they are all inter-related and, in fact, interchangeable to such an extent that they cannot be isolated from one another.

A. General

Ibn Muqaffaʿ, a secretary of state in late Umaiyad and early ʿAbbāsid times, subjected the old idea of *sunna* to sharp criticism. Anticipating Shāfiʿī he realized that *sunna* as it was understood in his time, was based not on authentic precedents laid down by the Prophet and the first Caliphs, but to a great extent on administrative

[1] See above, p. 1.
[2] *Muh. St.* ii. 11 ff.; a short statement: *Principles*, 294 f.
[3] *Early Development*, 69 f., 75.

regulations of the Umaiyad government. In contrast to Shāfiʿī, however, he did not fall back on traditions from the Prophet but drew the contrary conclusion that the Caliph was free to fix and codify the alleged *sunna*.[1]

The early texts contain numerous traces of the process by which traditions from the Prophet imposed themselves on the old idea of *sunna* and thereby prepared the ground for Shāfiʿī's identification of *sunna* with them. In the time of Shāfiʿī, traditions from the Prophet, particularly 'isolated' ones, were still felt to be something recent which disturbed the 'living tradition' of doctrine in the ancient schools. In *Ikh.* 284, the Iraqian opponent points out that Shāfiʿī's reasoning, which starts from traditions, is new compared with that of Shāfiʿī's companions, the Medinese, who base themselves on practice. Shāfiʿī replies: 'I have told you before that practice means nothing, and we cannot be held responsible for what others say; so stop arguing about it.'

Similarly, in *Tr. III*, 148 (p. 243), Shāfiʿī addresses a Basrian opponent: 'If you answered consistently with your principle, you ought to hold that men are obliged to act, not according to what is related from the Prophet, but according to a corresponding practice or lack of practice after him.' The opponent replies: 'I do not hold that.' But this refers only to the negative consequence which Shāfiʿī forces on him, as appears from his further reply: 'There can be no *sunna* of the Prophet on which the Caliphs have not acted after him.'

In *Ris.* 58, commenting on a tradition which makes ʿUmar change his decision when a decision of the Prophet to the contrary became known to him, Shāfiʿī says: 'A tradition from the Prophet must be accepted as soon as it becomes known, even if it is not supported by any corresponding action of a Caliph. If there has been an action on the part of a Caliph and a tradition from the Prophet to the contrary becomes known later, that action must be discarded in favour of the tradition from the Prophet. A tradition from the Prophet derives its authority from itself and not from the action of a later authority. The Muslims [when informed of a tradition from the Prophet] did not make the objection that ʿUmar had acted differently in the midst of the Companions.'[2] The opponent acknowledges that if this were correct, it would prove that the *sunna*, in Shāfiʿī's sense, superseded all contrary practice, that one could not pretend that the validity of the *sunna* required confirmation by evidence of its subsequent application, and that nothing contradictory to the *sunna* could affect it in any way.[3] This shows what the actual doctrine of the opponents is.

[1] *Ṣaḥāba*, 126. See further below, pp. 95, 102 f.

[2] This is exactly what the opponents say, as Shāfiʿī implies a few lines farther on.

[3] The text is to be corrected after *ed. Shākir*, p. 425.

We now realize that the arguments, which were adduced by the ancient schools of law against traditions from the Prophet, for instance, the assumption of repeal and the consideration that the Companions would not have been unaware of the Prophet's decisions, were directed against traditions from the Prophet, not as such but only in so far as by their recent growth they tended to disrupt the 'living tradition' of the schools. This explains the apparent inconsistency of sometimes referring to traditions from the Prophet, and sometimes rejecting them in favour of the established doctrine.

Among the earliest authentic illustrations of the ancient attitude to practice are two statements of Ibrāhīm Nakha'ī. Ibrāhīm is aware that the imprecation against political enemies during the ritual prayer is an innovation introduced only under 'Alī and Mu'āwiya some considerable time after the Prophet. He confirms this by pointing out the absence of any information on the matter from the Prophet, Abū Bakr and 'Umar.[1] It follows that the tradition, which claims the Prophet's example for this addition to the ritual and which Shāfi'ī of course accepts,[2] must be later than Ibrāhīm.[3] On another point of ritual, Ibrāhīm refers to the varying practice during the life of the Prophet and under Abū Bakr and 'Umar, and to the Companions' adoption, under 'Umar, of an agreed ruling with reference to the alleged practice of the Prophet on the latest relevant occasion.[4] This story of an agreed ruling is obviously not historical and merely tends to invest the doctrine with the authority of the Companions. But in so far as they relate to Ibrāhīm Nakha'ī, both reports seem to be authentic.

Contrary to the historical development, Shāfi'ī charges the adherents of the old idea of *sunna* as something which takes its highest authority from Companions, with following an innovation (*muḥdath*) of 'Umar,[5] or even flings at them the opprobrious term *bid'a*, that is, a reprehensible innovation.[6] In this connexion (*Ikh.* 36) Shāfi'ī states that the followers of the ancient schools themselves, and the Kufians and Basrians in particular, reproach those who differ from one of

[1] *Āthār A.Y.* 349–52; *Āthār Shaib.* 37; *Tr. I*, 157 (*b*).

[2] *Tr. III*, 119; *Ikh.* 285 ff.

[3] The same applies to the corresponding information on Abū Bakr, 'Umar, and 'Uthmān to which Shāfi'ī refers, as well as to the pointed counter-statements concerning several Companions, particularly Ibn 'Umar, statements which appear from Abū Ḥanīfa onwards (*Tr. I*, 157 (*b*); *Muw.* i. 286; *Muw. Shaib.* 140; *Āthār Shaib.* 37).

[4] *Āthār A.Y.* 390; *Āthār Shaib.* 40.

[5] *Tr. IX*, 4. This is directed against Abū Yūsuf who had taken into account the existence of the state register (*dīwān*), an essential feature of Islamic administration the foundation of which was ascribed to 'Umar.

[6] *Ikh.* 34, explicitly directed against both Iraqians and Medinese.

their own traditions with *bidʿa*. This is not borne out by the ancient sources, which show the scholars prepared to accept the fact of local variants in the 'living tradition'.[1] At the very utmost, the insistence of the Medinese on their local practice and consensus[2] might imply a criticism of other local practices. But nothing seems to justify Shāfiʿī's reproach, addressed in the first line to the Iraqians, that they defend their *bidʿas* with language so immoderate that he is unwilling to reproduce it (*Ikh.* 34)—unless it were that the followers of the ancient schools had called the recent traditions from the Prophet an innovation, which in fact they were. No doubt this would have seemed immoderate language to Shāfiʿī, and he would be merely returning the attack.

B. The Medinese

Shāfiʿī addresses the Egyptian Medinese: 'You claim to establish the *sunna* in two ways: one is to find that the authorities among the Companions of the Prophet held an opinion that agrees with the doctrine in question, and the other is to find that men did not disagree on it; and you reject it [as not being the *sunna*] if you do not find a corresponding opinion on the part of the authorities or if you find that men disagree' (*Tr. III*, 148, p. 240).

This is borne out by many passages in the ancient Medinese texts, for instance, *Muw.* iii. 173 f., where Mālik quotes a *mursal* tradition on pre-emption, on the authority of the Successors Ibn Musaiyib and Abū Salama b. ʿAbdalraḥmān from the Prophet, and adds: 'To the same effect is the *sunna* on which there is no disagreement amongst us.' In order to show this, he mentions that he heard that Ibn Musaiyib and Sulaimān b. Yasār were asked whether there was a *sunna* [that is, a fixed rule] with regard to pre-emption, and both said yes, and gave the legal rule in question.[3]

The wording here and elsewhere implies that *sunna* for Mālik is not identical with the contents of traditions from the Prophet.

[1] See below, pp. 85, 96.

[2] See below, pp. 64 f, 83 f.

[3] When this statement on the *sunna* was made by, or ascribed to, Ibn Musaiyib and Sulaimān b. Yasār, there existed no traditions from the Prophet or from Companions on the problem in question. The *mursal* tradition from the Prophet is therefore later, and the *isnād* containing Ibn Musaiyib and Abū Salama spurious. This *mursal* tradition is also more detailed than the other statement and represents a later stage in the discussion.

In *Muw.* iii. 181 ff., Mālik establishes the *sunna* by a tradition from the Prophet and by references to the opinions of 'Umar b. ʿAbdalʿazīz, Abū Salama b. ʿAbdalraḥmān, and Sulaimān b. Yasār. He adds systematic reasoning because 'one wishes to understand', but he returns to the *sunna* as decisive: 'the *sunna* is proof enough, but one also wants to know the reason, and this is it.' It does not occur to Mālik to fall back on the tradition from the Prophet as such, as the decisive argument, a thing which Shāfiʿī does in *Tr. III*, 148 (p. 249).

In *Muw.* i. 196, Mālik quotes a decision of Zuhrī, ending with the words: 'this is the *sunna*'; and Mālik adds that he has found this to be the doctrine of the scholars of Medina.

In *Muw.* iii. 110, Mālik speaks of the '*sunna* in the past' (*maḍat al-sunna*) on a point of doctrine on which there are no traditions.

Mud. i. 115 establishes the practice of Medina as *sunna* by two traditions transmitted by Ibn Wahb, which Mālik had as yet ignored,[1] and by references to the first four Caliphs and to other old authorities.

In *Mud.* v. 163, Ibn Qāsim says: 'So it is laid down in the traditions (*āthār*) and *sunnas* referring to the Companions of the Prophet.'

The expression '*sunna* of the Prophet' occurs only rarely in the ancient Medinese texts. In *Muw.* iv. 86 f., Mālik says that he has heard it related that the Prophet said: 'I leave you two things after my death; if you hold fast to them you cannot go astray; they are the Book of Allah and the *sunna* of his Prophet.'[2] Mālik gives no *isnād*, and this use of *sunna* is not part of Medinese legal reasoning proper. The same applies to the tradition, related with a full *isnād* through Mālik in *Muw. Shaib.* 389, that 'Umar b. ʿAbdalʿazīz instructed Abū Bakr b. ʿAmr b. Ḥazm to write down all the existing traditions and *sunnas* of the Prophet, traditions of ʿUmar and the like, lest they got lost.[3] For a third case, see below, p. 155.

The element of 'practice' in the Medinese 'living tradition' is expressed by terms such as *ʿamal* 'practice', *al-ʿamal al-mujtamaʿ ʿalaih* 'generally agreed practice', *al-amr ʿindanā* 'our practice',

[1] See *Muw.* i. 370; *Muw. Shaib.* 146; *Tr. III*, 22.

[2] This is the prototype of the traditions in favour of the *sunna* of the Prophet and of the well-guided Caliphs; see above, p. 25, n. 1.

[3] On the tendency underlying this spurious tradition, see Goldziher, *Muh. St.* ii. 210 f.; Mirza Kazem Beg, in *J.A.*, 4th ser., xv. 168.

al-amr al-mujtamaʿ ʿalaih ʿindanā 'our generally agreed practice', *al-amr alladhī lā khilāf fīh ʿindanā* 'our practice on which there is no disagreement', terms which occur *passim* in the *Muwaṭṭa'* and elsewhere.[1] It is called 'ancient practice' (*al-amr al-qadīm*) in a quotation from Yaḥyā b. Saʿīd in *Tr. VIII*, 14, and this, Shāfiʿī points out, may either be something that one must follow [when it is based on a tradition from the Prophet], or else it may proceed from governors whom one is not obliged to follow. The best the opponent can do, Shāfiʿī says, is to suppose that the case in question belongs to the first kind.

That the 'practice' existed first and traditions from the Prophet and from Companions appeared later, is clearly stated in *Mud.* iv. 28, where Ibn Qāsim gives a theoretical justification of the Medinese point of view. He says: 'This tradition has come down to us, and if it were accompanied by a practice passed to those from whom we have taken it over by their own predecessors, it would be right to follow it. But in fact it is like those other traditions which are not accompanied by practice. [Here Ibn Qāsim gives examples of traditions from the Prophet and from Companions.] But these things could not assert themselves and take root (*lam tashtadd wa-lam taqwa*), the practice was different, and the whole community and the Companions themselves acted on other rules. So the traditions remained neither discredited [in principle] nor adopted in practice (*ghair mukadhdhab bih wa-lā maʿmūl bih*), and actions were ruled by other traditions which were accompanied by practice. These traditions were passed on from the Companions to the Successors, and from these to those after them, without rejecting or casting doubt on others that have come down and have been transmitted.[2] But what was eliminated from practice is left aside and not regarded as authoritative, and only what is corroborated by practice is followed and so regarded. Now the rule which is well established and is accompanied by practice is expressed in the words of the Prophet . . . and the words of Ibn ʿUmar to the same effect. . . .'[3]

The Medinese thus oppose 'practice' to traditions. The dead-

[1] For another ancient term see below, p. 245 f.

[2] This lip-service paid to traditions shows the influence they had gained in the time of Ibn Qāsim.

[3] It deserves to be noted that Ibn Qāsim relies on 'practice' although he might have simply referred to the tradition from the Prophet.

lock between the two principles is well illustrated by the following anecdote, related in Ṭabarī (*Annales*, iii. 2505) on the authority of Mālik: Muḥammad b. Abī Bakr b. Muḥammad b. ʿAmr b. Ḥazm was judge in Medina, and when he had given judgment contrary to a tradition and come home, his brother, ʿAbdallāh b. Abī Bakr, who was a pious man, would say to him: 'My brother, you have given this or that judgment to-day.' Muḥammad would say: 'Yes, my brother.' ʿAbdallāh would ask: 'What of the tradition, my brother? The tradition is important enough to have the judgment based on it.' Muḥammad would reply: 'Alas, what of the practice?'—meaning the generally agreed practice in Medina, which they regard as more authoritative than a tradition.

That the Medinese resolved this deadlock by preferring 'practice' to traditions from the Prophet and from Companions, can be seen from the following examples, which are only a few out of many.[1]

Mālik (*Muw.* iii. 134, 136; *Mud.* x. 44) and Rabīʿ (*Tr. III*, 48) admit the sale of bales by specification from a list, because it is the current practice in the past and present by which no uncertainty (*gharar*) is intended (Mālik), or because men consider it as valid (Rabīʿ). *Mud.* x. 44 considers Mālik's statement as authoritative (*ḥujja*), particularly because he states the practice, and finds it confirmed by traditions (*āthār*)—not from the Prophet but from authorities such as Yaḥyā b. Saʿīd who establishes the same practice. 'Practice' therefore decides the extent to which the general prohibition of *gharar*, incorporated in a tradition from the Prophet, is to be applied.

Mālik (*Muw.* iii. 136) and Rabīʿ (*Tr. III*, 47) declare, against a tradition from the Prophet which gives the parties to a sale the right of option as long as they have not separated: 'We have no fixed limit and no established practice for that.' Ibn ʿAbdalbarr (quoted in Zurqānī, iii. 137) comments: 'The scholars are agreed that the tradition is well-attested, and most of them follow it. Mālik and Abū Ḥanīfa and their followers reject it, but I know of no one else who does so. Some Mālikīs say that Mālik considered it superseded by the consensus of the Medinese not to act upon it, and this consensus is in Mālik's opinion more authoritative than an 'isolated' tradition. As Abū Bakr b. ʿAmr b. Ḥazm says: "If you see the Medi-

[1] See further *Tr. III*, 22 (cf. *Muw.* i. 370), 29 (cf. *Mud.* i. 65), 68 (cf. *Mud.* xiv. 224; xv. 192), 69 (cf. *Muw.* iii. 211), 144 (cf. *Muw.* ii. 333).

nese agree on something, know that it is the truth." But others say that this claim of a Medinese consensus is not substantiated, because the decision[1] to act upon the tradition is related explicitly from Ibn Musaiyib and Zuhrī who are among the most prominent scholars of Medina; further because nothing against acting upon the tradition is explicitly related from the other Medinese, excepting Mālik and Rabī'a b. Abī 'Abdalraḥmān, and not even uniformly from the latter; and finally because Ibn Abī Dhi'b who is a Medinese scholar of the time of Mālik, objected to Mālik's decision not to act upon the tradition, and in his anger used against him hard and unbecoming words.' In other words: by the time of Ibn 'Abdalbarr, spurious information regarding old Medinese authorities had been put into circulation, so as to bring their doctrine into line with the tradition, and we find more of the same kind, regarding the 'seven scholars of Medina' and others, in 'Iyāḍ (quoted in Zurqānī, ibid.). The tradition is certainly later than the ancient doctrine common to the Medinese and Iraqians. Ibn Abī Dhi'b is not a member of the Medinese school of law but a traditionist and disseminator of traditions.[2]

Mālik in *Muw*. iii. 219 ff. prefers the practice, 'what people used to do', as expressed in a statement ascribed to Qāsim b. Muḥammad and a concurring action reported from Ibn 'Umar, to a tradition related from the Prophet. Shāfi'ī comments on this (*Tr. III*, 41): 'Qāsim's statement cannot prevail over a tradition from the Prophet. . . . If it is suggested that Qāsim's reference to the practice of men can refer only to a group of Companions or of scholars who could not possibly be ignorant of the *sunna* of the Prophet, and who did not arrive at their common doctrine because of their personal opinion (*ra'y*) but only on account of the *sunna*, it can be objected that in another case you do not share the opinion of Qāsim and say: "We do not know who the 'people' are to whom Qāsim refers." If Qāsim's statement does not prevail there over your personal opinion, it is surely even less qualified to prevail here over a tradition from the Prophet.' This shows that the 'practice' of the Medinese is not necessarily identical with the authentic or alleged opinions of the old authorities of their school. Shāfi'ī goes on to quote a tradition through Ibn 'Uyaina—'Amr b. Dīnār—Sulaimān b. Yasār, to the effect that Ṭāriq gave judgment in Medina in accordance with[3] the decision related from the Prophet. We must regard this as a spurious statement on an old Medinese, of the same kind as, but older than, those we have met with in the preceding paragraph. As

[1] Delete *tark* from the printed text.

[2] See above, p. 54 f., and below, p. 256, n. 6.

[3] Read *'alā* instead of *'an* which gives no sense.

Qāsim b. Muḥammad and Sulaimān b. Yasār were contemporaries, the responsibility for it can be fixed on either Ibn 'Uyaina or 'Amr b. Dīnār who were both members of the traditionist group.[1]

On the other hand, 'practice' is explicitly identified with those traditions which the Medinese accept, for instance in *Muw.* ii. 368 (= *Muw. Shaib.* 314): Mālik—Zuhrī—Qabīṣa b. Shu'aib—'Umar gave the grandfather the same share in the inheritance which men give him nowadays. In other words: Medinese contemporary 'practice' is projected back into the time of 'Umar. If 'Umar and Ibn 'Umar are the particular authorities of the Medinese,[2] this means only that their names were used in order to justify doctrines which reflected the current 'practice' or which were meant to change it; it does not mean that the traditions going under their names were more or less authentic and formed the basis on which the doctrine was built.[3] (The same applies to Ibn Mas'ūd, 'Alī, and 'Umar as authorities of the Iraqians.)[4] We shall be able to prove the late origin of many of these traditions in detail.[5] We should not, of course, be justified in assuming an absolute identity of legal doctrine and formal traditions for any school at any period.

After the first legitimization of doctrine by reference to Companions of the Prophet had been achieved, the further growth of traditions from Companions and also from the Prophet went partly parallel with the further elaboration of doctrine within the 'living tradition' of the ancient schools, but partly also represented the means by which definite changes in the accepted doctrine of a school were proposed and supported. These efforts were sometimes successful in bringing about a change of doctrine, but often not, and we find whole groups of 'unsuccessful' Medinese and Iraqian doctrines expressed in traditions.[6] I need hardly point out that we must regard the interaction of legal doctrines and traditions as a unitary process, the several aspects and phases of which can be separated only for the sake of analysis. The greatest onslaught on the 'living tradition' of the ancient schools of law was made by the traditionists in the

[1] See below, p. 256, n. 6.

[2] See above, p. 25 f.

[3] See below, p. 156 f.

[4] See above, p. 31 f.

[5] See below, p. 176 ff.

[6] For details on all this, see part II of this book; on 'unsuccessful' doctrines in particular, below, pp. 240 and 248 f.

name of traditions going back to the Prophet.[1] Their attack was well on its way when Shāfi'ī appeared. He accepted their essential thesis and thereby cut himself off from the development of the doctrine in the ancient schools. This view of the development of the function of legal traditions is the only alternative to considering the doctrine of the ancient schools, as Shāfi'ī does, a mass of inconsistencies and contradictions.

We have already encountered cases in which Medinese 'practice' reflects directly the actual custom.[2]

Shāfi'ī discusses another significant example in *Tr. III*, 46. According to him, the Medinese allow for practical reasons the exchange of bullion for a smaller amount of coin of the same metal, so as to cover the minting expenses. This is a serious infringement of the general rules for the exchange of precious metals, and it is little wonder that no parallel exists in *Muw.*, *Muw. Shaib.*, and *Mud.*, although *Mud.* iii. 107, 109, allows some little latitude in similar transactions. But Ibn 'Abdalbarr[3] mentions it as a 'bad and discreditable doctrine' ascribed by a group of Mālikīs to Mālik and Ibn Qāsim who, it is stated, make a concession for this transaction if there is no means of avoiding it. We must regard this decision not as a passing concession on the part of Mālik, but as the original doctrine of the Medinese, and its deliberate obliteration from most of the old sources as an indication of growing strictness in the enforcement of the prohibition of 'usury'. This strictness was advocated in traditions which were collected by Mālik in *Muw.* iii. 111 ff. but prevailed only after him.

As parallel cases, Shāfi'ī mentions (*Tr. III*, 46) concessions of the Medinese to custom with regard to the sale of meat for meat in equal quantities by estimate without weighing, called by Mālik (*Muw.* iii. 127) 'our generally agreed practice', and of bread for bread, eggs for eggs, &c. (cf. *Muw.* iii. 122).

The Medinese in the generation before Mālik, in common with Auzā'ī (*Tr. IX*, 14), allowed soldiers to take food back from enemy country, without dividing it as part of the booty, and to consume it at home. The explicit reason given is that this was the usual custom. Several relevant traditions are to be found in *Mud.* iii. 38 f. Only Mālik (*Muw.* ii. 299), following his own opinion (*ra'y*), restricted the permission to very small amounts.

[1] See below, p. 253 ff. [2] Above, p. 64 f.

[3] *Istidhkār*, MS. Or. 5954 of the British Museum. The question here is whether one may exchange bullion for the same amount in coins and at the same time pay a minting fee; this is legally the same as the problem in the text. For minting fees in the Umaiyad period, see Balādhurī, *Futūḥ*, 468 f.

Shaibānī relates in *Tr. VIII*, 21: 'Mālik declared once: "We did not apply the *lex talionis* to [broken] fingers, until 'Abdal'azīz b. Muṭṭalib, a judge,[1] applied it; since then, we have applied it." But the opinion of the Medinese does not become right because an official (*'āmil*) has acted thus in their country.' This shows the relatively recent origin of parts of the Medinese 'practice' and doctrine.[2]

But the 'practice' of the Medinese does not simply reflect the actual custom, it contains a theoretical or ideal element.

In *Mud.* i. 65, Mālik opposes the 'practice' to a tradition from Abū Bakr (*Muw.* i. 149). But he thinks of the practice as it ought to be, and therefore says: 'The practice, in my opinion, is . . . .' In *Mud.* iii. 12, Mālik says: 'This is how it is' (*huwa l-sha'n*). But the picture he gives is not one of the actual custom. It is, rather, an ideal, fictitious picture of the practice at the beginning of Islam, as is shown by *Tr. IX*, 1.[3] In *Muw.* iii. 39, Mālik states: 'This is our practice.' But it was not yet so in the time of Zuhrī, shortly before Mālik. So Mālik's recurrent expression *al-amr 'indanā*, literally 'the practice with us', may mean here and in other places only 'the [right] practice in our opinion', although Zurqānī as a rule carefully explains it as meaning 'the practice in Medina'.

At this point, we see the 'practice' of the Medinese merge into the common opinion of the recognized scholars, which becomes the final criterion of the 'living tradition' of the school.[4] The continuous doctrine of Medina prevails over the strict and literal interpretation of a tradition (*Muw.* iii. 259). Mālik follows what he has seen the scholars approve, and uses a tradition from Ibn 'Umar only as a subsidiary argument (*Muw.* ii. 83). He counters a tradition from 'Ā'isha, which he does not follow, with the accepted doctrine of the school (*Muw.* ii. 336), and introduces the latter with the words 'the best that I have heard'.[5] He calls a doctrine 'our generally agreed practice, that which I have heard from those of whom I approve, and that on which both early and late authorities are agreed', and again 'a *sunna* on which there

[1] See Ṭabarī, *Annales*, iii. 159, 198, years 144 and 145.

[2] See *Muw.* iv. 51; *Mud.* xvi. 112, 122.

[3] See below, p. 205.

[4] Shāfi'ī himself identifies the two when he says, referring to *Muw.* i. 49: 'If your "practice" (*al-amr 'indakum*) means the consensus of the Medinese . . .' (*Tr. III*, 148, p. 249, and similarly elsewhere).

[5] On the meaning of this formula, see below, p. 101, n. 1.

is no disagreement amongst us, and one to which men's practice has always corresponded (*Muw.* iv. 55 f.)'. This shows the close connexion between the old idea of *sunna*, 'practice', and the common opinion of the recognized scholars, which together constitute the 'living tradition' of the school.

Shāfiʿī attacks this idea of 'living tradition' in *Tr. III*, 147: 'You claim that the judges give judgment only in accordance with the opinion of the scholars, and you claim that the scholars do not disagree. But it is not so. . . . Where is the practice? . . . We do not know what you mean by practice, and you do not know either, as far as we can see. We are forced to conclude that you call your own opinions practice and consensus, and speak of practice and consensus when you mean only your own opinions.'

The 'practice' of the school is not identical with the opinions ascribed to ancient authorities.[1] Shāfiʿī says quite correctly to the Egyptian Medinese: 'You believe in taking knowledge from the lowest source' (*Tr. III*, 148, p. 246), and Rabīʿ and his Egyptian companions find the doctrine of their school laid down authoritatively in Mālik's *Muwaṭṭaʾ* (ibid., p. 248). They claim the essential unity of the 'living tradition' of the school, or as Shāfiʿī puts it, they 'contend that knowledge is transmitted in Medina as if by inheritance, and that the authorities do not disagree on it' (*Tr. III*, 77). So Rabīʿ, still speaking as a Medinese, can ask confidently: 'Can you show me a single case in Medina where an opinion held by the great majority (*al-aghlab al-akthar*) of the Successors and rejected only by a minority, has been abandoned by us for the opinion of one of their predecessors, contemporaries, or successors?' (*Tr. III*, 148, p. 246). The growth of 'unsuccessful opinions' ascribed to Companions, Successors, and later authorities, not to mention traditions from the Prophet, enables Shāfiʿī to take up this challenge, but he acknowledges the Medinese principle implicitly when he blames them for following 'the practice of the majority of those from whom opinions are related in Medina' rather than a tradition from the Prophet (ibid., p. 247).[2]

[1] See above, p. 65, and also *Tr. III*, 27, 77, 94, 143, &c.

[2] The theory of the Medinese 'living tradition' is clearly stated by Ibn Qutaiba, 331 ff. and by Ibn ʿAbdalbarr, quoted in Zurqānī, iv. 36, l. 1.

C. The Syrians

Auzā'ī knows the concept of '*sunna* of the Prophet' (§ 50),[1] but does not identify it with formal traditions. He considers an informal tradition without *isnād*, concerning the life-story of the Prophet, sufficient to establish a 'valid *sunna*' (§ 37), and an anonymous legal maxim sufficient to show the existence of a 'valid *sunna* going back to the Prophet' (§ 13).[2]

His idea of 'living tradition' is the uninterrupted practice of the Muslims, beginning with the Prophet, maintained by the first Caliphs and by the later rulers, and verified by the scholars. The continuous practice of the Muslims is the decisive element, reference to the Prophet or to the first Caliphs is optional, but not necessary for establishing it. Examples occur in almost every paragraph of *Tr. IX*.

Auzā'ī's 'living tradition' is based partly on actual custom; he says so clearly in § 6, and the same can be inferred from §§ 14,[3] 16, 18, 25, 27 (see the parallel passage in Ṭabarī, 52). At the same time, it has become idealized by being projected back to 'Umar b. 'Abdal'azīz (§ 25), or is being idealized by Auzā'ī himself who lays down fixed rules (§ 27). He exaggerates the unanimity of doctrine (§§ 31, 32); the stage reached by his immediate predecessors becomes for him the continuous and unanimous practice.

Auzā'ī opposes the fictitious 'constant usage of the Prophet and of the Caliphs' to the actual administrative practice (§ 4).[4] He infers the existence of a normative usage of the Muslims or of the Caliphs from informal traditions on the history of the Prophet (§§ 7, 10),[5] or even from a legal maxim (§ 13).

The legal maxim which Auzā'ī in § 13 takes as proof of a 'valid *sunna* going back to the Prophet', says that 'he who kills a foreign enemy [in single combat] has the right to his spoils'. Auzā'ī does not say that this is related on the authority of the Prophet; and Abū Yūsuf, who must certainly have mentioned it if he had known it as a tradition on the authority of the Prophet, is silent. The maxim appears, as part of a tradition concerning the Prophet and Abū Qatāda at the battle of Ḥunain, for the first time in Mālik (*Muw.* ii.

[1] All quotations in this section refer to *Tr. IX*, unless the contrary is stated. Most questions have parallels in Ṭabarī.

[2] See farther down on this page.

[3] See above, p. 67.

[4] See below, p. 205.

[5] See below, p. 261.

301) who interprets it restrictively.[1] He denies knowledge of any other tradition from the Prophet (ibid. 305), but knows a statement on Abū Bakr and 'Umar in favour of the contrary doctrine (Ṭabarī, 87): this statement, being a denial, presupposes the doctrine expressed in the legal maxim, and is the result of a religious scruple at infringing the strict division of booty. The scruple arises from the Koran, and is shared by the Iraqians. The statement may therefore be taken as confirming the authentic character of the practice as alleged by Auzā'ī. Auzā'ī (Ṭabarī, 87) knows the scruple in an earlier form in which it was given the authority of 'Umar. This form subjects the spoils at least to the deduction of one-fifth as the share of the Prophet, a deduction which is also based on the Koran.

The tradition on the announcement of the Prophet at the battle of Bi'r Ma'ūna, again in favour of the legal maxim, appears for the first time in Shāfi'ī (*Tr. IX*, 13), and so does the reference to the action of Sa'd b. Abī Waqqāṣ at Qādisīya, which is intended to rebut the earlier negative statement on Abū Bakr and 'Umar. Later than Shāfi'ī are several traditions mentioned in Zurqānī, ii. 306, and in *Comm. ed. Cairo* on *Tr. IX*, 13; they make the Prophet award the spoils to the killer on a number of other occasions. Some of these have found a place in one or other of the classical collections.[2] The practice was certainly old, it found expression in a legal maxim, Auzā'ī identified it with the '*sunna* going back to the Prophet', a religious scruple regarding it was in part acknowledged by the Iraqians and Mālik, and only Shāfi'ī, under the spell of formal traditions from the Prophet, fell back on the old doctrine.

In § 1 (and in the parallel in Ṭabarī, 89), Auzā'ī refers to actions of the Prophet in general terms without giving *isnāds*, and alleges the uninterrupted practice of the Muslims under 'Umar and 'Uthmān and so on, until the civil war and the killing of the Umaiyad Caliph Walīd b. Yazīd (A.H. 126).[3] In

[1] Shāfi'ī (*Tr. IX*, 13) calls it already 'well-attested, reliable, and not contradicted as far as I know'. It appears in an improved form, providing Abū Qatāda with legal proof of his deed, in Wāqidī.

[2] The tradition on Khālid b. Walīd and the Prophet (in Ibn Ḥanbal, Muslim, and others) favours the restrictive Mālikī and Ḥanafī doctrine. The tradition on Sa'd b. Abī Waqqāṣ at the battle of Uḥud improves the reference to his action at Qādisīya, referred to above, by projecting the incident back into the time of the Prophet.

[3] Ibn Wahb in *Mud.* iii. 12 quotes the same statement of Auzā'ī, but instead of the passage on 'Umar and so on until the killing of Walīd, he says: 'from the Caliphate of 'Umar to the Caliphate of 'Umar b. 'Abdal'azīz'; the name of impious Walīd was changed into that of pious 'Umar b. 'Abdal'azīz in early 'Abbāsid times.

§ 3 (*b*) he refers to the alleged early practice of the Caliphs of the Muslims in the past, until the civil war (in the parallel text in Ṭabarī, 68, he adds: after the death of Walīd b. Yazīd). And in § 24 he says: 'The Muslims always used to . . ., no two men disagreed on this until Walīd was killed.' The parallel passage to § 1 in Ṭabarī, 89, contains an even stronger condemnation of the recent practice. Here Auzā'ī contrasts recent practice with what he alleges to have been the custom since the time of the Prophet, and even accepts a practically undesirable consequence of the old practice.

The civil war which began with the death of Walīd and marked the beginning of the end of the Umaiyad dynasty, was a conventional date for the end of the 'good old time' and not only with regard to the *sunna*.[1]

In view of what we have already seen, we must regard Auzā'ī's 'recent' custom as the real practice (which is indeed admitted and regulated by the Iraqians in the case of § 1), and his alleged 'old' custom as an idealized picture of the 'good old time'.[2] It is relevant to note here that the Syrian Auzā'ī still accepts practically the whole of the Umaiyad period, including even the reign of the 'impious' Walīd, as a normative model on an equal footing with the earliest period of Islam. There is as yet no trace of anti-Umaiyad feeling in him, and several anecdotes, although they cannot be taken as historical, reflect this fact.[3] The real practice as it appears in Auzā'ī's doctrine may be dated towards the end of the Umaiyad period.

Auzā'ī shows a particular kind of dependence on the authority of the Prophet: on the one hand, he is far from Shāfi'ī's insistence on formally well-attested traditions with full *isnāds* going back to the Prophet;[4] on the other, he is inclined to project the whole 'living tradition', the continuous practice of the Muslims, as he finds it, back to the Prophet and to give it the Prophet's

[1] See above, p. 36 f., and the anecdote from Dhahabī, in Fischer, *Biographien von Gewährsmännern*, 71, where Ma'mar relates: 'We were under the impression that we had heard much from Zuhrī, until Walīd was killed and the scrolls containing Zuhrī's traditions were carried on beasts of burden from his treasury' (falsely amended by the editor).

[2] See below, p. 205.

[3] Dhahabī, *Tadhkira*, s.v. Auzā'ī, i. 168 ff. An anecdote on his having had to hide when the 'Abbāsids entered Syria, is given by Yāqūt, *Mu'jam al-Buldān*, ii. 110 (cf. Barthold, in *Islam*, xviii. 244).

[4] See above, p. 34.

authority, whether he can adduce a precedent established by the Prophet or not. He has this feature in common with the Iraqians.[1]

D. The Iraqians

The Iraqians, in their view of *sunna*, no more think it necessarily based on traditions from the Prophet than do the Medinese.

Thus in *Tr. II*, 4 (*f*), in a tradition from ʿAlī, representing an 'unsuccessful' Iraqian doctrine, *sunna* occurs in the sense of 'established religious practice'. And *Tr. III*, 148 (p. 249) makes the Iraqians say: 'We do this on account of the *sunna* [i.e. they give judgment on the defendant's refusal to take the oath when the plaintiff can produce no legal proof, and they do not demand from the plaintiff a confirmatory oath as do the Medinese]. There is no mention of the oath, or of the refusal to take it, in the Koran. This is a *sunna* which is not in the Koran, and it does not come into the category of evidence from witnesses [which is provided for by Koran ii. 282]. We hold that the Koran orders us to give judgment on the evidence of witnesses, either two men or one man and two women, and the refusal to take the oath does not come under this.'

The essential point is that the Iraqians use *sunna* as an argument, even when they can show no relevant tradition. But long before Shāfiʿī, they had coined the term '*sunna* of the Prophet'. It appears in a number of Iraqian traditions.

Tr. II, 9 (*b*): Shāfiʿī—Abū Kāmil and others—Ḥammād b. Salama Baṣrī—Thumāma [of Basra]—his grandfather Anas b. Mālik—his father Mālik gave him the copy of a decree of Abū Bakr on the *zakāt* tax and said: 'This is the ordinance of Allah and the *sunna* of the Prophet.' A parallel version in § 9 (*c*) has: 'Abū Bakr gave him the *sunna* in writing.' This tradition can be dated to the time of Ḥammād b. Salama; the connexion between Ḥammād and Thumāma is very weak.[2]

Tr. II, 18 (*a*): Shāfiʿī—a man—Shuʿba—Salama b. Suhail—Shaʿbī—ʿAlī said [referring to an adulteress]: 'I flog her on the basis of the Koran, and lapidate her on the basis of the *sunna* of the Prophet.' The full text of this tradition[3] shows that it depends on the wording of a group of traditions from the Prophet on the punishment

[1] See below, p. 76.
[2] See also below, p. 167.
[3] See below, p. 106.

of an adulterer (Māʿiz); it must therefore be later. The *isnād* shows that it cannot be older than Shaʿbī at the best; but the relative chronology of the traditions on this subject makes it impossible to assign it even this date.[1]

Ṭaḥāwī, i. 241, gives several traditions in which Companions refer to the orders, or to the *sunna*, of the Prophet. Ṭaḥāwī remarks correctly that these traditions are Iraqian. They do indeed represent the Iraqian doctrine on the problem in question. The *isnāds* of parallel versions and other indications enable us to date them to the beginning of the second century.

The earliest evidence for the Iraqian term '*sunna* of the Prophet' occurs in a dogmatic treatise which Ḥasan Baṣrī wrote at the command of the Umayyad Caliph ʿAbdalmalik, and which therefore cannot be later than the year 86.[2] The author shows himself bound, in a general way, by the example of the forebears (*salaf*) and refers explicitly to the *sunna* of the Prophet. But his actual reasoning is based exclusively on the Koran, and he does not mention any tradition from the Prophet or even from the Companions. It is only his adversaries who refer in general terms to the opinions of the Companions, and these they oppose to the unguided opinion (*ra'y*) of the individual. But the author also charges his opponents with *ra'y*, that is, arbitrary interpretation of the Koran.

We now come to statements of individual Iraqians on *sunna*.

Abū Yūsuf, it is true, declines to accept Auzāʿī's general reference to the uninterrupted custom, questions the reliability of the unidentified persons on whose authority Auzāʿī claims the existence of a *sunna*, and asks for formal *isnāds*.[3] And the Hijazis, Abū Yūsuf says, 'when asked for their authority for their doctrine, reply that it is the *sunna*, whereas it is possibly only the decision of a market-inspector (*ʿāmil al-sūq*) or some provincial agent (*ʿāmilum-mā min al-jihāt*)'. But this is only part of the usual polemics between followers of the ancient schools, who do not hesitate to find fault with others for arguments which they use themselves.

Abū Yūsuf's own idea of *sunna* appears from *Tr. IX*, 5, where

[1] In the same way, Koran and *sunna* are opposed to each other in a statement ascribed to Shaʿbī and quoted in Ṭaḥāwī, i. 20.

[2] Text, ed. Ritter, in *Islam*, xxi. 67 ff.; summary and commentary by Obermann, in *J.A.O.S.* lv. 138 ff.

[3] *Tr. IX*, 1, 3 (*b*), 9.

he opposes *sunna* to isolated traditions;[1] from §§ 7, 8, where he refers to *sunna* beside traditions; from § 14 where he distinguishes between what he has heard on the authority of the Prophet, the traditions (*āthār*), and the well-known and recognized *sunna* (*al-sunna al-maḥfūẓa al-maʿrūfa*). This last is simply the doctrine of the school, the outcome of religious and systematic objections against the ancient lax practice.

In *Tr. IX*, 18, Abū Yūsuf applies the term '*sunna* of the Prophet' to a case in which nothing to the contrary is known on the authority of the Prophet and of the Companions. In § 21 he refers to 'the *sunna* and the life-history (*sīra*) of the Prophet', quoting several traditions on history without *isnād*, and says: 'The Muslims and the pious forebears, the Companions of the Prophet, have never ceased to do the same, and we have not heard that any of them ever avoided doing so.' In this case, where Auzāʿī's doctrine happens to represent the religious scruple against the rough-and-ready practice, Abū Yūsuf's reasoning is of the same kind as that of Auzāʿī elsewhere.

In *Tr. IX*, 24, Auzāʿī had referred to the unanimous practice 'until Walīd was killed'. Abū Yūsuf retorts: 'One does not decide a question of allowed and forbidden, by simply asserting that people always did it. Most of what people always did is not allowed and ought not to be done. There are cases which I could mention, . . . where the great mass (*ʿāmma*) acts against a prohibition of the Prophet. In these questions one has to follow the *sunna* which has come down from the Prophet and the forebears, his Companions and the lawyers (*al-sunna ʿan rasūl Allāh wa-ʿan al-salaf min aṣḥābih wa-min qaum fuqahāʾ*).' This shows that Abū Yūsuf's idea of *sunna*, notwithstanding his polemics, was essentially identical with that of Auzāʿī. There was only a greater degree of technical documentation on the part of the Iraqian scholar.

In *Kharāj*, 99, Abū Yūsuf relates a tradition from ʿAlī, according to which the Prophet used to award 40 stripes as a punishment for drinking wine, Abū Bakr 40, and ʿUmar 80. He comments: 'All this is *sunna*, and our companions are agreed that the punishment for drinking wine is 80 stripes.'

The degree to which Shaibānī puts the doctrine of the Iraqians under the aegis of the Prophet becomes clear from

[1] Quoted above, p. 28.

Muw. Shaib. 361, where he calls it 'something we have heard on the authority of the Prophet'; but his whole evidence for this consists in statements of Zuhrī and 'Aṭā' on a change of practice in Umaiyad times.

In his long reasoning in *Tr. VIII*, 13, Shaibānī, as it happens, does not use the term *sunna*. But the whole passage, as far as legal arguments are concerned, might have been written by Auzā'ī. Shaibānī refers to the Koran, to traditions from the Prophet (in general terms), to traditions from Companions, and to a later authority (Zuhrī), and claims that the practice changed under Mu'āwiya.

To sum up, the '*sunna* of the Prophet', as understood by the Iraqians, is not identical with, and not necessarily expressed by, traditions from the Prophet; it is simply the 'living tradition' of the school put under the aegis of the Prophet. This concept is shared by Auzā'ī, but not by the Medinese. It cannot be regarded as originally common to all ancient schools of law, and as between the Syrians and the Iraqians, the evidence points definitely to Iraq as its original home. In any case, it was the Iraqians and not the Medinese to whom the concept of '*sunna* of the Prophet' was familiar before the time of Shāfi'ī. The common opinion to the contrary has taken at its face value a later fiction, some other aspects of which we have discussed already.[1]

The Iraqians hardly use the term '*amal*, 'practice', even where their doctrine endorses actual administrative procedure.[2] We have seen Abū Yūsuf inveigh against Auzā'ī's concept of practice, although his own idea of *sunna* comes down to the same. Shāfi'ī's Basrian opponent, when charged with making the 'practice' prevail over traditions from the Prophet, replaces this term in his own answer by *sunna*.[3]

However it be formulated, the Iraqian idea of 'living tradition' is essentially the same as that of the Medinese, and Shāfi'ī can say, addressing the Egyptian Medinese: 'Some of the Easterners have provided you with an argument and hold the same view as you' (*Tr. III*, 148, p. 242). This 'living tradition' is meant when an Iraqian opponent of Shāfi'ī says that there

[1] See above, p. 8, on Medina as the true home of the *sunna*, and p. 27 on the interest of the Medinese in traditions, compared with that of the Iraqians.

[2] See above, p. 60, n. 5.

[3] See above, p. 59.

would be nothing to choose between two doctrines, each of which is represented by a tradition, 'if there were nothing to go by but the two traditions' (*Ikh.* 158 f.). It corresponds to the accepted doctrine of the school, and a scholar from Kufa, presumably Shaibānī himself, can comment on the fact that a well-authenticated tradition from the Prophet is not acted upon because 'all people' have abandoned it, saying: 'By "people" I mean the muftis in our own time or [immediately] before us, not the Successors'; he specifies the people of Hijaz and Iraq; for Iraq, he can only mention Abū Ḥanīfa and his companions, and he is aware that Ibn Abī Lailā holds a different opinion which, however, 'we do not share'; he knows nothing about the muftis in Basra (*Ikh.* 336 f.). The Iraqians, therefore, like the Medinese, take their doctrine 'from the lowest source'. The scholars of Kufa in particular find this doctrine expressed in the opinions ascribed to Ibrāhīm Nakhaʿī.[1]

E. Shāfiʿī

For Shāfiʿī, the *sunna* is established only by traditions going back to the Prophet, not by practice or consensus (*Tr. III*, 148, p. 249). Apart from a few traces of the old idea of *sunna* in his earlier writings,[2] Shāfiʿī recognizes the '*sunna* of the Prophet' only in so far as it is expressed in traditions going back to him. This is the idea of *sunna* which we find in the classical theory of Muhammadan law, and Shāfiʿī must be considered as its originator there.[3]

Sunna and traditions are of course not really synonymous.[4] Keeping this in mind, we notice that Shāfiʿī restricts the meaning of *sunna* so much to the contents of traditions from the Prophet, that he is inclined to identify both terms more or less completely.[5]

In the preceding sections we had occasion to refer to Shāfiʿī's attacks against the old ideas of *sunna*, 'practice' and 'living

[1] See above, p. 33. [2] See below, p. 79 f.

[3] It is also the idea of the traditionists, as explicitly stated in Ibn Qutaiba, 215 f.

[4] See above, p. 3.

[5] The following are some of the most telling passages: *Ris.* 30, 31, 58; *Tr. I*, 9, 138; *Tr. II*, 5 (*c*), 15, 19 (*e*); *Tr. III*, 65, 105, 114, 122, 125, 130; *Tr. VI*, 266; *Tr. VIII*, 6, 7, 8, 12; *Tr. IX*, 39; *Umm.* iv. 170; *Ikh.* 27, 51, 57, 357. Shāfiʿī projects this identification of *sunna* with the contents of traditions from the Prophet back into the time of the Successors: *Ikh.* 24.

tradition'. His main line of argument starts from the traditions from the Prophet (and the Companions) which the Medinese themselves transmitted but did not follow, those traditions which had grown up in Medina beside the 'living tradition' of the school and had not succeeded in modifying it. In *Tr. III*, 68, he addresses the Egyptian Medinese: 'So you relate in this book [the *Muwaṭṭa'*] an authentic, well-attested tradition from the Prophet and two traditions from 'Umar, and then diverge from them all and say that judgment is not given according to them and that the practice is not so, without reporting a statement to the contrary from anyone I know of. Whose practice then have you in mind when you disagree on the strength of it with the *sunna* of the Prophet—which alone, we think, ought to be sufficient to refute that practice—and disagree not only with the *sunna* but with 'Umar also? . . . At the same time, you fall back on practice, but we have not discovered to this very day what you mean by practice. Nor do I think we ever shall.'[1]

The spurious information on the opinions of old Medinese authorities, which by Shāfi'ī's time had grown up beside traditions from the Prophet (and from Companions), provides him with another argument against the Medinese 'living tradition', as expressed in the generally recognized doctrine of the school.[2] So he finds that Mālik and the (Egyptian) Medinese diverge from '*sunna*, practice, and *āthār* [that is, traditions from persons other than the Prophet] in Medina' (*Tr. III*, 54) and that their practice is not uniform as they always claim (ibid. 119). And he considers that their alleged 'ancient practice' is something introduced by governors, an argument which had already appeared in the polemics between the ancient schools.[3]

Logically from his point of view, Shāfi'ī appeals from the actual to an ideal and fictitious doctrine of the Medinese which he reconstructs, just as Auzā'ī had opposed the alleged custom of the 'good old time' to the real and 'recent' practice: 'There is no one in stronger opposition to the [hypothetical] people of Medina than you. . . . You disagree with what you relate from the Prophet . . . and from authorities whose equals cannot be found. One might even say that you are self-confessedly and

[1] Similar passages: *Tr. III*, 29, 47, 67, 89, 148 (p. 249), &c.

[2] See below, p. 85 and n. 1.

[3] See above, pp. 63, 74.

most stubbornly opposed to the [hypothetical] people of Medina, and you could not deny it. You are much more in the wrong than others because you claim to continue their doctrine and to follow them, and then differ from them more than those who do not make this claim.'[1]

As the recognized doctrine of the Medinese school had, by Shāfiʿī's time, acquired a considerable body of *loci probantes* in traditions from the Prophet, his Companions, and later authorities, Shāfiʿī was able to charge them with inconsistency in maintaining their 'living tradition' in the face of other traditions of the same kind. This argument of his merges with his criticism of the attitude of the ancient schools to traditions:[2] 'Mālik sometimes rejects a tradition from the Prophet in favour of the doctrine of a Companion, and then he rejects the Companion's doctrine in favour of his own opinion (*ra'y*); that is to say, everything is at his discretion (*fal-ʿamal idhan ilaih*)[3] and he can act as he likes. But to do this is not proper for people of our generation (*wa-laisa dhālik li-aḥad min ahl dahrinā*).' This implies that Shāfiʿī's theory is something new.[4]

The earlier writings of Shāfiʿī contain a few traces of the old concept of *sunna*. The following passage deserves to be quoted: 'Ibn Musaiyib states that the weregeld for three fingers of a woman is 30 camels and for four fingers 20, and in answer to the objection of inconsistency he replies that it is the *sunna*; further a tradition to the same effect is related from Zaid b. Thābit. One cannot therefore declare this doctrine erroneous from the systematic point of view (*min jihat al-ra'y*), because this objection can be made only to an opinion which is itself based on systematic reasoning, where one reasoning could be considered sounder than another. But here the only possible objection would be a traditional one (*ittibāʿan*), based on something from which one may not diverge; and as Ibn Musaiyib said that it is the *sunna*, it is probable that it comes from the Prophet or from the majority of his Companions. Moreover Zaid [b. Thābit] is not likely to have based his doctrine on systematic reasoning, because it can have no such basis. Should someone quote against this the tradition from ʿAlī to the contrary, the answer is that this is well authenticated neither from ʿAlī nor from ʿUmar; even if it were,

[1] *Tr. III*, 29 (*c*). See further §§ 30, 34, 148 (p. 246 f.).

[2] See above, pp. 21, 26.

[3] This alludes to the Medinese concept of 'practice' (*ʿamal*), and we might also translate: 'the practice is at his discretion'.

[4] *Tr. III*, 65. See further §§ 69, 85, 128, 145 (*a*).

it is probable that it is the result of the only possible and reasonable systematic consideration; whereas the *sunna*, as quoted by Ibn Musaiyib, disagrees with analogy and reason, and must therefore stand on a traditional basis, as far as we can see.' In a later addition Shāfiʿī says that this was his former opinion, but that he abandoned it because he found no proof that the alleged *sunna* actually went back to the Prophet, and so he now prefers analogy; also, he says, the tradition from Zaid is even less well attested than that from ʿAlī.[1]

We find the old idea of the decisive authority of 'practice' surviving even in Abū Dāwūd, the author of one of the classical collections of traditions and in law a follower of Shāfiʿī, who concludes that a tradition from the Prophet has been repealed because the [idealized] practice, which he finds expressed in a tradition from ʿUrwa, is different (*Bāb man raʾa l-takhfīf fil-qirāʾa fil-maghrib*; cf. the comment of Zurqānī, i. 149).

F. Conclusions

The ancient schools of law shared the old concept of *sunna* or 'living tradition' as the ideal practice of the community, expressed in the accepted doctrine of the school. It was not yet exclusively embodied in traditions from the Prophet, although the Iraqians had been the first to claim for it the authority of the Prophet, by calling it the '*sunna* of the Prophet'. The continous development of doctrine in the ancient schools was outpaced by the development of traditions, particularly those from the Prophet, in the period before Shāfiʿī, and the ancient schools were already on the defensive against the rising tide of traditions when Shāfiʿī appeared. This contrast between doctrine and traditions gave Shāfiʿī his opportunity; he identified the '*sunna* of the Prophet' with the contents of traditions from the Prophet to which he gave, not for the first time,[2] but for the first time consistently, overriding authority, thereby cutting himself off from the continuous development of doctrine before him. If the 'living tradition' diverges constantly from traditions, this shows that the traditions are, generally speaking, later.

The generally accepted doctrine of a school merges in the

[1] *Tr. VIII*, 5. See further *Tr. II*, 21 (*d*); *Tr. IX*, 13, 23, 27; *Tr. VII*, 275 (top); *Ris.* 28; *Ikh.* 184, 409.

[2] See above, p. 28.

consensus.[1] The idea of consensus, as used in the ancient schools, is in fact another aspect of their concept of 'living tradition', and it is only because it has become an independent principle in the classical theory of Muhammadan law, that we shall discuss it in a separate chapter.

[1] See above, pp. 62 f., 64 f., 68, n. 2, 69, 70.

CHAPTER 8

CONSENSUS AND DISAGREEMENT

A. The Old Idea of Consensus

WE have seen that the legal theory of the ancient schools of law is dominated by the idea of consensus; that they distinguish between the consensus of all Muslims, both the scholars and the people, on essentials, and the consensus of the scholars on points of detail; that they consider the consensus in both forms as the final argument on all problems, and not subject to error; and that it represents the common denominator of doctrine achieved in each generation, as opposed to individual opinions (*ra'y*) which make for disagreement.[1]

The follower of the ancient schools with whom Shāfi'ī discusses consensus (*Tr. IV*, 256), defines the scholars whose opinions are authoritative and to be taken into account as those whom the people of every region recognize as their leading lawyers (*man naṣabah ahl balad min al-buldān faqīhan*), whose opinion they accept and to whose decision they submit.[2] Small minorities of muftis, he says, must not be taken into account, but only the majority (*lā anẓur ilā qalīl al-muftīn wa-anẓur ilal-akthar*).

This concept of consensus is common to the Iraqians and the Medinese.[3] Both these ancient schools claim the sanction of a consensus of the Companions for the doctrine ascribed to their particular authority among the Companions of the Prophet, thereby projecting the final criterion of their doctrine back to its alleged origins. This consensus of the Companions takes, in the nature of things, the form of a silent approval (*ijmā' sukūtī* in later terminology).

In *Tr. III*, 69, Shāfi'ī addresses the Medinese: 'A decision given by 'Umar, according to you, is public and notorious (*mashhūr ẓāhir*), and can only have proceeded from a consultation with the Companions of the Prophet; therefore his decision, according to you, is equivalent to their opinion or to the opinion of the majority of them,

[1] See above, p. 42 f.
[2] For a list of these local authorities, see above, p. 7 f.
[3] See above, p. 41, n. 5, and *Tr. III*, 148 (p. 243).

... and you say that his decision given in Medina is the same as their general consensus.'

For the Iraqians, see above, p. 44, and Shāfi'ī's discussion with a Basrian opponent, couched in Medinese terms, in *Tr. III*, 148 (p. 244). Shāfi'ī: 'There were in Medina some 30,000 Companions of the Prophet, if not more. Yet you are not able to relate the same opinion from perhaps as few as six, nay, you relate opinions from only one or two or three or four, who may disagree or agree, but they mostly disagree: where then is the consensus?[1] Give an example of what you mean by majority.' Opponent: 'If, for example, five Companions hold one opinion in common, and three hold a contrary opinion, the majority should be followed.' Shāfi'ī: 'This happens only rarely, and if it does happen, are you justified in considering it a consensus, seeing that they disagree?' Opponent: 'Yes, in the sense that the majority agree.' But he concedes that of the rest of the 30,000 nothing is known. Shāfi'ī: 'Do you think, then, that anyone can validly claim consensus on points of detail? And the same applies to the Successors and the generation following the Successors.'

The idea of the general consensus of the community is so natural that the question of foreign influence does not arise. But things are different for the highly organized concept of the 'consensus of the scholars', which consists in the considered opinion of their majority and expresses the 'living tradition' of their school. This concept corresponds to the *opinio prudentium* of Roman law, the authority of which was stated by the Emperor Severus in the following terms: 'In ambiguitatibus quae ex legibus proficiscuntur, consuetudinem aut rerum perpetuo similiter iudicatarum auctoritatem vim legis obtinere debere.'[2] Goldziher has suggested an influence of Roman on Muhammadan law in this case.[3] This concept may well have been transmitted to the Arabs by the schools of rhetoric.[4]

B. The Medinese and Consensus

One feature in which the Medinese idea of consensus differs from the Iraqian is that the Medinese restrict themselves to a local consensus, that is, count only the authorities in Medina. We have come across several passages which show this provin-

[1] Shāfi'ī implies, of course, that nothing is known of the opinions of the majority.

[2] *Digest* i. 3, 38.

[3] In *Proceedings of the Hungarian Academy, Class of Linguistics and Moral Sciences*, xi, no. 9 (1884), pp. 11, 18 (in Hungarian).

[4] See below, p. 99 f.

cialism,[1] and in *Tr. III*, 22, Shāfiʿī states that he has confined himself in his argument to the premisses of the Medinese, and spoken of the consensus only as the consensus of Medina. In his reply to the Medinese Rabīʿ in *Tr. III*, 148 (p. 242) Shāfiʿī points out that men in other countries do not acknowledge the local consensus of Medina as a real one. This Medinese provincialism certainly does not imply any pretension on their part that their city was the true home of the *sunna*,[2] although it may have become one of the starting-points for this later claim. It is, more likely, just a crude remnant of the original geographical character of the ancient schools of law,[3] a provincialism which had been superseded, in the case of the Iraqians, by a wider outlook and—not an isolated case—a more highly developed theory. Furthermore, some Medinese share the Iraqian idea of consensus.[4]

Rabīʿ, speaking for the Medinese, declares in *Tr. III*, 22, that 'there is consensus only when there is no disagreement', but points out at the same time that this test is not applied indiscriminately, but only to 'approved scholars'. Even so, only the agreement of the majority is demanded (*Tr. III*, 148, p. 248). Mālik, in *Muw.* iii. 183, makes the far-reaching claim that 'no one anywhere disagrees' with a certain doctrine,[5] but Ibn ʿAbdalbarr (quoted in Zurqānī, *ad loc.*) points out that this claim is not quite correct. More moderately, Mālik says in *Muw.* ii. 83, that he has seen the scholars approve of a doctrine, or, in *Muw.* ii. 171: 'This is what the scholars in our city have always held.'

The Medinese consensus is to a great extent anonymous, and Shāfiʿī attacks it for this reason. In *Tr. III*, 71, he says: 'I wish I knew who they are whose opinions constitute consensus, of whom one hears nothing and whom we do not know, Allah help us! Allah has obliged no man to take his religion from [private] persons whom he knows.[6] Even if Allah had done so, how would this justify taking one's religion from persons unknown?'[7] The alleged Medinese consensus resolves itself for Shāfiʿī into the claim of 'hereditary transmission of knowledge in Medina'.[8]

[1] See above, pp. 23, 64 f., 69; also *Ris.* 73.
[2] See above, p. 8.
[3] See above, p. 7.
[4] *Tr. IV*, 257; and see below, p. 95 f.
[5] This shows further that the Medinese do not, on principle, reject a broader consensus.
[6] Delete *lā* in the printed text.
[7] Similarly, *Tr. III*, 22, 88, 102; *Ris.* 73, &c.
[8] See above, p. 69.

In ascertaining consensus, the Medinese take no account of the (generally spurious) information on the alleged opinions of their authorities which had been put into circulation by the time of Mālik and Shāfi'ī.[1] But the particular followers of Mālik amongst the Medinese regard their master's doctrine, as expressed in the *Muwaṭṭa'*, as the only authoritative statement of the consensus in Medina.[2]

The systematic collection of alleged ancient authorities in favour of the common Medinese doctrine starts only with Ibn Wahb. Typical examples are the lists found in *Mud.* v. 87, 90; viii. 78 f., and elsewhere. We are not justified in considering them more authentic than the lists of fictitious old Medinese authorities to which Shāfi'ī appeals from the actual Medinese doctrine. We shall discuss the old Medinese authorities in detail below, pp. 243 ff.

The consensus in Medina supersedes, of course, 'isolated' traditions from the Prophet and from Companions.

C. The Iraqians and Consensus

In contrast to the Medinese concept, the Iraqian idea of consensus is not provincial, but extends in theory to all countries. *Ris.* 73 opposes it to that of the Medinese, and Shāfi'ī's Iraqian opponents argue with the 'consensus of [all] people' (*Ikh.* 71), and the 'consensus of the scholars in all countries' (*Tr. IV*, 256). Abū Yūsuf admits an exception from a rule established by systematic reasoning 'because the Muslims have allowed it' (*Tr. IX*, 5), and Shaibānī refers to 'all Muslims without a contradicting voice, that is, all Hijazis and Iraqians' (*Tr. VIII*, 1).

This is the Iraqian theory. But in practice the consensus of the Iraqians shows the same local character as that of the Medinese. This is implied by Shāfi'ī in *Tr. III*, 148 (p. 246, at the beginning) and in *Ris.* 73; and it underlies Abū Yūsuf's reference to 'the consensus of all our scholars' (*Tr. IX*, 42), and Shaibānī's standing reference to 'the opinion of Abū Ḥanīfa and of our scholars in general' in *Muw. Shaib.* This last expression means the same as Mālik's repeated references to 'our agreed practice' in *Muw.*

The words of Shāfi'ī's Basrian opponent in *Tr. III*, 148 (p. 245), show the conclusions which were drawn from the

[1] See above, pp. 65, 69, 78 f., and below, pp. 195, 206, n. 5.
[2] See above, p. 6 f.

natural assumption that the consensus was not subject to error: 'Whenever I find a generation of scholars at a seat of knowledge, in their majority, holding the same opinion, I call this "consensus", whether their predecessors agreed or disagreed with it, because the majority would not agree on anything in ignorance of the doctrine of their predecessors, and would abandon the previous doctrine only on account of a repeal or because they knew of some better argument, even if they did not mention it.' Shāfi'ī calls this an unfounded assumption (*tawahhum*) and points out that their successors would then also be free to diverge from them without mentioning their argument. This means, he says, leaving the decision always to the last generation: a point his opponents must concede if they are not to set themselves up as the only standard of knowledge. But this they could hardly do without making the same concession to scholars elsewhere. This is a fair, though polemical, summing-up of the attitude of the Iraqians.

The first external justification of the principle of consensus occurs in *Muw. Shaib.* 140, where Shaibānī says with regard to a particular decision: 'The Muslims are agreed on this and approve of it, and it is related on the authority of the Prophet that everything of which the Muslims approve or disapprove, is good or bad in the sight of Allah.' This informal tradition, still without an *isnād*, was no doubt relatively recent in the time of Shaibānī.[1]

The consensus of the Iraqians is originally just as anonymous as that of the Medinese (*Ris.* 73); it represents the average opinion, and the Iraqians take as little account of the views of minorities as the Medinese do (*Ikh.* 119). Now Shaibānī, who in *Muw. Shaib.* constantly refers to 'the opinion of Abū Ḥanīfa and of our scholars in general', gives in *Āthār Shaib.* a collection of decisions given and traditions transmitted by Ibrāhīm Nakha'ī, together with the opinions of Abū Ḥanīfa. *Āthār A.Y.* is a largely coextensive collection of Ibrāhīm's alleged opinions and traditions, made by Abū Yūsuf. We must therefore conclude that Abū Ḥanīfa, Abū Yūsuf, Shaibānī, and their companions found the consensus, as their group understood it, represented by the body of doctrine associated with the name

[1] See *Comm. Muw. Shaib.*, *ad loc.*, on its doubtful authenticity, even by the standards of the Muhammadan scholars.

of Ibrāhīm Nakhaʿī.[1] This did not prevent them from differing occasionally from Ibrāhīm and from one another.

On the whole we find that although there is not much difference between the Iraqians and the Medinese in the way their consensus works in practice, the Iraqians developed its theory much farther, overcame theoretically at least its original provincialism, and were the first to identify it with the teaching of individual authorities.

In *Tr. IV*, 258, Shāfiʿī addresses an Iraqian opponent: 'Your idea of consensus is the consensus of the Companions or the Successors or the following generation and finally the contemporaries. . . . For example you take Ibn Musaiyib the scholar of Medina, ʿAṭā' the scholar of Mecca, Ḥasan the scholar of Basra, and Shaʿbī the scholar of Kufa among the Successors, and regard as consensus that on which they agree. You state that they have never met as far as you know, and you infer their consensus from what is related from them. . . . But no one amongst them, as far as we know, has ever used the word consensus, although it would cover most legal knowledge if it were as you claim. Is it not sufficient to discredit your idea of consensus, that no one since the time of the Prophet is related to have claimed it, apart from cases in which nobody holds a diverging opinion, except your contemporaries?'

This agrees well with the idea of Iraqian consensus which we have gained so far, except for the hard-and-fast rule of establishing a consensus, which Shāfiʿī attributes in the course of his polemics to the Iraqians and which is not confirmed by the other indications on how their consensus is ascertained. Ḥasan and Shaʿbī do not play the important role in the Iraqian tradition which Shāfiʿī assigns to them, and he neglects Ibrāhīm Nakhaʿī, who in their doctrine takes a place even more important than that of Ibn Musaiyib for the Medinese. Moreover, the subservience of Iraqian consensus to the doctrine of other 'geographical' schools which Shāfiʿī implies, is not borne out by the facts; the broader, non-provincial character of the Iraqian idea of consensus is confined to their theory and does not extend to their practice. We must therefore consider this hard-and-fast rule not genuinely Iraqian, but rather a logical consequence which Shāfiʿī forced on his opponents. There are other traces of Shāfiʿī's editing in this passage.[2]

For the predominance of consensus, in the doctrine of the Iraqians, over 'isolated' traditions from the Prophet and from Companions, see above, p. 28.

[1] On this body of doctrine see below, pp. 233 ff.
[2] See below, p. 109, n. 2.

D. The Mu'tazila and Consensus

The Mu'tazila, or *ahl al-kalām* as Shāfi'ī calls them, acknowledge consensus and share the Iraqian concept of it as the general agreement of the people of all countries.[1]

They apply this idea of consensus to traditions: if the whole community transmits a certain tradition from the Prophet, it cannot be mistaken.[2] This constitutes an extreme case of the 'wide spread' (*tawātur*) of traditions demanded by them.[3]

As regards the consensus of the community on questions left to personal opinion and systematic reasoning (*ra'y* and *qiyās*), the prominent Mu'tazilite Naẓẓām considered it fallible.[4] This seems to have been a personal doctrine of Naẓẓām, notwithstanding the statement which Ibn Qutaiba, 241, quotes from a Mu'tazilite source, to the effect that legal rules which are unanimously accepted are nevertheless often refuted by the Koran. This statement is directed against the technical consensus of the scholars as accepted by the ancient schools. Of the numerous examples which Ibn Qutaiba adds, one at least (p. 256) is obviously an argument *ad hominem*, and others seem to be of the same kind.

E. Shāfi'ī and Consensus

Shāfi'ī's doctrine of consensus shows a continuous development throughout his writings.[5] We have seen that the followers of the ancient schools distinguish between the consensus of all Muslims on essentials and the consensus of the scholars on points of detail.[6] What follows tends to confirm the suggestion that it was Shāfi'ī who, using a favourite debating device of his, imposed this clear-cut distinction on a less sharply defined, two-sided idea of his opponents. Whether this is so or not, we have seen both Iraqians and Medinese making extensive use of the consensus of the scholars or even of the 'approved' scholars. Shāfi'ī started by recognizing and using this old concept of the

[1] See above, p. 41; *Tr. III*, 148 (p. 242).

[2] *Tr. III*, loc. cit.; Khaiyāṭ, 94 f.

[3] See above, p. 51 f.

[4] Khaiyāṭ, 51, and, relating to questions of dogma, Ibn Qutaiba, 21.

[5] See the chronology of Shāfi'ī's writings in Appendix I, below, p. 330. The chronology is independent of this development of Shāfi'ī's doctrine, except for the exact place of *Tr. VIII* within Shāfi'ī's earlier period.

[6] See above, p. 42.

consensus of the scholars without misgivings. Later he came more and more to qualify it. Finally he reached the stage of refusing it any authority and even denying its existence. But so deeply ingrained was the habit of referring to it that he did not completely abandon it, but went on using it, mostly as a subsidiary argument and as an argument *ad hominem*.

In the first group of treatises Shāfi'ī's use of the argument of consensus is indistinguishable from that of the ancient schools.

Tr. I, 127: an analogy with a doctrine based on the consensus, 'which no one can be allowed to neglect'; Shāfi'ī states explicitly farther on that this is the consensus of the scholars (although he calls it *madhhab al-'āmma*), and not the consensus of the community on essentials. § 182: Shāfi'ī refers to the scholars in general.

Tr. II, 16 (*e*): 'Neither we nor anyone we know holds this. The general opinion is (*yaqūl al-nās*). . . .' § 17 (*c*): 'This is the opinion of the muftis in general (*muftu l-nās*), and we know of no disagreement in this respect.' § 19 (*p*): 'Neither we nor any mufti we know [except the Iraqians] holds this. . . . I am not aware that they [the Iraqians] relate this from anyone in the past (*mimman maḍā*) whose word carries authority (*qauluh ḥujja*).' § 19 (*r*): 'Our opinion—and Allah knows best—comes nearest to what is recognized by the scholars.' § 21 (*g*): 'They [the Iraqians] . . . do not follow the opinion of any predecessor (*aḥad min al-salaf*), as far as I know . . . . [The opinion which we hold] is the opinion of our scholars in general [that is, the Medinese].'

Tr. VIII, 6: 'This is also the opinion of Ibn Musaiyib, Ḥasan, Ibrāhīm Nakha'ī, and the majority of the muftis among the Hijazis and the traditionists of whom we have heard.' § 7: 'The argument is the *sunna* [or, rather, an analogy based on traditions from the Prophet] and the lack of disagreement among the scholars, to the best of my knowledge.' § 11: '[Who holds this], puts himself outside the several possible opinions (*kharaj min qaul al-muttafiqīn wal-mukhtalifīn*).' § 14: 'The doctrine of the mass of the scholars in all countries (*qaul 'awāmm ahl al-buldān min al-fuqahā'*).'

Tr. IX, 10: 'It is established by tradition and by fetwas [opinions given by scholars].' § 25: 'The authorities of the Muslims are agreed (*ajma'at a'immat al-Muslimīn*).'

In the following two treatises, Shāfi'ī still holds essentially the old idea of consensus, but qualifies it; the consensus of the Muslims gains prominence.

Tr. VII, 271 ff.: Nobody is authorized to give a judgment or a fetwa 'unless he bases himself on . . . what the scholars agree in saying'.—'He disagrees with the general doctrine of the body of learned men whose decisions have been transmitted.'—'*Q.*: What is the proof for the authority of that on which men are agreed? *A.*: When the Prophet ordered men to hold fast to the community of Muslims, this could only mean that they were to accept the doctrine of the community; it is reasonable, too, to assume that the community cannot [p. 272] as a whole be ignorant of a ruling given by Allah and the Prophet. Such ignorance is possible only in individuals, whereas something on which all [Muslims] are agreed cannot be wrong and whosoever accepts such a doctrine does so in conformity with the *sunna* of the Prophet.'[1]—'This is neither reasonable nor in keeping with the decisions of those who have given decisions from the first time of Islam onwards.'—P. 275: It is not permissible to disagree with an unambiguous text of the Koran, nor an established *sunna*, 'nor, I think, with the community at large (*jamā'at al-nās*), even when there is no Koran or *sunna*'.

Ris.: the consensus of the scholars or of their majority appears explicitly on pp. 19, 21, 21 f., 24, 25, 32, 40, 46, 48 ult., 72 (at the end), 73 (at the beginning), 82 (at the beginning). The consensus of the Muslims at large occurs on pp. 46, 58, 72. Shāfi'ī contrasts both kinds of consensus and obviously ascribes higher authority to the consensus of the Muslims at large on p. 63. There he claims that one might almost say that the Muslims in both early and later times are agreed on a point of theory, but he will go only so far as to say that he has not heard that the Muslim scholars were divided on the issue.

In the main passage on consensus, on p. 65, Shāfi'ī discusses only the consensus of the community at large and severs its historical connexion with the old idea of *sunna* or 'living tradition'. '*Q.*: What is your argument for following the consensus of the public (*ma jtama' al-nās 'alaih*) on a question where there is no explicit command of Allah [in the Koran] and where no decision of the Prophet is related: do you, as others do, hold that the consensus of the public is always based on an established *sunna*[2] even if it is not related? *A.*: That on which the public are agreed and which, they state, is related from the Prophet, that is so, I trust. But as to that which the public do not [explicitly] relate [from the Prophet], which they may or may not assert on the basis of a tradition from the Prophet, so that we cannot consider it as [certainly] transmitted on the authority of the Prophet

[1] This is, after Shaibānī's tradition from the Prophet (above, p. 86), the second external justification of the principle of consensus. See below, p. 91, on the traditions in which Shāfi'ī finds this *sunna* expressed.

[2] In the opinion of the ancient schools, this means their 'living tradition', but Shāfi'ī takes it in the sense of a formal tradition from the Prophet. See also above, p. 43, n. 1.

—because one may transmit only what one has heard—in cases where the transmission [on the authority of the Prophet] is only an assumption which may or may not be true: [as to that,] we accept the decision of the public because we follow their authority, knowing that, wherever there are *sunnas* of the Prophet, their whole body cannot be ignorant of them, although it is possible that some are, and knowing that their whole body cannot agree on something contrary to the *sunna* of the Prophet and on an error, I trust.'

In confirmation, Shāfi'ī quotes two traditions which state that the Prophet ordered men to hold fast to the community, and which he explains as referring to the consensus. 'The error comes from separation, but in the community as a whole there is no error with regard to the meaning of the Koran, the *sunna*, and analogy, I trust.'

Contrary to the old idea of consensus and also to the later system, Shāfi'ī here restricts its function to the interpretation of Koran and *sunna* and to drawing conclusions from them. He has not succeeded in clarifying his idea of consensus of the community at large, and it remains in an uneasy relationship with the new dominating element, the traditions from the Prophet. Shāfi'ī does not know yet the *locus classicus* in favour of consensus: 'My community will never agree on an error.' As a tradition from the Prophet, it appears only in the time of the classical collections,[1] and its wording is directly derived from statements such as that of Shāfi'ī.

Tr. VI contains only one reference to the consensus of the community at large, on p. 265: 'We know that the Muslims as a body cannot be ignorant of a *sunna*, whereas it is possible that some, individually, are.'

From *Tr. IV* onwards, Shāfi'ī rejects the consensus of the scholars explicitly, at least in theory, and even denies its existence.

Tr. IV, 256: Shāfi'ī twice uses the argument of the *sorites* against the consensus of the majority of scholars.[2] He considers the alleged consensus of the majority only as a pretext for accepting or rejecting doctrines at pleasure. The consensus of the scholars can never be realized as they are never found together,[3] nor can common information (*naql al-'āmma*) be had about them. On p. 257, the opponent asks whether in Shāfi'ī's view a real consensus exists at all. Shāfi'ī replies: 'Certainly, there is much in the essential duties on which no one who knows anything will pretend that there is no consensus, and this applies also to certain general principles'; but he defies him to find a consensus when he comes to controversial questions of detail

[1] Also in Ibn Qutaiba, 24, and in Ibn Rawandī, quoted in Khaiyāṭ, 97.

[2] In another connexion, the *sorites* occurs in *Ikh.* 324.

[3] This contradicts Shāfi'ī's own reasoning, with regard to the community, in *Ris.* 65.

in his own and in the preceding generation. Shāfiʿī denies its existence on questions of detail, which are the concern of specialists, in Medina, and still more in the community at large. The consensus of the majority of those scholars on whom one happens to possess information cannot be used as an argument, and no inference may be drawn regarding the opinion of those scholars of whom nothing is known.[1]

In *Tr. III*, 129, Shāfiʿī maintains the authority of the consensus of the community at large: 'It is impossible that the community should agree on something contrary to the words of the Prophet.' In § 148 (p. 244), he gives his theory in detail. No consensus, whether of the Companions or of the Successors or of the generation after them, can be validly claimed on questions of detail. '*Q.*: How can you validly claim consensus at all? *A.*: It can be validly claimed with regard to duties that no one may neglect, such as prayers, *zakāt* tax, and the prohibition of what is forbidden. But as regards questions concerning specialists, the ignorance of which does not harm the great public and the knowledge of which is to be found with specialists . . ., we can only say one of two things: if we are not aware that they have disagreed, we say so, and if they have disagreed we say that they have done so. . . . We follow whichever of their opinions is more in keeping with Koran and *sunna*. If there is no such indication—and this is rarely the case—then . . . [we follow] the one which is considered better in all its implications by the scholars. If they disagree as described, it is correct to say: [opinions on] this problem are related from a number of persons who disagree, and we follow the opinion of three against that of two, or of four against that of three; but we do not claim that this is a consensus, because to claim a consensus is to make a statement about those who have not expressed an opinion. . . .[2] The consensus comprises the greatest possible number of different groups of people.' Shāfiʿī insists on strict unanimity (ibid., p. 248): 'If the contrary opinion were related only from one or two or three, one could not say that men are agreed, because they are divided. . . . I do not claim consensus unless no one denies that it exists.'

In numerous passages, however, Shāfiʿī uses the old concept of the consensus of the majority of scholars as a subsidiary argument or an argument *ad hominem* against the Medinese. But he explicitly rejects

[1] Shāfiʿī's insistence on positive unanimity has been prepared already in *Ris.*

[2] Shāfiʿī declares repeatedly that one must not claim the consensus 'unless the scholars confirm it explicitly or at least state that they know of no scholar who contradicts it' (§ 22), or without the existence of traditions from the Companions or the Successors sufficient to establish their unanimous agreement (§ 88), or without positive information (*khabar*) to this effect (§ 120).

the Iraqian concept of consensus of scholars in each generation.[1] Basing himself on the traditions expressing 'unsuccessful' Medinese opinions and on recent (mostly spurious) information regarding old Medinese authorities, he denies the existence of real consensus in Medina and charges the contemporary Medinese with diverging from the consensus of their old authorities.[2] He tends to replace the old concept of consensus, on which the Medinese rely, by his idea of *sunna* (§ 71). Against the provincialism of the Medinese in their concept of consensus, he points out that the Medinese are only a minority and claims that, if a consensus exists in Medina, it exists also in the other countries, and if there is disagreement in Medina, the other countries also disagree.[3]

Ikhtilāf al-Ḥadīth, itself the latest of the treatises, contains early passages, and we find both the old concept of consensus and Shāfiʿī's new one. Some typical examples of the former (which are, however, not all necessarily early) occur on pp. 5, 37, 73, 170, 176, 207, 246, 262. For the latter see, for instance, pp. 141 ff., which is directed against the assumption of a silent consensus of the Companions, and of a consensus of Companions in general: 'the alleged consensus [of Companions and later authorities] on many points of detail cannot be properly claimed'; Shāfiʿī considers the opinion of his opponents to the contrary as ill-advised, ignorant, and pretentious. 'The forebears never, if I am right,[4] held that all details of law are based on consensus in the same way in which there is consensus on the Koran, the *sunna*, and the essentials.' Apart from the essential duties which the public at large are obliged to observe, no consensus has been claimed by any of the Companions or of the Successors or of the following generation or of those after them, or by any scholar on earth whom Shāfiʿī has known, or by anyone who was regarded as a scholar by the public, except occasionally when someone claimed it after a fashion approved by no scholar Shāfiʿī can think of, and to his personal knowledge rejected by many.[5]

But Shāfiʿī was unable to dispense completely with the idea of consensus of the scholars; he tried to reconcile it with his concept of the consensus of the community at large by opposing the opinion of the generality of scholars (*ʿawāmm ahl ahl-ʿilm*) to that of the specialists (*khāṣṣa*) among them (pp. 56 f.).[6] The unanimous opinion of the

[1] § 148 (p. 245), quoted above, p. 85 f.

[2] §§ 121, 148 (p. 247), and often.

[3] §§ 22, 77, 134, 148 (p. 248, at the end).

[4] This shows that Shāfiʿī's doctrine is something new.

[5] This exaggeration is refuted by Shāfiʿī's own statement on the doctrine of the ancient schools, above, pp. 42 f.

[6] See also below, p. 136.

scholars merges into the consensus of the Muslims at large and serves to eliminate stray opinions by showing them to be below the general scholarly standard. Shāfiʿī says on pp. 309 f.: 'If someone were to take a *sunna* of the Prophet or a doctrine unanimously acknowledged by the scholars in general, would he be justified in adducing his own disagreement as proof [that the point is contested] or would he be simply an ignoramus who has still to learn? If the first were the case, everyone might invalidate any rule without reference to a *sunna* or to a disagreement among the scholars.' Shāfiʿī gives as an example the paternity of a child: whosoever does not consider it cancelled by the procedure of *liʿān* diverges from the *sunna* of the Prophet, and Shāfiʿī knows of no disagreement among the Muslims about it. These passages, which presuppose Shāfiʿī's final concept of the consensus of the community at large, seem to be late.[1]

Umm is composite, containing passages of various dates and partly revised. Both the old and the new idea of consensus are expressed in it.

F. The Later Doctrine of Consensus

The classical theory of consensus falls outside the scope of this inquiry.[2] From what has been said, it is clear that the classical theory represents essentially a return to the old concept; in other words, Shāfiʿī's rejection in principle of the consensus of the scholars, and his restriction of consensus to the unanimous doctrine of the community at large, were unsuccessful.[3] But the later doctrine does not simply continue the old concept, it accepts Shāfiʿī's identification of *sunna* with the contents of traditions from the Prophet and covers it with the authority of the consensus of the scholars. So the main result of Shāfiʿī's break with the principle of 'living tradition' became itself part of the 'living tradition' at a later stage. The price that had to be paid for this recognition was that the extent to which traditions from the Prophet were in fact accepted as a foundation of law was in future to be determined by consensus; and Shāfiʿī's

[1] The context of the second passage expresses hostility towards the use made of consensus by the ancient schools.

[2] See above, p. 2, and Goldziher, in *Nachr. Ges. Wiss. Gött.*, 1916, 81 ff.

[3] Graf, *Wortelen*, 65, sums up the differences between Shāfiʿī's doctrine in *Ris.* and the later theory. The later idea of consensus is already fully developed in Ṭabarī; see Kern, in *Z.D.M.G.* lv. 72. Ibn Qutaiba, 326, regards the consensus, although it be not based on the Koran or on a tradition, as a valid argument; it is difficult to say which stage of doctrine this statement represents.

endeavour to erect the traditions from the Prophet, instead of the 'living tradition' and the consensus, into the highest authority in law was short-lived.

G. Disagreement

Shāfiʿī states repeatedly that the ancient schools of law are hostile to disagreement.[1] So are, according to Ibn Qutaiba, 7, the *ahl al-kalām*. The followers of the ancient schools refer to Koranic passages, such as sura iii. 105; xcviii. 4, where Allah blames disagreement in matters of religion; they refuse to concede any kind of disagreement and say that had the old authorities met, they would have come to an agreement by convincing one another (*Tr. IV*, 261). There is also a tradition which makes Ibn Masʿūd conform to a practice which does not correspond to his doctrine, and when this is pointed out to him say: 'Disagreement is bad.'[2]

Hostility to disagreement, on the ground of administrative convenience, was voiced by Ibn Muqaffaʿ, a secretary of state.[3] He pointed out the wide divergencies in jurisprudence and in administration of justice existing between the several great cities and between the schools of law such as the Iraqians and the Hijazis. These divergencies, he said, either perpetuated different local precedents[4] or came from systematic reasoning, which was sometimes faulty or pushed too far. The Caliph should review the different doctrines with their reasons and codify and enact his own decisions in the interest of uniformity. This code ought to be revised by successive Caliphs. These considerations of Ibn Muqaffaʿ lie quite outside the compass of the ancient lawyers and traditionists; they are obviously influenced by Persian administrative tradition.

On the other hand, we find Medinese traditions in favour of disagreement and against uniformity. One of these traditions expresses the reaction of the Medinese to an extreme proposal such as that of Ibn Muqaffaʿ, projected back into the Umaiyad

[1] *Tr. IV*, 255, 258, 275.

[2] *Tr. II*, 19 (*aa*); *Tr. III*, 117; *Ikh.* 74. A tradition from ʿAlī with the same tendency, in Bukhārī, is discussed by Goldziher, *Ẓâhiriten*, 98.

[3] *Ṣaḥāba*, 126 f. As this treatise was addressed to the Caliph Manṣūr (A.H. 136–58) and Ibn Muqaffaʿ was killed between 139 and 142, it can be dated about A.H. 140.

[4] *Shaiʾ maʾthūr ʿan al-salaf ghair mujmaʿ ʿalaih yudabbiruh qaum ʿalā wajh wa-yudabbiruh ākharūn ʿalā wajh ākhar.*

period. It relates that it was suggested to ʿUmar b. ʿAbdalʿazīz to bring about uniformity of doctrine; but he said: 'I should not like it if they had not disagreed,' and sent letters to the several provinces ordering that each region should decide according to the consensus of its scholars.[1] On the side of the Iraqians, the *Fiqh Akbar* expresses the doctrine that disagreements in the community are a concession from Allah.[2]

These two groups of evidence are not necessarily contradictory, and both tendencies expressed by them are complementary to the concept of consensus in the ancient schools of law. On one side, they accept the geographical differences of doctrine as natural; on the other, they uphold their consensus, disparage irregular opinions which are apt to break it,[3] and state unambiguously what they consider to be right. The rising tide of traditions from the Prophet in particular threatened the continuity and uniformity of doctrine; so Shāfiʿī rightly connected the rejection of 'isolated traditions' by the ancient schools with their aversion to disagreement (*Tr. IV*, 258). The adherents of the ancient schools logically insisted that a qualified lawyer (*mujtahid*)[4] might be wrong in his conclusions (ibid. 274). Against the underlying attitude to error and disagreement is directed a tradition to which Shāfiʿī refers in his reply and which makes the Prophet say: 'If a *mujtahid* is right he receives two rewards, and if he is mistaken he receives one reward.'

The *isnād* of this tradition (*Tr. IV*, 275 and *Ris*. 67, where further details of this discussion are recorded) runs: Shāfiʿī—ʿAbdalʿazīz b. Muḥammad—Yazīd b. ʿAbdallāh b. Hād—Muḥammad b. Ibrāhīm Taimī—Busr b. Saʿīd—Abū Qais—ʿAmr b. ʿĀṣ—Prophet, and after giving the text, Yazīd claims that he mentioned this tradition to Abū Bakr b. Muḥammad b. ʿAmr b. Ḥazm, who confirmed it on the authority of Abū Salama b. ʿAbdalraḥmān—Abū Huraira. This kind of artificial confirmation is typical of the first appearance

[1] This and two other traditions of similar tendency in Dārimī, *Bāb ikhtilāf al-fuqahā'*. See also the anecdote on Mālik and an early ʿAbbāsid Caliph, discussed in *E.I.*, s.v. *Mālik b. Anas*.

[2] Wensinck, *Creed*, 104, 112 f. This maxim became, much later, a saying of the Prophet, but neither Abū Ḥanīfa, nor Shāfiʿī, nor the classical collections of traditions knew it as such.

[3] The term *ikhtilāf* 'disagreement' means occasionally 'inconsistency, self-contradiction'; see, e.g., *Tr. IX*, 12, 14 (quotations from Abū Yūsuf), and the title of Shāfiʿī's *Ikhtilāf al-Ḥadīth*.

[4] See below, p. 99.

of traditions which had to overcome opposition, and we can safely conclude that this tradition originated in the time of Yazīd, that is, in the generation before Mālik. It found its way into the classical collections.[1] A later form, not yet known to Shāfi'ī, which gives spurious circumstantial detail and mentions ten rewards as against one, is quoted by Ibn Qutaiba, 182.[2]

Shāfi'ī acknowledges disagreement as the necessary result of systematic reasoning (*ijtihād*); it existed already in the time of the Companions, and it is to be resolved by reference to Koran and *sunna*; referring to the tradition on one and two rewards, he denies the existence of a fundamental disagreement even when there are contradictory opinions, because every *mujtahid* fulfils his duty by drawing the conclusion which he considers right.[3]

All this is meant to justify Shāfi'ī's break with the doctrine of the ancient schools and his insistence on the supreme authority of the traditions from the Prophet, beside which the results of systematic reasoning become irrelevant. He says in *Tr. IV*, 261: 'On points on which there exists an explicit decision of Allah or a *sunna* of the Prophet or a consensus of the Muslims, no disagreement is allowed; on the other points, scholars must exert their own judgment in search of an indication (*shubha*) in one of these three sources; he who is qualified for this research is entitled to hold the opinion which he finds implied in Koran, *sunna*, or consensus; if a problem is capable of two solutions, either opinion may be held as the result of systematic reasoning, but this occurs only rarely.'

To sum up: Shāfi'ī advances a fresh and independent study of traditions from the Prophet as against the established doctrine of the ancient schools.

[1] e.g. Bukhārī, *Kitāb al-i'tiṣām bil-kitāb wal-sunna, Bāb ajr al-ḥākim idha jtahad.*

[2] An earlier statement of the same thesis, to the effect that every *mujtahid* is rewarded, is ascribed to Ibn Musaiyib, but is hardly authentic; see below, p. 114.

[3] *Tr. III*, 148 (p. 244); *Tr. IV*, 262; *Tr. VII*, 275; *Ris.* 68; *Ikh.* 149.

CHAPTER 9

ANALOGY, SYSTEMATIC REASONING, AND PERSONAL OPINION

THE result of our inquiry so far has been that the real basis of legal doctrine in the ancient schools was not a body of traditions handed down from the Prophet or even from his Companions, but the 'living tradition' of the school as expressed in the consensus of the scholars. The opinion of the scholars on what the right decision ought to be precedes systematically, and also historically, its expression in traditions. We shall see[1] that the material on which the ancient lawyers of Islam started to work was the popular and administrative practice as they found it towards the end of the Umaiyad period. At present we are concerned with their systematizing activity itself. It started with the exercise of personal opinion and of individual reasoning on the part of the earliest cadis and lawyers. It would be a gratuitous assumption to consider the arbitrary decision of the magistrate or the specialist as anterior to rudimentary analogy and the striving after coherence. Both elements are found intimately connected in the earliest period which the sources allow us to discern. Nevertheless, all this individual reasoning, whether purely arbitrary and personal or inspired by an effort at consistency, started from vague beginnings, without direction or method; and it moved towards an increasingly strict discipline until Shāfiʿī, consistently and as a matter of principle, rejected all individual arbitrariness and insisted on strict systematic thought.[2]

Individual reasoning in general is called *ra'y*, 'opinion'. When it is directed towards achieving systematic consistency and guided by the parallel of an existing institution or decision it is called *qiyās* 'analogy'. When it reflects the personal choice of the lawyer, guided by his idea of appropriateness, it is called *istiḥsān* or *istiḥbāb* 'preference'. The term *istiḥsān* therefore came

[1] Below, pp. 190 ff.

[2] These remarks show how far the sources now available compel me to place the emphasis differently from Goldziher, *Ẓâhiriten*, 5 ff. In what follows, I have endeavoured to study the development in detail rather than to duplicate Goldziher's discussion of its outlines for the early period. See also *E.I.* ii. s.v. *Fikh*.

to signify a breach of strict analogy for reasons of public interest, convenience, or similar considerations. The use of individual reasoning in general is called *ijtihād*, and *mujtahid* is the qualified lawyer who uses it. These terms are to a great extent synonymous in the ancient period, and remained so even after Shāfi'ī. Individual reasoning, both in its arbitrary and in its systematically disciplined form, is freely used by the ancient schools, often without being called by any of the terms mentioned. It is typical of the lack of differentiation between the two elements that, if any term is used at all, it is mostly the generic term *ra'y*. In this chapter we are concerned only with the function of individual reasoning as a source of law; for the development of technical legal thought as such, see below, pp. 269 ff.

Qiyās is derived from the Jewish exegetical term *hiqqīsh*, *inf. heqqēsh*, from the Aramaic root *nqsh*, meaning 'to beat together'. This is used: (*a*) of the juxtaposition of two subjects in the Bible, showing that they are to be treated in the same manner; (*b*) of the activity of the interpreter who makes the comparison suggested by the text; (*c*) of a conclusion by analogy, based on the occurrence of an essential common feature in the original and in the parallel case.[1] The third meaning, in which Hillel uses the term (Palestinian Talmud, *Pesachim*, 6, *fol.* 33 a 14), is identical with that of *qiyās*. The existence of an original concrete meaning in Aramaic but not in Arabic (where *qiyās* belongs to the root *qys*), makes the foreign provenance of the term certain. Margoliouth has recognized this origin of *qiyās*, and tentatively suggested the further filiation of *hiqqīsh*, in its technical meanings, from *συμβάλλειν*.[2]

Conclusions *a maiore ad minus* (and negatively *a minore ad maius*) which fall under *qiyās* and are familiar to Shāfi'ī and his Iraqian predecessors,[3] form one branch of Hillel's exegetical rules.[4] D. Daube has pointed out that some of these rules occur, almost literally, in earlier Roman legal classics, and has suggested the 'plausible explanation . . . that there were pretty much the same rhetorical schools in Rome and in the provinces'.[5] The same conclusions occur in Shāfi'ī's older Christian contemporary Theodore Abū Qurra (ed. Migne, *Patr. Gr.* xcvii. 1556), and Theodore's whole technique of

[1] See W. Bacher, *Die älteste Terminologie der jüdischen Schriftauslegung* (1899), 44 f.

[2] In *J.R.A.S.*, 1910, 320.

[3] See below, pp. 110, 124 f.

[4] See H. L. Strack, *Introduction to the Talmud and Midrash* (1931), 93 f. Bergsträsser, in *Islam*, xiv. 81, regards this as a case of technical influence of Jewish on Muhammadan jurisprudence.

[5] In *Law Quarterly Review*, lii. 265 f., in *Hebrew Union College Annual*, xxii, 239 ff., and in *Festschrift Hans Lewald*, Basle 1953, 27 ff.

discussion is the same as that of Shāfiʿī. This influence of Graeco-Roman rhetoric might also account for other traces of Greek logic and Roman law in early Muhammadan legal science,[1] including the particular kind of analogical reasoning known as *istiṣḥāb*[2] which we find for the first time in Shāfiʿī,[3] and perhaps even the reasoning called *istiṣlāḥ*.[4]

A. The Umaiyad Period

The information on the early judges of Egypt in Kindī can hardly be considered as authentic throughout as far as the first century is concerned; but it agrees with that relating to the first half of the second century in making the judges rely on their personal opinion to the exclusion of traditions. This ancient feature, therefore, still persisted at the time in which the information on the first century originated, and it certainly existed in the earlier part of the second century.

P. 312, A.H. 65: among the desirable qualifications of a judge are mentioned knowledge of the Koran and knowledge of how to distribute the shares of inheritance; the judge in question did not have either, but 'judged according to what he knew [that is, what he had heard from others], and inquired [that is, consulted others] about what he did not know'; there is no question yet of knowledge of *sunna* or traditions. If it is stated (p. 313) that this judge was illiterate but nevertheless successful because he used to frequent the company of two Companions of the Prophet, the evidence to the contrary from a much later period compels us to regard this as a secondary explanation.

Pp. 314–20, on ʿAbdalraḥmān b. Ḥujaira, judge A.H. 69–83: several decisions are ascribed to him, and the context shows that they are regarded as the result of his own discretion. They are so irregular by all later standards that it is possible or even likely that they reflect authentic legal opinions of the first century, even if their ascription to this particular judge is not beyond doubt.[5] His alleged

[1] See Margoliouth, *Early Development*, 97; above, pp. 83, 91, below, p. 125; *Ikh.* 339 (*regressus ad infinitum*). See also my papers in *J. Comparative Legislation*, 1950, Nos. 3–4, pp. 9–16, in *Histoire de la Médecine*, ii, 1952, No. 5, pp. 11–19, and in *XII Convegno 'Volta'*, Rome, 1957, 197–230.

[2] See Goldziher, in *Vienna Oriental Journal*, i. 231 ff.

[3] See below, p. 126.

[4] See below, p. 111, n. 1.

[5] This disproves the later idea that the Egyptians in the beginning followed mostly the decisions of the Companion ʿAbdallāh b. ʿAmr b. ʿĀṣ (Maqrīzī, ii. 332).

reference to a tradition from ʿUmar (p. 319) is certainly spurious, because this tradition expresses a secondary and 'unsuccessful' Medinese doctrine (*Muw.* iii. 86; *Muw. Shaib.* 271; *Mud.* v. 87; *Tr. III*, 56). The same applies, for similar reasons, to Ibn Musaiyib's protest to Ibn Ḥujaira against an Egyptian practice relating to the contract of sale (p. 316), and to Ibn Ḥujaira's alleged decision on the obligatory gift from husband to wife in the case of divorce (p. 317), the model for which occurs on p. 309.

Pp. 334 ff., A.H. 99: the Caliph ʿUmar b. ʿAbdalʿazīz left it to a judge to decide at his own discretion (*ra'y*) a question of injury on which no precedent was known to the Caliph (*lam yablughnī fī hādhā shai'*). When the same judge submitted a question of pre-emption to the Caliph, ʿUmar b. ʿAbdalʿazīz referred in general terms to 'what he had heard' (*kunnā nasmaʿ*). This expression does not imply the existence of a tradition, but is regularly used in ancient terminology of opinions that commend themselves.[1] In answering two other problems submitted by the same judge, the Caliph did not refer to traditions but gave his own independent decisions.[2]

P. 344, on Tauba b. Nimr, judge A.H. 115–20: he imposed an obligatory gift from husband to wife in every case of divorce, but did not insist in the face of persistent refusal; this shows that this doctrine, based on a sweeping interpretation of Koran ii. 236, 241, was an innovation.

P. 350, on Khair b. Nuʿaim, judge A.H. 120–7: he gave the same decision as Tauba, and the context implies beyond doubt that it was the result of his own discretion. Kindī's authority states that no other judge gave this decision, which seems to contradict the former statement. The same doctrine was reported from Khair's Medinese contemporary Zuhrī and projected back to Qāsim b. Muḥammad, one generation earlier (*Muw.* iii. 55). But it did not prevail in the Medinese school, which imposed the obligatory gift only when the divorce originated from the husband and not from the wife (*Tr. III*, 141). Another unsuccessful Medinese opinion, which is based on a

Maqrīzī states (loc. cit.) on the authority of Kindī that Yazīd b. Abī Ḥabīb (d. A.H. 128) was the first to introduce the study of legal traditions into Egypt.

[1] See above, p. 68; below, pp. 208, n. 8; 211; further, *Muw.* iii. 16; *Tr. III*, 38, where Rabīʿ speaks as a Medinese; and Goldziher, *Ẓâhiriten*, 15. Mālik's formula *aḥsan mā samiʿt* (or *alladhī samiʿt*) has regularly the same meaning; see below, pp. 180, 313; also the typical cases, *Muw.* iii. 8, 16, 68, 259 and particularly 37, where one of several examples occurs in a tradition which runs: Mālik—ʿAbdalraḥmān b. Qāsim—his father Qāsim b. Muḥammad—Marwān b. Ḥakam gave judgment on a question of divorce. ʿAbdalraḥmān comments: 'Qāsim liked this decision and considered it the best that he had heard (*wa-yarāh aḥsan mā samiʿ fī dhālik*).' For another formula with a similar meaning ('it was said', 'they used to say') see ibid. 35 and below, p. 184.

[2] References to ʿUmar b. ʿAbdalʿazīz are generally spurious; see below, p. 192.

more meticulous interpretation of the Koranic verses and also tends to extend the sphere of the obligatory gift, though not quite as far as Khair and Zuhrī do, is expressed in a tradition related by Nāfiʿ from Ibn ʿUmar. This tradition, and one from another Companion in favour of the obligatory gift, were put into circulation between Zuhrī and Mālik, in whose *Muwaṭṭa'* they appear for the first time. Shāfiʿī follows the tradition from Ibn ʿUmar and attacks the current Medinese doctrine as systematically inconsistent. All Medinese opinions, starting with the *ra'y* of Tauba and Khair, share the tendency to impose the obligatory gift in a wider range of cases than the Iraqians (*Muw. Shaib.* 262); these last give the Koranic verses a narrow interpretation, which is also the natural one, and their doctrine probably represents the oldest stage.

Pp. 348–52: a considerable number of decisions given by the same Khair b. Nuʿaim are reported; it is evident from the context that they are regarded as the result of his own discretion, and no references to traditions are given in this connexion.

It is significant that this kind of information ceases soon afterwards.

The position of *r'ay* in Muhammadan jurisprudence immediately after the end of the Umaiyad period is discussed at length by Ibn Muqaffaʿ in his *Risāla fil-Ṣaḥāba*, which can be dated about A.H. 140.[1] According to Ibn Muqaffaʿ, the Caliph, whatever the flatterers may say, cannot interfere with the major duties of religion, and a wrongful order coming from him must not be obeyed. But he possesses supreme authority and can give binding orders at his discretion (*ra'y*) on military and civil administration and generally on all matters on which there is no precedent (*athar*), basing himself on Koran and *sunna*.[2] No one but the Caliph has this right (pp. 122 f.). Reason and personal opinion (*ʿaql* and *ra'y*) have a restricted but necessary function in religion. The final discretionary decision belongs only to the ruler, but he must endorse and carry out the positive commandments and *sunnas* (p. 123). Systematic reasoning (*ra'y*) ruthlessly pursued leads to the drawing of remote conclusions which are based neither on Koran nor on *sunna*, are acceptable to no one except their author, and lead to disagreement (p. 126).

[1] See above, p. 95, n. 3.

[2] Ibn Muqaffaʿ uses *athar* for an authoritative precedent, practically as a synonym of *sunna* or 'living tradition'; cf. above, p. 95, n. 4. He does not mention formal traditions.

The distinction which Ibn Muqaffaʿ makes here between those who base themselves on *sunna*[1] and those who use *ra'y* has nothing to do with the distinction between the Hijazis and the Iraqians which he has introduced before, or even with that between the traditionists and the adherents of the ancient schools. It is, as the evidence collected in this and the preceding chapters shows, merely a distinction between two still-connected and complementary tendencies which the shrewd secretary of state, anticipating Shāfiʿī, isolated from each other and saw as destined to clash.

As an observer from outside, Ibn Muqaffaʿ disparages *ra'y* as it is used in the ancient schools of law, and suggests that the Caliph should supersede and regulate it.[2] He shows that human imperfections are inherent in systematic reasoning although the person who undertakes it applies strict analogy, particularly when this reasoning is pushed to its extreme limits. He gives a common-sense but non-technical description of the proper function and limitations of analogy and the proper use of *ra'y* and *istiḥsān*, by which undesirable consequences of strict systematic reasoning can be avoided (p. 126).

By his very attacks on *ra'y* Ibn Muqaffaʿ acknowledges its importance in the ancient schools of law. Apart from using the term, as we saw, for the supreme discretionary decision of the ruler, he uses it for a suggestion of his own on taxation (p. 130), and even mentions it repeatedly as an essential part of the activity of the lawyers, who must possess knowledge of *sunna* and precedents (*ahl al-fiqh wal-sunna wal-siyar*). The emphasis which he lays on the *ra'y* of the Caliph, as opposed to that of the lawyers, is caused by his special position as a secretary of state and the particular political situation at the beginning of the ʿAbbāsid dynasty.

B. The Iraqians

The Iraqians do not invalidate the decision of a judge who decides according to his discretion (*ra'y*), even if they regard it as unjust (*Ikh.* 54). But whilst they use *ra'y* themselves, they do not consider it as a valid argument on the part of others (ibid. 378). This inconsistency and the resultant

[1] See above, pp. 58 f.

[2] See above, p. 95.

inconclusive character of *ra'y* provide Shāfi'ī with an argument against it.[1]

The earliest documents of Iraqian *ra'y* consist of a number of traditions from Companions, one of which has been quoted above, p. 29. Further examples in *Tr. II* are:

§ 12 (*a*): 'Alī credits himself and 'Umar with *ra'y*. Sha'bī appears in the *isnād*.

§ 12 (*g*): Ibn Mas'ūd expresses his *ra'y*, but in view of the opposition of some Companions of the Prophet he forgoes acting upon it. This is a counter-tradition against the Iraqian doctrine which goes under the name of Ibn Mas'ūd.

§§ 14 (*e*), 18 (*n*): *ra'y* is ascribed to 'Alī.

§ 18 (*w*): *ra'y* is used by Ibn Mas'ūd in a tradition which expresses the oldest Iraqian doctrine. Its *isnād* is *munqaṭi'*, and it is not earlier than the time of Sha'bī, who appears in its *isnād*.

§ 18 (*y*): Ibn Mas'ūd and 'Umar, who approves of Ibn Mas'ūd's decision, express their *ra'y* that the punishment by *ta'zīr*, which is awarded by the judge, is not to exceed half the Koranic *ḥadd* punishment. This Iraqian principle is an early arbitrary decision, and the tradition endeavours to enlist the authority of 'Umar for the doctrine which is attributed to Ibn Mas'ūd.

The Basrian version of a tradition against the sale of fruit before it is ripe even puts into the mouth of the Prophet an argument with *ara'aita*, which is typical of the discussions based on *ra'y* (*Tr. I*, 19; *Tr. III*, 12).

To a later period belong traditions in the classical collections and other works, such as that which makes Ibn Mas'ūd come out boldly in favour of the use of one's own *ra'y*, after following first the Koran, then the decisions of the Prophet, then the decisions of pious men;[2] or that which declares that the Companions, when confronted with a question on which they had no tradition from the Prophet, used to come together and arrive at a decision in common (*ajma'ū*), and that their opinion was right (*fal-ḥaqq fīmā ra'au*);[3] or 'Umar's alleged instructions to the old judges in Iraq, Shuraiḥ, and Abū Mūsā Ash'arī.[4]

[1] Below, pp. 121 f. We have observed the same kind of inconsistency in the technical criticism of traditions by the ancient schools: above, pp. 38 f.

[2] Nasā'ī, *Kitāb ādāb al-quḍāt, al-ḥukm bi-ttifāq ahl al-'ilm*. This can be dated in the time of A'mash.

[3] Dārimī, *Bāb al-tawarru' 'an al-jawāb*.

[4] Goldziher, *Ẓâhiriten*, 9; Margoliouth, in *J.R.A.S.*, 1910, 307 ff. On the famous tradition on Mu'ādh and the Prophet, see below, pp. 105 f.

Ra'y *of individual Iraqians*

Ibrāhīm Nakha'ī. The main body of decisions ascribed to Ibrāhīm as the eponym of a certain strand of Iraqian doctrine[1] is to a great extent pure *ra'y*, often expressing systematic thought.

Abū Ḥanīfa. He extends a time limit as a precaution (*Muw. Shaib.* 274); this is typical *ra'y*. He often uses the expressions *ara'aita* and *alā tarā* (*turā*), which are etymologically connected with *ra'y* and mean 'what do you think of...', 'do you not think', in order to introduce systematic reasoning, parallels, extreme and borderline cases, reductions *ad absurdum*, &c. (*Tr. I, passim*). But he hardly ever says directly: 'This is my opinion (*ra'y*)', 'I am of the opinion (*arā*)', &c.

Abū Yūsuf. An example of his explicit use of *ra'y* occurs in *Tr. I*, 169. The same treatise contains numerous examples of *ara'aita* and *alā tarā*, which Abū Yūsuf uses for the same purpose as Abū Ḥanīfa, and also in order to introduce strict analogical reasoning.

Shaibānī. In *Muw. Shaib.* 142, he calls *ra'y* his gratuitous theory of repeal or, alternatively, his arbitrary interpretation of traditions that do not agree with the common doctrine of his school. In *Muw. Shaib.* 153, he maintains as his *ra'y* the systematic reasoning ascribed to Ibrāhīm Nakha'ī (*Āthār A.Y.* 144; *Āthār Shaib.* 27), as against a tradition from 'Umar which points to the contrary. This tradition, and another from 'Alī to the same effect (*Tr. II*, 3 (*m*)), obviously did not yet exist when the Iraqian doctrine was attributed to Ibrāhīm. *Ara'aita* and *alā tarā* serve to introduce systematic reasoning in *Tr. VIII*, 19; *Muw. Shaib.* 289.

The use of *ra'y* is called *ijtihād* in the title of Shaibānī's book, *Kitāb ijtihād al-ra'y*.[2] This term occurs also in the later group of Iraqian traditions referred to above (p. 104). But this meaning of *ijtihād* is secondary, and its original meaning 'discretion, estimate', has been preserved in Medinese usage, and even to some extent in Shāfi'ī.[3]

The main *locus probans* for *ijtihād al-ra'y* is a tradition according to which Mu'ādh b. Jabal was sent by the Prophet as a judge to Yemen, and in answer to the question of the Prophet about the principles which he intended to follow as a judge, replied that he would use his own discretion (*ajtahid ra'yī*) if he found no guidance in the Koran or in the *sunna* of the Prophet, a programme which the Prophet

[1] See above, pp. 33, 86 f. These decisions belong mostly not to the historical Ibrāhīm but only to the time of Ḥammād; see below, pp. 233 ff.

[2] *Fihrist*, 204, l. 18.

[3] See below, pp. 116 and 127. The word *ra'y* itself often shows the same ancient meaning; see, e.g., *Kharāj*, 35 f. and above, p. 102.

approved warmly. Goldziher has given the general reasons which speak for a late origin of this tradition.[1] Shāfiʿī refers to it, without *isnād*, in *Tr. VII*, 273, but not in the other passages, where he speaks of *ijtihād*. It reappears in Ibn Ḥanbal, v. 230, 236, 242, transmitted by, respectively, Muḥammad b. Jaʿfar Hudhalī, Wakīʿ, and ʿAffān b. Muslim—Shuʿba—Abū ʿAun Muḥammad b. ʿUbaidallāh—Ḥārith b. ʿAmr—several companions of Muʿādh—Muʿādh. This *isnād* is fictitiously Syrian in its upper part, down to Ḥārith b. ʿAmr, who is 'unknown', and in its lower part Iraqian; and Iraqian also is the reference to the *sunna* of the Prophet.[2] The *isnād* becomes real beyond doubt only from Shuʿba onwards, from whom three transmitters relate it. This, together with the obviously doubtful character which the tradition still possessed in the time of Shāfiʿī, enables us to conclude that it originated in the generation before him, in the period of Shuʿba.

Iraqian qiyās

The general conclusion which will emerge from what follows is that the ancient Iraqians were familiar with the method, but used the term only exceptionally in their writings.

The oldest examples of Iraqian *qiyās* show a crude and primitive reasoning. Some are typical of a group of 'unsuccessful' traditions from ʿAlī,[3] and Shāfiʿī calls the primitive analogy in one of them *raʾy*.

An old *qiyās* which prevailed in the Iraqian doctrine was to demand a fourfold confession of the culprit before he incurred the *ḥadd* punishment for adultery, by analogy with the four witnesses prescribed by Koran xxiv. 4. This was originally pure *qiyās*, and the only Iraqian tradition on this subject of which I am aware is one of the 'unsuccessful' traditions from ʿAlī, which makes him turn away an offending woman four times and only punish her after her fifth confession:[4] this presupposes the *qiyās* and exaggerates the underlying tendency. This doctrine spread into Hijaz, and was put there under the aegis of the Prophet, in a group of traditions the final outcome of which in the classical collections is the tradition of Māʿiz, who was turned away three times by the Prophet and punished after his fourth confession. Most versions go so far as to state that the confessions were made on four separate occasions.[5] Although expressed in traditions, the doctrine remained

[1] *Ẓâhiriten*, 10.
[2] See above, pp. 73 f.
[3] *Tr. II*, 4 (*c*), (*d*), (*f*), 18 (*g*); cf. below, p. 241.
[4] See above, pp. 73 f.
[5] This detail was not part of the original Iraqian doctrine. Abū Ḥanīfa, basing

confined to Iraq (*Tr. I*, 104, 105, 200) and did not prevail in the Medinese school. The oldest variant of this group of traditions, a *mursal* ascribed to Ibn Musaiyib and in itself evidently unhistorical (*Muw.* iv. 4), does not yet know the name of Mā'iz and the fourfold confession as such; another version which mentions the fourfold confession without naming the culprit is even a *mursal* of Zuhrī (ibid. 5 f.). It is obvious that the classical tradition of Mā'iz is late, and that its prototype became known in Hijaz, as the justification of an Iraqian *qiyās*, only in the generation preceding Mālik.

This *qiyās* provoked another, to the effect that the *ḥadd* punishment for theft could be applied only after a twofold confession of the culprit, by analogy with the two witnesses demanded in this case. This doctrine is expressed in a tradition from 'Alī (*Tr. II*, 18 (*s*)), but not all Iraqians hold it.[1]

The minimum value of stolen goods, for the *ḥadd* punishment for theft to be applicable, was fixed in Iraq, by a crude analogy with the five fingers, at 5 dirham. This is the doctrine of Ibn Abī Lailā (*Tr. I*, 198) and one of the doctrines ascribed to Ibn Mas'ūd (*Tr. II*, 18(*x*)), and the parallel is explicitly drawn in a tradition from 'Uthmān (quoted in Sarakhsī, ix. 137). The generally accepted Iraqian *ra'y*, however, was to fix the minimum value of stolen goods arbitrarily at 10 dirham, and as a justification of this, traditions from Ibn Mas'ūd, 'Alī, and the Prophet were produced (*Tr. I*, 198). We have to consider this as the original doctrine, and the *qiyās* as a refinement which remained unsuccessful.

The minimum value of stolen goods provided the starting-point for fixing, by a crude analogy, the minimum amount of *ṣadāq*, the contractual payment to be made by the bridegroom to the bride which is an essential element of the marriage contract (*donatio propter nuptias*). Here, too, the original Iraqian reasoning was arbitrary *ra'y*, such as Shāfi'ī ascribes to 'some followers of Abū Ḥanīfa' who say: 'We think it shocking that intercourse should become lawful for a trifling amount' (*Tr. III*, 54). This stage of doctrine is represented by the opinion ascribed to Ibrāhīm Nakha'ī in a late source ('Iyāḍ, quoted in

himself on the wording of these Medinese versions, tried to introduce it in Iraq but was not successful (see below, p. 300, on *Tr. I*, 104).

[1] *Tr. I*, 196, and below, p. 297 f.; *Kharāj*, 102 f.

Zurqānī, iii. 9): 'Ibrāhīm disapproved of a *ṣadāq* of less than 40, and once he said: of less than 10, dirham.'[1] This arbitrary *ra'y* was later modified, not for the better, by a crude analogy, according to which the use of part of the body of the wife by the husband ought not to be made lawful for an amount less than that legalizing the loss of a limb through the *ḥadd* punishment for theft, and the minimum amount of *ṣadāq* was fixed at 10 dirham (*Muw. Shaib.* 237).[2] This was expressed in a tradition from 'Alī, through Sha'bī (*Tr. III*, 54).[3] The Medinese recognized originally no minimum amount of *ṣadāq*; only Mālik, followed by his personal disciples, adopted the Iraqian analogical reasoning, and starting from his own minimum value of stolen goods for the application of the *ḥadd* punishment, which was ¼ dīnār = 3 dirham, fixed the minimum *ṣadāq* at the same amount (*Muw.* iii. 9). Shāfi'ī states polemically that Mālik diverged from the earlier Medinese opinion under the influence of Abū Ḥanīfa. At the same time, the Iraqians had found this crude *qiyās* unsatisfactory, and fell back on the authority of traditions which had appeared in the meantime in favour of their doctrine (*Tr. III*, 54).

The Iraqians, as opposed to the Medinese (*Muw.* iii. 129), extended the prohibition against re-selling food before taking possession of it to all objects (Abū Ḥanīfa excepted only immovables); this analogical reasoning was put into the mouth of Ibn 'Abbās (he says *aḥsib* 'I think'), in a tradition which Shaibānī adduces as his argument (*Muw. Shaib.* 331).[4] The Iraqians likewise disallowed the sale of animals against animals on credit, bringing this contract under the general rule against uncertainty (*Tr. IX*, 5).

It was the administrative practice that the rider received two shares for his mount in addition to his own share of the booty (ibid., 3). Auzā'ī recognized it as the continuous practice, and found its alleged starting-point in informal traditions on the

[1] The second half of this statement is certainly spurious, as it reflects the second stage of the Iraqian doctrine.

[2] The Iraqian Ibn Shubruma, who put the minimum value of stolen goods for purposes of *ḥadd* punishment at 5 dirham, consistently fixed the minimum *ṣadāq* at the same amount ('Iyāḍ, loc. cit.).

[3] For the *isnād*, see *Comm. Muw. Shaib.* 238, n. 17.

[4] Shāfi'ī (*Ikh.* 328) introduces the word *ra'y* into the text. On the date of this tradition, see below, p. 143.

military expeditions of the Prophet. The ancient Iraqians found it illogical that the share of an animal should be greater than the share of a Muslim, and reduced the portion of the rider to one share for his mount, in addition to his own share. This was still the doctrine and the argument of Abū Ḥanīfa, who also knew a tradition from ʿUmar to this effect (*Comm. ed. Cairo*, loc. cit.). Abū Yūsuf, however, returned to the Syrian (and Medinese) doctrine. His ostensible reasons were Syrian and Medinese traditions, which he relates in detail in *Kharāj*, 11 f. But Shaibānī (*Siyar*, ii. 176) gives, besides the reference to traditions, the argument that the older Iraqian doctrine would put the animal and the Muslim on the same footing. In this case, therefore, the refinement of reasoning led to the rejection of a crude *qiyās*.

Shāfiʿī calls the Iraqians 'adherents of *qiyās*' (*ahl al-qiyās*) in *Tr. I*, 137, and in several other passages he represents the *qiyās* as one of their fundamental principles. For example, ibid., 89: 'They do not allow anyone to diverge from *qiyās*.' Or *Tr. IV*, 258: 'If they [the Successors] express opinions on questions on which there is no Koranic text and no *sunna*, you infer that they have arrived at their decision by *qiyās*, and you say: "*Qiyās* is the established knowledge which knowledgeable people agree is right."' The opponent agrees. Shāfiʿī points out that it is possible that they based their opinions on *ra'y* and not on *qiyās*. The opponent agrees that this is possible, but does not think that they could have expressed opinions except on the basis of *qiyās*. Shāfiʿī replies: 'You . . . imagine that they used *qiyās*, and you make its use obligatory. . . .'[1] These statements are materially correct, but Shāfiʿī formulates them in a pointed manner for purposes of polemics.[2] Shāfiʿī was the first to distinguish on principle between general *ra'y* and strict *qiyās*, and he imposed this distinction on his opponents by a favourite debating device of his.

In the actual reasoning of the Iraqians *qiyās* is simply a more or less clearly defined kind of *ra'y*, and the term *qiyās* is used rarely. In *Ikh.* 116 f., the Iraqian opponent agrees that a certain doctrine of his is based neither on tradition or *sunna* nor on

[1] See also *Tr. I*, 51; *Tr. VIII*, 13 (quoted above, p. 27); *Ris.* 81 (referred to above, p. 48), &c.

[2] The passage in *Tr. IV*, 258, bears also other traces of Shāfiʿī's editing; see above, p. 87.

qiyās, but claims that it is 'reasonable' (*ma'qūl*). In *Tr. III*, 11, the Iraqians look for the element common to both the original and the assimilated case, which justifies the use of analogy, but they do not use *'illa*, which is the later term for it.

The Iraqians base their doctrine on *qiyās* and systematic reasoning[1] rather than on traditions, and they use *qiyās* as an instrument in criticizing traditions.[2] The Iraqian opponent states in *Ikh.* 117 f. that no *qiyāṣ* is valid against a binding tradition (*khabar lāzim*), but the word 'binding' is operative,[3] and how this rule works in practice appears from *Ris.* 75, where the Iraqian opponent follows the opinion of Ibn Mas'ūd, which reflects the Iraqian doctrine, against an analogy drawn from traditions from the Prophet.

Qiyās *of individual Iraqians*

Ibn Abī Lailā. Tr. I, 171 (*a*): Ibn Abī Lailā uses analogical reasoning and expresses it by saying: 'This is the same as . . .' (*hādhā . . . bi-manzilat . . .*), without using the term *qiyās*.

§ 216: he gives general systematic reasoning, based on an analogy, but does not use the term *qiyās*.

Abū Ḥanīfa. Ibid., 107: Abū Ḥanīfa gives a systematically consistent decision, and Shāfi'ī calls it *qiyās*.

§ 200: Abū Ḥanīfa acknowledges the implication of a tradition, and Shāfi'ī, who draws the same conclusion, calls it *qiyās*.

§ 219: a conclusion *a maiore ad minus*.

§ 229: an analogical conclusion from the Koran.

Tr. IX, 15: Shāfi'ī calls Abū Ḥanīfa's reasoning *qiyās*. Abū Ḥanīfa does not use the term *qiyās* in any of these cases.

Abū Yūsuf. Tr. I, 27: Abū Yūsuf draws an analogy but calls it *mithl* ('the same as . . .').

§ 71: he draws a conclusion from the doctrine of Ibn Abī Lailā and calls it *qiyās qaulih* ('a consequence of his doctrine').

Tr. IX, 2: Abū Yūsuf has two arguments *a maiore ad minus*; only Shāfi'ī calls this *qiyās*.

§ 38: Abū Yūsuf gives analogical reasoning, without using the term *qiyās*.

Shaibānī. Tr. VIII, 1: Shāfi'ī calls Shaibānī's wider systematic reasoning *qiyās*.

[1] An example of systematic reasoning which goes much farther than a simple analogy occurs in *Tr. III*, 17.

[2] See above, p. 30. Many of these cases have been obliterated by the subsequent growth of traditions in favour of the Iraqian doctrine.

[3] For its meaning, see below, p. 136, n. 2.

§ 6: Shaibānī uses analogical reasoning and calls it a *qiyās* based on the *sunna*; he also calls it *ma'qūl* 'reasonable', but Shāfi'ī claims that Shaibānī has perverted the *qiyās* and turned it upside down.

§ 7: Shaibānī is able to support the Iraqian doctrine by analogical reasoning starting from a Medinese tradition (*Muw.* iv. 40).

§ 21 and often elsewhere in *Tr. VIII*: conclusions *a maiore ad minus*.

Siyar, iv. 376: a weak analogy against Abū Ḥanīfa's and Abū Yūsuf's consistent doctrine (*Tr. IX*, 24).

Iraqian istiḥsān

According to Shāfi'ī (*Tr. III*, 66), the Iraqians are accustomed to say: 'The *qiyās* would be . . ., but we practise *istiḥsān*.' Ṭabarī (§ 101) says that according to Abū Ḥanīfa and his companions a certain act 'is considered valid by *istiḥsān*, although it is against the *qiyās*'; this decision is taken for purely practical reasons; the terms are of Ṭabarī's choosing and do not occur in the parallel passage, *Tr. IX*, 15.

Some old cases of *istiḥsān* are expressed in, and therefore obliterated by, traditions. For example, strict analogy justifies the application of the *lex talionis* to only one culprit for one victim, and this is indeed the Iraqian doctrine in the case of wounds; but as regards capital crimes, the Iraqians have several culprits executed for the murder of one. *Comm. Muw. Shaib.* 292, n. 3, states that this doctrine is held in deference to a [Medinese] tradition from 'Umar in which the consideration of the public interest is expressed clearly (*Muw.* iv. 48; *Muw. Shaib.* 291). In other words, the ancient Iraqians diverged from the *qiyās* for reasons of public policy, a decision which in Medina was embodied in the tradition from 'Umar. But Shāfi'ī takes the tradition from 'Umar as his starting-point, builds on it another *qiyās* to the effect that the *lex talionis* for wounds is also applicable to several culprits for one victim, and then blames the Iraqians for their inconsistency (*Tr. II*, 18 (*h*)). Properly speaking, this goes against Shāfi'ī's own rule that no *qiyās* is to be based on an exception, but for him the tradition is the basis of his doctrine.[1]

A practical concession to the *mukātab*, the slave whose

[1] This aspect of *istiḥsān*—the consideration of the public interest—was later called *istiṣlāḥ* by the Mālikīs; see Goldziher, in *Vienna Oriental Journal*, i. 229.

master has allowed him to purchase his liberty by instalments, is expressed in a tradition from ʿAlī (*Tr. II*, 17 (*c*)), and acknowledged by Ibn Abī Lailā (*Tr. I*, 139); Sarakhsī, vii. 207, calls it *istiḥsān*. Abū Ḥanīfa is systematically consistent, but still makes a very slight concession (at the end of ibid., 140). Abū Yūsuf followed Abū Ḥanīfa at first; in his later opinion he made a concession to the *mukātab*, though not so wide and so formal a one as did Ibn Abī Lailā, leaving the matter rather to the discretion of the judge. Shāfiʿī, who rejects *istiḥsān* on principle, becomes thoroughly consistent.

Goldziher, judging from the sources at his disposal, concluded that Abū Ḥanīfa himself established the principle of *istiḥsān*.[1] We now find that it already existed, as part of the actual reasoning of the Iraqians, before him, although the technical term for it appears, as far as I know, for the first time in Abū Yūsuf. This is confirmed by the following examples.

Ibn Abī Lailā. Tr. I, 92, 93, 94: he shows regard for the practice and gives a common-sense decision which is later called *istiḥsān* (see below, p. 273).

§ 153: he makes an inconsistent exception on account of *vis maior*, out of regard for material justice.

Abū Ḥanīfa. Ibid., 131: Sarakhsī, xxviii. 34, clearly shows the *istiḥsān* in Abū Ḥanīfa's reasoning.

§ 178: Abū Ḥanīfa disapproved of the old custom of *ishʿār* (making incisions in the flesh of sacrificial animals) because it was cruelty; Ibn Abī Lailā and Abū Yūsuf, however, approved of the custom, and authority for it was found in several traditions; Ṭaḥāwī (quoted in Sarakhsī, iv. 138) calls Abū Ḥanīfa's opinion *ra'y*, and the reasons which he gives for this opinion show it to be *istiḥsān*.

Tr. IX, 2: a consideration of Abū Ḥanīfa is based on common sense.

§ 15: neither here nor elsewhere does Abū Ḥanīfa use the term *istiḥsān*.

Abū Yūsuf. Tr. I, 2: he makes a concession in a case of *vis maior*; Sarakhsī, xv. 103, calls it *istiḥsān*.

Goldziher[2] has collected from *Kharāj* and from Shaibānī's *Jāmiʿ al-Ṣaghīr* several examples where Abū Yūsuf and Shaibānī respectively use the term *istiḥsān* and oppose it to *qiyās*.

Shaibānī. Muw. Shaib. 197, 226: Shaibānī gives an arbitrary opinion and chooses his traditions accordingly; he calls this *ra'y*.

[1] Loc. cit. 228.

[2] Ibid., and in *E.I.*, s.v. *Fiḳh*.

C. The Medinese

Shāfiʿī charges the Medinese with arbitrary *ra'y*.[1] He does so polemically and without real justification in cases where they have other, and for them valid, reasons for their doctrine. But everything that is not based on a tradition from the Prophet is in the last resort *ra'y* for Shāfiʿī, and he calls even the opinions of Companions of the Prophet *ra'y*. *Ra'y* is, indeed, the foundation of a great part of the Medinese doctrine, and in *Ikh.* 197 Shāfiʿī calls the Medinese with whom he disputes 'some scholars learned in traditions and *ra'y*'.

In the argument which Shāfiʿī puts into their mouth in *Tr. III*, 41, they give to the *sunna* higher authority than to *ra'y*; this becomes obvious if we take *sunna* in the old sense of 'living tradition' of the school,[2] which superseded individual opinion. But the doctrine of the school is itself based on the opinion of the recognized scholars, and we find reference being made to what the scholars hold (*ahl al-ʿilm yaraun*) as a decisive argument.[3] In this particular case, the opinion in question is a primitive analogical reasoning by which pregnancy is assimilated to illness. This old *ra'y*, which was originally to a great extent anonymous, as the consensus of Medina of which it formed a part was anonymous,[4] was frequently ascribed to individual ancient authorities. So we find that Shāfiʿī, in the same particular case, singles out Qāsim b. Muḥammad as holding the opinion in question. These ascriptions cannot in general be considered authentic unless they are proved so, as the analysis of two typical examples will show.

Mud. iii. 34: Ibn Wahb—Ibn Lahīʿa—Khālid b. Abī ʿImrān—Qāsim b. Muḥammad and Sālim were of the opinion (*ra'y*) that the minor who is taken on a raid or who is born during it receives no share of the booty. This is simply the Medinese doctrine, formulated polemically against the opinion of Auzāʿī (*Tr. IX*, 10), and not a straightforward expression of opinion. It is, indeed, likely that Qāsim and Sālim held this opinion, but then this could also be said of their Medinese contemporaries.

Muw. iv. 40 = *Tr. III*, 77: Mālik—Yaḥyā b. Saʿīd—Ibn Musaiyib

[1] *Tr. III*, *passim*, e.g. §§ 44, 124 (general criticism of the Medinese reasoning).

[2] See above, pp. 61 f.

[3] *Muw.* ii. 115 = *Tr. III*, 128.

[4] See above, p. 84 f.

—'Umar fixed the compensation for a molar at one camel,[1] Mu'āwiya at five camels;[2] Ibn Musaiyib would personally have preferred to fix it at two camels, and remarks that every *mujtahid* is rewarded. This harmonizing but unsuccessful opinion, which presupposes the two other doctrines, can hardly go back to Ibn Musaiyib. The remark on the reward of the *mujtahid* expresses opposition to the doctrine of the school and, though earlier, is hardly much earlier than the tradition from the Prophet on this matter, a tradition which we can date in the generation before Mālik.[3] The common ancient doctrine which fixed the compensation at five camels can safely be dated in Umaiyad times, and the mention of Mu'āwiya as the authority for it points in the same direction; it was possibly, but not necessarily, an administrative regulation.[4] It was given a higher authority in a tradition in which Marwān b. Ḥakam (whose name is another hall-mark of traditions connected with Umaiyad doctrines) consults Ibn 'Abbās, who replies: five camels, and on another aspect of the problem draws an analogy with the fingers;[5] and in the still later traditions from the Prophet to the same effect, either through Ibn 'Abbās or with a new *isnād* through 'Amr b. Shu'aib—his father—his grandfather.[6] The common ancient doctrine was also projected back to individual early Iraqian authorities: Sha'bī, Ibrāhīm Nakha'ī, Ibrāhīm—Shuraiḥ.[7]

But even if ascriptions of *ra'y* to Medinese authorities of the first century are not as a rule authentic, they show its importance in the doctrine of the Medinese school.[8]

As regards the generation before Mālik, it does not seem likely that Rabī'a b. Abī 'Abdalraḥmān, who later received the nickname *Rabī'at al-Ra'y*, showed an inclination to *ra'y* stronger than his contemporaries. Indeed, this would have been difficult for him in view of the role which *ra'y* played even in Mālik's doctrine; his nickname

[1] This is the opinion of 'some other Medinese' in *Tr. VIII*, 10.

[2] This is the opinion of 'some Medinese', including Mālik, ibid. It is shared by the Iraqians, *Muw. Shaib.* 290.

[3] See above, p. 96 f. *Ra'y* and its reward are mentioned together in an anecdote on 'Umar b. 'Abdal'azīz and the lawyers of Medina: Ṭabarī, *Annales*, ii. 1183 (year 87). This anecdote is later than 'Umar b. 'Abdal'azīz, and therefore later than Ibn Musaiyib.

[4] See below, p. 208.

[5] *Muw.* iv. 40; *Muw. Shaib.* 290; *Tr. VIII*, 10. On another tradition in which Ibn 'Abbās expresses his *ra'y*, see above, p. 108, n. 4.

[6] Traced by *Comm. Muw. Shaib.* 290, to some of the classical and other collections.

[7] *Āthār Shaib.* 83, 95; *Tr. VIII*, 10.

[8] The old Meccan authority Mujāhid, a 'rationalist' in the interpretation of the Koran, was reported also in law to have accorded to *ra'y* a very high position (Goldziher, *Richtungen*, 110).

seems to be part of the misleading picture created after Shāfi'ī's time of the character of the Medinese school.[1]

Zuhrī, who belongs to the same generation, is quoted both in favour and in disparagement of *ra'y*. On one side he is related, on the authority of Auzā'ī, to have said: 'What an excellent minister of knowledge is sound opinion';[2] on the other he is alleged to have said: 'The [traditional] scholar (*al-'ālim*) is superior to the *mujtahid* by a hundred degrees.'[3] In view of the importance of *ra'y* in the Medinese school, the second statement can at once be dismissed as spurious; but the first, too, the self-conscious wording of which goes beyond the simple and natural use of *ra'y* by Mālik and Ibn Qāsim, is probably spurious.

Mālik's older contemporary Mājashūn called the final doctrine on a particular problem, at which the reasoning of the Medinese school had arrived, *ra'y*.[4]

Mālik's ra'y

The use of *ra'y* by Mālik is well known,[5] and Shāfi'ī, in a polemical passage, reproaches him for making *ra'y* his final criterion (*Tr. III*, 65). Mālik credits Companions of the Prophet with *ra'y*, which he follows (e.g. *Muw.* ii. 69). He uses his *ra'y* on points on which there are no traditions (e.g. ibid. ii. 307), expresses it in confirming traditions from Companions and later authorities (e.g. ibid. iii. 260), uses it in order to interpret traditions restrictively (e.g. ibid. iii. 129), and in connexion with the practice makes it prevail over traditions (e.g. *Mud.* i. 65). His *ra'y* may be a strict analogy (e.g. *Muw.* ii. 268), or an arbitrary, inconsistent decision which may be called *istiḥsān*.[6] Occasionally it stands for broader systematic reasoning (e.g. Ṭabarī, 61), and Mālik uses *ara'aita* for introducing systematic arguments (e.g. *Muw.* iii. 183).

Ibn Qāsim's ra'y

Ibn Qāsim expresses his *ra'y* in the *Mudauwana*, *passim*, either confirming Mālik's doctrine (e.g. iii. 33), or contradicting it (e.g. i. 42), or discussing points not decided by Mālik (e.g. ii. 229). On one of these last he gives his '*ra'y* and *istiḥsān*' (xvi. 203). But where there are traditions and well-established *sunnas* on the authority of the Prophet, analogy and reasoning (*naẓar*) are out of place (iv. 151).

[1] See above, pp. 8, n. 2, 27, 76. On Rabī'a, see below, p. 247 f.

[2] Dārimī, *Bāb fi jtināb al-ahwā'*: *ni'm wazīr al-'ilm al-ra'y al-ḥasan.*

[3] Ibid., *Bāb fī faḍl al-'ilm wal-'ālim.*

[4] See below, p. 221.

[5] Goldziher, *Muh. St.* ii. 217.

[6] See below, pp. 118 f.

This is the reply of Ibn Qāsim to a systematic reasoning of Saḥnūn, and shows the influence of Shāfiʿī.

Medinese ijtihād

The ancient Medinese use *ijtihād* not in the general sense of exercising one's own opinion, but in the rather more specialized one of technical estimate, discretion of the expert. There are positive indications that this narrower meaning of *ijtihād* as a technical term is older than the broader one.

In Mālik *ijtihād* often means estimate by experts.[1] Mālik further knows the *ijtihād* of the Caliph or government (*sulṭān*),. meaning either their endorsement of the technical estimate of the experts, as in *Muw.* iv. 39,[2] or their fair, discretionary judgment, as ibid. ii. 305 = Ṭabarī, 87; *Mud.* iii. 29, 30.[3] In *Mud.* ii. 194 he enjoins on the arbiter, who is called upon to fix the fine for a transgression of ritual, to follow his own fair judgment (*ijtihād*) and not traditions on the decisions of Companions in similar cases.

Rabīʿ, in *Tr. III*, 61, uses '*ijtihād* of the Caliph' with the same meaning, and in § 77 he says: 'There is no fixed decision (*ḥukm maʿrūf*) here, but a compensation (*ḥukūma*) must be fixed by fair estimate (*ijtihād*).[4]

Ibn Qāsim, in *Mud.* iv. 29, uses *ijtihād ahl al-ʿilm* for 'estimate of knowledgeable people, experts'.

Medinese qiyās

In many passages in *Tr. III* Shāfiʿī credits the Medinese with using analogy, and attacks them for using it improperly.[5] According to them, Shāfiʿī says, one must not diverge from traditions except for sound reason and *qiyās* (§ 145 (*a*)). But we find them using the term *qiyās* themselves only in § 36, where Rabīʿ states that Mālik does not extend the effect of a tradition by analogy, as Shāfiʿī does, although he extends one of the categories mentioned there by subsumption; some of Mālik's followers hold that the specific mention of five categories in that

[1] *Muw.* iv. 34 (*bis*), 37, 38, 39 (*bis*); *Mud.* xvi. 121, and *passim.*

[2] But the words 'the Caliph has to exercise *ijtihād*' seem to have been added by the editor, Yaḥyā, as they are lacking from Mālik's text as quoted by Shaibānī in *Tr. VIII*, 9; see also *Mud.* xvi. 121.

[3] See also above, p. 48.

[4] The Iraqians (*Tr. VIII*, 21 and elsewhere) say 'fair compensation' (*ḥukūmat ʿadl*) where the Medinese would, and do, say *ijtihād*.

[5] e.g. §§ 31, 34 (Shāfiʿī calls their reasoning arbitrary *qiyās* and *raʾy*), 143; also *Ris.* 27 and elsewhere.

tradition implies that all others are excluded; at the same time the Medinese, without using the later technical term *ʿilla*, look for the motive which underlies the mention of those categories in the tradition; but again they fall back on the opinion that this is not a case in which one must look for implications and that the tradition has to be accepted as it stands (*lā bal al-ḥadīth jumla lā li-maʿnā*). This shows that reasoning by analogy, as used by the Medinese, is still an undisciplined part of their general *ra'y*, and the term *qiyās* was no doubt forced on Rabīʿ by Shāfiʿī.

Mālik, in *Mud.* ii. 268, reasons by analogy on a point of detail, introducing it by 'I am of the opinion' (*arā*). According to *Tr. III*, 97, Mālik bases 'any number of analogies' on a tradition from Ibn ʿAbbās, but these are Shāfiʿī's words. *Mud.* ii. 94 uses *shabbah* 'to assimilate', in describing Mālik's analogical reasoning.

The use of analogical reasoning, but not the term *qiyās*, is also ascribed to ancient Medinese authorities such as Sālim (*Muw.* i. 260) and Ibn Musaiyib (ibid. ii. 307). In the first case there is an analogy based on an exception from a general rule, which is an undisciplined form of *qiyās*. Whereas these ascriptions must be regarded with the same suspicion as those discussed above (pp. 113 f.), the following story related by Mālik (ibid. iv. 39) is certainly spurious: Rabīʿa b. Abī ʿAbdalraḥmān asked Ibn Musaiyib about the compensation for the fingers of a woman; Ibn Musaiyib replied that it was 10 camels for one finger, 20 for two, 30 for three, but 20 for four; when Rabīʿa expressed his astonishment, Ibn Musaiyib asked him whether he was an Iraqian, and assured him that it was the *sunna*.[1] The actual Medinese doctrine followed by Mālik was, however, to fix the compensation for the fingers of a woman at 10 camels each, according to analogy.

Among the Companions, analogical reasoning is ascribed to Ibn ʿAbbās in a Medinese tradition which makes him fix the same amount of compensation for each tooth, whatever its position in the mouth, with reference to the fact that the compensation for each finger is the same (ibid. iv. 40). This is also the doctrine of the Medinese and of the Iraqians. But as regards the compensation for the lips, the Iraqians, carrying farther the analogy in the tradition from Ibn ʿAbbās, hold, indeed, that half the weregeld is due for each lip, whereas the ancient Medinese award one weregeld for both lips,

[1] This opinion follows from the Medinese principle that the compensation for injuries caused to a woman is half of that for injuries caused to a man, if it amounts to one-third of the weregeld or more, but the same as that for injuries caused to a man, if it amounts to less than one-third of the weregeld; see below, p. 217.

but two-thirds of the weregeld for the loss of the lower lip alone; Mālik and his disciples, however, share the doctrine of the Iraqians, presumably under their influence (*Muw.* iv. 40; *Tr. VIII*, 7).[1]

Medinese istiḥsān

According to *Tr. III*, 24 the doctrine of the Medinese on a certain point is *istiḥsān*; Shāfiʿī uses this term as a synonym of *ra'y*. Ibn Qāsim, in the *Mudauwana*, often uses *istiḥsān*.[2] He also ascribes it to Mālik.[3] But in most passages there is nothing to show whether the term *istiḥsān* was used by Mālik himself or only introduced by Ibn Qāsim, and in one at least (xiv. 109) Ibn Qāsim gives as his own opinion (*ra'ait*) that Mālik used *istiḥsān*; the term does not, as far as I know, occur in Mālik's *Muwaṭṭa'* or in other ancient quotations from Mālik; and where Mālik uses reasoning which might, indeed, be termed *istiḥsān* he does not mention the term. We are therefore justified in concluding that Mālik does not use the term, and that in the solitary passage in which Ibn Qāsim gives it as part of Mālik's words he has put it into the mouth of his master.

This passage is xiv. 134, where Ibn Qāsim says: 'I only know that Mālik distinguished [between the two cases in question], and used to say: "This is a point which has not been made, as far as I know, by any scholar before me . . . but it is a decision on which I have used my *istiḥsān* and my *ra'y*, and I am of the opinion (*arā*) that the practice ought to be accordingly. . . ." ' We have seen above, (p. 115) that Ibn Qāsim uses *ra'y* and *istiḥsān* as synonyms. This is one of the four cases in which the later Mālikī school ascribes to its founder *istiḥsān* as opposed to *ra'y*, a systematic distinction which did not exist in the early period.[4] These alleged cases of Mālik's *istiḥsān* do not include the following, which are authentic:

(*a*) *Muw.* iii. 10 and *Mud.* v. 2: Mālik expresses his *ra'y*; his reasoning is typical *istiḥsān*, and Ibn Qāsim (*Mud.* v. 4 f.) calls it so.

(*b*) *Mud.* ix. 138: this is an exception from a strict analogy based on a tradition: a loan with restitution in kind, which is permissible in the case of male slaves, is not allowed in the case of slave-girls.

[1] For another tradition which credits Ibn ʿAbbās with analogical reasoning, see above, p. 108.

[2] For references, see Santillana, *Istituzioni*, i. 57, n. 170 (reprint: 73, n. 170).

[3] Sometimes *istiḥsān* has a non-technical meaning, e.g. *Mud.* ii. 130 for Mālik's approval (*istiḥbāb* and *istiḥsān*) of a doctrine; ibid. xvi. 228 for a tentative opinion of Mālik on a point on which there is no certainty, such as is provided by a *sunna*.

[4] See, on these four alleged cases of Mālik's *istiḥsān*, Guidi–Santillana, ii. 451, nn. 44 and 49, and for the later Mālikī doctrine of *istiḥsān*, Santillana, *Istituzioni*, i. 57.

(*c*) *Tr. III*, 36: here we have another exception from strict analogy; this is also projected back to Mujāhid and ʿAṭāʾ (Zurqānī, ii. 195).[1]

D. The Syrians

Raʾy, under the name of *naẓar*, is acknowledged in a tradition which the *isnād* shows to be Syrian;[2] according to it, the Prophet was asked what one was to do with a problem on which there was nothing in Koran or *sunna*, and he said: 'The pious men among the believers shall consider it' (*yanẓur fīh*).

Another tradition[3] makes Auzāʿī relate that ʿUmar b. ʿAbdalʿazīz wrote in one of his instructions: 'No one has the right to personal *raʾy* on [points settled in] the Koran; the *raʾy* of the Caliphs concerns those points on which there is no revelation in the Koran and no valid *sunna* from the Prophet; no one has the right to personal *raʾy* on [points settled in] a *sunna* enacted by the Prophet.' This shows essentially the same acceptance of *raʾy*, although the emphasis is laid on its limitations. It represents Auzāʿī's attitude correctly, although whether the tradition as such is authentic must remain doubtful, and the reference to ʿUmar b. ʿAbdalʿazīz is in any case spurious.[4]

Auzāʿī uses *raʾy*, with explicit mention of the term, in Ṭabarī, 97 (p. 148) and elsewhere. He draws a conclusion *a minore ad maius* in *Tr. IX*, 12, and other conclusions by analogy, without using the term *qiyās*, in § 41 (which is crudely reasoned) and repeatedly in § 42. More or less rudimentary systematic reasoning occurs in §§ 34–6 and 44 f. On the other hand he quotes in § 50, without *isnād*, an alleged saying of Shuraiḥ: 'The *sunna* came before your *qiyās*; follow it and do not introduce innovations; you cannot go astray as long as you hold fast to traditions (*athar*).'[5] This picture agrees well with Auzāʿī's attitude to traditions and his concept of *sunna*.[6]

The statements which are attributed to Auzāʿī himself in late sources, representing him as directly hostile to *raʾy*, are certainly spurious.

[1] See, further, below, p. 314.

[2] Dārimī, *Bāb al-tawarruʿ ʿan al-jawāb*.

[3] Ibid., *Bāb mā yuttaqā min tafsīr ḥadīth al-nabī*.

[4] See below, p. 192. The mention of Auzāʿī in the *isnād* of a tradition in favour of sound *raʾy* is also not historical; see above, p. 115.

[5] This is one of a group of Iraqian traditions against *raʾy* and *qiyās*, and later than Shaʿbī (see below, pp. 130 f.).

[6] See above, pp. 34 f., 70 ff. The passage quoted from Ibn Qutaiba (above, p. 35) summarizes Auzāʿī's attitude correctly.

E. Shāfi'ī

Shāfi'ī and ra'y

In his earliest period Shāfi'ī uses *ra'y* in the same loose way as the ancient schools. Straightforward examples of this will be found in *Tr. I*, *Tr. VIII*, and *Tr. IX*.[1] It so happens that *Tr. II*, which belongs to the same period, does not contain equally telling passages, but only the ascription of *ra'y* to Companions, which is irrelevant in this connexion and occurs, indeed, in early and late contexts. There are further numerous passages from all periods where Shāfi'ī formulates his conclusions cautiously by giving them as his opinion in a non-technical sense.[2] He also uses *ara'aita* and *alā tarā* for introducing systematic arguments.[3]

In *Tr. IV*, 261, which belongs to Shāfi'ī's middle period, he says: 'When there is no explicit text in the Koran and no *sunna*, the *mujtahids* [scholars] may use their *ijtihād* and hold what they think right (*mā ra'auhu ḥaqqan*).' But this has to be interpreted in the light of Shāfi'ī's polemics, in the same treatise, against *istiḥsān* and arbitrary *ijtihād*, and in favour of disciplined *qiyās*. In *Tr. III*, 148 (p. 244), Shāfi'ī still recognizes that one has to make decisions on points of detail on which there is no consensus and no guidance in Koran and *sunna*, but he claims that this occurs only rarely.

From *Tr. VII* onwards Shāfi'ī rejects arbitrary *ra'y* in favour of strict analogy, for which he even claims a consensus of the scholars.[4] Ibid. 273: Shāfi'ī knows of no scholar who would authorize an intelligent and cultured man to give a judgment or a fetwa by his own opinion, if he did not know the bases of *qiyās*, which are Koran, *sunna*, consensus, and reason (*'aql*). *Ris.* 58: Shāfi'ī uses the term *qiyās*, whereas his opponent, a representative of the ancient schools, calls it *ra'y*. *Tr. III*, 77: Shāfi'ī refuses to set his *ra'y* against a tradition from a Companion. *Ikh.* 21: 'No one is authorized to apply reasoning (*li-ma*) or questioning (*kaif*) or anything tainted by personal opinion

[1] *Tr. I*, 182: Shāfi'ī expresses his own *ra'y*. *Tr. VIII*, 5: Shāfi'ī uses the term *ra'y* for 'systematic reasoning', which he later calls *qiyās*. Ibid., 14: 'It is to be decided by the use of one's own opinion (*ijtihād al-ra'y*), and to be judged by *qiyās*.' *Tr. IX*, 42: 'In my opinion it is not . . . (*lam ara*).'

[2] e.g. *Tr. I*, 18; *Tr. III*, 55, 64, 114; *Tr. IV*, 260; *Tr. VIII*, 11; *Ris.* 78, 79; *Ikh.* 229; *Umm.* iv. 170.

[3] *Ara'aita*: *Tr. I*, 132, 133; *Ikh.* 386, 394, 395. *Alā tarā*: *Tr. I*, 27, 47, 49, 72, &c.

[4] As early as *Tr. I*, 127, he opposes analogy to surmise (*ẓann*).

(*ra'y*) to a tradition from the Prophet.' This excludes the use of systematic reasoning as a means of criticizing traditions, a purpose to which it is put by the ancient schools, particularly the Iraqians.[1] Whenever Shāfi'ī disagrees with an opinion he is inclined to call it *ra'y*, even in cases where his Medinese opponents refer to consensus and practice.[2] In most cases, however, his rejection of *ra'y* takes on the more specialized form of rejection of *istiḥsān*.

Shāfi'ī and istiḥsān

Ra'y and *istiḥsān* are the same for Shāfi'ī, and he uses both terms indiscriminately.[3] The whole second part of *Tr. VII* (pp. 270–7) is devoted to the refutation of *istiḥsān*. No one is authorized to give a judgment or a fetwa unless he bases himself on the Koran, the *sunna*, the consensus of the scholars, or a conclusion drawn by analogy from any of these, and so it follows that no one may give a judgment or fetwa based on *istiḥsān*. The Koran (lxxv. 36) declares that man is not left without guidance; but he who uses *istiḥsān* acts as if he were left without guidance and comes to whatever conclusion he pleases. The Koran in many passages makes it a duty to follow Allah's commandments and to give the right decision; no one can do this unless he knows what the right decision is, and he can know it only from Allah as laid down by Him, either explicitly or by implication, in the Koran and in the *sunna* of the Prophet; no one can find himself confronted by a problem for which provision is not made by Allah directly or indirectly. To admit opinions not based on a principle or on analogy with a principle —not based, that is, on Koran, *sunna*, consensus, or reason (*'aql*)— would be equivalent to admitting the opinions of non-specialists. Moreover, the expert on questions of fact is not authorized to give an arbitrary opinion, or to set aside reasoning by analogy for *istiḥsān*. If one were authorized to use *istiḥsān* one would have to acknowledge that others are free to use another *istiḥsān*, so that every judge and mufti in every town might use his own *istiḥsān*, and there would be several right decisions and

[1] See above, pp. 110, 115, and below, p. 123.

[2] *Tr. III*, 117, 121, 122, 124, &c. See also the passages quoted above, pp. 26, 69, 79. Ibn Qutaiba, 62, takes up Shāfi'ī's recurrent reproach against the adherents of *ra'y*.

[3] *Tr. VII*, 273; *Ris*. 69.

fetwas on one and the same problem. In *Tr. IV*, 253, Shāfiʿī states that no decisions by arbitrary *istiḥsān* are allowed, only reasoning by analogy on points on which there is no text in the Koran, no *sunna*, and no consensus—that is, no binding information (*khabar yalzam*);[1] 'we and the people of our time (*ahl zamāninā*) are obliged to observe this.' Shāfiʿī recognizes here that the earlier generations used a freer kind of reasoning, and he is the first to confine it on principle within the limits of strict analogy.[2]

But in *Tr. III*, 14, Shāfiʿī uses what is, in fact, an *istiḥsān*; and in *Umm.* iii. 114, where he discusses the same problem, his reasoning is clearly arbitrary *ra'y*, that is, *istiḥsān*. Mālik (*Mud.* ix. 138) had given the same decision by *istiḥsān*,[3] and Shāfiʿī no doubt retained it from his early Medinese period.[4]

Shāfiʿī and qiyās

The only kind of reasoning which Shāfiʿī admits is conclusion by analogy. He takes *qiyās* for granted in his polemics against the ancient schools. *Qiyās* is obligatory (*Tr. IV*, 258), and is resorted to when there is no relevant text in the Koran, no *sunna*, and no consensus (*Ris.* 65); all are agreed on this (*Tr. IV*, 260). But *qiyās* remains subordinate to, and is weaker than, these sources of law (*Ris.* 82); Shāfiʿī does not reckon it as one of the sources (*uṣūl*), but considers it derivative (*farʿ*) (*Tr. VII*, 274). It must be based on Koran, *sunna*, or consensus; it cannot supersede them and is in its turn superseded by them (*Tr. III*, 61 and *passim*). *Sunnas*, that is, traditions from the Prophet, are not subject to analogical reasoning, and their wording must not be interpreted away by *qiyās*.[5] Nothing that the Prophet has forbidden can be allowed by *qiyās* (*Tr. I*, 51). But Shāfiʿī uses *qiyās* in support of traditions,[6] and in *Ris.* 76 he says: 'Unquestioning submission to traditions (*ittibāʿ*) and *qiyās*

[1] On the meaning of this term, see below, p. 136.

[2] For another passage with a similar remark directed against *ra'y*, see above, p. 79.

[3] See above, p. 118.

[4] In *Tr. III*, 135, 146, Shāfiʿī uses the word *istiḥsān* for expressing his approval of an opinion, not in its technical meaning.

[5] Ibid., 11, 17; *Tr. V*, 262; *Ris.* 31. Only human opinions derived from traditions or themselves based on systematic reasoning are subject to it: *Ikh.* 339 (translated above, p. 13); *Tr. VIII*, 5 (translated above, p. 79 f.).

[6] *Tr. III*, 33; *Tr. IX*, 47.

are two separate aspects: the tradition is always followed unquestioningly, whether it agrees with *qiyās* or not; if it does not agree, *ittibā'* becomes the opposite of *qiyās*; there are also cases where one set of circumstances falls under both rules.'

Shāfi'ī gives the following example. The Prophet decided that the buyer can either keep a *muṣarrāt*, that is, an animal which the seller has not milked for some time before the sale so as to make its yield of milk appear greater, or return it together with one *ṣā'* of dates if he has milked it; he also gave the ruling that 'profit follows responsibility' (*al-kharāj bil-ḍamān*).[1] In cases to which this rule applies there is no [ideal] part of the price corresponding to the profit [which accrues after the sale in the possession of the buyer], and this rule is extended by *qiyās* to all parallel cases. In the case of the *muṣarrāt*, the decision of the Prophet is followed and not extended by *qiyās*, the Prophet having fixed the unknown quantity of milk in the animal, which has an [ideal] part of the price corresponding to it. Now if someone buys an animal which turns out to be a *muṣarrāt* and decides to keep it nevertheless, but after a month finds another hidden fault for which he decides to return it, he can do so, and the milk which has accrued to him during the month belongs to him according to the rule of *al-kharāj bil-ḍamān*; but he must also give one *ṣā'* of dates for the milk which was in the *muṣarrāt* [at the time of sale]. This detail is decided according to the tradition, and the ownership of the milk which has accrued during the month by analogy with the general rule.

Qiyās is, however, used as a criterion for choosing between conflicting traditions.[2] Moreover, in *Tr. III*, 23, Shāfi'ī confirms by analogical reasoning his rejection of a tradition, although he does not call his argument *qiyās* but 'the decisive proof in our opinion' (*al-ḥujja al-thābita 'indanā*). These are survivals of the earlier use of systematic reasoning for criticizing traditions.[3]

The consensus of the Muslims decides which *qiyās* is right and which is wrong (*Ris.* 72). The consensus supersedes an analogy based on a tradition from the Prophet (*Tr. III*, 129).[4] But *qiyās* supersedes the 'practice' which may have been introduced only by some Successor (*Tr. VIII*, 14).

Shāfi'ī's most important methodical rule regarding the use of

[1] See below, p. 181.
[2] See above, p. 14, and *Tr. I*, 115; *Ikh.* 96, 98, 220.
[3] See above, p. 121.
[4] This is what Shāfi'ī says; in fact, he goes even farther and follows the implication of the consensus as against the implication of the tradition.

qiyās is that a *qiyās* cannot be based on a special case which constitutes an exception from a general rule; in other words, that exceptions cannot be extended by analogy.[1] This rule is valid within the sphere of the *sunna* of the Prophet, and between Koran and *sunna* (*Ris.* 75). It is also valid as regards consensus: a decision of an exceptional and unsystematic character, sanctioned by consensus, must not be extended by analogy beyond its original field; but within this, *qiyās* may be used (ibid. 81). The necessary corollary is that an exemption from a general rule must be based on incontrovertible proof (*Ikh.* 256). Shāfiʿī formulates the principle underlying his rule as: 'Legal institutions must not be treated by analogy with one another' (*lā tuqās sharīʿa ʿalā sharīʿa*) (*Tr. III*, 34).

Qiyās is used on questions of detail, which are the concern of specialists only (*Ris.* 50). It is the opposite of *istiḥsān* because it is based on indications (*dalāʾil*) and parallels (*mithāl*), and it is comparable to the opinions of experts on questions of fact (*Tr. VII*, 272 f.). But being subject to differences of opinion it does not convey certainty (*iḥāṭa*) (*Tr. IV*, 255). Shāfiʿī recognizes its limits, in opposition to the *ahl al-kalām* (*Tr. I*, 122), and no further *qiyās* can be based on the result of a *qiyās* (ibid. 51).

A particular kind of *qiyās* is represented by conclusions *a potiori*[2] and by conclusions *a maiore ad minus* or, conversely, *a minore ad maius*. Shāfiʿī gives the theory in *Ris.* 70 f.: 'The strongest kind of *qiyās* is the deduction, from the prohibition of a small quantity, of the equally strong or stronger prohibition of a great quantity; from the commendation of a small act of piety, of the presumably stronger commendation of a greater act of piety; from the permission of a great quantity, of the presumably even more unqualified permission of a smaller quantity. . . . Some scholars do not call this *qiyās*, but consider it to fall under the original ruling, and likewise when something is equivalent to (*fī maʿnā* . . .) something allowed or forbidden, so that it is also allowed or forbidden; they reserve the term *qiyās* for cases where there is a possible parallel which can be construed in two ways, one of which is chosen to the exclusion

[1] *Tr. I*, 12 (translated below, pp. 326 f.), 215 (at the end of § 216), 253 (Shāfiʿī shows by brilliant systematic reasoning why *qiyās* cannot be used here); *Ris.* 73, 76, &c.

[2] *Tr. I*, 138; *Tr. III*, 36 (*aulā*), 48 (*adkhal fī maʿnā* . . .).

of the other. Others regard everything that goes beyond the explicit text of Koran and *sunna* and is only its equivalent as *qiyās*.' Shāfi'ī considers the conclusion *a maiore ad minus* 'a binding rule of *qiyās*' (*Tr. VIII*, 12), but in most cases where he draws it he does not call it by this name.

The element common to the original and to the parallel case on which a *qiyās* is based Shāfi'ī calls either informally *ma'nā* 'idea',[1] or more technically *aṣl* 'basis';[2] he does not use the later term *'illa*. In the case of organs of the body, this common element is supplied by their common names; for example, the common name 'lip' justifies the award of the same compensation for injuries to the upper and to the lower lip, and Shāfi'ī states explicitly that 'the weregeld is based on names and not on the degree of usefulness'.[3] But in another case he avoids reasoning 'based on the similarity of names', because it would lead him into a dilemma.[4] If a ruling covering two species of a genus is to be extended, by analogy, to another species, it ought to be extended consistently to all species of that genus, or not at all (*Ris.* 27). The substitute (*badal*) must be treated in analogy with its original (*mubaddal 'anhu*) (*Ikh.* 97).

As a general safeguard against arbitrariness Shāfi'ī insists that analogy must start from the outward and obvious meaning (*ẓāhir*) of the passages on which it is based. This consideration, which corresponds to Shāfi'ī's rule of interpreting traditions according to their outward meaning,[5] occurs in numerous passages, and is set forth in detail in the first part of *Tr. VII* (pp. 267–70).[6] The whole of law, Shāfi'ī points out, is concerned with the *forum externum*; he proves this from passages in the Koran and from traditions from the Prophet, and gives examples.[7]

We have noticed cases where Shāfi'ī's *qiyās* falls short of his own

[1] *Ris.* 8, 31, 76.

[2] *Ikh.* 320.

[3] *Tr. VIII*, 7, 9, 10. The theory, later ascribed to Shāfi'ī, that the *qiyās* must be based [exclusively] on names (Aghnides, 86 f.), is not borne out by the texts.

[4] *Tr. VIII*, 9 (at the end).

[5] See above, p. 56.

[6] *Fihrist*, 210, mentions among Shāfi'ī's writings a *Kitāb al-ḥukm bil-ẓāhir* (l. 28) and a *Kitāb ibṭāl al-istiḥsān* (l. 29). It is likely that these two titles correspond to the two parts of *Tr. VII*, the whole of which is called *Kitāb ibṭāl al-istiḥsān* in the printed edition.

[7] Shāfi'ī's argument is not as inconclusive as it seems, because Muhammadan law does not distinguish on principle between the finding of general rules and the decision of individual cases.

theoretical requirements.[1] Another case, which was, however, eliminated by Shāfiʿī in his later doctrine, occurs in *Tr. I*, 98. There was an ancient common tendency to apply the *ḥadd* punishment for drinking wine only if the culprit was taken *flagrante delicto*, that is, in a state of drunkenness. This was the doctrine of Ibn Abī Lailā. Abū Ḥanīfa, followed by Abū Yūsuf, extended this principle by analogy to all *ḥadd* punishments, which according to him lapse after a short period of prescription. Shāfiʿī did not admit this principle, which conflicted with the system, but he made allowances for the common tendency by letting all *ḥadd* punishments lapse through intervening repentance (*tauba*), by analogy with the Koranic ruling on banditry (Koran v. 34). This is an analogy based on an exceptional case. In his later opinion, however, as related by Rabīʿ, Shāfiʿī ruled that repentance had no effect on the *ḥadd* punishment (excepting, of course, the particular case of Koran v. 34), and found this decision implied in traditions from the Prophet.

Qiyās often means not a strict analogy, but consistent systematic reasoning in a broader sense, as in *Tr. I*, 123, 133, 184, 200, and often.

Shāfiʿī and istiṣḥāb

Istiṣḥāb is the conclusion by which one 'attaches' a later stage to a former—in other words, one does not presume any changes in the legal situation unless they are proved for certain. Shāfiʿī applies this principle in *Umm*, iv. 170 without, however, using the term *istiṣḥāb*; he obviously regards it as part of *qiyās* and 'reason' (*maʿqūl*).

Shāfiʿī and ʿaql, maʿqūl

Shāfiʿī often refers to *ʿaql* 'reason' or *maʿqūl* 'what is reasonable', sometimes as a synonym of *qiyās*, as in *Tr. I*, 160, and in the numerous cases where he speaks of *qiyās* and *ʿaql* or *qiyās* and *maʿqūl*, sometimes in a broader meaning, implying that a doctrine is consistent and stands to reason.[2] So *maʿqūl* can be opposed to *qiyās* proper (ibid. 121), or be used to show that there is no place for *qiyās* (ibid. 253).[3] *Ijtihād* must be exercised by *ʿaql* (*Ris.* 5); Allah has endowed mankind with *ʿaql* and guides them either by an explicit text or by indications on which to base their *ijtihād* (ibid. 69).

[1] See above, pp. 111, 123.

[2] e.g. *Tr. I*, 73; *Tr. III*, 44; *Tr. VII*, 272; *Tr. VIII*, 21; *Tr. IX*, 16; *Ris.* 79; *Ikh.* 113, 222, 234 (*al-maʿrūf fil-maʿqūl*, 'what agrees with the wider systematic implications').

[3] Naubakhtī, *Firaq*, 7, opposes *ijtihād al-raʾy* to *ʿaql*.

Shāfi'ī and ijtihād

'The use of *qiyās* is *ijtihād*' (*Tr. VII*, 272 f.); or even: '*Qiyās* and *ijtihād* are two terms with the same meaning; on all problems which confront the Muslim there is either a binding decision or an indication of the right solution; this must be sought by *ijtihād*, and *ijtihād* is *qiyās*' (*Ris.* 66). *Ijtihād* is the preliminary of *qiyās*, and opposed to arbitrary *istiḥsān* (*Tr. IV*, 253). It implies reasoning, is based on indications, and excludes following one's own whims and preferences (*Tr. VII*, 274 f.). It is obligatory, and in exercising it one obeys Allah's commands (*Ris.* 5). It is obvious that Shāfi'ī opposes his *ijtihād* of *qiyās* to the Iraqian *ijtihād al-ra'y*,[1] and in *Tr. III*, 61, he also rejects the Medinese idea of *ijtihād* or discretion.[2]

Shāfi'ī gives his detailed theory of *ijtihād*, which is in many respects similar to that of *qiyās*, in the two main passages, *Tr. IV*, 253 f., and *Tr. VII*, 272 ff. The decisions on those points on which there exists no text in the Koran, no *sunna*, and no consensus, and on which a conclusion by analogy must be drawn from Koran or *sunna*, are also covered by the general authority of Allah, because *ijtihād* is vouchsafed by Koran and *sunna*. The Koran authorizes *ijtihād* when it prescribes finding the direction of the Ka'ba from the indications given by the stars, &c. (Koran ii. 144, in conjunction with vi. 97; xvi. 16), but not arbitrarily, or verifying the good character of witnesses from outward criteria (Koran ii. 282, in conjunction with lxv. 2), without regard to their hidden character.[3] The *sunna* authorizes *ijtihād* in the traditions on the Prophet and Mu'ādh,[4] and on the single and double reward of the *mujtahid*.[5] No one may give an opinion on law except by *ijtihād*, that is, *qiyās* as opposed to *ra'y* or *istiḥsān*, and he who is not qualified by the knowledge of Koran, traditions, and consensus, on which he must base his *ijtihād*, has no right to an opinion. The parallel of the opinions of experts on questions of fact[6] applies to *ijtihād* as well as to *qiyās*. It is agreed that in the former generations judges gave judgments and muftis decisions on points on which there was

[1] See above, p. 105. [2] See above, p. 116.

[3] This argument is far-fetched, as the Koranic passages refer to material decisions; but see above, p. 125, n. 7.

[4] See above, pp. 105 f. [5] See above, pp. 96 f.

[6] See above, p. 121.

no text in the Koran and no *sunna*, and they must have arrived at them by *ijtihād*.

Ijtihād leads to disagreement.[1] Because of the tradition on the single or double reward of the *mujtahid*, every *mujtahid* who has done his best to arrive at the correct solution is considered to be right, in so far as he has discharged his obligation, even if the result of his *ijtihād* is wrong.[2]

F. The Muʿtazila

The *ahl al-kalām*, that is, the Muʿtazila,[3] base their whole doctrine on reasoning (*naẓar*) and *qiyās*, aiming at consistency. They hold that *qiyās* and *naẓar* lead to truth, and consider themselves as particularly adept in their use.[4]

The names by which Shāfiʿī and Ibn Qutaiba call them, *ahl al-kalām* and *ahl al-naẓar* or *ahl al-qiyās*, mean 'adherents of systematic reasoning, rationalists'. Shāfiʿī, in *Tr. I*, 122, reports their analogical reasoning on a question of law and refutes it. They reject traditions on account of *naẓar* and reason, and use *qiyās* as a basis for criticizing traditions.[5]

Naẓẓām sought to discredit the statements hostile to *qiyās* and *ra'y* which were ascribed to some Companions; he also blamed Ibn Masʿūd for a decision based on an arbitrary assumption (ibid. 24 f.), and believed that the Companions committed mistakes in their fetwas when they followed their personal opinion (*ra'y*) (Khaiyāṭ, 98). The context of Ibn Qutaiba shows that this was meant to discredit the ancient schools of law whose main authorities were Companions, and was not directed against the use of systematic reasoning as such. Only Ibn Qutaiba, who upheld the case of the traditionists and opponents of human reasoning in law, and particularly Khaiyāṭ, who represented a later stage of the Muʿtazilite doctrine,[6] misrepresented Naẓẓām as wishing to exclude *ra'y* and *qiyās*.

G. The Traditionists

The traditionists[7] are hostile to all reasoning and try to rely exclusively on traditions. They do not refer anything in matters

[1] See above, p. 97.

[2] *Tr. IV*, 253; *Tr. VII*, 274 f.

[3] See below, p. 258.

[4] Ibn Qutaiba, 16, 20, 74, 76. Ibid. 17, they are charged with using *istiḥsān*, but this is polemical.

[5] Ibid., 104, 151, 182, and elsewhere.

[6] See below, p. 259.

[7] See below, p. 253.

of religion to *istiḥsān*, *qiyās*, or *naẓar* (Ibn Qutaiba, 103). They are weak in systematic reasoning, and Shāfiʿī charges them with wilful ignorance.[1] The following details on their doctrine are taken from Ibn Qutaiba.

Ibn Qutaiba spurns systematic reasoning (*qiyās* and *ḥujjat al-ʿaql*) even as an additional argument (p. 234). He concedes that *ra'y* on the details of law, on which there is no explicit enactment, is less important than the neglect of the Koran and of the traditions from the Prophet; but the right way to arrive at general rules, main duties, and *sunnas* is not by *qiyās* and human reasoning (p. 68). How can *qiyās* apply to the details when it does not agree with the principles (p. 70)? Ibn Qutaiba gives examples where *qiyās* does not apply (pp. 71 ff.). On the other hand, Ibn Qutaiba recognizes that the Companions used their discretion (*ẓann*, *ijtihād al-ra'y*) on questions which were not settled by the Koran and by traditions from the Prophet (p. 367), and he justifies this by saying that they were the leaders of the community (p. 30). Finally, he concedes that there are forbidden things which are prohibited neither in the Koran nor in the *sunna*, but for which man is left to his instinct (*fiṭra*) and his nature (p. 342 and elsewhere).

H. Traditions against Human Reasoning in Law

Goldziher has shown that *ra'y* meant originally 'sound opinion', as opposed to an arbitrary and irresponsible decision.[2] But since the activity it denoted was purely human and therefore fallible, it soon acquired, in polemics, the derogatory meaning of 'arbitrary opinion', particularly when it was opposed to the doctrine of the forebears and the *sunna* of the Prophet. We find this derogatory meaning present already in the dogmatic treatise ascribed to Ḥasan Baṣrī.[3] This does not prevent those who reproach their opponents with *ra'y* from using it themselves.

A further step is represented by the objection to *ra'y* and *qiyās* on principle, an objection which, as Goldziher has seen,[4] is secondary and posterior to their general use. The anecdotes

[1] *Ikh.* 323, 367 f. (quoted above, p. 56 f.).

[2] *Ẓâhiriten*, 10.

[3] See above, p. 74. Ibn Muqaffaʿ, *Ṣaḥāba*, 120, opposes *ra'y* to [authoritative] information (*khabar*).

[4] *Ẓâhiriten*, 13 ff.

expressing this objection, which have been collected by Goldziher, are clearly apocryphal and occur only in late sources. This attitude is typical of the traditionists, and the traditionists were also responsible for a whole body of traditions from the Prophet, from Companions, and from Successors, disparaging *ra'y* and *qiyās* and often opposing it to the *sunna* of the Prophet. The statements hostile to reasoning which they put into the mouth of old authorities of the ancient schools themselves, are certainly not authentic, and the Iraqian and Medinese *isnāds* affixed to them are spurious.

Traditions with Iraqian isnāds

One of the oldest traditions of this kind is an alleged saying of Shuraiḥ against *qiyās*, quoted above (p. 119). It is already known to Auzā'ī (*Tr. IX*, 50), and appears in Dārimī (*Bāb taghaiyur al-zamān*) with an *isnād* through the Iraqian Sha'bī, who adds a remark of his own against *qiyās*. But the doctrine connected with these statements contradicts the uniform opinion of the Iraqians (*Muw. Shaib.* 289; *Tr. VIII*, 7), and we must conclude that the names of Sha'bī and Shuraiḥ were borrowed by the traditionists.[1]

We saw that the *isnād* of the main tradition in favour of *ijtihād al-ra'y*, containing the instructions of the Prophet to Mu'ādh b. Jabal, is Iraqian, though fictitiously Syrian in its upper part.[2] A counter-tradition, the *isnād* of which is also (pseudo-)Iraqian in its lower and fictitiously Syrian in its upper part, replaces the recommendation of *ijtihād al-ra'y* by the order given to Mu'ādh to report to the Prophet in cases of doubt (Ibn Māja, *Bāb ijtināb al-ra'y wal-qiyās*).

Bukhārī (*Kitāb al-i'tiṣām bil-kitāb wal-sunna, Bāb mā yudhkar min dhamm al-ra'y*) gives a tradition with an Iraqian *isnād*, according to which Sahl b. Ḥunaif warns himself against *ra'y*, reminding himself of his own experience on the day of Ḥudaibiya during the lifetime of the Prophet, and applying it to his present situation on the day of Ṣiffīn. Here *ra'y* is identified with political disloyalty and made responsible for the civil wars in early Islam.

Dārimī (*Bāb al-tawarru' 'an al-jawāb*; *Bāb taghaiyur al-zamān*; *Bāb fī karāhiyat akhdh al-ra'y*) gives a number of traditions against *qiyās*, *ra'y*, and *ijtihād* from old Iraqian authorities, particularly Sha'bī. Others adduced are Ibn Mas'ūd, Masrūq, Ibrāhīm Nakha'ī, Ḥasan

[1] Shuraiḥ is also the recipient of alleged instructions from 'Umar which include *ijtihād al-ra'y* (see above, p. 104, n. 4); this is an authentically Iraqian tradition.

[2] Above, p. 106.

Baṣrī, Ibn Sīrīn, Qatāda. Some of these traditions presuppose the role of Ibn Mas'ūd and Ibrāhīm Nakha'ī as main authorities of the Iraqians; one in particular endeavours to minimize the doctrine which goes under the name of Ibrāhīm, by a self-deprecating statement which it puts into his mouth. The picture of Sha'bī as 'the strongest critic of *ra'y* and *qiyās* among the Iraqians' (Ibn Qutaiba, 69 f.) was created by the traditionists, but we find that Sha'bī occurs in the *isnāds* of traditions which ascribe early Iraqian *ra'y* and *qiyās* to Companions.[1]

A tradition with an Iraqian *isnād* which is extremely doubtful in all its links higher than Ibn 'Uyaina, makes 'Alī point out that reasoning by analogy has no place in a certain question of ritual (*Tr. II*, 2 (*a*)). This is a counter-move against the Iraqian traditions which ascribe *ra'y* and *qiyās* to 'Alī and other Companions.[2]

Traditions with Medinese (Meccan, Syrian) isnāds

See several of the traditions discussed above, pp. 54 f., 117 (on *Muw.* iv. 39), 119 (on 'Umar b. 'Abdal'azīz), and further:

Bukhārī (*Kitāb al-i'tiṣām bil-kitāb wal-sunna, Bāb mā yudhkar min dhamm al-ra'y*): 'Urwa b. Zubair connects *ra'y* with the time of ignoramuses after real scholars have become extinct.

Dārimī (*Bāb al-tawarru' 'an al-jawāb*): 'Urwa b. Zubair warns against *ra'y* and suspects foreign influence in it.

Dārimī (ibid.): a tradition the *isnād* of which in its lower, historical, part is typical of the traditionists (all men from the town of Raiy), ascribes to the Meccan scholar 'Aṭā' the saying: 'I should be ashamed before Allah if my *ra'y* were taken as a norm on earth.' This is not genuine because we find 'Aṭā' use both *qiyās* (*Tr. I*, 124) and *istiḥsān* (Ibn 'Abdalbarr, quoted in Zurqānī, i. 108).[3]

Dārimī (*Bāb mā yuttaqā min tafsīr ḥadīth al-nabī*): 'Umar b. 'Abdal'azīz said in a sermon: 'There is no Prophet after ours, and no holy book after ours; what Allah has allowed or forbidden through our Prophet, remains so forever; I am not one who decides (*qāḍī*) but only one who carries out (*munfidh*), no innovator but a follower.' This tradition in the *isnād* of which occurs Mu'tamir b. Sulaimān, who was responsible for several traditions with a traditionist bias,[4] is directed

[1] See above, p. 104, on *Tr. II*, 12 (*a*), 18 (*w*); p. 108, on *Tr. III*, 54. On Sha'bī in general, see below, p. 230 f.

[2] See above, pp. 104, 106.

[3] This *istiḥsān* is a genuine old opinion, though not necessarily authentic for the scholars to whom it is ascribed. On 'Aṭā' in general, see below, p. 250 f.

[4] See above, p. 56.

against the old idea of *ijtihād*. The doctrine expressed here, with all its implications, became part of the classical theory of Muhammadan law, but only after the time of Shāfi'ī. Bukhārī separated *ijtihād* from its old connexion with *ra'y* and *qiyās*,[1] and Ibn Qutaiba, 19, 30, restricted the term *mujtahid* to the great scholars of the past who cannot be equalled, denying *ijtihād* to the contemporaries.

[1] *Kitāb al-i'tiṣām bil-kitāb wal-sunna, Bāb mā jā' fi-jtihād al-qaḍā' bimā anzal Allāh.*

CHAPTER 10

FINAL REMARKS ON LEGAL THEORY

WE found that the theory of the Iraqians was in several respects more highly developed than that of the Medinese, for instance with regard to the theory of traditions, the *sunna* of the Prophet, consensus, and *ijtihād*.[1] But the statement of Khaṭīb Baghdādī (xiv. 245 f.), that Abū Yūsuf was the first to compose books on the theory of law on the basis of the doctrine of Abū Ḥanīfa, is not confirmed by the old sources.

Later legal theory subsumes every relevant act under one of the 'five legal categories' which are: obligatory, recommended, indifferent, disapproved, and forbidden, and discusses the relationship between these categories and the concepts of validity, nullity, and intermediate degrees. The 'five categories' as such are as yet unknown to Shāfi'ī and his predecessors.

Shāfi'ī discusses several aspects of this subject in the whole of *Tr. VI* (pp. 265–7), in *Tr. VII*, 270, and in *Ris.* 48 f.; it is obvious that he does not know 'disapproved' as a separate category, and I do not remember having met *makrūh*, which is the term for it, in his writings. *Mustaḥabb*, which is a later term for 'recommended', occurs with this meaning in *Tr. III*, 25, but it is obvious from the context as well as from *Tr. VI* that it is not yet part of Shāfi'ī's technical terminology. Another term for 'recommended' is *sunna*, in later terminology strictly distinguished from '*sunna* of the Prophet'; Shāfi'ī seems to use it with this meaning in *Ikh.* 184, but again clearly not as part of his technical terminology. In *Ris.* 43 he distinguishes between 'obligatory proper' (*wājib*) and 'obligatory by choice' (*wājib fil-ikhtiyār*) which is the same as 'recommended'.[2] Muzanī's terminology is not more precise than that of his master.[3]

Shaibānī, too, has no fixed terms for 'recommended' and 'disapproved', and the tradition of the Ḥanafī school is presumably right when it holds that Shaibānī used the term *makrūh* as meaning 'forbidden'.[4] In *Muw. Shaib.* 225, Shaibānī, quoting a tradition from Ibn 'Umar, comments 'this is the *sunna*', but explains that one may also act differently; this shows that the two meanings of *sunna* were not yet clearly separated, and the same can be assumed for Shāfi'ī's usage in *Ikh.* 184.

[1] See above, pp. 29, 76, 87, 105.
[2] See also p. 322 (on *Tr. III*, 111).
[3] *K. al-Amr wal-Nahy*, *passim*.
[4] *Comm. Muw. Shaib.*, *passim*.

The same ambiguous use of *sunna* occurs in *Mud.* i. 128, where Saḥnūn quotes a tradition from ʿAlī to the effect that the *witr* prayer is not absolutely obligatory like the prayers ordained in the Koran, but is a *sunna* introduced by the Prophet. Quotations in Zurqānī, i. 184, show Mālik's fluctuating terminology for 'recommended'.[1]

Shāfiʿī's discussion of the relationship between the categories of allowed and forbidden and the concepts of validity and nullity[2] shows that opinions were divided on this problem of legal theory, but does not enable us to trace the development of doctrine. It appears, however, from Shāfiʿī's use of the term *fāsid*, approximately 'voidable', as a synonym of *bāṭil* 'null and void', that he abandoned the never very clear distinction between *fāsid* and *bāṭil* which was familiar to the ancient schools before him.[3]

Another subject discussed at length in later legal theory is the validity of judgments in general, and in particular the annulment of judgments given against explicit rulings of Koran, *sunna*, and consensus. Shāfiʿī gives the general rule that a judgment is to be rescinded if it disagrees with a text in the Koran, a *sunna*, a consensus, or one of their necessary implications (*Tr. I*, 56). *Qiyās* is significantly absent from this list, and even Shāfiʿī recognizes the old freedom of *ra'y* to this extent.

Legal philosophy is concerned with the question whether every act is to be regarded as allowed on principle, unless it is specifically forbidden, or as forbidden on principle, unless it is specifically allowed. Shāfiʿī does not consider this theoretical problem, and in *Ris.* 48 f., where he discusses the general relationship between the categories allowed and forbidden, he keeps his feet firmly planted on positive law.

As regards the hierarchy of sources, Shāfiʿī refers to them as a rule, with variations in detail, in the following order: Koran, *sunna* or traditions from the Prophet, *āthār* or traditions from Companions and others, consensus, *qiyās* and reason (*maʿqūl*). He says in *Ris.* 70: 'The basis of legal knowledge (*jihat al-ʿilm*) is the Koran, the *sunna*, the consensus, the *āthār*, and the *qiyās* based on these. The scholar must interpret the ambiguous passages of the Koran according to the *sunna* of the Prophet, and if he does not find a *sunna*, according to the consensus of the Muslims, and if there is no consensus, according to the *qiyās*.'

[1] '*Ḥasan*, not *wājib*', as related by Ashhab; '*sunna*, *maʿrūf*', as related by Ibn Wahb.

[2] *Tr. VI*; *Tr. VII*, 270; *Ris.* 48 f.

[3] See, e.g., Shaibānī, *Jāmiʿ al-Ṣaghīr*, 33, 78 f.; Dimitroff, in *M.S.O.S.* xi (1908), 147 ff.; Santillana, *Istituzioni*, i. 176 ff.

The quaternion Koran, *sunna*, consensus, and *qiyās*, which comprises the recognized sources or principles (*uṣūl*) of law in the classical theory,[1] occurs in *Ris.* 8, but Shāfiʿī's references to it are rare, and he certainly did not put all these four concepts on the same level as sources.

On the contrary, he calls Koran and *sunna* 'the two sources' (*aṣlān*) (*Umm*, vi. 203); everything else is subsidiary (*tabaʿ*) to them (*Tr. IV*, 52); nothing else can add to or subtract from their authority (*Tr. IX*, 29). They are peremptory statements (*qaul farḍ*) to which no question of 'why' applies, and the final authority (*al-qaul al-ghāya*) by which the derivative statements are to be measured (*Ikh.* 340). In *Ris.* 82, Shāfiʿī defends himself against the charge of putting consensus and *qiyās* on the same plane as Koran and *sunna.* While recognizing that the decisions deriving from all of them are equally binding, he points out the difference existing between them as sources or bases (*uṣūl, asbāb*): what is based on the Koran, and on the unanimously recognized *sunna*, is true on the face of it and in reality (*fil-ẓāhir wal-bāṭin*); what is based on the *sunna*, transmitted in 'isolated' traditions, and not unanimously recognized, is true only on the face of it, because an error in transmission is possible;[2] Shāfiʿī also decides on the basis of consensus, and then of *qiyās*; but this basis is weaker, comes into play only in the case of necessity, and is inadmissible if there is a *khabar*, that is a ruling in Koran or *sunna.*

The *sunna* of the Prophet, according to Shāfiʿī, ranks below the Koran.[3] What is not to be found in the Koran, is to be taken from the *sunna* and the consensus (*Ikh.* 3). Shāfiʿī paid lip-service to the overruling authority of the Koran, which he did not recognize in practice.[4]

The consensus ranks below the *sunna* in Shāfiʿī's opinion,[5] which is opposed equally to the doctrine of the ancient schools and to the final classical theory of law.[6] In these last, the consensus guarantees the whole system of law; for Shāfiʿī it guarantees only the result of analogical reasoning (*Ris.* 65).

Last in Shāfiʿī's hierarchy of sources comes analogy (*Tr. I*,

[1] See above, p. 1. The later opposition of *uṣūl* 'legal theory' to *furūʿ* 'positive law' is also unknown to Shāfiʿī; for his various uses of *farʿ* and *furūʿ*, see above, p. 122 and below, p. 136.

[2] See above, p. 52.

[3] e.g. *Ris.* 14; *Ikh.* 68; also *Ikh.* 409 where *sunna* is used in the old meaning of 'living tradition'.

[4] See above, p. 15.

[5] e.g. *Ris.* 12, 58; *Ikh.* 409.

[6] See above, pp. 82, 94 f.

52), and Shāfiʿī is conscious of its precarious character, even when it is used correctly (*Ris.* 66).[1] As opposed to analogy, Shāfiʿī groups Koran, *sunna*, and consensus together under the name of 'binding information' (*khabar lāzim* or *khabar yalzam*).[2]

Shāfiʿī distinguishes between the knowledge of the general public and the knowledge of the specialists (*ʿilm al-ʿāmma* and *ʿilm al-khāṣṣa*).[3] The former comprises the essential duties (*jumal al-farāʾiḍ*) of which no responsible person may be ignorant; this 'absolutely certain' kind of knowledge (*iḥāṭa*) is explicitly stated in the Koran and transmitted by the community at large in traditions from the Prophet which are related, in every generation, by many from many, so that no error in their transmission is possible. The second kind of knowledge comprises questions of detail (*furūʿ*, *khāṣṣ al-aḥkām*) on which there is no explicit text in the Koran, which are expressed in traditions less widely attested or 'isolated', and which are partly the result of reasoning by analogy and subject to disagreement; this kind of knowledge is beyond the reach of the general public, and not even obligatory for all specialists;[4] if a sufficient number of specialists cultivate it, the others may consider themselves excused.[5]

Finally, Shāfiʿī holds that the divine revelation, as expressed in Koran and *sunna*, provides for every possible eventuality.[6] He refers to Koran lxxv. 36 and to a tradition which makes the Prophet say that he received no command and no prohibition from Allah which he did not hand on.[7] From this thesis Shāfiʿī draws a number of conclusions, including the rejection of the 'living tradition', of the consensus of the scholars, and of *istiḥsān*. Similarly, his theory of legal knowledge connects his doctrines on traditions, consensus, disagreement, and analogy.

On the whole, and notwithstanding the evidence of its

[1] Ṭabarī still refuses to give to analogy the same character as a source of law as he does to Koran, *sunna* (that is traditions from the Prophet), and consensus (of the scholars and of the general public); see Kern, in *Z.D.M.G.* lv. 72.

[2] *Tr. VII*, 271, and elsewhere. In the terminology of the ancient schools, *khabar lāzim* (*yalzam*) seems to be restricted to the Koran and to those traditions which they recognize; see above, pp. 27, 110.

[3] *Ris.* 50, 63, 66 (main passages); see also *Tr. III*, 148 (p. 246); *Tr. IV*, 255; *Ikh.* 101, 271.

[4] According to the ancient schools, the consensus of the scholars is a rule (*ḥujja*) for those who lack the knowledge: *Tr. IV*, 255. See also above, p. 93.

[5] Shāfiʿī does not yet use the later term *farḍ kifāya*, and for its opposite he does not use the later term *farḍ ʿain*, but says *farḍ ʿalal-ʿāmma*. Even Khaiyāṭ, 100, apparently does not know yet the technical term *farḍ kifāya*.

[6] *Tr. IV*, 250; *Tr. VII*, 271.

[7] See above, p. 53.

gradual development, traces of the influence of earlier doctrines, and occasional inconsistencies,[1] Shāfiʿī's legal theory is a magnificently consistent system and superior by far to the doctrines of the ancient schools. It is the achievement of a powerful individual mind, and at the same time the logical outcome of a process which started when traditions from the Prophet were first adduced as arguments in law. The development of legal theory is dominated by the struggle between two concepts: that of the common doctrine of the community, and that of the authority of traditions from the Prophet. The doctrine of the ancient schools of law represents an uneasy compromise; Shāfiʿī vindicated the thesis of the traditionists; and the classical legal theory extended the sanction of consensus to the traditionist principle.

The most important outside witness for the development of Muhammadan legal theory is the secretary of state Ibn Muqaffaʿ in his *Risāla fil-Ṣaḥāba.*[2] According to him, it is part of the duty of the government to teach the Koran, to be well-versed in the *sunna*, to uphold the standards of trustworthiness and integrity, particularly in the dispensation of administrative justice and the examination of complaints, and to avoid irresponsible persons (pp. 124, 129 f.). The Caliph ought to admit to his company righteous lawyers who might serve as a model for the people (p. 129). The lawyers ought to be the educators of every town and ought to prevent the spread of [political] heresies (*bidaʿ*) (p. 130). These counsels reflect the conscious encouragement of Muhammadan law by the first ʿAbbāsid Caliphs.

[1] See above, pp. 11 f., 15, 18, 19 f., 38, 79 f., 88 ff., 120, 125 f.

[2] See above, pp. 58 f., 95, 102 f.

PART II

THE GROWTH OF LEGAL TRADITIONS

CHAPTER 1

PRELIMINARY REMARKS

THE current opinion regarding the growth of traditions is, roughly, that there originally existed an authentic core of information going back to the time of the Prophet, that spurious and tendentious additions were made to it in every succeeding generation, that many of these were eliminated by the criticism of *isnāds* as practised by the Muhammadan scholars, that other spurious traditions escaped rejection, but that the genuine core was not completely overlaid by later accretions.[1] Most of these and similar assumptions, by which some later writers tended to minimize Goldziher's fundamental discovery of the character of the traditions from the Prophet,[2] are unwarranted and certainly do not apply to legal traditions. One of the main conclusions to be drawn from Part I of this book is that, generally speaking, the 'living tradition' of the ancient schools of law, based to a great extent on individual reasoning, came first, that in the second stage it was put under the aegis of Companions, that traditions from the Prophet himself, put into circulation by traditionists towards the middle of the second century A.H., disturbed and influenced this 'living tradition', and that only Shāfiʿī secured to the traditions from the Prophet supreme authority.[3] The aim of Part II is to show that a considerable number of legal traditions, which appear in the classical collections, originated after Mālik and Shāfiʿī; to study the growth of legal traditions and of their *isnāds* in detail; to draw conclusions on their origins in the pre-literary period; and thereby to work out and test a method which enables us to trace the development of legal doctrine during this period for which traditions are our only contemporary evidence; in other

[1] The current opinion is well summarized by Lammens, *Islām*, 69 f.

[2] See above, p. 4.

[3] See above, pp. 20, 57, 66 f., 80 f., 98, &c.

words, to replace the static picture of conflicting tendencies which has prevailed so far, by one showing the historical process.

Traditions regarding the biography of the Prophet (*maghāzī*, *sīra*) generally lack proper *isnāds*. Shāfiʿī differentiates between them and legal traditions on this account.[1] On the special subject of the law of war, 'historical' traditions were already used by Auzāʿī to a great extent;[2] but the gradual introduction of 'historical' material into legal discussions continued in the period between Auzāʿī and Shāfiʿī.[3] This reception of 'historical' traditions into legal discussion went parallel with their acquiring increasingly elaborate *isnāds*.[4] All this time, the body of 'historical' information was still growing, and both Abū Yūsuf and Shāfiʿī object to 'historical' traditions adduced by their opponents, because they are unknown to, or not accepted by, the specialists on *maghāzī*.[5] This process was reciprocal, and we find traditions of a properly legal character, but with an 'historical' background, penetrating more or less successfully into the biography of the Prophet.[6]

[1] *Tr. III*, 44; *Tr. IX*, 8, 9 (cf. *Umm*, iv. 69); *Ris.* 21 f.; *Ikh.* 388 f. Also Abū Yūsuf differentiates between *sunna* and *sīra* in *Tr. IX*. 6. 21.

[2] See above, p. 34.

[3] 'Historical' traditions introduced by Mālik: Ṭabarī, 81, and *Mud.* iii. 7 f. (see also above, p. 23, n. 5, on Mālik's imperfect knowledge of the biography of the Prophet); introduced by Abū Yūsuf: *Tr. IX*, 1, 11, 30, 36; introduced by Shaibānī: *Siyar*, iii. 94 (cf. *Tr. IX*, 25); ibid. iv. 238 (cf. *Tr. IX*, 39); introduced by Shāfiʿī: *Tr. VIII*, 12, 13; *Tr. IX*, 19, 23, 25, 39, 44; *Umm*, iv. 170, &c.

[4] Compare Mālik in *Mud.* iii. 8, Abū Yūsuf in *Tr. IX*, 28 and the biographers of the Prophet (Ibn Hishām, 653, 872 f.; Wāqidī, 163, 369 f.; Ibn Saʿd, ii_1. 41, 114), with the *isnāds*, through Nāfiʿ, in *Umm*, iv. 161, 174 and *Mud.* iii. 8.

[5] Abū Yūsuf: *Tr. IX*, 10; Shāfiʿī: *Tr. IX*, 6; *Umm*, iv. 66.

[6] e.g. details of the marriage of the Prophet to Maimūna (below, p. 153); the alleged temporary permission of the *mutʿa* marriage by the Prophet (below, p. 267); the alleged *qunūt* of the Prophet (below, p. 267 f.); episodes illustrating the effect of conversion to Islam on a previous marriage (below, p. 276). See further the tradition, put into circulation by the traditionists, on the prayer of the Prophet while incapacitated by an accident; this was opposed to the originally biographical tradition on his prayer during his last illness (*Muw.* i. 248; *Muw. Shaib.* 113; *Mud.* i. 81; *Tr. III*, 19; *Ris.* 36 f.; *Ikh.* 98 ff., 136); the full *isnāds* of this last biographical tradition in the legal sources are secondary and borrowed from the other tradition.

CHAPTER 2

THE GROWTH OF LEGAL TRADITIONS IN THE LITERARY PERIOD. CONCLUSIONS ON THE PRE-LITERARY PERIOD

THE aim of the present chapter is to provide a firm starting-point for the systematic use of traditions as documents for the development of legal doctrine, by investigating the growth of legal traditions in the literary period, roughly from A.H. 150 to 250, between Abū Ḥanīfa and the classical collections of traditions, with a few extensions into the first half of the second century.[1] The evidence presented here is only the most significant part of what could be collected, and the most important result is that whereas the growth of legal traditions from the Prophet went on over the whole period, it was particularly vigorous in the fifty years between Shāfiʿī and the classical collections, a result which can be ascribed to the joint influence of Shāfiʿī and the traditionists. The evidence must, in the nature of things, be cumulative, and whilst care has been taken to verify the presence or absence of the traditions in question in or from the sources available, an occasional oversight or the well-known incompleteness of our sources does not invalidate the general conclusions. The best way of proving that a tradition did not exist at a certain time is to show that it was not used as a legal argument in a discussion which would have made reference to it imperative, if it had existed. The evidence collected in the present chapter has been chosen with particular regard to this last point, and in a number of cases one or the other of the opponents himself states that he has no evidence other than that quoted by him, which does not include the tradition in question. This kind of conclusion *e silentio* is furthermore made safe by *Tr. VIII*, 11, where Shaibānī says: '[This is so] unless the Medinese can produce a tradition in support of their doctrine, but they have none, or they would have produced it.' We may safely assume that the legal traditions with which we are concerned were quoted as arguments by those whose

[1] This kind of investigation was desired by Goldziher, *Muh. St.* ii. 218, n, 1.

doctrine they were intended to support, as soon as they were put into circulation.

Traditions later than Ḥasan Baṣrī

Although the dogmatic treatise of Ḥasan Baṣrī[1] is not concerned with matters of law, it is appropriate to begin with it, because it shows that even dogmatic traditions which are, generally speaking, earlier than legal ones, hardly existed at the time of its composition, that is, in the later part of the first century A.H. There is no trace of traditions from the Prophet, and the author states explicitly: 'Every opinion which is not based on the Koran, is erroneous.'

Tradition originating between "Ibrāhīm Nakhaʿī" and Ḥammād

Āthār A.Y. 206: Abū Ḥanīfa—Ḥammād—Ibrāhīm—Ibn Masʿūd did not follow a certain practice. *Āthār Shaib.* 37: Abū Ḥanīfa—Ḥammād—Ibrāhīm did not follow it; the same is related from Ibn Masʿūd. But there is a tradition from the Prophet to the contrary. *Āthār A.Y.* 207: Abū Ḥanīfa—Ḥammād—ʿAbdalkarīm[2]—with an *isnād* going back to the Prophet, that he did follow it. *Āthār Shaib.* 37: Shaibānī—ʿUmar b. Dharr Hamdānī—his father—Saʿīd b. Jubair—Ibn ʿAbbās—Prophet: a tradition in favour of the practice, polemically directed against the other opinion. The same tradition with another Iraqian *isnād* occurs in *Tr. II*, 19 (*t*).

It will be shown that the name of Ibrāhīm Nakhaʿī is often a label for the ancient Iraqian doctrine.[3] This and the then recently produced tradition from the Prophet to the contrary were transmitted by Ḥammād to Abū Ḥanīfa, and the tradition from the Prophet soon acquired better *isnāds*.

Traditions originating between "Ibrāhīm Nakhaʿī" and Abū Ḥanīfa

A certain tradition from the Prophet is unknown to Ibrāhīm (*Āthār Shaib.* 22), known to Abū Ḥanīfa without *isnād* (*Āthār A.Y.* 251), and appears with a full *isnād* in *Muw.* i. 275; *Muw. Shaib.* 122; *Tr. II*, 19 (*g*) and in the classical collections.[4]

For another example, see above, p. 60. It has been shown there that certain traditions from the Prophet on a question of ritual were as yet unknown to Ibrāhīm, but that one version in favour of a certain practice was followed by Shāfiʿī. Another version which, by implica-

[1] See above, p. 74.
[2] This link is very weak, see the Commentary.
[3] See below, p. 233.
[4] The link between Mālik and the Companion who relates it from the Prophet is very weak.

tion, is directed against that practice, appears first in Abū Ḥanīfa (*Tr. I*, 157 (*b*)), and a third version in *Muw. Shaib.* 382.

Tradition originating between "Ibrāhīm Nakha'ī" and Mālik

Āthār A.Y. 98: Ibrāhīm says: 'There is nothing with regard to prayer on which the Companions of the Prophet agreed so fully as saying the morning prayer in full daylight.' This seems to be an authentic statement of Ibrāhīm. Later than this and in favour of saying it in early dawn are traditions from 'Alī and Ibn Mas'ūd (ibid.) and from the Prophet (first in *Muw.* i. 19).

Tradition originating between "'Aṭā'" and Shāfi'ī

Tr. I, 181: Abū Yūsuf refers to and follows the opinion of 'Aṭā' which he heard personally from Ḥajjāj b. Arṭāt. It is likely that this opinion goes back not even to 'Aṭā' himself but only to Ḥajjāj.[1] But in Shāfi'ī's time it was expressed in a tradition from the Prophet.

Traditions originating between Ibn Abī Lailā and Abū Ḥanīfa

Tr. I, 176: Ibn Abī Lailā does not consider it necessary to fast two *consecutive* months for having broken the fast of Ramadan by intercourse (see Sarakhsī, iii. 72 on a still milder opinion of Rabī'a); he obviously did not yet know the tradition from the Prophet to this effect, based on an analogy with Koran lviii. 4. Abū Ḥanīfa considers that the two months must be consecutive, and is the first to refer to the tradition from the Prophet, *mursal* and with the suspected transmitter 'Aṭā' Khurāsānī in the *isnād*. The tradition acquires an uninterrupted *isnād* only in the time of Mālik (*Muw.* ii. 99; *Muw. Shaib.* 177).

§ 193: Ibn Abī Lailā does not yet know a tradition from the Prophet which appears in Abū Ḥanīfa (or Abū Yūsuf), Shāfi'ī, and the classical collections.

Tradition originating between Auzā'ī and Mālik

See above, p. 70. It is stated there that Abū Yūsuf does not yet know a tradition from the Prophet, although Mālik, his contemporary, does. Whereas this calls for caution in the use of the argument *e silentio*, it also shows that the tradition was not yet widely known in the time of Mālik.

Tradition originating between Auzā'ī and Ibn Sa'd

See below, p. 180, n. 1.

[1] See below, p. 250.

Traditions originating between Abū Ḥanīfa and Abū Yūsuf

Tr. IX, 42: Abū Yūsuf adduces a tradition with an imperfect *isnād*, not through Abū Ḥanīfa who obviously did not yet know it, but through an anonymous sheikh. Several similar cases occur in *Āthār A.Y.*

See also below, p. 158.

Traditions originating between Abū Ḥanīfa and Shaibānī

Tr. II, 18 (*y*): Abū Ḥanīfa, for a rule of penal law, can refer only to a tradition from Sha'bī. Shaibānī gives a tradition from the Prophet, not through Abū Ḥanīfa but through another transmitter. The underlying doctrine was not yet acknowledged by Ibn Abī Lailā (see *Tr. I*, 112). Similar cases occur in *Āthār Shaib.*

Tradition originating between Abū Ḥanīfa and the Classical Collections

Tr. I, 169: Abū Ḥanīfa can refer only to Ibrāhīm Nakha'ī (also in *Kharāj*, *Āthār A.Y.*, and *Āthār Shaib.*); traditions from the Prophet to the same effect appear in the classical works and, with a fictitious *isnād* in which Abū Ḥanīfa himself appears, in a late version of the *Musnad Abī Ḥanīfa* (see *Comm. ed. Cairo*, p. 125, n. 1).

Tradition originating between Mālik and Shaibānī

Mālik (*Muw.* iii. 129) knows a tradition only from Ibn 'Abbās in a short version which he interprets restrictively, in keeping with his own doctrine. But Shaibānī (*Muw. Shaib.* 331, without *isnād*) and Shāfi'ī (*Tr. III*, 95, with full *isnād*) know a fuller version which implicates the Prophet and is followed by Ibn 'Abbās's own extensive interpretation.

Traditions originating between Mālik and Shāfi'ī

Tr. II, 2 (*g*): Neither the Iraqians who refer to the consensus of the scholars as against a tradition from Ibn Mas'ūd nor the Medinese (*Muw.* i. 100; *Mud.* i. 31) know traditions from the Prophet on the problem in question. Only Shāfi'ī gives a tradition from the Prophet.

§ 19 (*ee*): The recommendation to invest the property of orphans, so that the *zakāt* tax may not consume it, is known to Mālik (*Muw.* ii. 49) only as a saying of 'Umar, but to Shāfi'ī already as a saying of the Prophet, with full *isnād*.

Tr. IX, 10: Auzā'ī had referred to an 'historical' tradition from the Prophet, without *isnād*, but Abū Yūsuf had rejected it as not acceptable to specialists and referred to a tradition from Ibn 'Abbās in favour of his own, different doctrine, shared by Mālik and

Shāfiʿī. It was therefore imperative for Mālik to mention a tradition from the Prophet, if he knew one, but he adduces only the alleged opinion of the ancient Medinese scholars Qāsim b. Muḥammad and Sālim (*Mud.* iii. 34),[1] and *Mud.* adds only a circumstantial but certainly spurious tradition which is set in the time of the Companions. The classical tradition from the Prophet on the problem in question, through Nāfiʿ—Ibn ʿUmar, was still unknown to Mālik and appears for the first time in Shāfiʿī. It is added that Nāfiʿ related this tradition to ʿUmar b. ʿAbdalʿazīz who gave instructions accordingly; this expresses the attitude of the traditionists.

Ikh. 96: a tradition from the Prophet on an important point of ritual purity, the sound *isnād* of which Shāfiʿī commends, is still unknown to and not followed by Mālik (*Muw.* i. 100; *Muw. Shaib.* 76).

Traditions originating between Mālik and the Classical Collections

Muw. iii. 134: Mālik adds to the text of a tradition from the Prophet his own definition of the aleatory contracts *mulāmasa* and *munābadha*; the same definition appears as a statement of Mālik, not in connexion with any tradition, in *Mud.* x. 37 f. It is, in fact, a current Medinese formula, ascribed to Rabīʿa in *Mud.* x. 38, and also occurring as an explanatory addition to the text of two parallel versions of the same tradition, where Mālik does not appear in the *isnād* (ibid.). But this interpretation has become part of the words of the Prophet in Bukhārī and Muslim (see Zurqānī, iii. 134); at the same time, Bukhārī and Muslim relate the same tradition without the interpretation, and in Nasā'ī where the addition is slightly longer, it is clearly separated from the text.

Tr. III, 22: Mālik's own words, technically formulated (*Muw.* i. 372; *Mud.* i. 109) and repeated by Rabīʿ in a discussion which turns on the traditional authority for the doctrine in question, without any suggestion that these words are part of a tradition, have become a tradition from the Prophet in Ibn Māja's collection (quoted *Comm. Muw. Shaib.* 148, n. 3; also in Ṭaḥāwī, i. 207).

§ 36: Mālik had to rely on a *mursal* tradition from ʿUmar, and on a subsumption which Shāfiʿī refutes as contrary to Arabic usage. There are two traditions from the Prophet with Medinese *isnāds* in Muslim's collection (quoted by Zurqānī II. 196).

Traditions originating between Abū Yūsuf and Shaibānī

Tr. IX, 29: Auzāʿī refers to the alleged instruction of Abū Bakr not to lay waste the enemy country; this invokes the authority of a Caliph and Companion of the Prophet in favour of the doctrine of

[1] See above, p. 113.

the Syrians who accepted the practice current under the Umaiyads. Abū Yūsuf has the counter-tradition (on the authority of Ibn Isḥāq) that Abū Bakr instructed one of his commanders to lay waste every village where he did not hear the call to prayer. In the time of the classical collections, this had produced a tradition from the Prophet, to the effect that the Prophet, on his raids, stopped at dawn, in order to ascertain whether the morning call to prayer was said in the place he intended to attack (see the details in *Comm. ed. Cairo*).[1] The original instruction of Abū Bakr was interpreted away, (*a*) by making Abū Bakr say that Syria would certainly be conquered [so that there was no point in laying it waste] (*Siyar*, i. 35)—this can be dated between Abū Yūsuf and Shaibānī[2]—and (*b*) by *mursal* traditions regarding the instructions which the Prophet gave to the leader of an expedition sent against Syria (Ibn Wahb in *Mud.* iii. 8). Several early Medinese authorities were incorporated in the *isnāds* of these last traditions.

§ 38: Abū Yūsuf could reject a tradition as irregular (*shādhdh*), but Shaibānī knew more of the same kind and therefore followed them (*Siyar*, iv. 87).

Tradition originating between Shaibānī and Shāfi'ī

Shāfi'ī and his predecessors discuss the question whether the major ritual ablution (*ghusl*) is necessary before the Friday prayer or not. The traditions on this point are difficult to reconcile. A harmonizing tradition from the Prophet to the effect that the minor ablution (*wuḍū'*) is sufficient but the major ablution better, is known neither to Mālik (*Muw.* i. 184) nor to Shaibānī (*Muw. Shaib.* 72). It occurs first in Shāfi'ī (*Ikh.* 181). *Āthār A.Y.* 357 knows this solution simply as the opinion of Ibrāhīm Nakha'ī, that is, the doctrine of the Iraqian school, and Shaibānī (loc. cit.) gives his opinion to the same effect.

Tradition originating between Shaibānī and the Classical Collections

Tr. VIII, 1: The fixing of the rate of exchange of gold and silver for purposes of weregeld is ascribed to 'Umar both by the Iraqians and the Medinese; Shāfi'ī too, although he knows a tradition from the Prophet in favour of the Medinese rate, bases himself on the decision of 'Umar. The Iraqian rate (1 dīnār = 10 dirham) underlies traditions from the Prophet in the classical collections (see the details in Guidi–Santillana, ii. 680). It was imperative for Shaibānī

[1] The original instruction of Abū Bakr was also projected back to the Prophet: Sarakhsī in *Siyar*, i. 35 f.

[2] Also Shāfi'ī refers to it in *Tr. IX*, 29 and in *Umm*, iv. 173 ff.

to quote them as a necessary part of his argument in *Tr. VIII*, 1, had he known them; they must therefore be later.[1]

Traditions originating between Shāfiʿī and Ibn Ḥanbal

Tr. III, 31: Compared with *Muw.* ii. 9 and Shāfiʿī's text, the traditions known to Ibn Ḥanbal are more numerous, and still more are known to Ibn ʿAbdalbarr (see Zurqānī, ii. 9).

§ 143: Neither Shāfiʿī nor the Medinese (see also *Muw.* iii. 124, 126) know a tradition from the Prophet, forbidding the sale of animals with anticipated payment and deferred delivery; it occurs in Ibn Ḥanbal and the classical collections (see Zurqānī, iii. 126). Shaibānī (*Muw. Shaib.* 344) knows this only as a tradition from ʿAlī, and adds that he heard that the Prophet prohibited it; also Abū Yūsuf (*Tr. IX*, 5) refers to the prohibition given by the Prophet, but without an *isnād*.

Ikh. 59: Shāfiʿī gives as his own opinion a harmonizing interpretation of traditions, and so does Shaibānī for himself and for Abū Ḥanīfa in *Muw. Shaib.* 47; the same doctrine is expressed in traditions from the Prophet in Ibn Ḥanbal and later collections (see *Comm. Muw. Shaib.* 47).

Ibid. 149: Neither Shāfiʿī nor Mālik (*Muw.* iv. 204) nor Shaibānī (*Muw. Shaib.* 280) know the traditions according to which the Prophet prohibited eating lizards because they might be a lost tribe changed into animals; they occur in Ibn Ḥanbal, the classical collections and others (see *Comm. Muw. Shaib.* 280; also Ṭaḥāwī, ii. 314). This kind of tradition, beloved by Ibn Qutaiba, seems to become prominent early in the third century A.H. (see also the following remark).

Ibid. 162: The tradition declaring that a black dog is a devil is still unknown to Shāfiʿī, as well as to Mālik (*Muw.* i. 277) and to Shaibānī (*Muw. Shaib.* 148). But Ibn Ḥanbal knows it (see Zurqānī, i. 277), and so does Jāḥiẓ (*Ḥayawān*, i. 141 ff.).

Ibid. 310: Shāfiʿī knows no explicit tradition from the Prophet, to the effect that the triple divorce, pronounced in one session, counts as a single divorce, apart from the implication of a tradition from Ibn ʿAbbās which he is at pains to explain away.[2] Neither does Mālik (*Muw.* iii. 36). But Ibn Ḥanbal (see Zurqānī, iii. 36) has a tradition through Ibn ʿAbbās from the Prophet, who declares that the triple divorce, pronounced in one session, counts as a single divorce and is revocable. Shāfiʿī also states explicitly (p. 315) that

[1] See below, p. 204.

[2] The several *isnāds* of this tradition converge in Ibn Juraij, and we may conclude that it originated in his time, i.e. in the generation preceding Mālik.

as far as he knows the Prophet never blamed the triple divorce; but a tradition condemning it occurs in some classical and other collections (Zurqānī, ibid.).

Traditions originating between Shafiʿī and the Classical Collections

Tr. I, 109: Shāfiʿī states explicitly that the oldest authority of the Iraqians for their doctrine on the evidence of non-Muslims, in lawsuits between themselves, is Shuraiḥ; the tradition from the Prophet to the same effect in Ibn Māja (see *Comm. ed. Cairo*) is later.

Tr. III, 21: Shāfiʿī adduces traditions from others than the Prophet as a confirmation; this shows that the traditions from the Prophet which he mentions are all that he knows. But further traditions occur in the classical and other collections (see *Comm. Muw. Shaib.* 103).

§ 29 (*a*): Shāfiʿī is positive that there exists no authority in traditions from the Prophet for a certain ancient doctrine which is based on practice; Rabīʿ can adduce none, and there is no trace of any in *Muw.* i. 149 or in *Muw. Shaib.* 101. But Bukhārī, Muslim, and others know a tradition from the Prophet to this effect (see Zurqānī and *Comm. Muw. Shaib.*, loc. cit.).

§ 29 (*c*): Zurqānī, i. 155, states correctly that Mālik in the whole relevant section does not mention one tradition from the Prophet; neither does Shāfiʿī nor Shaibānī in *Muw. Shaib.* 128. Zurqānī and *Comm. Muw. Shaib.* supply several from the classical and other collections. Considering Shāfiʿī's vehement polemics, it is certain that these traditions were still unknown to him and his predecessors.

§ 40: The Medinese follow traditions from ʿUmar, through Ibn ʿUmar, as against a tradition from the Prophet, through ʿĀ'isha; or historically speaking, the Medinese doctrine found its expression in traditions from ʿUmar, and the tradition from the Prophet is later. This doctrine was justified by a harmonizing interpretation of the tradition from the Prophet (*Muw. Shaib.* 197; Ṭaḥāwī, i. 363; Zurqānī, ii. 152), and this interpretation underlies a tradition in Muslim (see Zurqānī, loc. cit.) which must be later than the discussion between Shāfiʿī and Rabīʿ. Shāfiʿī follows the tradition from the Prophet, through ʿĀ'isha, and disregards the traditions from ʿUmar on principle; this attitude was also embodied in a tradition in Bukhārī and Muslim (see *Comm. Muw. Shaib.* 197), according to which Ibn ʿUmar decided in keeping with what was the Medinese doctrine, but was contradicted by ʿĀ'isha who referred to the example of the Prophet. This, too, is later than Shāfiʿī who would not have failed to refer to it in his polemics with the Medinese, had he known it.

§ 43: Shāfiʿī states that there is no tradition from the Prophet on the weregeld for a Jew or a Christian; but the classical collections (see Zurqānī, iv. 41) have a tradition from the Prophet in favour of a doctrine for which Mālik (*Muw.* iv. 41) could only refer, without *isnād*, to ʿUmar b. ʿAbdalʿazīz.

§ 60: Mālik and Shāfiʿī know only one tradition from the Prophet, with a very imperfect *isnād*, on an important point of ritual (see Zurqānī, i. 70). Several other traditions from the Prophet, with improved *isnāds*, occur in the classical collections (see *Comm. Muw. Shaib.* 67).

§ 89 (*a*): Shāfiʿī is explicit that there is no directly relevant tradition from the Prophet, and only a tradition from Ibn ʿUmar, in favour of the Medinese doctrine; but it appears, in the form of a tradition from the Prophet, in the classical collections (see Zurqānī, ii. 151).

§ 111: Mālik and Shāfiʿī know only a tradition through Nāfiʿ from Ibn ʿUmar in favour of a certain practice on the pilgrimage, and Rabīʿ adds that Mālik alone relates it. The classical collections (see Zurqānī, ii. 257), however, have, (*a*) a tradition through Nāfiʿ to the effect that Ibn ʿUmar did not regard it as *sunna*, together with the statement of the transmitter Nāfiʿ that the Prophet and the Caliphs after him performed it; (*b*) a version, through Nāfiʿ—Ibn ʿUmar, from the Prophet together with the statement that the practice of Abū Bakr and ʿUmar was the same; (*c*) a tradition to the effect that ʿĀʾisha and Ibn ʿAbbās did not regard it as *sunna*, but as an accidental action of the Prophet; and (*d*) a tradition explaining how the action of the Prophet came about accidentally. All this is later than Mālik and Shāfiʿī.

§ 144: Neither Mālik (*Muw.* ii. 333), nor Shaibānī (*Muw. Shaib.* 323), nor Shāfiʿī, nor Rabīʿ know a tradition from the Prophet which would be decisive; it occurs in Abū Dāwūd (see *Comm. Muw. Shaib.* 323).

§ 146: Shāfiʿī can quote from the Prophet only a tradition on the Prophet and Ibn ʿAbbās; but Bukhārī (see Zurqānī, ii. 83) has a more outspoken tradition on the Prophet and Abū Huraira; this was certainly not yet known to Shāfiʿī.

Ikh. 236: Shāfiʿī knows two contradictory traditions from the Prophet, not explicit and with unsatisfactory *isnāds*; Mālik had contented himself with traditions from Companions (*Muw.* ii. 103; *Muw. Shaib.* 181). An explicit tradition from the Prophet occurs in Nasāʾī and other collections (see Zurqānī, ii. 103). A series of gradual stages of the development of traditions, first from Companions and then from the Prophet, can be established with the material given by Zurqānī.

See also above, pp. 71, 91, 114, n. 6, and below, p. 155.

Traditions originating between Shāfi'ī and Ibn Qutaiba

Ibn Qutaiba, 113, has a tradition, through Zuhrī—'Urwa—'Ā'isha, to the effect that the Prophet ordered the hand of a woman who had borrowed ornaments and sold them to be cut off. This is unknown to Mālik, Shaibānī (*Muw. Shaib.* 303), and Shāfi'ī, but occurs in an improved form, with the explicit mention of theft, in the classical collections.

Ibn Qutaiba, 206, knows the saying of the Prophet: 'I was given the Koran, and together with it its equivalent', referring to the *sunna*. This was certainly unknown to Shāfi'ī who would not have failed to mention it, had he known it (see above, p. 16).

See also above, p. 97.

On the whole, the traditions contained, respectively, in the legal works of the second half of the second century, in the classical collections of the second half of the third century, and in the later collections of Ṭaḥāwī and others represent three successive stages of growth. The same process appears in the several versions of the *Musnad Abī Ḥanīfa*, which were collected by Khwārizmī: the later versions contain many more traditions than the early and authentic ones, the contents of which are confirmed by *Āthār A.Y.* and *Āthār Shaib*. We must postulate the same process of growth for the pre-literary period, and formulate again the methodical rule which follows from Goldziher's results but which has been neglected lately: that every legal tradition from the Prophet, until the contrary is proved, must be taken not as an authentic or essentially authentic, even if slightly obscured, statement valid for his time or the time of the Companions, but as the fictitious expression of a legal doctrine formulated at a later date. Its date can be ascertained from its first appearance in legal discussion, from its relative position in the history of the problem with which it is concerned, and from certain indications in text and *isnād* which will be discussed in the following chapters. The sources available enable us to draw these conclusions in many cases. We shall find that the bulk of legal traditions from the Prophet known to Mālik originated in the generation preceding him, that is in the second quarter of the second century A.H., and we shall not meet any legal tradition from the Prophet which can be considered authentic.

So far we have discussed the growth of legal traditions from the Prophet only. The following examples will show that traditions from Companions, too, were put into circulation during the whole of the literary period, including the time after Shāfiʿī. This does not contradict our previous conclusion that traditions from Companions precede, generally speaking, traditions from the Prophet,[1] but shows that the insistence of Shāfiʿī and the traditionists on the overriding authority of the traditions from the Prophet did not prevail at once. Traditions from Companions are as little genuine as traditions from the Prophet, and must be subjected to the same scrutiny in order to ascertain their place in the development of legal doctrine.[2]

Traditions from Companions originating:

Between "Ibrāhīm Nakhaʿī" and Abū Ḥanīfa:

See above, p. 60, n. 3.

Between "Ibrāhīm Nakhaʿī" and Mālik:

See *Āthār Shaib.* 80, compared with *Muw.* iii. 41: a tradition from ʿAlī.

See also above, p. 142.

Between "Ibrāhīm Nakhaʿī" and Shaibānī:

See above, p. 105.

Between Zuhrī and Mālik:

See above, p. 102.

Between Auzāʿī and Shāfiʿī:

See *Tr. IX*, 15: a tradition from ʿUmar.

Between Mālik and Ibn Wahb:

Muw. i. 247: Mālik reasons in favour of the Medinese 'practice', as against a tradition from Nāfiʿ—Ibn ʿUmar. Shaibānī (*Muw. Shaib.* 133) makes a pointed remark against the Medinese doctrine. This and Shāfiʿī's polemics against it (*Tr. III*, 27) make it certain that there existed no foundation for it in the form of traditions. But Ibn Wahb (*Mud.* i. 88) gives a tradition through Mālik from Nāfiʿ—Ibn ʿUmar, in favour of that doctrine. This and similar mentions of Mālik in the *isnāds* of Ibn Wahb are obviously not authentic.[3]

[1] See above, pp. 30, 33, &c.
[2] See below, p. 169 f.
[3] For a parallel case in Shāfiʿī, see below, p. 151.

Muw. i. 263: Mālik opposes his own opinion (*ra'y*) to a tradition from the Prophet, and quotes a tradition from Ibn 'Umar in support. But Ibn Wahb gives (*a*) a tradition with a formal *isnād* to the effect that 'the *sunna* corresponds to what they do in Medina; Abū Bakr, 'Umar, and 'Uthmān did it, and they still do it in Medina'; (*b*) a statement without *isnād* to the effect that Ibn 'Umar, Ibn Musaiyib, Qāsim, Sālim, 'Urwa, 'Umar b. 'Abdal'azīz, Yaḥyā b. Sa'īd, Rabī'a, and Abul-Aswad did the same (*Mud.* i. 115).

See *Muw.* ii. 51 (and *Tr. III*, 105), compared with *Mud.* ii. 41: a tradition (through Rabī'a) from 'Umar.

See *Tr. III*, 72, compared with *Mud.* xv. 141: traditions from 'Umar (through Zuhrī) and from 'Umar b. 'Abdal'azīz.

The same can be shown for numerous other traditions adduced by Ibn Wahb in *Mud.*

Between Mālik and Shāfi'ī:

See *Muw.* iv. 39, compared with *Tr. III*, 148 (p. 249): a tradition from 'Umar and 'Uthmān. The roundabout *isnāds* from Shāfi'ī to Mālik are spurious, and Shāfi'ī's reference to 'a reliable man' is worthless.[1]

Between Abū Yūsuf and Shaibānī:

See *Tr. IX*, 18, compared with *Siyar*, iii. 107 (together with *Mud.* iii. 13): a tradition from 'Umar.

Between Shaibānī and Ṭaḥāwī:

See *Muw. Shaib.* 193 ff. (together with *Tr. III*, 39), compared with Ṭaḥāwī, i. 374 ff: traditions from 'Umar.

See *Muw. Shaib.* 266, compared with Ṭaḥāwī, ii. 149: a tradition from Ibn 'Umar.

Traditions from Successors, containing their alleged opinions, underwent the same process of growth during the literary period, and there are many cases of spurious information concerning them in our earliest literary sources.[2] The 'living tradition' of the school of law in question enables us to recognize doctrines for which the authority of its ancient representatives was claimed illegitimately, by their irregular character, with due regard to the possibility of individual divergences and the development of doctrine within the school.

[1] See above, p. 38.

[2] See above, pp. 65 f., 69, 78, 85, 101, 114, 117, 130 f., 151, and below, pp. 157 f., 159, 160 f., 167 f., 193 f., 195, 197, 200, 207, 211, 222, 229 ff., 235 f., 244 ff.

CHAPTER 3

THE CONFLICT OF DOCTRINES AS REFLECTED IN THE GROWTH OF TRADITIONS

WE often find that traditions are formulated polemically with a view to rebutting a contrary doctrine or practice. Some of these counter-traditions, as we may call them, are obvious; others are cleverly disguised but can be detected by analysis and comparison with parallel traditions. Counter-traditions are of course later than the doctrine or practice which they are meant to rebut. In addition to the cases noted before,[1] the following simple examples will show how counter-traditions can be found and used for ascertaining the development of doctrine.

Muw. ii. 14: 'Ā'isha relates that the Prophet said the funeral prayer over Suhail b. Baiḍā' only *in* the mosque. The wording shows that this is directed against the Medinese practice of saying the funeral prayer outside the mosque (*Tr. III*, 33). The *isnād* of this tradition is incomplete (it was later completed in an unsatisfactory manner, see Zurqānī, ii. 14), and as the only person between Mālik and 'Ā'isha is Mālik's immediate authority Abul-Naḍr the client of 'Umar b. 'Ubaidallāh, it must have originated in the generation before Mālik. In view of this, the tradition through Mālik—Nāfi'—Ibn 'Umar, to the effect that the funeral prayer over 'Umar was said in the mosque (*Muw.* ii. 15), should likewise be taken not as a bona fide historical statement, but as a counter-statement against the Medinese practice, and the parallel version in *Muw. Shaib.* 165 has in fact the same polemical wording as the 'Ā'isha tradition. The reference to the funeral of 'Umar is older than the reference to the Prophet and served as a model for it.

Muw. ii. 89 and *Muw. Shaib.* 178 contain an imposing array of traditions of two types, both obviously polemical, directed against the doctrine ascribed to Abū Huraira, that he who starts a day in Ramadan in the state of major ritual impurity cannot make a valid fast. One type seeks to establish that starting the fast in this condition was not a personal privilege of the Prophet; the other claims the acquiescence of Abū Huraira in a doctrine opposite to that

[1] See above, p. 46, 48 ff., 57, 104, 129 ff., 141 f., 145; also below, pp. 225 f., 265.

ascribed to him; some versions in the classical collections (see Zurqānī, ii. 89 and *Comm. Muw. Shaib.* 178) make him change his opinion or affirm emphatically that not he but the Prophet says so. The ascetic refinement ascribed to Abū Huraira was unsuccessful and was repelled by traditions which used his own name.

Muw. ii. 103: the first tradition from Ibn 'Umar is a typical counter-tradition, alleging a change in his practice.

The Medinese regard the marriage concluded by a pilgrim as invalid, the Meccans and the Iraqians regard it as valid (*Muw. Shaib.* 208). Mālik (*Muw.* ii. 183) has heard that Ibn Musaiyib, Sālim, and Sulaimān b. Yasār, in answer to a question, said that the pilgrim must not marry nor give in marriage.[1] This doctrine was projected back to Ibn 'Umar and, with spurious circumstantial details, to 'Umar (*Muw.* and *Muw. Shaib.*, loc. cit.). The opposite doctrine was expressed in a tradition to the effect that the Prophet married Maimūna as a pilgrim (*Muw. Shaib.*). This tradition is related by Ibn 'Abbās who is the traditional authority of the Meccans.[2] This was countered, on the part of the Medinese, by a *mursal* tradition related by Sulaimān b. Yasār who was a freedman of Maimūna, to the effect that the Prophet married her in Medina, and therefore not as a pilgrim (*Muw.*),[3] and a more outspoken tradition related by Yazīd b. Aṣamm, a nephew of Maimūna, to the same effect (*Ikh.* 238). We see that even the details of this important event in the life of the Prophet are not based on authentic historical recollection, but are fictitious and intended to support legal doctrines. There is, finally, in favour of the Medinese doctrine an alleged discussion between Abān b. 'Uthmān and 'Umar b. 'Ubaidallāh with circumstantial detail (*Muw.*, *Muw. Shaib.* and *Ikh.*), where Abān invokes the ruling of the Prophet as related by his father 'Uthmān and in one version[4] calls his adversary who died, and presumably lived, in Damascus, 'a rude Iraqian'. We have here a Medinese refinement which can hardly be earlier than the second century.

Muw. iii. 106: Mālik—Dāwūd b. Ḥuṣain—Abū Sufyān the client of Ibn Abī Aḥmad—Abū Sa'īd Khudrī: the Prophet prohibited the *muzābana*, a kind of aleatory transaction. Ibid. 102: a tradition with the same *isnād*, only with Abū Huraira instead of Abū Sa'īd Khudrī: the Prophet allowed the sale of *'arāyā*, a transaction on

[1] This general reference to the old authorities shows the doctrine, but is not necessarily genuine information on any of them; see below, p. 159.

[2] See below, p. 249 f.

[3] It appears with more or less successfully completed *isnāds* in the classical collections; see Zurqānī, ii. 183.

[4] In Muslim, quoted in Zurqānī, loc. cit.

dates which falls under the definition of *muzābana*. Both traditions represent opposite doctrines and were only later harmonized artificially by Mālik and Shāfi'ī (*Ikh.* 322). One of the two had the *isnād* of the other grafted on it; this seems to have been the tradition against *muzābana*, because it occurs also as a *mursal* through Mālik—Zuhrī—Ibn Musaiyib from the Prophet (*Muw.* iii. 106).[1] This then is the oldest authority in the form of a tradition; it was countered by the tradition in favour of the sale of *'arāyā*, and finally acquired the *isnād* of the latter.

The Medinese (*Muw.* iv. 48) hold that a person who has committed murder by guile, is to be executed by the authorities on grounds of public policy, and base themselves on a tradition from 'Umar. The Iraqians (*Āthār Shaib.* 87 and *Tr. VIII*, 17) counter this conclusion from the 'Umar tradition which they recognize and follow in another respect,[2] by a different tradition according to which 'Umar intended to execute a murderer who had been pardoned by one of the next-of-kin, but desisted on hearing Ibn Mas'ūd's reasoned objection.

Muw. Shaib. 87: Ibrāhīm Nakha'ī doubts the decisive character of a tradition from the Prophet, transmitted by 'Alqama b. Wā'il from his father, as being perhaps an isolated occurrence and unknown to Ibn Mas'ūd and his Companions.[3] But two other persons of the name of 'Alqama, 'Alqama b. Qais, and 'Alqama b. Yazīd, belong to the Companions of Ibn Mas'ūd,[4] and 'Alqama b. Yazīd appears in the *isnād* of a tradition from Ibn Mas'ūd in favour of the usual Iraqian doctrine in *Mud.* i. 68. 'Alqama b. Wā'il's tradition from the Prophet is a counter-tradition against the Iraqian doctrine, and was in its turn countered by the reference to Ibrāhīm Nakha'ī; nothing of this is authentic.

Muw. Shaib. 190: Ibn 'Umar protests against untrue statements regarding the actions of the Prophet and gives the alleged correct information. The wording shows this to be a counter-tradition. It was harmonized with the opposite doctrine in a tradition with the *isnād* Mālik—Nāfi'—Ibn 'Umar—'Umar (*Muw. Shaib.*, loc. cit.).

The common ancient doctrine that prayer without recitation of the Koran is valid, is expressed in traditions from 'Alī (*Tr. II*, 3 (*k*)) and from 'Umar (*Tr. III*, 84; *Mud.* i. 65). Against this is directed the composite and polemically worded tradition from the Prophet in *Āthār A.Y.* 1, and the sweeping maxim 'no prayer [is valid] without recitation', which Shāfi'ī (*Tr. III*, 84) knows as a tradition

[1] This version acquired a full *isnād* later; see Ibn 'Abdalbarr in Zurqānī, iii. 106.

[2] See above, p. 111.

[3] Cf. above, p. 31.

[4] See below, p. 232.

from the Prophet. Ṭaḥāwī (i. 120) still takes the old doctrine seriously.

Tr. III, 56: Shāfiʿī quotes a tradition through Ibn Zubair from the Prophet; as he is at pains to establish that Ibn Zubair, who was only a child, could have heard and remembered the words of the Prophet, it is certain that Shāfiʿī did not yet know the parallel versions through ʿĀ'isha and through Umm Faḍl in Muslim (see Zurqānī, iii. 87). On the other hand, *Mud.* v. 87 gives a tradition through Umm Faḍl from the Prophet to the contrary. The version in Muslim turned this into its opposite.

Tr. IX, 1, 5: these purely negative statements on the Prophet are obviously counter-traditions.

Most of the traditions in which conflicting doctrines are ascribed to the same authority, are to be explained in this way.

A favourite device in the creation of counter-traditions consists of borrowing the name of the main authority for, or transmitter of, the opposite doctrine.[1]

Muw. ii. 152 and *Ikh.* 290: the first stage is represented by an opinion ascribed to Sālim; in the second stage, Sālim appears in the *isnād* of a version of a tradition from ʿUmar, who blames Muʿāwiya for his failure to conform; both traditions represent a pious reaction against the practice, current in Umaiyad times, of using perfume before entering the state of ritual consecration for the pilgrimage. But Sālim appears also as the transmitter of a tradition from the Prophet favouring the less strict practice, and he is made to add: 'The *sunna* of the Prophet has the better claim to be followed.'[2] But this reference to the *sunna* of the Prophet made no impression on the Medinese doctrine, and only Shāfiʿī felt obliged to follow it.

Tr. II, 18 (*r*): Shāfiʿī refers to the doctrine of Ibn ʿAbbās; during his lifetime, there came into circulation a tradition from the Prophet transmitted by Ibn ʿAbbās, so that he changed his doctrine as stated by Rabīʿ.

Ikh. 259, 264: Jābir, who is the main authority for the exclusion of a neighbour from the right of pre-emption, is made to relate a tradition from the Prophet which gives a neighbour this right; Shāfiʿī mentions that the specialists on traditions suspect it because of Jābir's doctrine to the contrary.

The names of the Iraqian authorities Shuraiḥ and Shaʿbī were

[1] Cf. Nöldeke, in *Z.D.M.G.* lii. 31.

[2] This can be dated in the generation preceding Mālik, because ʿAmr b. Dīnār is the common transmitter of this and of another tradition to the same effect in *Ikh.* 288.

borrowed by the traditionists in their polemics against reasoning in law.[1]

The circumstantial details in many traditions, which are meant to provide an authentic touch, often reveal their fictitious character and must not be taken as an indication of authenticity.

An Iraqian tradition from ʿUmar in *Muw.* ii. 296 and *Tr. III*, 88, contains a Persian expression and is disconcertingly vague in its accumulation of pretended details. A Medinese tradition from the Prophet in *Muw.* iv. 13 and *Ris.* 21 is transmitted by Zuhrī; Zuhrī expresses his uncertainty on a minor point of wording, and adds the explanation of a word; whilst the pretended scrupulousness regarding a minor point is meant to show that the transmission was correct, the explanation indicates that the text was novel in the generation preceding Mālik.[2]

The circumstantial details of one tradition are often repeated in its successors; traditions are modelled on one another, whether they be counter-traditions or not.

The same story, in different settings, is ascribed to Ibn Masʿūd (*Āthār A.Y.* 644; *Āthār Shaib.* 76) and to ʿUmar (*Muw.* iii. 74); both versions represent a later development of doctrine, common to the Iraqians and the Medinese.

Another story is related with a Medinese *isnād* from ʿAbdalraḥmān b. ʿAuf (*Muw.* iii. 99; *Muw. Shaib.* 343), and with an Iraqian *isnād* from ʿAlī (*Āthār Shaib.* 69); closely modelled on the Iraqian version and with the mention of Basra in the text, but with a Medinese *isnād*, is a third version which relates the same from ʿUthmān (*Muw.* and *Muw. Shaib.*, loc. cit.).[3]

In the course of polemical discussion, doctrines are frequently projected back to higher authorities: traditions from Successors become traditions from Companions, and traditions from Companions become traditions from the Prophet.[4] Whenever we find, as frequently happens, alleged opinions of Successors, alleged decisions of the Companions, and alleged traditions from the Prophet side by side, we must, as a rule and until

[1] See above, p. 130 f. See further Nau, in *J. A.* ccxi. 313 and n. 2.

[2] See also above, p. 153.

[3] See also above, pp. 53, n. 3, 55, n. 2 ; below, pp. 157 f., 164, 171, 183; and Lammens, *Fāṭima*, 136.

[4] This has already been pointed out by Goldziher in *Muh. St.* ii. 157 and *Z.D.M.G.* l. 483 f.

the contrary is proved, consider the opinions of the Successors as the starting-point, and the traditions from the Companions and from the Prophet as secondary developments, intended to provide a higher authority for the doctrine in question. When the opinion of a Successor coincides with a tradition, it would be unwarrantable to conclude, in the absence of an explicit reference or some other positive indication, that he knew and followed it.[1] In other words: we must follow the ancient schools of law in that historically legitimate procedure for which the systematic innovator Shāfi'ī blames them, and 'take our knowledge from the lowest source'.[2] We have met numerous examples of this backward projection of doctrines in the preceding and in the present chapter, and shall meet others in what follows.

A frequent device for enlisting some higher authority in favour of a doctrine is to make him confirm it after it has been formulated by someone of lower rank. Here are a few examples. Zaid b. Thābit orders Ḥajjāj b. 'Amr b. Ghāziya to give a decision, and confirms it (*Muw. Shaib.* 248). 'Alī puts a problem to Shuraiḥ and approves of his decision, using the Greek word *καλόν* (*Tr. II*, 10 (*o*)). The Prophet approves of Mu'ādh's proposed principles of legal reasoning (above, p. 105 f.). An independent witness confirms that the doctrine of Ibn Mas'ūd coincides with the decision of the Prophet (above, p. 29). Ibn Mas'ūd confirms as correct a decision given by others (*Muw.* iii. 35).[3]

Traditions are improved in various ways in order to obviate possible objections, as will be seen from the following examples.

Mālik in *Muw.* ii. 111, and Shāfi'ī in *Tr. III*, 129, know only a tradition which relates how 'Umar acted when he broke the fast inadvertently. Ibn Wahb in *Mud.* i. 193 gives the tradition in a modified form which avoids implicating 'Umar himself. Bukhārī (quoted in Zurqānī, ii. 111) gives a tradition, with an *isnād* through Hishām b. 'Urwa and with the same circumstantial details, to the effect that this mistake happened frequently in the time of the Prophet; but two different opinions are related from Hishām. The problem of inadvertent breaking of the fast was discussed in the generation preceding Mālik, Hishām was quoted as an authority for two differing opinions, and one of these found expression in three successive forms of traditions.

[1] I must diverge here from the assumption of Bergsträsser in *Islam*, xiv. 79.
[2] See above, p. 69. See also p. 66, and Part I, Chapters 4 and 7 in general.
[3] See also above, p. 96 f., and below, pp. 225 f., 263.

The main tradition in *Tr. III*, 5, represents ʿUrwa b. Zubair as being converted to a certain doctrine by a tradition from the Prophet which he came to know (this is obviously already a counter-tradition). *Muw.* i. 79 has a statement, through ʿUrwa's son Hishām, on ʿUrwa's doctrine which he had heard from his father Zubair, to the same effect as ʿUrwa's revised opinion in the first tradition. This obviates the claim of a change in ʿUrwa's doctrine. The first tradition occurs in a more elaborate form, designed to give it greater authority, in Ṭaḥāwī, i. 43.

The essential features of the common ancient doctrine on slaves captured by the enemy and recaptured by the Muslims, a doctrine for which Auzāʿī and Abū Ḥanīfa did not yet know a tradition, are expressed in an Iraqian tradition from the Prophet which appears for the first time in Abū Yūsuf in *Tr. IX*, 18. The ruling is given in general terms which do not well agree with the circumstantial story which has been added in order to provide an authentic touch. This form is improved and a further personal touch is added in the versions in Dāraquṭnī and Baihaqī respectively (see *Comm. ed. Cairo*, loc. cit.). Ḥasan b. ʿUmāra, in the generation preceding Abū Yūsuf, is the lowest common link in the three *isnāds*, and he or a person using his name must be responsible for the creation of this tradition and the fictitious higher part of the *isnād*. But Ibn ʿUmāra was impugned, and the tradition is therefore related alternatively, on hearsay authority, through ʿAbdalmalik b. Maisara who is, however, also considered weak.

The same doctrine is expressed in two Medinese traditions with the first-class *isnād* Abū Yūsuf—ʿUbaidallāh b. ʿUmar—Nāfiʿ—Ibn ʿUmar, both quoted for the first time by Abū Yūsuf in *Tr. IX*, 18, and in *Kharāj*, 123,[1] respectively. The first gives it as a general ruling of Ibn ʿUmar, the second purports to describe the loss by Ibn ʿUmar of a slave and a horse to the enemy, and the subsequent restitution of the one during the lifetime of the Prophet and of the other after his death, by Khālid b. Walīd who had recaptured them. In its older forms, which are preserved, without an *isnād*, in *Muw.* ii. 299 and in *Siyar*, iii. 107, this anecdote lacks the indirect reference to the Prophet[2] or is even explicitly dated to the time of ʿUmar.[3] None of this is genuine, and the fact that Mālik, who relates many traditions from Nāfiʿ—Ibn ʿUmar, does not yet know it as a formal tradition from Ibn ʿUmar, makes it likely that the *isnād* with Nāfiʿ

[1] Read *ʿUbaidallāh* and *Ibn ʿUmar* in the printed text of *Kharāj*.

[2] The Prophet is made directly responsible for the ruling in a later version in Bukhārī (see *Comm. ed. Cairo*, loc. cit.).

[3] Another version, in Bukhārī (see ibid., loc. cit.), dates it to the time of Abū Bakr.

in it was created by ʿUbaidallāh b. ʿUmar or a person using his name.

The common doctrine on property lost to the enemy and recaptured from them, of which the problem already discussed is a special case, was put under the aegis of Ibrāhīm Nakhaʿī and Mujāhid (*Kharāj*, 123). Shaibānī (*Siyar*, iii. 107) relates three divergent opinions which are ascribed to Zaid b. Thābit and Ibn Musaiyib, to Ḥasan Baṣrī and Zuhrī, and to Abū Bakr[1] respectively. Shaibānī's contemporary Ibn Wahb (*Mud.* iii. 13), however, quotes the alleged opinions of Zaid b. Thābit, Sulaimān b. Yasār, Abū Bakr, ʿUbāda b. Ṣāmit, Yaḥyā b. Saʿīd and Rabīʿa in favour of the common doctrine. The contradictions show that the names of Companions, Successors, and other ancient authorities were freely adduced in support of existing doctrines, and we cannot, until the contrary is proved, regard references to Successors as any more authentic than traditions from Companions and from the Prophet.[2]

Traditions are also adapted to the development of doctrine, as the following examples will show.

Tr. II, 18 (*q*): there are two versions of a tradition from ʿAlī; the second, by an addition, has been made to conform with the later general doctrine.

A tradition which appears in its full form in *Tr. III*, 126 and in *Muw. Shaib.* 87, is progressively shortened in *Muw.* i. 142 and in *Mud.* i. 68, so as to bring it into line with the Medinese doctrine.

Shaibānī, in *Tr. VIII*, 16, relates a tradition from Ibn ʿAbbās who, when consulted on the case of a man who had killed his brother accidentally, decided: 'The killer inherits nothing.' Another tradition, in *Muw.* iv. 44, refers to the case of a man who was killed by his father accidentally; ʿUmar handed the whole of the weregeld over to the brother of the victim and said: 'The Prophet said: "The killer receives nothing."'[3] The import of the legal maxim is mitigated here, so as to make it compatible with that one of the two Medinese opinions which Mālik follows, to the effect that the person who has killed the *de cuius* accidentally, inherits other property but not weregeld.

The following examples will show how a critical analysis of traditions can elucidate the history of legal doctrines.

Khiyār al-Majlis is the right of option given to the parties to a sale

[1] Zurqānī, ii. 299, adds ʿAlī and ʿAmr b. Dīnār.

[2] See also above, p. 71, n. 1–3.

[3] On the later development of this tradition see below, p. 166.

as long as they have not separated. This right is not recognized by the ancient schools of law, as is shown by *Muw. Shaib.* 338 for the Iraqians, by *Muw.* iii. 136 for the Medinese. But a tradition from the Meccan scholar 'Aṭā' in *Umm*, iii. 3 contains a detailed statement in its favour; it shows as yet no trace of the legal maxim embodied in the tradition from the Prophet (see what follows), and must therefore be considered genuine. On the other hand, the ascription of a similar doctrine to Shuraiḥ (ibid.) is obviously spurious and an effort to project it back on to an ancient Iraqian authority.

The *khiyār al-majlis* is enjoined in a tradition expressing a legal maxim: Mālik—Nāfi'—Ibn 'Umar—the Prophet said: 'The two parties to a sale have the right of option as long as they have not separated' (*Muw.* and *Muw. Shaib.*, loc. cit.; *Tr. III*, 47). This is certainly later than 'Aṭā' and must have been put into circulation by Nāfi' or someone who used his name.[1] Mālik states that there is no such practice, Rabī' confirms this for the Egyptian Medinese, and Shaibānī, who pays lip-service to the tradition, explains it away by a far-fetched interpretation.[2] Shāfi'ī's discussion shows that the Medinese used the same explanation, and Shaibānī ascribes it to Ibrāhīm Nakha'ī. This cannot be an authentic opinion of Ibrāhīm, but is the reaction of the Iraqians to the relatively late tradition, projected back on to their ancient authority. Both arguments, the reference to the different practice and the far-fetched interpretation, were countered by an addition which purports to describe Ibn 'Umar's own practice, added to the text of the tradition from the Prophet, with the *isnād* Ibn 'Uyaina—Ibn Juraij—Nāfi'—Ibn 'Umar. This presupposes the tradition from the Prophet and is therefore later. It does not appear in Mālik but is quoted by Shāfi'ī (*Umm*, iii. 3), and seems to have been put into circulation by Ibn 'Uyaina. On the other hand, the tradition from the Prophet was made agreeable to the common Iraqian and Medinese opinion by an addition which appears in the classical collections (see Zurqānī, iii. 138).

Shāfi'ī (*Umm*, iii. 3) is also the first to quote two further traditions from the Prophet in favour of the *khiyār al-majlis*; these are later elaborations with exhortations and circumstantial detail added. Their *isnāds* had been recently composed, and Shāfi'ī's immediate authority is in both cases anonymous. Shāfi'ī claims that the majority of the Hijazis and of the traditionists in all countries are in favour of the *khiyār al-majlis*. He arrives at his statement on the

[1] See also below, p. 167.

[2] Zurqānī, iii. 138 ascribes the same explanation to Abū Ḥanīfa, on the authority of Shaibānī.

Hijazis by judging from the *isnāds* of the traditions, and more of this kind of spurious information on the ancient Medinese authorities is collected by Ibn ʿAbdalbarr.[1] But Shāfiʿī's reference to the traditionists is correct.

We conclude that the idea of the *khiyār al-majlis* started from Mecca, was taken up by the traditionists and finally acknowledged, on the strength of the traditions from the Prophet, by Shāfiʿī. It did not exist in the common doctrine of the Iraqians and Medinese, and may well have been based on some local custom in Mecca.

Walā', the relationship of patron and client, is created by law between the manumitter and his manumitted slave; it is important for purposes of inheritance, *ius talionis*, weregeld and giving in marriage of women. A similar relationship is presumed between persons who have no Muslim next of kin and the state as representing the community of Muslims. History shows that conversion to Islam of non-Arabs during the Umaiyad period necessitated the creation of *walā'* between the convert and a Muslim member of one of the Arab tribes, usually the individual before whom he adopted Islam. This procedure is called *muwālāt*, and it was particularly frequent in the recently conquered countries. The Iraqians recognize the legal effects of *muwālāt*,[2] and Abū Ḥanīfa quotes traditions in which this doctrine is projected back to the Prophet, ʿUmar and Ibn Masʿūd. But in the time of Abū Ḥanīfa, *muwālāt* had already fallen into desuetude, and his contemporary Ibn Abī Lailā, who was a judge, did not recognize its legal effects (*Tr. I*, 128).[3] Neither did the Medinese (*Mud.* viii. 73), and this doctrine was projected back on the Iraqian side to Shaʿbī, and on the Medinese to ʿUmar and ʿUmar b. ʿAbdalʿazīz, whose name is intended to lend it an Umaiyad flavour. The Medinese have in fact preserved no trace of the state of affairs under the Umaiyads. Shāfiʿī did not regard the tradition from the Prophet as reliable (*Umm*, vi. 186 f.), and therefore rejected *muwālāt*.

With the foundling, the problem arises whether his *walā'* belongs to the person who finds him, or to the state. Mālik states the consensus of the Medinese in favour of the second doctrine (*Tr. III*, 71). This has the corollary that the expenses of his maintenance are a charge on the treasury, and this is projected back to ʿUmar b. ʿAbdalʿazīz (*Mud.* vii. 76). There exists, however, a tradition (*Muw.* iii. 196) according to which the Caliph ʿUmar assigned the *walā'* of a foundling to the person who had picked him up but, illogically,

[1] See above, p. 64 f.

[2] See *Tr. I*, 128 (for Abū Ḥanīfa); *Āthār A. Y.* 772; Shaibānī, *Makhārij*, xv. 27 ff.

[3] Shaibānī (*Makhārij* xv. 30) does not consider it obligatory.

undertook the expenses of maintenance himself (that is to say, as a charge on the treasury). This tradition is later than the two doctrines which it combines; its *isnāds* converge in Mālik's immediate authority Zuhrī.[1]

There are two Iraqian opinions as to whether the *ḥadd* punishment ought to be applied in the mosque or not (*Tr. I*, 255 (*b*)). Abū Ḥanīfa answers in the negative, and refers to a tradition from the Prophet; it occurs in Ibn Māja with an *isnād* through Ibn ʿAbbās (see *Comm. ed. Cairo*). Abū Yūsuf (*Kharāj*, 109) has a tradition from ʿAlī to the same effect, and a tradition in which the Successor Mujāhid declares: 'People used to disapprove of applying the *ḥadd* punishments in the mosque.' The same doctrine is ascribed to Ibrāhīm Nakhaʿī (*Āthār Shaib.*, quoted in *Comm. ed. Cairo*). The opposite opinion was held and applied in practice by Abū Ḥanīfa's contemporary, the judge Ibn Abī Lailā. This was the old-established practice, in keeping with the original function of the mosque as the place for the assembly of the community and the transaction of its official business, and the other opinion was the result of a religious objection, based on the consideration of the dignity of the mosque. The tradition from Mujāhid represents it still as anonymous; it was projected back to Ibrāhīm as the eponym of the Iraqians, and provided with the authority of ʿAlī and the Prophet. Mujāhid is the main transmitter from Ibn ʿAbbās, and this explains the appearance of Ibn ʿAbbās in the *isnād*.

[1] In a later version, quoted by Zurqānī, iii. 196, ʿUmar uses a proverb from the story of Zenobia.

CHAPTER 4

THE EVIDENCE OF *ISNĀDS*

WE have often had occasion, particularly in the preceding chapter, to use indications contained in the *isnāds* for the dating of traditions. In the present chapter we shall consider some of these indications in detail. Although the *isnāds* constitute the most arbitrary part of the traditions, the tendencies underlying their creation and development, once recognized, enable us to use them for the dating of traditions in many cases. It is common knowledge that the *isnād* started from rudimentary beginnings[1] and reached perfection in the classical collections of traditions in the second half of the third century A.H. This, together with our previous results concerning the growth of traditions, makes it impossible for us to share the confidence of the Muhammadan scholars in what they consider first-class *isnāds*. Their whole technical criticism of traditions, which is mainly based on the criticism of *isnāds*,[2] is irrelevant for the purpose of historical analysis. In particular, we shall see in the following chapter that some of those *isnāds* which the Muhammadan scholars esteem most highly are the result of widespread fabrications in the generation preceding Mālik[3].

The *isnāds* were often put together very carelessly.[4] Any typical representative of the group whose doctrine was to be projected back on to an ancient authority, could be chosen at random and put into the *isnād*. We find therefore a number of alternative names in otherwise identical *isnāds*, where other considerations exclude the possibility of the transmission of a genuine old doctrine by several persons. Such alternatives are particularly frequent in the generation preceding Mālik, for instance Nāfiʿ and Sālim (*passim*), Nāfiʿ and ʿAbdallāh b. Dīnār (*Muw.* iv. 204 and *Ikh.* 149 f.), Nāfiʿ and Zuhrī (*Muw.*

[1] On the time of its origin, see above, p. 36 f.

[2] See above, p. 36 ff.

[3] Caetani has studied the *isnāds*, with particular reference to historical traditions (*Annali*, i, Introduction, §§ 9–28). In so far as his conclusions apply to legal traditions, I find myself in substantial agreement with his analysis, except in one respect for which see below, p. 169.

[4] See significant examples above, p. 53 f. and below, p. 263.

iii. 71 and *Muw. Shaib.* 258), Yaḥyā b. Sa'īd and 'Abdallāh b. 'Umar 'Umarī (*Muw.* ii. 197 and *Muw. Shaib.* 207), Yaḥyā b. Sa'īd and Rabī'a (*Muw.* ii. 362 and *Tr. III*, 42). An example from the generation before that is the alternation between Muḥammad b. 'Amr b. Ḥazm and Abū Bakr [b. 'Amr] b. Ḥazm (*Muw.* i. 259 and *Tr. III*, 101). The following are further examples of the general uncertainty and arbitrary character of *isnāds*.

In *Muw.* iv. 49 we find: Mālik—Muḥammad b. 'Abdalraḥmān b. Sa'd b. Zurāra—Ḥafṣa killed a *mudabbar* slave of hers who had bewitched her. But in *Muw. Shaib.* 359 and in *Tr. III*, 93 we find: Mālik—Abul-Rijāl Muḥammad b. 'Abdalraḥmān [b. Jāriya]—his mother 'Amra—'Ā'isha sold a *mudabbar* slave of hers who had bewitched her. One of these versions is modelled on the other, and neither can be regarded as historical. It is obvious that the story was put into circulation in the generation preceding Mālik on the fictitious authority of one Muḥammad b. 'Abdalraḥmān, and this name was completed in such a way as to refer to two different persons in the two versions; it is at least doubtful whether Mālik met either of them.[1]

A tradition in *Muw.* i. 371 reads: Mālik—Hishām—his father 'Urwa—'Umar prostrated himself [on a certain occasion which is described], and the people prostrated themselves together with him. As 'Urwa was born in the caliphate of 'Uthmān, this *isnād* is 'interrupted' (*munqaṭi'*). Bukhārī has a different, uninterrupted *isnād*. But old copies of the *Muwaṭṭa'* have 'and we did it together with him', which is impossible in the mouth of 'Urwa. This of course is the original text of the *Muwaṭṭa'*. The same words occur in the text of a different tradition from the Prophet on the authority of Abū Huraira. This shows that the formulation of the text of the tradition came first, the *isnād* was added arbitrarily and improved and extended backwards later.

The Iraqian doctrine which extends the right of pre-emption to a neighbour is expressed in two legal maxims: 'the neighbour is entitled to the benefit of his proximity' (*al-jār aḥaqq bi-ṣaqbih*), and 'the neighbour of the house is entitled to the house of the neighbour' (*jār al-dār aḥaqq bi-dār al-jār*). The first has the *isnād* 'Amr b. Sharīd—Abū Rāfi'—Prophet (*Tr. I*, 49; *Ikh.* 260), the second the *isnād* Qatāda—Ḥasan Baṣrī—Samura—Prophet (Ibn Ḥanbal, v. 8 and often; Ibn Qutaiba, 287). But the second was also provided with

[1] Zurqānī, ii. 268, points out that the name and identity of 'Abdalmalik b. Qurair, another immediate authority of Mālik, are uncertain. See further above, p. 154, on the two different 'Alqamas.

an alternative form of the *isnād* of the first: 'Amr b. Shu'aib—'Amr b. Sharīd—Sharīd—Prophet (*Tr. I*, 50; Ibn Ḥanbal, iv. 389, 390), and with the mixed *isnād* Qatāda—'Amr b. Shu'aib—Sharīd—Prophet (Ibn Ḥanbal, iv. 388).[1]

A significant example of the arbitrary creation of *isnāds* occurs in *Tr. II*, 6 (*a*) and (*b*). Here we have first three versions of an Iraqian tradition that 'Alī said, or gave orders to say, prayers over the tomb of Sahl b. Ḥunaif. The prayer over the tomb was an Iraqian invention, but did not become prevalent in Iraq (*Muw. Shaib.* 166 and Shāfi'ī, loc. cit.). Nor did it become prevalent in Medina, although a tradition from the Prophet in its favour found currency there (*Muw.* ii. 11 and Zurqānī, ad loc.; *Muw. Shaib.*, loc. cit.). The *isnād* of this tradition uses the son of Sahl b. Ḥunaif: Mālik—Zuhrī—Abū Umāma b. Sahl—the Prophet said prayers over the tomb of a poor woman. This can be dated with certainty in the generation preceding Mālik. It is *mursal*; the *isnād* was later completed by inserting Sahl himself and by creating new *isnāds* through other Companions (*Comm. Muw. Shaib.*, loc. cit.).

The gradual improvement of *isnāds* goes parallel with, and is partly indistinguishable from, the material growth of traditions which we have discussed in the preceding chapters; the backward growth of *isnāds* in particular is identical with the projection of doctrines back to higher authorities.[2] Generally speaking, we can say that the most perfect and complete *isnāds* are the latest. As is the case with the growth of traditions, the improvement of *isnāds* extends well into the literary period, as the following examples will show. The Muhammadan scholars chose to take notice of one particular kind of interference with *isnāds*, the *tadlīs*;[3] we saw that Shāfi'ī disapproved of it, but minimized its occurrence.

Āthār A.Y.: the editor has collected in the Commentary the parallels in the classical and other collections; a comparison shows the extent of the progressive completion, improvement, and backward growth of *isnāds*.

Muw. iii. 172 and *Muw. Shaib.* 364: Mālik—Zuhrī—Ibn Musaiyib and Abū Salama—Prophet; this tradition is *mursal*. Shāfi'ī (*Ikh.* 258 f.) has the same, but knows it also with the full *isnāds* Zuhrī—Abū Salama—Jābir—Prophet, and Ibn Juraij—Abul-Zubair—Jābir—Prophet. According to *Comm. Muw. Shaib.*, Ibn Mājashūn,

[1] For other examples of borrowed *isnāds* see above, pp. 139, n. 6, 154.
[2] See above, p. 156 f.
[3] See above, p. 37.

Abū ʿĀṣim Nabīl, and Ibn Wahb give it with a full *isnād* through Abū Huraira instead of Jābir, and so it occurs in Ṭaḥāwī, ii. 265: Abū ʿĀṣim Nabīl—Mālik—Zuhrī—Ibn Musaiyib and Abū Salama —Abū Huraira—Prophet. But Ṭaḥāwī remarks that the most reliable of Mālik's companions, including Qaʿnabī and Ibn Wahb, relate it with an imperfect *isnād*, that is, *mursal*.

Muw. iv. 35 and *Muw. Shaib.* 239: Mālik—Zuhrī—Ibn Musaiyib —Prophet; this tradition is *mursal*. Shāfiʿī (*Tr. VIII*, 14) has it with a complete *isnād* through 'a reliable man' (identified by Rabīʿ as Yaḥyā b. Ḥassān)—Laith b. Saʿd—Zuhrī—Ibn Musaiyib—Abū Huraira—Prophet. The name of Abū Huraira was inserted in the period between Mālik and Shāfiʿī and taken from the *isnād* of a parallel version with a sensibly different text (*Muw.* and *Muw. Shaib.*, loc. cit.). In the same context, Shāfiʿī records the doubts of some Medinese regarding *isnāds* in general.

Muw. iv. 44: Yaḥyā b. Saʿīd—ʿAmr b. Shuʿaib—ʿUmar gives a decision, referring to an inconclusive statement of the Prophet.[1] Ibn Māja (*Abwāb al-farāʾiḍ, Bāb mīrāth al-qātil*), however, has a tradition with the *isnād* Muḥammad b. Saʿīd or ʿUmar b. Saʿīd—ʿAmr b. Shuʿaib—his father [Shuʿaib b. Muḥammad]—his grandfather ʿAbdallāh b. ʿAmr—Prophet: a wordy, explicit statement, part of a composite speech.

Ris. 45: Shāfiʿī does not remember having heard a certain tradition with a reliable *isnād* and doubts whether it is well authenticated. But it exists in Bukhārī and Muslim with a first-class *isnād* (see *ed. Shākir*, p. 315).

Ibid. 59: Mālik—Rabīʿa—several scholars—ʿUmar; Shāfiʿī states that this *isnād* is 'interrupted'. But it has become complete in Ibn Ḥanbal, Bukhārī, and Muslim (see Zurqānī, iv. 200 and *ed. Shākir*, p. 435).

Ibid. 64: Shāfiʿī states that a tradition is *mursal* and generally not acted upon, implying that it is not confirmed by any version with a complete *isnād*. But it appears with a different, full *isnād* in Ibn Ḥanbal (see *ed. Shākir*, p. 467) and Ibn Māja (see Graf, *Wortelen*, 63, n. 1).[2]

Parallel with the improvement and backward growth of *isnāds* goes their spread, that is the creation of additional authorities or transmitters for the same doctrine or tradition. The spread of *isnāds* was intended to meet the objection which used to be made to 'isolated' traditions.[3]

[1] See above, p. 159.
[2] See also above, pp. 141, 147, 153, n. 3, 158; below, p. 265.
[3] See above, pp. 50 ff.

Mālik (*Muw.* ii. 54) refers, without *isnād*, to the instructions on the *zakāt* tax which ʿUmar gave in writing. The same instructions are projected back to the Prophet, with *isnāds* through ʿUmar and through other Companions, in Ibn Ḥanbal and the classical collections (see Zurqānī, ad loc.). The two oldest examples are two traditions in *Tr. II*, 9 (*b*): the one Medinese, through Ibn ʿUmar from the Prophet, with the added remark that ʿUmar instructed his agents to the same effect; the other Iraqian, quoted above, p. 73. An earlier form of traditional authority for the identical Iraqian doctrine is represented by a tradition through Ibrāhīm Nakhaʿī from Ibn Masʿūd (*Āthār A.Y.* 423; *Āthār Shaib.* 49); the tradition from ʿAlī in *Tr. II*, 9 (*b*) represents an unsuccessful primitive effort to systematize.[1]

Mālik's tradition on the *khiyār al-majlis*,[2] with the *isnād* Nāfiʿ—Ibn ʿUmar—Prophet, must be later than the doctrine to the contrary which is common to the Medinese and the Iraqians (*Muw.* iii. 136; *Muw. Shaib.* 338). The classical collections (quoted in Zurqānī, iii. 136) have additional *isnāds*, some of which eliminate Nāfiʿ and branch off directly from Ibn ʿUmar, or even eliminate Ibn ʿUmar and go back to the Prophet through another Companion. These are certainly later developments.

The creation of new *isnāds* and additional authorities in Shāfiʿī's time can be observed in the traditions in favour of the important doctrine that the evidence of one witness and confirmed by the oath of the plaintiff constitutes legal proof. The judgments of Tauba b. Nimr, judge of Egypt A.H. 115–20 (Kindī, 344 ff.), show the gradual growth of this doctrine out of the practice; no traditions are adduced in this connexion. In the middle of the second century, we find that the Medinese and the Meccans hold, and the Iraqians and the Syrians reject it.[3]

The Iraqians claimed correctly that the doctrine was unknown to Zuhrī, ʿAṭāʾ, the old Medinese authorities, and the first Caliphs (*Tr. III*, 15; *Umm*, vii. 10); but this does not of course imply the existence of positive information on their attitude to a problem which did not yet exist in their time. The Medinese and Meccans projected their doctrine back to the old authorities Abū Salama b. ʿAbdalraḥmān and Sulaimān b. Yasār (*Muw.* iii. 182), to ʿAṭāʾ (*Umm*, vii. 8),[4] and to the Umaiyad Caliphs ʿUmar b. ʿAbdalʿazīz

[1] This does not mean, of course, that the tariff of the *zakāt* tax was not in fact fixed by ʿUmar, but this cannot be concluded from the traditions.

[2] See above, p. 160.

[3] For the Syrians, see Ibn ʿAbdalbarr, quoted in Zurqānī, iii. 181.

[4] But Shāfiʿī's quotation from ʿAṭāʾ in *Tr. I*, 124, which shows a different tendency, is presumably authentic.

(*Muw.*, loc. cit.),[1] ʿAbdalmalik and Muʿāwiya (*Muw. Shaib.* 361). At the next stage they ascribed their own doctrine fictitiously to the old Iraqian authorities Shuraiḥ and Shaʿbī,[2] to the Kufian ʿAbdallāh b. ʿUtba b. Masʿūd, and to the judge of Basra Zurāra b. Aufā (*Umm*, vi. 274 f.). Several of these references to old authorities describe the Medinese doctrine as *sunna*, thereby claiming that it represents the 'living tradition'.

The first tradition from the Prophet in favour of the Medinese doctrine, and the only one known to Mālik, is *mursal* (*Muw.* iii. 181). As Mālik undertakes to justify this doctrine by an elaborate argument, he would certainly have mentioned other traditions from the Prophet, had he known them. In Mecca, the tradition was provided with an uninterrupted *isnād* of Meccan authorities (*Ikh.* 345): this was the only additional version which Shāfiʿī knew when he wrote *Tr. III*, 15. When he wrote *Ikh.* 346, he knew a further version with a Medinese *isnād*, relating it from the Prophet on the authority of two Companions. In *Umm*, vi. 273 ff. he quotes the following additional versions.

Ibrāhīm b. Muḥammad—ʿAmr b. Abī ʿAmr the freedman of Muṭṭalib[3]—Ibn Musaiyib—Prophet. This is *mursal*, and introduces the old Medinese authority Ibn Musaiyib into the *isnād*.

Darāwardī—Rabīʿa—Saʿīd b. ʿAmr b. Shuraḥbīl b. Saʿīd b. Saʿd b. ʿUbāda—his father—his grandfather said he found it stated in the papers of Saʿd b. ʿUbāda that the Prophet gave the decision in question.

Darāwardī—Rabīʿa—Suhail b. Abī Ṣāliḥ—his father—Abū Huraira—Prophet. Darāwardī mentions that when he asked Suhail about this tradition, Suhail did not remember it but had had it repeated back to him by Rabīʿa and consequently related it 'from Rabīʿa from myself'. We must conclude that Darāwardī who was a contemporary of Mālik, or a person using his name, put this story with the two *isnāds* into circulation; it acquired an additional transmitter in the following slightly differing version:

ʿAbdalʿazīz b. Muṭṭalib—Saʿīd b. ʿAmr—his father said he found it stated in the papers of Saʿd b. ʿUbāda that the Prophet instructed ʿAmr b. Ḥazm to judge accordingly.

Shāfiʿī has also mixed and derived forms; the *isnāds* of some of these are influenced by the *isnād* of the general tradition on evidence.[4]

The old Medinese authority Rabīʿa who appears in the *isnāds* of Darāwardī's story, was also directly implicated and was reported to

[1] This is polemically turned against the Iraqians.

[2] Shaʿbī is even made to refer to the Medinese.

[3] See on him below, p. 172.

[4] See below, p. 187.

have said: 'We impose the oath when there is only one witness; we found this doctrine in the papers of Sa'd' (*Tr. III*, 15). This information on Rabī'a is clearly not authentic.

In the classical collections the *isnād* of the tradition in favour of the Medinese doctrine has become complete and 'widely spread';[1] but Ibn Ḥanbal at one time still cast doubt on the tradition.[2]

We sometimes find that *isnāds* which consist of a rigid and formal chain of representatives of a school of law and project its doctrine back to some ancient authority, are duplicated by others which go back to the same authority by another way. This was intended as a confirmation of the doctrine of the school by seemingly independent evidence.

A Medinese example is: Ibn 'Uyaina—'Abdalraḥmān b. Qāsim —his father Qāsim b. Muḥammad—the opinions of 'Uthmān, Zaid b. Thābit and Marwān b. Ḥakam (*Tr. III*, 89 (*a*)). The interruption in the *isnād* above Qāsim was remedied, and 'Abdalraḥmān b. Qāsim eliminated, in: Mālik—Yaḥyā b. Sa'īd—Qāsim b. Muḥammad—Furāfiṣa b. 'Umair—'Uthmān (*Muw.* ii. 151). Finally there appeared: Mālik—'Abdallāh b. Abī Bakr—'Abdallāh b. 'Āmir b. Rabī'a—'Uthmān, with a composite anecdote (*Muw.* ii. 192).[3]

An Iraqian example is: Abū Ḥanīfa—Ḥammād—Ibrāhīm Nakha'ī—'Alqama b. Qais and Aswad b. Yazīd—Ibn Mas'ūd (*Āthār Shaib.* 22). This became: Muḥammad b. 'Ubaid—Muḥammad b. Isḥāq—'Abdalraḥmān b. Aswad—his father Aswad b. Yazīd—Ibn Mas'ūd with Aswad and 'Alqama (*Tr. II*, 19 (*g*)).[4]

This artificial growth of *isnāds*, together with the material growth of traditions in the pre-literary and in the literary period, shows that it would be idle to try to reconstruct the tendencies and characteristics of the doctrine of any particular Companion from the traditions in which he appears as the final authority or of which he is the first transmitter.[5] Wherever the sources available enable us to judge, we find that the legal traditions from Companions are as little authentic as those from the Prophet. We can indeed recognize the existence of certain groups of legal traditions which go under the name of individual

[1] See Ibn 'Abdalbarr, quoted in Zurqānī, iii. 181.

[2] See Goldziher, in *Z.D.M.G.* l. 481.

[3] For two further Medinese examples, see *Ris.* 44, 45.

[4] Later developments of this second form are found in some classical and other collections.

[5] In this particular respect, I disagree with Caetani (*Annali*, i, Introduction, §§ 19, 24–8).

Companions; they are the products of schools of thought which put their doctrines under the authority of the Companions in question.[1] Even here we find that the names of 'Alī and of Ibn 'Umar were used both by the ancient Iraqian and Medinese schools of law and by their opponents.[2] On the other hand, the name of 'Umar was used both by the ancient Iraqians and Medinese, but this does not make the traditions related from him by both groups any more authentic. The use made by certain schools of the names of individual Companions as authorities for their doctrines accounts for the existence of common tendencies and characteristics, but it would be unwarranted to project these features back to the Companions themselves. It is significant that the earliest authorities of the Iraqians and of the Meccans, respectively, were originally not Ibn Mas'ūd and Ibn 'Abbās themselves, but the 'Companions of Ibn Mas'ūd' and the 'Companions of Ibn 'Abbās'. This makes it pointless to consider the Companions of the Prophet personally responsible for the large-scale circulation of spurious traditions.

There are numerous traditions which claim an additional guarantee of soundness by representing themselves as transmitted amongst members of one family, for instance from father to son (and grandson), from aunt to nephew, or from master to freedman. Whenever we come to analyse them, we find these family traditions spurious,[3] and we are justified in considering the existence of a family *isnād* not an indication of authenticity but only a device for securing its appearance.

Muw. i. 108 and 111 gives two traditions whose family *isnāds* have identical lower parts (Mālik—Hishām—his father 'Urwa). Both deal with the same problem, but there is a different woman in the generation of the Companions involved in each case. The version of p. 111 where the Prophet is not mentioned, contains an obvious confusion of persons (see Zurqānī, ad loc.), and it was passed over in silence by Shāfi'ī in *Tr. III*, 30; the version of p. 108 improves this by a change of persons and by introducing the Prophet, but it does not thereby become any more authentic.

The Iraqian and the different Medinese doctrine on a question of divorce are both ascribed to Zaid b. Thābit, the former with the

[1] See above, pp. 25, 31 f.; below, p. 249 f.

[2] See below, pp. 240, 249.

[3] See above, pp. 73, 114, 153, 158, 164, 166, 168 f.; below, 173.

usual Iraqian *isnād* Abū Ḥanīfa—Ḥammād—Ibrāhīm (*Āthār A.Y.* 633; *Āthār Shaib.* 79), the latter with the *isnād* Mālik—Sa'īd b. Sulaimān b. Zaid b. Thābit—Khārija b. Zaid—Zaid b. Thābit (*Muw.* iii. 37; *Muw. Shaib.* 254). The Iraqian *isnād* is *mursal*, and, as such, older than the Medinese family *isnād*. Both doctrines are harmonized in a tradition with the *isnād* Nāfi'—Ibn 'Umar (*Muw.* and *Muw. Shaib.*, loc. cit.).

Muw. iii. 38 gives two traditions on 'Ā'isha's interference in matters of marriage, both with the *isnād* Mālik—'Abdalraḥmān b. Qāsim—his father Qāsim b. Muḥammad—Qāsim's aunt 'Ā'isha, but in one case with 'Abdalraḥmān b. Abī Bakr and his wife, and in the other with Mundhir b. Zubair and his wife who was the daughter of 'Abdalraḥmān b. Abī Bakr. Both are parallel but incompatible versions of the same anecdote; a legal point on a question of divorce is made in an additional remark which is out of place in the second version.

Zurqānī discusses the contradictions in the family *isnāds* of the several versions of a tradition in *Muw.* i. 39, regarding Mālik's immediate authority 'Amr b. Yaḥyā Māzinī; this tradition is a compromise between several doctrines.

Whereas late traditions, as we saw, were provided with first-class *isnāds*, relatively old traditions sometimes failed to develop satisfactory *isnāds* and were therefore passed over by Bukhārī and Muslim.[1]

These results regarding the growth of *isnāds* enable us to envisage the case in which a tradition was put into circulation by a traditionist whom we may call N.N., or by a person who used his name, at a certain time. The tradition would normally be taken over by one or several transmitters, and the lower, real part of the *isnād* would branch out into several strands. The original promoter N.N. would have provided his tradition with an *isnād* reaching back to an authority such as a Companion or the Prophet, and this higher, fictitious part of the *isnād* would often acquire additional branches by the creation of improvements which would take their place beside the original chain of transmitters, or by the process which we have described as spread of *isnāds*. But N.N. would remain the (lowest) common link in the several strands of *isnād* (or at least in most of them, allowing for his being passed by and eliminated in additional strands of *isnād* which might have been introduced later).

[1] See, e.g., *Tr. IX*, 7–10, with *Comm. ed. Cairo.*

Whether this happened to the lower or to the higher part of the *isnād* or to both, the existence of a significant common link (N.N.) in all or most *isnāds* of a given tradition would be a strong indication in favour of its having originated in the time of N.N. The same conclusion would have to be drawn when the *isnāds* of different, but closely connected traditions showed a common link.

The case discussed in the preceding paragraph is not hypothetical but of common occurrence. It was observed, though of course not recognized in its implications, by the Muhammadan scholars themselves, for instance by Tirmidhī in the concluding chapter of his collection of traditions. He calls traditions with N.N. as a common link in their *isnāds* 'the traditions of N.N.', and they form a great part of the traditions which he calls *gharīb*, that is transmitted by a single transmitter at any one stage of the *isnād*.

A typical example of the phenomenon of the common transmitter occurs in *Ikh.* 294, where a tradition has the following *isnāds*:

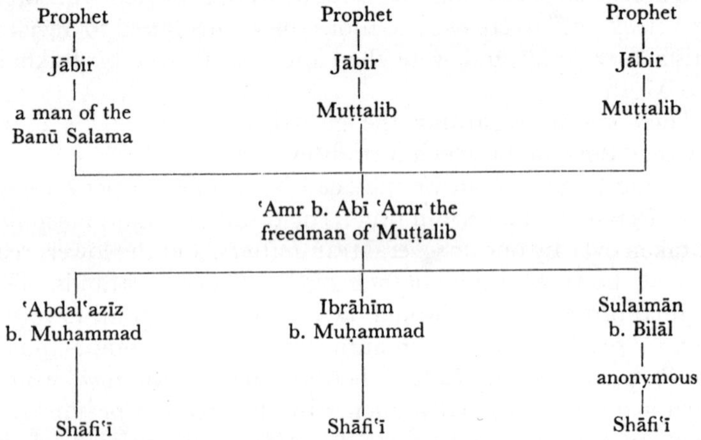

'Amr b. Abī 'Amr is the common link in these *isnāds*. He would hardly have hesitated between his own patron and an anonymous transmitter for his immediate authority.

The following example will show how the argument drawn from a common transmitter can be used, together with other considerations, in investigating the history of legal doctrines.

In the first half of the second century A.H., the sale of the *walā'* of a manumitted slave[1] was customary and considered valid. Ibn Sa'd, v. 309, relates of Abū Ma'shar: 'He was the *mukātab* slave[2] of a woman belonging to the Banū Makhzūm; he paid [the stipulated instalments] and became free; later, Umm Mūsā bint al-Ḥimyarīya [the mother of the Caliph Mahdī] bought his *walā'*, and he considered himself henceforth a client of the ruling house.' The common reaction of the Iraqians and the Medinese was to forbid this practice; see *Muw. Shaib.* 343 for the Iraqians, *Muw.* iii. 257 for the Medinese.[3] This common doctrine was expressed in a Medinese tradition (*Muw.*, loc. cit.), with the *isnād* Mālik—'Abdallāh b. Dīnār—Ibn 'Umar—Prophet, to the effect that the Prophet prohibited selling or giving away the right of *walā'*. As Zurqānī points out, 'Abdallāh b. Dīnār is the common link in the *isnāds* of its several versions, and it can therefore be dated in the generation preceding Mālik. The reason for this doctrine appears in one of the versions quoted by Zurqānī, which considers *walā'* as a kind of kinship (*luḥma*), in the same way as relationship by blood.

But the Medinese still allowed the sale of the *mukātab* slave.[4] This doctrine is expressed in a tradition with the *isnād* Mālik—Hishām—his father 'Urwa—his aunt 'Ā'isha—Prophet, to the effect that a certain Barīra, a *mukātab* slave-woman, found it difficult to meet her obligations under the contract, that 'Ā'isha offered to pay for her, provided she ('Ā'isha) could have the right of *walā'*, that the owners of Barīra were willing to sell her to 'Ā'isha, provided they retained the right of *walā'*, and that the Prophet advised 'Ā'isha to agree to their condition because it would be invalid and the right of *walā'* would belong to her by law, as she was the actual manumitter; and the Prophet afterwards proclaimed this rule of law (*Muw.* iii. 251). Hishām is the common link in the several versions of this family *isnād*, although a parallel version, through Zuhrī—'Urwa—'Ā'isha, passes him by (see Zurqānī ad loc.). As this tradition shows the Prophet and 'Ā'isha in a disconcerting light, the crucial point was formally mitigated in a version with the new *isnād* Mālik—Yaḥyā b. Sa'īd—'Amra—'Ā'isha, and a shortened one with the *isnād* Mālik—Nāfi'—Ibn 'Umar—'Ā'isha (*Muw.* iii. 255, 256).

1 See above, p. 161.

2 See below, p. 279.

3 But the Meccan scholar 'Aṭā' seems to have held that a master could allow his manumitted slave to enter into *walā'* with whom he wished; this information is presumably genuine. A tradition which implicates Ibn 'Abbās, the customary authority of the Meccans, in a contract of sale of *walā'*, seems to show that no objections were raised in Mecca. See *Comm. Muw. Shaib.* 343.

4 Or of the rights accruing to the master from the contract of manumission; see Zurqānī, iii. 256, 265.

The whole Barīra tradition is artificial, and later than the legal maxim 'the Muslims must abide by their stipulations' (*al-Muslimūn ʿalā shurūṭihim*), because it makes the Prophet refer to that maxim polemically in his final speech. The maxim itself is put into the mouth of Qāsim b. Muḥammad, who belongs to the generation preceding Hishām (*Muw.* iii. 220; *Tr. III*, 41). Shāfiʿī knows it also as a tradition from the Prophet, but doubts its authenticity (*Ikh.* 32); it is likely that it had been put into the form of a tradition from the Prophet only recently.[1]

The Iraqians, on the other hand, prohibit the sale of the *mukātab* (Zurqānī, iii. 256, 265), and dispense with the Barīra tradition; Shaibānī (*Muw. Shaib.* 344) quotes only the third, shortened version which does not contradict his doctrine explicitly. The introduction of Ibrāhīm Nakhaʿī into two *isnāds* of the Barīra tradition (Ṭaḥāwī, ii. 220) is a late counter-move.

Some significant common transmitters are:

ʿAbdallāh b. Dīnār: see above, p. 173; below, p. 199.

Aʿmash: see below, p. 209, n. 8.

ʿAmr b. Dīnār: see above, p. 155, n. 2.

ʿAmr b. Yaḥyā Māzinī: see below, p. 184.

Darāwardī: see above, p. 168; he gave spurious information on old Medinese authorities (see below, p. 195); he was an adversary of Mālik (*Tr. III*, 148, p. 248), but followed some of Mālik's opinions (see above, p. 7).

Ḥajjāj b. Arṭāt: see *Tr. IX*, 36 and *Comm. ed. Cairo.*[2]

Ḥasan b. ʿUmāra: see above, p. 158.

Ibn Abī Dhi'b: see above, p. 54 f.; below, p. 181.

Ibn Juraij: see above, p. 146, n. 1.

Ibn ʿUyaina: he appears in the *isnād* of a tradition from the Prophet praising the 'scholar of Medina', who was usually identified with Mālik, but also with ʿAbdalʿazīz b. ʿAbdallāh ʿUmarī: Ibn Ḥanbal ii. 299 and Tirmidhī, *Abwāb al-ʿilm*, *Bāb mā jā' fī ʿālim al-Madīna.* As Shāfiʿī, who is Ibn ʿUyaina's contemporary and often relates traditions from him, does not, as far as I know, refer to this tradition in his polemics, Ibn ʿUyaina himself seems hardly to be responsible for it.

Ibrāhīm b. Saʿd: see below, p. 182.

Muʿtamir b. Sulaimān: see above, p. 56.

Saʿd b. Isḥāq b. Kaʿb b. ʿUjra: see below, p. 198, n. 2.

Shaʿbī: his name was used for the *isnāds* of several groups of traditions; see above, p. 131; below, p. 203 n. 4, 231, 241.

[1] It had gained full status in the time of Ṭaḥāwī (ii. 246) and Ibn ʿAbdalbarr (quoted in Zurqānī, iii. 219).

[2] See below, p. 250.

Shuʿba: see above, p. 106.

Zaid b. Aslam: see *Muw.* i. 20 and Zurqānī, ad loc.; and below, p. 251 f.

Zuhrī: he is the common transmitter of most Medinese traditions directed against the temporary marriage (*mutʿa*): see below, p. 267. See further above, p. 162; below, pp. 186, 199, 222, 246. Zuhrī himself is hardly responsible in the greater part of these cases.

The existence of common transmitters enables us to assign a firm date to many traditions and to the doctrines represented by them. This consideration which takes into account the fictitious character of the higher parts of *isnāds*, must replace the uncritical acceptance at their face value of *isnāds*, as far back as the time of the Companions.[1] We must, of course, always reckon with the possibility that the name of a common transmitter was used by other, anonymous persons, so that its occurrence gives only a *terminus a quo*. This applies particularly to the period of the Successors. We shall discuss the typical case of Nāfiʿ in the following chapter.

Similar considerations apply to the *isnāds* of traditions relating to history.[2]

[1] See above, pp. 169 f.

[2] See above, p. 139, and my paper in *Acta Orientalia*, xxi, 1953, 288–300.

CHAPTER 5

THE ORIGIN OF LEGAL TRADITIONS IN THE FIRST HALF OF THE SECOND CENTURY A.H.

MOST of the 'common transmitters', whose importance for the dating of traditions we discussed at the end of the preceding chapter, occur in the generation preceding Mālik and his contemporary Abū Yūsuf, and we have found numerous traditions for which other considerations pointed to the same period of origin.[1] On the other hand, we have found genuine legal traditions from Companions as elusive as those from the Prophet.[2] We have even seen that the traditions pretending to express the doctrines of the Successors, in the second half of the first century A.H., are to a great extent fictitious.[3] Without attempting a rash generalization, we are therefore justified in looking to the first half of the second century A.H. for the origin of the bulk of legal traditions with which the literary period starts. The present chapter is intended to show this in detail on the test case of the traditions related by Mālik on the authority of Nāfiʿ from Ibn ʿUmar. We choose this group of Medinese traditions (*a*) because the available sources are most complete on the Medinese, (*b*) because the Nāfiʿ traditions are the most important single group of Medinese traditions, (*c*) because the *isnād* Mālik—Nāfiʿ—Ibn ʿUmar is one of the best, if not the very best, according to the Muhammadan scholars.

Already Shāfiʿī considers the transmission of traditions from Nāfiʿ to Mālik as very reliable, and he says in *Ikh.* 378 f., where he has to choose between two traditions related on the authority of Nāfiʿ by Mālik and by Aiyūb respectively: 'I think no one who knows traditions and their transmission can doubt that Mālik remembers the traditions of Nāfiʿ better than Aiyūb, because Mālik was more closely associated with him, and had the merit of remembering the traditions of his associates particularly well.' But as Nāfiʿ died in A.H. 117 or thereabouts, and Mālik in A.H. 179,[4] their association can have taken place, even

[1] See above, pp. 97, 107, 141, n. 4, 152, 156 f., 163 ff.; below, p. 212, n. 2.
[2] See above, p. 169 f.
[3] See above, p. 151 and n. 2.
[4] Nothing authentic is known of Mālik's date of birth.

at the most generous estimate, only when Mālik was little more than a boy. It may even be questioned whether Mālik, whom Shāfi'ī charged elsewhere with concealing imperfections in his *isnāds*,[1] did not take over in written form traditions alleged to come from Nāfi'.[2]

As Nāfi' was a freedman of Ibn 'Umar, the *isnād* Nāfi'—Ibn 'Umar is a 'family *isnād*', a fact which, as we have seen, is generally an indication of the spurious character of the traditions in question.[3] We saw further that Nāfi' often alternates with Sālim,[4] 'Abdallāh b. Dīnār, and Zuhrī, in other words, that these transmitters of traditions from Ibn 'Umar appear at random.[5] This makes us doubt whether the historical Nāfi' is responsible for everything that was ascribed to him in the following generation, and we shall find this doubt confirmed later in this chapter.

Wherever the sources available enable us to trace the development of doctrines, we find that the Nāfi' traditions, as a rule, express a secondary stage;[6] we have noticed cases in which they are later than doctrines or traditions which can be dated in the time of 'Aṭā', Zuhrī, and Hishām b. 'Urwa respectively.[7] Many Nāfi' traditions represent unsuccessful attempts at influencing the doctrine of the Medinese school, and Shāfi'ī in *Tr. III* discusses numerous examples of this kind from his own point of view which is biased in favour of the traditions. The very fact that the Medinese disagree to a considerable extent with alleged traditions of Nāfi' from their own authority Ibn 'Umar (or through Nāfi'—Ibn 'Umar from 'Umar or the Prophet), shows that these traditions are later than the established Medinese doctrine.[8]

[1] See above, p. 37.

[2] This procedure was customary in Shāfi'ī's time: see above, p. 38.

[3] See above, p. 170.

[4] A son of Ibn 'Umar; this gives another 'family *isnād*'. As Sālim died in A.H. 106 or thereabouts, it is even more likely that Mālik received the traditions from him in written form than it is in the case of Nāfi'.

[5] See above, p. 163. For further typical examples, compare *Muw.* iii. 204 with *Mud.* viii. 23; *Tr. III*, 47 with *Umm*, iii. 3.

[6] See above, p. 48, n. 1, 154, 167, 171; and below, pp. 208, 215, 265. The examples could be multiplied.

[7] See for 'Aṭā': above, p. 160; for Zuhrī: above, p. 102, and below, p. 266 f.; for Hishām: above, p. 173.

[8] See above, p. 25 f. on Ibn 'Umar as an authority of the Medinese, and p. 66 f. on the relation between traditions and the established doctrine of the school.

This effort to change the doctrines of the ancient schools of law by means of traditions is typical of the traditionists in the second century A.H.[1] We have noticed a Nāfiʿ—Ibn ʿUmar tradition which expressed their attitude explicitly.[2] There is also external evidence. Shāfiʿī himself stated that the *khiyār al-majlis*, which was prescribed in a Nāfiʿ tradition but not recognized by the Medinese, was accepted by the traditionists.[3] Furthermore, there are two traditions with the *isnād* Mālik—Nāfiʿ—Ibn ʿUmar, according to which the Prophet prohibited underbidding and overbidding, and certain practices which might create an artificial rise or fall in prices.[4] The traditions were obviously intended to make these practices illegal in the same way as, say, the taking of interest is illegal, so that contracts concluded in defiance of the prohibition would be invalid. With regard to the second of these two closely connected traditions, Ṭaḥāwī, ii. 199, states that this was indeed the doctrine of 'some', and Ibn Mundhir (quoted in *Comm. Muw. Shaib.* 333) identifies these as the traditionists. But again the traditions did not prevail with the Medinese; they, in common with the Iraqians, minimized them by interpretation, and Shāfiʿī distinguished clearly between the legal and the moral aspect. There exists a late counter-tradition, also with the *isnād* Nāfiʿ—Ibn ʿUmar (Ṭaḥāwī, loc. cit.).

We have noticed the gradual appearance of Nāfiʿ traditions in several cases,[5] and seen that existing traditions acquired *isnāds* with Nāfiʿ in them.[6] It is also not rare to find Nāfiʿ traditions advocating opposite doctrines, even at the beginning of the literary period.[7] In the time of Abū Ḥanīfa, Nāfiʿ—Ibn ʿUmar traditions were imitated in Iraq.[8] The Nāfiʿ traditions are not uniform, and "Nāfiʿ" is a label which was used for various purposes over a considerable period. It is certain that even the group of Nāfiʿ traditions in Mālik's *Muwaṭṭaʾ* represents the result of gradual growth. The historical Nāfiʿ was

[1] See below, pp. 249, 255.
[2] See above, p. 144.
[3] See above, p. 160.
[4] *Muw.* iii. 148, 152; *Muw. Shaib.* 333, 337; *Ikh.* 185 ff.
[5] See above, pp. 144, 148, 150, 160.
[6] See above, p. 139, n. 4, 158 f.
[7] See above, p. 150, and further: *Muw.* i. 245 f. with Zurqānī, ad loc.; *Muw. Shaib.* 126; *Mud.* i. 121 (= *Tr. III*, 117) and 172 (= *Muw.* ii. 253).
[8] See above, p. 32.

certainly not a representative of the ancient Medinese school of law, but beyond this his personality remains vague,[1] and the bulk of the traditions which go under his name must be credited to anonymous traditionists in the first half of the second century A.H.

[1] In *Mud.* iii. 8, Nāfi' is asked his opinion on the question whether one ought to lay waste enemy country; but his alleged answer is shown as spurious by the development of doctrine on this point since Umaiyad times (see above, p. 144 f., and below, p. 204 f.). Occasionally, remarks of Nāfi' appear appended to his traditions, but none of them seems to be authentic.

CHAPTER 6

LEGAL MAXIMS IN TRADITIONS

MUHAMMADAN jurisprudence in the pre-literary period often formulated legal maxims in the form of slogans most of which became traditions from the Prophet and from other authorities. A study of these legal maxims enables us to draw additional conclusions regarding the growth of legal traditions and the development of doctrine in the pre-literary period.

Not all legal maxims succeeded in becoming traditions with an acceptable *isnād*. This applies, for example, to the lawyers' maxim 'who joins a people belongs to them' which Auzā'ī uses as an argument (*Tr. IX*, 41),[1] and to the rule 'a sacrifice cannot be shared'. Mālik (*Muw.* ii. 348) refers to this last as 'the best that I have heard',[2] and interprets a tradition on the action of the Prophet and the Companions restrictively in its light. Shāfi'ī (*Tr. III*, 38) deprecates it as an anonymous saying which cannot overrule the action of the Prophet and of the Companions. The details of Mālik's doctrine go beyond the slogan, which, however, expresses the underlying idea in a short form.

Some maxims acquired the full status of a tradition from the Prophet rather late. The rhyming maxim 'there is no divorce and no manumission under duress' (*lā ṭalāq wa-lā 'atāq fī ighlāq*) appears as a tradition from the Prophet only in Ibn Ḥanbal and some of the classical collections;[3] Mālik (*Muw.* iii. 69) and an unsuccessful Iraqian opinion (*Tr. II*, 10 (*r*)) know only traditions from Ibn 'Umar and from 'Alī to the same effect, but still without the explicit maxim.

The process by which the maxim 'the spoils belong to the killer' was gradually provided with the authority of the Prophet and of Companions, has been described above (pp. 70 f.). It represented the old practice, but was interpreted restrictively by the ancient schools of law for a systematic reason, based on a religious scruple.

[1] It appears as a tradition from the Prophet only in a somewhat different form, from Ibn Sa'd onwards; cf. Wensinck, *Handbook*, s.v. *Mawlā*. It is inspired by Koran, iv. 115.

[2] See above, p. 101.

[3] See Zurqānī, iii. 70.

The maxim 'the Muslims must abide by their stipulations' has been discussed above (p. 174). It was put into the mouth of Qāsim b. Muḥammad, two generations before Mālik, and later ascribed to the Prophet. It is earlier than the tradition from the Prophet regarding the case of Barīra, which refers to it polemically and which can itself be dated in the generation preceding Mālik. The statement of Qāsim and the Barīra tradition refer to two separate problems, and the maxim was obviously intended as a general rule; the introductory words of the statement of Qāsim confirm this.

In most cases, however, legal maxims appear only as part of formal traditions. This is the case with the maxim 'profit follows responsibility',[1] which appears as a tradition from the Prophet in Iraqian and Medinese texts from the time of Abū Yūsuf onwards.[2] The *isnāds* of the Medinese version have a common link in the traditionist Ibn Abī Dhi'b.[3] But this shows only the origin of the Medinese tradition and not of the legal maxim.

Legal maxims can often be shown to be later than the earliest stage of legal doctrine and practice. This is the case even with as fundamental a rule on ritual as the maxim 'no prayer without recitation' (above, p. 154 f.).

The frequency of divorce with immediate re-marriage led to many cases of contested paternity in pre-Islamic Arab society and even during the first century of Islam.[4] The Koran (ii. 228 ff., lxv. 1 ff., xxxiii. 48) introduced the *'idda*, a waiting period during which a divorced woman and a widow were barred from re-marrying. But this rule was still disregarded in the middle Umaiyad period, as *Aghānī*, xi. 140, shows. The legal maxim 'the child belongs to the marriage bed' was intended to decide disputes about paternity which were likely to happen in these conditions, but which could hardly arise under the Koranic rule regarding *'idda*. The maxim is, strictly speaking, incompatible with the Koran, and it had not yet asserted itself in the time of the dispute recorded in *Aghānī*.[5] It was, however, in-

[1] See above, p. 123.

[2] *Āthār A. Y.* 828; *Mud.* x. 106; *Ikh.* 332; Ibn Ḥanbal, vi. 49, 208, 237, &c.

[3] The alternative family *isnād* Hishām—'Urwa is derived from the *isnād* of Ibn Abī Dhi'b which contains 'Urwa in its higher part.

[4] Cf. *Ḥamāsa*, i. 216; *Aghānī*, xi. 140; Wellhausen, in *Nachr. Ges. Wiss. Gött.*, 1893, 453.

[5] See Goldziher, *Muh. St.* i. 188, n. 2.

corporated in traditions from the Prophet.[1] Abū Ḥanīfa knows it as a saying of the Prophet and applies it literally with a surprising result; but Ibn Abī Lailā and Abū Yūsuf, followed by Shāfi'ī, interpret it differently (*Tr. I*, 224), so that there is hardly a case left to which it could be applied. In the time of Shāfi'ī, there are no scholars who take the legal maxim at its face value, and Shāfi'ī treats him who would do so, as an ignoramus (*Ikh.* 309 f.). This shows how incompatible the maxim was with the Muhammadan law of marriage, and since it also differed from the old Arab method of deciding disputes about paternity, it is possible that it was influenced by the rule of Roman law *pater est quem nuptiae demonstrant*,[2] as Goldziher has pointed out.[3]

The old Arab method of deciding disputes about paternity was by the decision of professional physiognomists.[4] This method was, on one side, declared superseded by the decision of the Prophet in favour of the legal maxim, and on the other, justified by making the Prophet himself use it.[5] The *isnāds* of the second of these traditions have a common link in Ibrāhīm b. Sa'd, a contemporary of Mālik, and the family *isnād* of the first points to its origin in the generation preceding him. The old Arab method was finally retained in Muhammadan law for those rare cases in which a dispute about paternity had to be decided.[6] But as the legal maxim had become a saying of the Prophet, lip-service continued to be paid to it, although it was not, in fact, acted upon.

The maxim that 'there is no [valid] marriage without a *walī*', that is, the nearest male relative of the bride who must give her in marriage, was not originally as self-evident as it became later in Muhammadan law. Mālik dispenses with the

[1] *Muw.* iii. 197; *Ikh.* 304.

[2] *Digest*, 2, 4, 5.

[3] *Muh. St.*, loc. cit.—Robertson Smith, *Kinship*, 132 ff., Wellhausen, ibid. 453, 457, n. 3, and Lammens, *Berceau*, 283, seem to consider the maxim as an authentic rule of pre-Islamic Arab practice; but there is no evidence for this, beyond the artificial theories of the later genealogists who of course knew the maxim, and a suspect tradition on the so-called *nikāḥ al-istibḍā'* (Bukhārī, *Kitāb al-nikāḥ, Bāb man qāl lā nikāḥ illā bi-walī*).

[4] See Goldziher, ibid. i. 184 f.; Robertson Smith, ibid. 169, n. 2; Lammens, loc. cit.

[5] Both traditions in *Ikh.* 305 f.

[6] The tradition from 'Umar in *Muw.* iii. 202, describing a case where the method of physiognomy breaks down, does not even mention the possibility of applying the legal maxim.

legal *walī* in the case of a lowly woman,[1] and Abū Ḥanīfa (and others, if Zurqānī, iii. 4, is right) if the bride marries a man of equal standing for the full *ṣadāq* or *donatio propter nuptias* which a woman of her standing can expect;[2] Zurqānī, iii. 17, refers to an unidentified doctrine according to which a woman who is not a virgin needs no *walī* for marriage. The marriage without a legal *walī*, which continued the easy-going practice of the pre-Islamic Arabs, was taken for granted in a tradition from 'Ā'isha which on account of its *isnād* can be dated in the generation preceding Mālik.[3]

The opinion that there is no valid marriage without a *walī* found its first expression in the alleged decision of 'Umar b. 'Abdal'azīz that such marriages must be dissolved (*Mud.* iii. 15). This is no doubt later than the Caliphate of 'Umar b. 'Abdal-'azīz, and dates only from the second century A.H. It was held in Iraq, Medina, and Mecca, projected back to 'Alī, 'Umar, and Ibn 'Abbās, and finally ascribed to the Prophet, on the authority of 'Ā'isha and of other Companions; the traditions which put it into the mouth of the Prophet appear only from Shāfi'ī onwards.[4] The legal maxim was coined at this later stage. Abū Yūsuf, having held an opinion near to that of Abū Ḥanīfa at first, adopted this doctrine,[5] Shaibānī held it, Shāfi'ī supported it with a brilliant systematic argument (*Tr. III*, 53), and Ibn Qāsim rejected the earlier tradition from 'Ā'isha as contrary to the 'practice' (*Mud.* iv. 281).

The alliterating maxim '[there shall be] no damage and no mutual infliction of damage' (*lā ḍarar wa-lā ḍirār*) is given as a saying of the Prophet in a tradition with the *isnād* Mālik—'Amr b. Yaḥyā Māzinī—his father.[6] This is *mursal*,[7] and is abstracted from two traditions with the same *isnād*, one on 'Umar with Ḍaḥḥāk b. Khalīfa and Muḥammad b. Maslama, the other on 'Umar with 'Abdalraḥmān b. 'Auf and Yaḥyā Māzinī's grandfather; both stories are parallel and express the

[1] *Tr. III*, 53; *Mud.* iv. 15, 20, 27.

[2] *Muw. Shaib.* 244. For the meaning of *ṣadāq* see above, p. 107.

[3] *Muw.* iii. 38; cf. above, p. 171.

[4] *Muw.* iii. 5; *Muw. Shaib.* 244; *Mud.* iv. 15; *Tr. II*, 10 (*a*); *Tr. III*, 53; also in Ibn Ḥanbal and the classical collections.

[5] Ṭaḥāwī, quoted in *Comm. Muw. Shaib.* 244.

[6] This and the other traditions mentioned in this paragraph occur for the first time in *Muw.* iii. 207 ff.

[7] The *isnād* was later completed and improved; see Zurqānī, ad loc.

same doctrine as applied to particular cases and not in the form of a general maxim. ʿAmr b. Yaḥyā Māzinī is the relevant common link in the family *isnād*. There is a further tradition from the Prophet, on the authority of Abū Huraira, again regarding a particular case, with a strongly worded additional remark of Abū Huraira who blames his audience for their reluctance to accept it; this shows that it had to overcome resistance. The *isnād* runs Mālik—Zuhrī—Aʿraj—Abū Huraira, with uncertainties regarding Zuhrī and Aʿraj,[1] and the tradition seems to have been recent in the time of Mālik. Zurqānī's comment shows that the rule was taken literally, and therefore presumably put into circulation, by the traditionists; it gained general acceptance as a saying of the Prophet, but did not succeed in changing the doctrine of the ancient schools of law who interpreted it as a recommendation.[2]

The maxim 'restrict *ḥadd* punishments as much as possible' started as an anonymous saying, was then ascribed to the 'Companions and Successors' in general, then to a number of individual Companions, and finally to the Prophet. These successive stages are recognizable in the words of Abū Yūsuf.[3] The maxim cannot be older than the end of the period of the Successors. As an anonymous slogan, the maxim is introduced with the words 'they used to say'; this is one of the formulas used of ancient opinions.[4]

On the maxim 'the two parties to a sale have the right of option as long as they have not separated', see above (pp. 160 f.). It is later than ʿAṭā', was put into circulation as a tradition from the Prophet by the traditionists, but did not succeed in changing the common doctrine of the Iraqians and Medinese.

A considerable number of legal maxims are Iraqian.[5] The oldest Iraqian reasoning regarding the position of the slave in the law of inheritance is expressed in the maxim, ascribed to Ibn Masʿūd (*Tr. II*, 16 (*j*)): 'the slave debars and does not cause to inherit [those who are related to the *de cuius* through a

[1] See Zurqānī, loc. cit.

[2] See *Muw. Shaib.* 346 for the Iraqians, *Mud.* xiv. 227 and xv. 192 for the Medinese; according to Zurqānī, loc. cit., Shāfiʿī adopted the same opinion in his later doctrine, having taken the tradition literally at first.

[3] *Kharāj*, 90 f.; *Tr. IX*, 15, and *Comm. ed. Cairo* for the later sources.

[4] See above, p. 101, n. 1.

[5] Two Iraqian maxims, one rhyming, on pre-emption: see above, p. 164.

slave]' (*al-'abd yaḥjub wa-lā yūrith*). This shows a primitive kind of legal reasoning, as if the right to inherit were a force transmitted from one person through another to a third. Another tradition from Ibn Mas'ūd (*Tr. II*, 16 (*l*)) shows the old, unsystematic concern for the just and morally right decision. But in the time of Shāfi'ī, the Iraqians had developed a strict and technical legal reasoning which they expressed in the maxim 'the slave cannot inherit and cannot leave inheritance' (*al-'abd lā yarith wa-lā yūrith*). This is derived from the first maxim (with a change of meaning in the word *yūrith*) and implies that the slave does not debar anyone from inheriting.

Iraqian legal maxims were sometimes taken over by the Medinese. The Iraqian maxim 'the killer inherits nothing' was transformed in Medina into 'the killer receives nothing [of the weregeld]', so as to agree with one of the two Medinese opinions (above, p. 159).

The maxim 'injury caused by an animal is not actionable' (*jarḥ al-'ajmā' jubār*), and the doctrine expressed by it, are Iraqian.[1] The Medinese held that damage caused by roving animals at night was actionable, and this doctrine was expressed in a tradition from the Prophet (*Muw.* iii. 211). But the Iraqian maxim penetrated into Hijaz and was provided with a Medinese *isnād* (*Muw.* iv. 46). Mālik, who relates both traditions, does not try to harmonize them; only Shāfi'ī (*Ikh.* 400) does so by using forced interpretation.[2]

'The Medinese say: "Talion depends on the weapon" (*al-qawad bil-silāḥ*)', meaning that talion takes place only when the murder has been committed with a weapon.[3] This does not fit the doctrine of the Medinese who have, therefore, to construe the use of a stick, stone, and so on as the equivalent of the use of a weapon. It does, however, fit the Iraqian doctrine,[4] and

[1] *Āthār Shaib.* 85 (with the *isnād* Abū Ḥanīfa—Ḥammād—Ibrāhīm Nakha'ī—Prophet); *Muw. Shaib.* 295.

[2] Zurqānī, iii. 212, states that Laith b. Sa'd of Egypt and 'Aṭā' of Mecca held that damage caused by animals both in daytime and at night was actionable; this is possibly authentic and may have corresponded with an original Medinese doctrine, so that the actual Medinese doctrine would represent a compromise under the influence of the Iraqian maxim.

[3] *Tr. VIII*, 18. See further *Muw.* iv. 49, *Mud.* xvi. 106 for the Medinese, and *Āthār A. Y.* 961, *Āthār Shaib.* 82, 84, Ṭaḥāwī, ii. 106 ff. for the Iraqians.

[4] We need not go into the differences of detail between Abū Ḥanīfa, Abū Yūsuf, and Shaibānī.

we might conclude that the Medinese borrowed the maxim from the Iraqians, although I find it attested on the Iraqian side, in the sources available, only at a later period.[1]

An old Iraqian maxim is countered by a later Medinese one in the following case:

In pre-Islamic Arab usage, *rahn* 'security' meant a kind of earnest money which was given as a guarantee and material proof of a contract, particularly when there was no scribe available to put it into writing.[2] The word occurs in this meaning in Koran ii. 283. But the institution of earnest money was not recognized by the ancient schools of law, although it left some traces in traditions,[3] and the common ancient doctrine knew *rahn* only as a security for the payment of a debt. The foreign origin of this doctrine which neglects old Arab usage and an explicit passage in the Koran, is probable. There arises the question of how far the security automatically takes the place of the debt, (*a*) if the security gets lost while it is in the possession of the creditor, (*b*) if the debtor fails to pay the debt within the stipulated time. The oldest opinion goes farthest and states that 'the security takes the place of that for which it is given' (*al-rahn bi-mā fīh*). This maxim is Iraqian (*Tr. I*, 68) and was projected back to Shuraiḥ (*Umm*, iii. 166); it was also known in Medina (*Muw.* iii. 190), and in Mecca where it was connected with 'Aṭā' and projected back to the Prophet (*Umm*, loc. cit.). The Iraqian school, however, mitigated this extreme doctrine.[4]

The old Iraqian maxim was countered in Medina by the opposite maxim 'the security is not forfeited' (*al-rahn lā yaghlaq*); it was put into the mouth of the Prophet in traditions whose *isnāds* have their common link in Zuhrī.[5] It is a late, polemical counter-statement and does not adequately express the Medinese doctrine which is considerably influenced by the mitigated doctrine of the Iraqian school.[6] The doctrines of the Iraqian

[1] Ṭaḥāwī, ii. 105 and Zurqānī, iv. 49, as a tradition from the Prophet: *lā qawad illā bil-saif*. It is applied here, perhaps secondarily, to the mode of execution by talion.

[2] Cf. Tyan, *Organisation*, i. 73, n. 3.

[3] See *Muw.* iii. 94 and Zurqānī, ad loc.

[4] *Muw. Shaib.* 362; Sarakhsī, xxi. 64. A further Iraqian mitigation in *Umm*, iii. 166, Sarakhsī, xxi. 65.

[5] *Muw.* iii. 188; *Muw. Shaib.* 362; *Umm*, iii. 147, 164, 167.

[6] *Muw.* iii. 189; *Umm*, iii. 165. The Medinese compromise is also ascribed to 'Aṭā' (*Umm*, iii. 166).

and of the Medinese school represent two successive stages in the abandonment of the opinion expressed by the first maxim. Shāfiʿī completed this process and was the first consistently to apply to securities the concept of a deposit on trust (*amāna*).[1]

The essential maxim of procedure in Muhammadan law, 'evidence [by witnesses] has to be produced by the plaintiff, and the oath [in denial] has to be taken by the defendant', became a tradition from the Prophet only at a relatively late period.[2] It is not mentioned as a tradition in *Muw.* and in *Muw. Shaib.*, although *Muw.* iii. 181 presupposes it as the accepted rule. Abū Ḥanīfa (*Tr. I*, 116) and Shāfiʿī's Iraqian opponent (*Ikh.* 354) refer to it as a saying of the Prophet, without an *isnād*.[3] *Āthār A.Y.* 738 gives it as a statement of Ibrāhīm Nakhaʿī, and only the later versions of the *Musnad Abī Ḥanīfa* in Khwārizmī have full *isnāds* from Abū Ḥanīfa back to the Prophet, mostly through Ibrāhīm. It appears as a formal tradition from the Prophet, with a Meccan *isnād*, for the first time in Shāfiʿī (*Ikh.* 345), and as part of the composite speech of the Prophet at the conquest of Mecca in Shāfiʿī's contemporary Wāqidī. It is later found in the classical collections.

The maxim presupposes that the plaintiff does not have to take the oath, but Abū Ḥanīfa's Iraqian contemporary, the judge Ibn Abī Lailā, demanded it from the plaintiff together with the evidence of witnesses (*Tr. I*, 116), and this doctrine was ascribed to Shuraiḥ and expressed in a tradition from ʿAlī (*Tr. II*, 14 (*e*)).[4] The Medinese, and Shāfiʿī after them, recognized the evidence of one witness together with the oath of the plaintiff, and we saw that this doctrine grew out of the judicial practice at the beginning of the second century A.H.[5] If the plaintiff has no evidence and the defendant refuses to take the oath in denial, the Medinese give judgment for the plaintiff only if he takes the oath himself;[6] Ibn Abī Lailā, in the same

[1] *Tr. I*, 68; *Umm*, iii. 147 ff., 164 ff.; Sarakhsī, xxi. 65.

[2] It was also known as a tradition from ʿUmar (e.g. *Umm*, vii. 11). Margoliouth, *Early Development*, 90, considers that this maxim was taken over from Jewish law.

[3] Also, by implication, *Mud.* xiii. 49.

[4] *Āthār A. Y.* 740: 'Abū Ḥanīfa did not demand the oath together with the evidence of witnesses, nor did Ḥammād demand it.' This reference to Ḥammād for a legal opinion seems to imply that "Ibrāhīm Nakhaʿī" demanded it; a remark on Ibrāhīm has perhaps dropped from the text.

[5] See above, p. 167.

[6] See *Muw.* iii. 183 f. and Zurqānī, ad loc., quoting Ibn ʿAbdalbarr.

case, used to demand the oath from the plaintiff if he doubted his good faith (*Tr. I*, 9, [82], 116).

All these are traces of the common tendency to impose a safeguard on the exclusive use of the evidence of witnesses as legal proof;[1] this tendency can be dated in the first half of the second century, and the legal maxim superseded it to a great extent, but not completely. The passage Koran v. 106 f. does not belong here; it reflects an earlier stage in which the 'witnesses' were concerned not so much with giving evidence as with affirming by oath the truth of the claims of their party, as compurgators. This stage had been superseded, and the function of witnesses restricted to the giving of evidence, before the question of a safeguard arose.[2]

As regards the restriction of legal proof to the evidence of witnesses and the denial of validity to written documents, it must go back to the first century.[3] This feature contradicts an explicit ruling of the Koran (ii. 282) which obviously endorsed the current practice of putting contracts into writing, and this practice did persist during the first century and later, and had to be accommodated with legal theory.[4] Nothing definite is known about the origin of this feature.

To sum up: legal maxims are rough and ready statements of doctrine in the form of slogans, sometimes rhyming or alliterating. They are not uniform as to provenance and period, and some important ones are rather late. But as a rule they are earlier than traditions, and they gradually take on the form of traditions. They date, generally speaking, from the time of the first primitive systematization of Muhammadan law in the first half of the second century A.H., but often represent a secondary stage of doctrine and practice. Some maxims express counter-doctrines and unsuccessful opinions, but if sufficiently well attested, they were harmonized with the prevailing doctrine. Also the traditionists used them occasionally, in the form of traditions, for voicing their point of view. Numerous maxims originated in Iraq, and they were sometimes taken over by the

[1] Cf. below, p. 272, n. 1.

[2] It is possible, of course, that the oath as a safeguard in the second stage was partly a survival from the first.

[3] Already John of Damascus mentions it as a characteristic feature: Migne, *Patr. Gr.* xciv. 768.

[4] See Tyan, *Notariat*, 8 f. and *passim*.

Medinese; but we find no traces of the opposite process. This shows the prevalent role of the Iraqians in the early period of Muhammadan jurisprudence. The legal maxims reflect a stage when legal doctrine was not yet automatically put into the form of traditions.[1]

[1] I do not exclude the possibility that some legal maxims may be older than the second century A.H., or may even go back to the pre-Islamic period, but this cannot be assumed but must be positively proved in each case, as R. Brunschvig has done for the maxim *al-walā' lil-kubr* (in *Revue Historique de Droit Français et Étranger*, 1950, 23–34).

PART III

THE TRANSMISSION OF LEGAL DOCTRINE

CHAPTER 1

UMAIYAD PRACTICE AS THE STARTING-POINT OF MUHAMMADAN JURISPRUDENCE

A. Preliminary Remarks

OUR conclusions so far have led us to the beginning of the second century A.H. as the time in which Muhammadan jurisprudence started. Occasionally, we have met or shall meet legal opinions which can probably be assigned to the end of the first century.[1] But the essential features of old Muhammadan jurisprudence, such as the idea of the 'living tradition' of the ancient schools of law; a body of common doctrine expressing the earliest effort to systematize;[2] legal maxims which often reflect a slightly later stage; and an important nucleus of legal traditions—all these features can be dated, roughly in this order, from the beginning of the second century onwards. In any case, it is safe to say that Muhammadan legal science started in the later part of the Umaiyad period, taking the legal practice of the time as its raw material and endorsing, modifying, or rejecting it, as the present chapter will show in detail. This is our starting-point for an historical study of the transmission of legal doctrine in the pre-literary period, which is the subject of Part III of this book.

As we are concerned with the early history of Muhammadan jurisprudence and not that of legal institutions as such, we need not attempt to analyse here the Umaiyad practice from which it started into its component parts. Two general remarks, however, are relevant. Firstly: legal practice in the several parts of the Umaiyad empire was not uniform, and this accounts for some of the original differences in doctrine between the ancient schools of law.[3] Secondly:

[1] See above, p. 100 f., and below, pp. 234, 245.

[2] See below, p. 214 ff.

[3] See above, p. 161, on a local Meccan custom.

although the dynasty and most of the Arab ruling class were Muslims, and although some elementary legal rules enacted in the Koran were more or less followed,[1] the legal practice during the earlier part of the Umaiyad period cannot yet be called Muhammadan law. Muhammadan law came into existence only through the application of Muhammadan jurisprudence to the raw material supplied by the practice.[2] It will be shown that legal norms based on the Koran, which go beyond the most elementary rules, were introduced into Muhammadan law almost invariably at a secondary stage.[3]

During most of the Umaiyad period the administration of justice lay in the hands of the provincial governors and, in so far as special judges were appointed, they were agents of the governors to whom these last delegated part of their functions.[4] The creation of a judiciary, separate from the political administration, dates only from ʿAbbāsid times. When John of Damascus refers to the law-givers (νομοθέται) of Islam, he means the governors and their agents, the judges, and his repeated statement, which cannot be a mistake, on flogging as the punishment for theft shows that their practice disregarded an explicit rule of the Koran (v. 38), which prescribes the cutting off of the hand.[5] In a number of passages, Shāfiʿī and his predecessors refer, for the most part polemically, to the origin of legal rules in decisions of governors and their agents.[6]

In assigning the origins of Muhammadan jurisprudence, which created Muhammadan law out of Umaiyad practice, to the later part of the Umaiyad period, I do not wish to deny that this practice contained earlier elements and, in particular, that some of its fundamental features were created by ʿUmar. The problems of the caliphate of ʿUmar, of pre-Umaiyad and Umaiyad administrative practice, and of the origins of Muhammadan law and jurisprudence have been discussed at length, but in rather general terms, by Caetani.[7] Parts II and III of this book will show how far my results have led me to agree or to disagree with him.[8]

[1] For examples of essential rules which were disregarded, see above, pp. 181, 188.

[2] See further below, pp. 283 ff.

[3] Below, pp. 224 ff.

[4] See Tyan, *Organisation*, i. 132 ff., 169; Bergsträsser, in *Z.D.M.G.* lxviii. 396 f.

[5] Migne, *Patr. Gr.* xciv. 1591; xcvi. 1337. John's references to the flogging of the πόρνος (loc. cit.) take no account of the lapidation of the adulterer which is certainly later than the time of the Prophet (cf. Caetani, *Annali*, iii, year 17, § 84, at the end). A governor, at the end of the first century A.H., punished drunkenness not by flogging but by the death penalty (Ṭabarī, *Annales*, ii. 1301: year 96); the punishment for drunkenness had not yet been fixed at that time (cf. Wensinck, in *E.I.*, s.v. *Khamr*).

[6] See above, pp. 58 f., 60, n. 5, 63, 68, 70, 72, 74, 78.

[7] *Annali*, v, year 23, §§ 517 ff.

[8] I disagree particularly with his reversion from the historical criticism of tradi-

We often find the names of 'Uthmān, of the Umaiyad Caliphs Mu'āwiya, Marwān b. Ḥakam, and 'Umar b. 'Abdal'azīz, and of other members of the family mentioned in traditions which directly or indirectly reflect Umaiyad practice, and the occurrence of these names in a tradition makes a prima-facie case for the origin of the problem in question in Umaiyad times. We must not, of course, conclude without positive proof that the decisions or opinions ascribed to these persons are authentic; their names were quoted sometimes in order to put a genuine old practice under their authority, but often in order to make them responsible for a rejected practice or opinion, or even in order to claim their authority in favour of a doctrine which superseded an older practice or opinion. The traditions which implicate 'Uthmān and the Umaiyads are therefore to a great extent, explicitly or implicitly, counter-traditions, and in so far as they represent an anti-Umaiyad tendency, which they often express strongly, they cannot be earlier than the rise of the 'Abbāsids, when everything to which exception was taken was blamed on the fallen dynasty of the Umaiyads.[1] The 'pious' Umaiyad 'Umar b. 'Abdal'azīz escaped this fate and became a favourite authority of Auzā'ī and of the Medinese for the fictitious 'good old' practice, which was opposed to the real practice as it existed at the end of the Umaiyad period. Examples of all this have occurred before,[2] and others will be found in the following sections.

B. Umaiyad Popular Practice

The present section is intended to illustrate the reactions of nascent Muhammadan jurisprudence to popular practice as it existed under the Umaiyads in general.

Cult and Ritual

Islamic cult and ritual were certainly rudimentary at the beginning of the Umaiyad period, and the Umaiyads and their

tions (§ 519); with his antedating the origin of Muhammadan jurisprudence to about A.H. 50; and with his belief in the existence of many authentic traditions from the Prophet at the beginnings of jurisprudence (§ 549).

[1] We saw (above, p. 72) that Auzā'ī, who was himself a Syrian, showed as yet no trace of anti-Umaiyad feeling. This applies to legal traditions only; it is agreed that political traditions directed against the ruling dynasty were put into circulation under the late Umaiyads.

[2] For 'Uthmān see above, p. 153; for Mu'āwiya, pp. 55, 114, 155; for Marwān b. Ḥakam, p. 114; for 'Umar b. 'Abdal'azīz, pp. 62, 71, n. 3, 101, 119, 131, 144, 161 (twice), 167 f., 183. On the fictitious character of references to 'Umar b. 'Abdal'azīz see further below, p. 206.

governors were responsible for the elaboration of some of their essential features, as Lammens and Becker have shown.[1] The first specialists on religious law were not satisfied with the practice as they found it, and their demands were incorporated in traditions which sometimes show a strong anti-Umaiyad bias.

Marriage

If divorce takes place before the consummation of the marriage, the husband has to pay only half of the *donatio propter nuptias* that has been fixed (Koran ii. 237). If husband and wife had been left together in private, the wife would normally claim that intercourse had taken place, which would give her the right to the full *donatio*. The judicial practice in Umaiyad times, however, seems to have been to reject this claim, and a decision to this effect is ascribed to 'Marwān b. Ḥakam or a governor before him' in a tradition with the *isnād* Ibn Wahb—Muḥammad b. ʿAmr—Ibn Juraij—ʿAmr b. Dīnār—Sulaimān b. Yasār.[2] In what is clearly a later addition, a distinction according to place and circumstances is made; this corresponds to a later, Medinese, stage of the doctrine.

But a presumption in favour of the claim of the wife prevailed both in Iraq (*Muw. Shaib.* 230) and, broadly speaking, in Medina, although here sometimes a distinction as to place and circumstances was made (*Muw.* iii. 10; *Mud.* v. 2). Ibn Musaiyib is adduced in favour both of the general claim and of the distinction. This presumption was projected back in Medina to ʿUmar and to Zaid b. Thābit (*Muw.*), and in Iraq to ʿAlī (*Mud.*) and to Ibn Masʿūd (Muzanī, iv. 38); later, it was ascribed to the first Caliphs.[3] The original tradition on the decision of Marwān b. Ḥakam was countered by a more detailed version of the same story, where Marwān sends to Zaid b. Thābit and the latter convinces him that the presumption in favour of the claim of the wife must be recognized (*Mud.*). The *isnād* runs: Ibn Wahb—Ibn Abil-Zinād—his father—Sulaimān b. Yasār; this

[1] Lammens, *Ṭâif*, 198, and in other places of his historical writings; Becker, *Islamstudien*, i. 465 f., 494 ff.

[2] *Mud.* v. 2. The doubt regarding the person shows the lack of positive knowledge; only the reference to the Umaiyad period is certain. The tradition, taken by itself, does not show whether this was Umaiyad practice or a counter-doctrine; the interpretation given to it here is based on the successive stages of doctrine.

[3] *Comm. Muw. Shaib.* 230, n. 7, quoting Baihaqī and others.

counter-tradition with a family *isnād* is later than the time of Sulaimān b. Yasār.

The opposite doctrine, rejecting the claim of the wife, did not disappear completely, but was projected back to Ibn ʿAbbās and Shuraiḥ;[1] it was also supported by reference to the literal meaning of Koran ii. 237 and xxxiii. 49. It was taken up, together with this argument, by Shāfiʿī who thus reverted unwittingly to the Umaiyad practice.[2]

Mālik and his followers were not clear whether the presumption which they recognized was rebuttable or conclusive (*Mud.*). In the Mālikī school, their doctrine was whittled down until the difference of principle as against Shāfiʿī disappeared (Zurqānī, iii. 10). But the doctrine of Abū Ḥanīfa and Shaibānī, based on the same principle as that of Mālik, is consistent (*Muw. Shaib.*).

Foster-relationship as an impediment to marriage was recognized by the pre-Islamic Arabs, and endorsed by Koran iv. 23 with regard to foster-mothers and foster-sisters.[3] Popular opinion in Umaiyad times incorporated relationship by marriage into the orbit of foster-relationship, so that the foster-son of the wife of a man was deemed to be the (foster-)brother of the man's daughter by another wife.[4] Both the Iraqians and the Medinese adopted this popular opinion;[5] it was ascribed to Zuhrī and found expression in traditions from Ibn ʿAbbās and, on the authority of ʿĀ'isha, from the Prophet.[6]

But this doctrine did not remain unchallenged. Shāfiʿī relates a tradition according to which Hishām b. Ismāʿīl, the governor of ʿAbdalmalik in Medina, in view of the popular objection to a marriage between persons connected in this way, referred the case to the Caliph who decided that this connexion did not constitute foster-relationship. It would be rash to deduce from this the existence of a government regulation at variance with the popular belief. Opposition to it became vocal

[1] *Tr. III*, 75. On the other hand, Shuraiḥ is claimed to have been essentially in favour of the presumption (*Mud.*); this shows how arbitrary and unreliable these references are.

[2] *Tr. III*, 55, 75; Muzanī, iv. 36 ff.

[3] See *E.I.*, s.v. *Raḍāʿ*.

[4] The underlying idea appears from the technical terms *laban al-faḥl* and *liqāḥ wāḥid*: the milk on which one child was suckled was produced by the same *semen genitale* by which the other child was begotten.

[5] *Muw. Shaib.* 275; *Mud.* v. 88.

[6] For these and the following traditions, see *Muw.* iii. 85 ff.; *Muw. Shaib.* 271; *Tr. III*, 148 (p. 246 f.).

in Medina only in Mālik's time, and Mālik's contemporary Darāwardī is the common transmitter in the *isnāds* of most traditions to this effect. These traditions, some of which are clearly counter-traditions, claim the authority of a number of Companions, including Ibn 'Abbās and 'Ā'isha, and of numerous old Medinese authorities of the generation of the Successors: all this is certainly spurious.

Divorce

The problem of the legal effects of a divorce pronounced as 'definite' (*batta*) was still unsettled in the generation preceding Mālik, and this uncertainty and several possible answers were projected back into earlier Umaiyad times in Medinese and Iraqian traditions.

The following two traditions are Medinese (*Muw.* iii. 36):

Mālik—Yaḥyā b. Sa'īd—Abū Bakr b. Muḥammad b. 'Amr b. Ḥazm informed 'Umar b. 'Abdal'azīz that Abān b. 'Uthmān considered the word *batta* as producing a single [revocable] divorce, but 'Umar b. 'Abdal'azīz insisted that it exhausted all possibilities of divorce [that is, was to be reckoned as a triple divorce].

Mālik—Zuhrī—Marwān b. Ḥakam decided that the word *batta* produced a triple [irrevocable] divorce.

The following tradition is Iraqian (*Āthār Shaib.* 74):

Abū Ḥanīfa—Ḥammād—Ibrāhīm Nakha'ī—'Urwa b. Mughīra as governor of Kufa was perplexed by the term *batta* and asked Shuraiḥ. The latter quoted the opinion of 'Umar that it produced a single revocable divorce, and the opinion of 'Alī who considered it as producing a triple divorce; pressed for his own opinion, Shuraiḥ held that the use of *batta* was a reprehensible innovation, but that it produced either a triple or a single definite divorce, according to the intention of the speaker.

This divorce with *batta* is a development from current practice and independent of the common ancient doctrine of Muhammadan law on divorce, a doctrine which is based on a not very obvious interpretation of Koran ii. 228–30.[1] Accord-

[1] It may fairly be doubted whether the Koran allows more than two divorces, and whether verse 230 does not refer to every divorce which has become definite, be it the first or the second. Cf. Bell, *The Qur'ān*, i. 32 and n. 4; *E.I.*, s.v. *Ṭalāḳ*, section IV.

ing to this common doctrine, the first and the second divorce pronounced by a husband over his wife are revocable and become definite only at the end of a waiting period (*'idda*);[1] the third divorce, however, is at once irrevocable and definite. By divorcing with *batta* the husband renounced his right to revoke the divorce and made it definite at once; it must therefore have been single but definite. This can safely be considered as part of the practice under the Umaiyads.[2] It was recognized by the Iraqians: they allow a single, definite divorce which is pronounced by using the word *batta* or similar expressions.[3]

Because divorce with *batta* did not fit well into the clear-cut scheme of the common doctrine, efforts were made in both Iraq and Medina to make it either single and revocable, or triple and definite, and the traditions quoted above reflect these efforts. They were successful in Medina, where Mālik preferred the second alternative (*Muw.* iii. 36).

When the old meaning of divorce with *batta* was no longer understood in Hijaz, the problem of its legal effects was conceived in terms of the single or triple validity of a triple divorce pronounced in one session. The memory of the old practice was harmonized with current doctrine by the fictitious statement that a triple divorce pronounced in one session counted only as a single divorce in the time of the Prophet, of Abū Bakr and the first three years of the caliphate of 'Umar, with the implication that 'Umar gave it triple validity (*Ikh.* 310). This statement, attributed to Ibn 'Abbās, can be dated immediately before Mālik; while a formal tradition through Ibn 'Abbās from the Prophet, to the effect that such a divorce counts as single and

[1] So far, the common doctrine doubtless reproduces the exact meaning of the Koranic passage.

[2] Tibrīzī in his commentary on *Ḥamāsa*, i. 203, relates how Murra b. Wāki' divorced his wife with *batta*, being under the impression that he had the power to revoke this divorce within a year; how his former wife was asked in marriage, whereupon Murra demanded her back, but she refused to return to him; and how Murra appealed in vain to Mu'āwiya or to 'Uthmān, in order to have his former wife prevented from re-marrying. The verses which are quoted in connexion with this story confirm it in its broad outlines but not in its details some of which are uncertain (cf. the doubt whether it was Mu'āwiya or 'Uthmān to whom he appealed). Supposing that the mention of *batta* is authentic, the point of the story is the ignorance of a rude bedouin (as Murra calls himself) of the legal consequences of a divorce, and what the bedouin thought is not evidence on the nature of the divorce with *batta*.

[3] *Āthār A.Y.* 632; *Āthār Shaib.* 78; *Muw. Shaib.* 255; *Tr. I*, 225; *Tr. II*, 11 (*d*), (*e*).

revocable, appeared only in the time between Shāfi'ī and Ibn Ḥanbal.[1] The Medinese considered the whole procedure a sin but valid as a triple divorce, and ascribed this doctrine to the same Ibn 'Abbās and even to the Iraqian Ibn Mas'ūd (*Muw.* iii. 35). This discussion later produced traditions from the Prophet approving or disapproving the pronouncing of a triple divorce in one session, and even declaring it altogether invalid, as well as a large number of spurious references to Companions and other authorities, including those of the Iraqians, in favour of the Medinese opinion.[2] The whole problem of the triple divorce pronounced in one session is secondary.

The following two traditions (*Muw.* iii. 34) show one of the reasons why divorce with *batta* was of practical importance; its identification in Medina with triple divorce; and the projection of this new problem back into the middle Umaiyad period.

Mālik—Rabī'a—Qāsim b. Muḥammad and 'Urwa b. Zubair held that a man married to four wives who divorces one of them with *batta*, is at once free to marry again, without waiting for her *'idda* to expire.

Mālik—Rabī'a—Qāsim b. Muḥammad and 'Urwa b. Zubair told this, their opinion, to the Umaiyad Caliph Walīd b. 'Abdalmalik when he visited Medina, but Qāsim stipulated that the three divorces must be pronounced in separate sessions.

In late Umaiyad times it must have been the practice for the divorced wife or widow to vacate the house of her husband immediately, without waiting for the end of her *'idda*. This practice is clearly stated in two Medinese traditions.[3] According to one, Yaḥyā b. Sa'īd b. 'Āṣ divorced his wife and her father took her away; 'Ā'isha complained to Marwān b. Ḥakam and asked him to have her returned to her house, but Marwān referred to the case of Fāṭima bint Qais who was divorced in the time of the Prophet; 'Ā'isha replied: 'Can you not forget the tradition of Fāṭima?', but Marwān was afraid of bad feeling between the former husband and wife. According to the other Medinese tradition, Ibn 'Umar disapproved of the divorced wife of a grandson of the Caliph 'Uthmān moving during her *'idda*.

[1] See above, p. 146.
[2] See *E.I.*, s.v. *Ṭalāḳ*, sections III and IV.
[3] *Muw.* iii. 62; *Muw. Shaib.* 263.

The same practice which the Medinese traditions ascribed to the Umaiyads, went under the name of 'Alī in Iraq.[1]

The Umaiyad practice was attacked more successfully with references to the Koran. A counter-tradition relating the decision of the Prophet in the case of a certain Furai'a referred to Koran lxv. 2, tried to explain the opposite doctrine away by implying second thoughts on the part of the Prophet, and even claimed that 'Uthmān during his caliphate decided accordingly.[2] An Iraqian tradition makes Ibrāhīm Nakha'ī quote Koran lxv. 1, which is directly relevant, and give it an arbitrary interpretation which makes it even stronger.[3] Koran lxv. 6 is also brought in.

This secondary doctrine prevailed both in Hijaz and Iraq, and was ascribed to 'Umar, Ibn 'Umar and Ibn Musaiyib, and to Ibn Mas'ūd and Ibrāhīm Nakha'ī respectively.[4]

Other points of Umaiyad practice regarding family law have been discussed before.[5]

C. Umaiyad Administrative Practice

The starting-point of Muhammadan jurisprudence is not only popular practice under the Umaiyads as discussed in the preceding section; it is often the administrative practice of the government. The existence of administrative regulations, sanctioning the practice from which Muhammadan jurisprudence started, is sometimes directly attested[6] and can sometimes be deduced from the subject-matter. Practically all individual cases in which we must postulate an Umaiyad administrative practice as the starting-point fall under the three great headings of fiscal law, law of war, and penal law; cases unconnected with one or other of these are few. This agrees well with the general character of Umaiyad government.

[1] *Āthār Shaib.* 76; *Tr. II*, 10 (*k*).

[2] *Muw.* iii. 74; *Muw. Shaib.* 263. The Furai'a tradition cannot yet have existed at the time when the tradition on 'Ā'isha and Marwān was put into circulation; its several *isnāds* (see Zurqānī, ad loc.) have a common transmitter in Mālik's immediate authority Sa'd b. Isḥāq b. Ka'b b. 'Ujra.

[3] *Āthār A.Y.* 643.

[4] *Muw.* iii. 62, 74; *Muw. Shaib.* 252, 263.—*Āthār A.Y.* 643 ff.; *Āthār Shaib.* 76.

[5] See above, p. 161 on *muwālāt*, p. 181 on disputes about paternity, p. 182 f. on marriage without a *walī*.

[6] See further on in this section and above, p. 191, n. 6.

Fiscal Law

The Umaiyad administration imposed the *zakāt* tax on horses; this tax was accepted in Syria and Iraq, but rejected, after some hesitation, in Medina. Both sides expressed their doctrine in traditions.[1] In favour of the tax are the following (in *Tr. III*):

Mālik—Zuhrī—Sulaimān b. Yasār—'Umar was unwilling to impose the *zakāt* on horses, but the Syrians insisted on paying it, and 'Umar finally agreed to accept it but ordered the takings to be spent locally.

Shāfi'ī—Ibn 'Uyaina—Zuhrī—Sā'ib b. Yazīd—'Umar imposed the *zakāt* on horses. Zuhrī is the common link in the *isnāds* of both traditions.

Against the tax are directed the following (in *Muw.*):

Mālik—'Abdallāh b. Dīnār—Sulaimān b. Yasār—'Irāk b. Mālik—Abū Huraira—the Prophet decided that no *zakāt* was to be imposed on horses. The reference to the Prophet is meant to supersede that to 'Umar. Sulaimān b. Yasār is taken from the *isnād* of the first tradition.

Mālik—'Abdallāh b. Dīnār—Ibn Musaiyib bases an analogy on the exemption of horses from the *zakāt*. 'Abdallāh b. Dīnār is the common link in the *isnāds* of these two traditions.

Mālik—'Abdallāh b. Abī Bakr b. 'Amr b. Ḥazm—his father—'Umar b. 'Abdal'azīz gave written instructions not to impose *zakāt* on horses. This tradition with a spurious family *isnād* tries to enlist the authority of an Umaiyad Caliph against the Umaiyad regulation.

The Iraqians, down to Abū Ḥanīfa,[2] accepted the *zakāt* on horses;[3] but Shaibānī,[4] under the influence of the recent tradition from the Prophet, which later appeared in the classical collections, changed the doctrine.

The Umaiyad administration used to deduct the *zakāt* tax from government pensions, and Mālik states on the authority of Zuhrī that Mu'āwiya was the first who did it. In Iraq, this procedure was put under the authority of Ibn Mas'ūd. But this practice was rejected by both schools[5] for the systematic reason

[1] *Muw.* ii. 71; *Muw. Shaib.* 173; *Āthār Shaib.* 47; *Tr. III*, 83.
[2] And Zufar: Zurqānī, ii. 71.
[3] Tradition from Ibrāhīm Nakha'ī to this effect: *Āthār Shaib.* 47.
[4] And Abū Yūsuf: Zurqānī, loc. cit.
[5] *Muw.* ii. 44; *Tr. II*, 19 (*dd*).

that the *zakāt* becomes due only after one year's uninterrupted ownership; this reason is given explicitly on behalf of the Iraqians, and on behalf of the Medinese implicitly in a statement of the general rule with the *isnād* Mālik—Nāfi'—Ibn 'Umar. The Medinese explained away the authorities that might be adduced in favour of the practice,[1] by a tradition to the effect that 'Uthmān deducted from the pension only the amount of *zakāt* due for other property, on the basis of the declaration of the recipient.[2] The same procedure was projected back to Abū Bakr in the following tradition:

Mālik—Muḥammad b. 'Uqba consulted Qāsim b. Muḥammad on the deduction of *zakāt* from pensions—Qāsim referred to Abū Bakr for the general rule regarding *zakāt*, and stated that Abū Bakr followed the procedure as mentioned. This can be dated in the generation preceding Mālik, when the proper decision was still in doubt.

The Umaiyad administration seems to have levied *zakāt* tax on the property of minors.[3]

When payments were made in kind, the Umaiyad administration issued assignments on its stores, and the speculative trade in these assignments, leading as it did to 'usury' (*ribā*), provoked a reaction on the part of the Iraqians and the Medinese. The Medinese prohibited re-selling food before one had taken possession of it, the Iraqians extended this prohibition to all objects.[4] Both the administrative practice and the objection raised against it are explicitly stated in a story which involves Marwān b. Ḥakam, and the objection against re-selling food before one has taken possession of it is ascribed to Ibn Musaiyib,[5] and expressed in traditions related by Nāfi' and 'Abdallāh b. Dīnār, from Ibn 'Umar, from the Prophet. Traditions in favour of the extension of the prohibition to all objects were known also in Medina; they start with a version according to which 'Umar ordered Ḥakīm b. Ḥizām not to re-sell before he had taken possession,[6] and this version develops into traditions from the

[1] Ibn 'Abdalbarr, quoted in Zurqānī, ii. 44, mentions Ibn 'Abbās.

[2] 'Uthmān was meant to supersede Mu'āwiya.

[3] See below, p. 216.

[4] *Muw.* iii. 117, 129; *Muw. Shaib.* 331; *Tr. III.* 50, 95; *Ris.* 47; *Ikh.* 327. Cf. above, p. 108.

[5] This is the oldest tradition on the problem.

[6] This is *munqaṭi'*, on the authority of Nāfi'.

Prophet transmitted by Ḥakīm b. Ḥizām.[1] The objection prevailed only in the generation preceding Mālik; the Kufian 'Uthmān Battī (d. A.H. 143) still allowed re-selling of all objects before one had taken possession (Zurqānī, iii. 118).

A vivid picture of the levying of tolls under Umaiyad administration is given in the following tradition (*Muw.* ii. 51):

Mālik relates on the authority of Yaḥyā b. Sa'īd that Zuraiq [or Ruzaiq] b. Ḥaiyān, the director of the toll-gates of Egypt under the Umaiyad Caliphs Walīd, Sulaimān, and 'Umar b. 'Abdal'azīz, was instructed by 'Umar b. 'Abdal'azīz to levy the appropriate amounts from Muslims and non-Muslims—nothing if the value of their merchandise was under the prescribed minimum by a third of a dīnār or more—and to give a receipt valid for one year. Whereas no reliance can be placed on the individual reference to 'Umar b. 'Abdal'azīz, the description of the procedure is certainly correct in the essentials. The third of a dīnār within which the exemption from toll does not become effective is an authentic feature;[2] it was disregarded by both the Iraqians and the Medinese.[3] For the rest, the Iraqians uphold the concession that the payment of toll frees the goods from further toll duties for a year;[4] the Medinese, however, subject them to toll duty every time they pass a toll-gate.[5]

It is possible that the restriction of legacies to one third of the estate, which is of Umaiyad origin, was connected with a fiscal interest.[6] The estate of a person who leaves no legal heirs falls to the treasury, and a restriction of legacies would therefore tend to increase its share. Whereas this is suggested only as a possible explanation, the Umaiyad origin of the restriction of legacies to one-third of the estate is explicitly stated in the following tradition (*Muw.* iii. 245):

Mālik—Rabī'a—a man on his death-bed, when Abān b. 'Uthmān was governor [of Medina], set free the six slaves who

[1] 'Aṭā' is the common link in the *isnāds* of two versions; a third, which by-passes him in the *isnād*, adds a technical definition of what is meant by the prohibition.

[2] Ibn 'Abdalbarr, quoted in Zurqānī, ii. 51, considers it as *ra'y* and *istiḥsān* on the part of 'Umar b. 'Abdal'azīz.

[3] But according to Ibn Qāsim, quoted ibid., Mālik let no exemption take place if the value was only a grain or two [of gold] less than the prescribed minimum; see also *Muw.* ii. 45, for dealing with underweight coins.

[4] *Kharāj*, 76; *Āthār Shaib.* 171.

[5] *Tr. III*, 105.

[6] For a parallel, see below, p. 206.

were his only property, but Abān drew lots and set free only the winning two.[1]

This was projected back to the Prophet, first of all as a *mursal*, both in Iraq and in Hijaz, with the *isnāds*: Mālik—Yaḥyā b. Saʿīd and others—Ḥasan Baṣrī and Ibn Sīrīn—Prophet (*Muw.*, ibid.), and Ibn Juraij—Qais b. Saʿd—Makḥūl—Ibn Musaiyib—Prophet (*Ikh.* 370). This tradition dates only from the second century, because Shāfiʿī states[2] that it is the only argument which can be adduced against the doctrine of Ṭāwūs on another problem of legacies; whether the alleged doctrine of Ṭāwūs is authentic or not, the tradition cannot have existed in the time of the historical Ṭāwūs who died in A.H. 101. The whole doctrine on legacies was still fluid at the beginning of the second century.

The restriction of legacies to one-third of the estate was the common ancient doctrine and was directly based on an Umaiyad administrative regulation. But as regards the manumission of slaves on the death-bed, the Iraqians, for systematic reasons, abandoned the drawing of lots and set one-third of each slave free (*Ikh.* 380 ff.).

For obvious fiscal reasons, the Umaiyad administration controlled the granting of ownerless and uncultivated land for purposes of cultivation.[3] As far as the disposal of land already under cultivation, abandoned by its former owners at the time of the great conquests, is concerned, Muhammadan jurisprudence gives only an artificially systematized picture, which as a whole is considerably later than the facts it purports to represent. At the beginning of the second century A.H., when Muhammadan legal science began, there remained only the question whether a grant of the administration was necessary for a valid title to uncultivated land brought under cultivation for the first time (*iḥyāʾ al-mawāt*). Both the Iraqians, down to Abū Ḥanīfa, and the Medinese answered in the affirmative, upholding the Umaiyad administrative practice which in this case was maintained by the ʿAbbāsids.[4]

In the generation preceding Mālik, however, traditions from

[1] The manumission on the death-bed counts as a legacy.

[2] *Ris.* 22; *Ikh.* 381.

[3] See Becker, *Islamstudien*, i. 218 ff.; Caetani, *Annali*, v, year 23, §§ 733 ff. As the result of the following analysis I must, however, disagree with Becker's over-simplified conclusion, ibid. 227.

[4] *Kharāj*, 36; *Muw. Shaib.* 356; *Tr. III*, 67.

the Prophet were put into circulation, mostly in Medina, to the effect that 'if someone brings uncultivated land under cultivation, it belongs to him', implying that no grant was necessary.[1] Mālik shows himself influenced by them when he adds 'and this is our practice', but he specifies (*Mud.* xv. 195) that they apply only to desert tracts, not to land near cultivated country, or as Ibn Qāsim adds on the authority of Mālik, not to land that has been granted as tribal quarters (*khiṭaṭ*). On the Iraqian side, Abū Yūsuf recognized the right of the ['Abbāsid] administration to the control and grant of titles, but on account of the traditions accepted the validity of the title of the cultivator without a grant, and Shaibānī followed him in this.

Connected with fiscal policy was the currency reform of the Umaiyad Caliph 'Abdalmalik. He fixed the official exchange ratio of gold to silver at 1 : 14, struck silver dirhams of 'standard seven', that is, weighing seven-tenths of one gold dīnār, and accordingly made 20 dirhams equivalent in value to one dīnār.[2] It is not surprising that in determining the amounts of weregeld in gold and silver, the ancient schools of law, for once, reflect an earlier stage. The Iraqians fixed it at 1,000 dīnār or 10,000 dirham, the Medinese at 1,000 dīnār or 12,000 dirham.[3] Both schools projected their tariffs back to 'Umar.[4]

But in the details of their doctrine, the ancient Iraqians presuppose 'Abdalmalik's reform. They specify that the dirhams must be of 'standard seven' which was introduced by 'Abdalmalik and which Shaibānī even calls 'the standard of Islam'. They further explain the different tariff of the Medinese by the artificial theory that the dirhams in this case must be of 'standard six', that is, weigh six-tenths of one dīnār. This kind of dirham never existed, but the reckoning results in approximately the same amount of silver for one dīnār;[5] this again presupposes

[1] *Muw.* iii. 204 and the passages referred to in the preceding note. The *isnāds* are quite fluid above Hishām b. 'Urwa.

[2] See *E.I.*, s.v. *Dīnār, Dirham*; J. Walker, *A Catalogue of the Arab-Sassanian Coins* (British Museum, 1941), cxlvi ff. The main Arabic source is a treatise by Maqrīzī, translated and annotated by de Sacy, *Monnaies*. See also E. von Bergmann, in *Sitzungsber. Wien*, lxv. 239 ff.; H. Sauvaire, in *J.A.*, 7th ser., vol. xiv ff.

[3] *Tr. VIII*, 1; *Āthār A.Y.* 980; *Āthār Shaib.* 81; *Muw.* iv. 32.

[4] The Iraqian *isnāds*, which alone are given in full in the sources available, have a common link in Sha'bī.

[5] Exactly the weight of 7.2 as against 7 dīnār (the dīnār being also a unit of weight). Rough reckonings like this are not uncommon in early legal texts.

'Abdalmalik's reform. This ancient Iraqian theory was first put into the mouth of Ibrāhīm Nakha'ī and then projected back to 'Uthmān who was alleged to have fixed the weregeld at 12,000 dirham of 'standard six'. Later still, an alleged currency reform of 'Umar on the basis of 'standard six' was deduced.[1] The reform of 'Abdalmalik was projected back to the Umaiyad governor Ziyād b. Abī Sufyān.[2] The traditions from the Prophet concerning the amount of weregeld in gold and silver, which occur in the classical traditions, were as yet unknown to Shaibānī.[3]

The minting fees of the Umaiyad administration gave the lawyers an occasion for elaborating strict rules on the exchange of bullion for coins.[4]

Law of War

It was the policy of the Umaiyads, for reasons of expediency, not to lay waste the enemy country wantonly. This was well known to Auzā'ī and to Abū Yūsuf.[5] In justification of the Umaiyad policy it was alleged that Abū Bakr instructed Yazīd b. Abī Sufyān, a member of the Umaiyad family, to adopt it when he sent him at the head of an army group against Syria.[6] Syrian doctrine acknowledged the Umaiyad practice, and Ibn Ḥanbal considered the Abū Bakr tradition a Syrian invention.[7]

The devastation of enemy country, on the other hand, was advocated by reference to Koran lix. 5 which authorizes the cutting down of trees in warfare, by counter-traditions from Abū Bakr and from the Prophet,[8] and by 'historical' traditions from the Prophet.[9]

Against this, the Syrians took the Abū Bakr tradition as an authoritative interpretation of the Koranic passage, referred to Koran ii. 205 which forbids the causing of devastation, and as far as the 'historical' traditions from the Prophet were concerned, concluded that there must have been a change of dispensation.[10]

1 See de Sacy, *Monnaies*, 13.
2 *Tr. VIII*, 1; de Sacy, ibid. 15.
3 See above, p. 145.
4 See above, p. 67.
5 Ṭabarī, 81; *Tr. IX*, 28.
6 *Muw.* ii. 295; *Mud.* iii. 7 f.; *Tr. III*, 65; *Tr. IX*, 28 f.; Ṭabarī, 81.
7 See *Comm. ed. Cairo* on *Tr. IX*, 28.
8 See above, p. 145.
9 See above, p. 139, n. 4.
10 *Tr. IX*, 29; Ṭabarī, 81; *Umm*, iv. 161, 173 ff.; *Siyar*, i. 35.

The Medinese, under the influence of the recent traditions, decided for unrestricted warfare,[1] and so did the main group of Iraqians, represented by Abū Ḥanīfa, Abū Yūsuf, and Shaibānī.[2] Some other Iraqians, however, shared the doctrine of the Syrians, and Sufyān Thaurī declared that were it not for the Abū Bakr tradition, he would have no objection to the cutting down of trees.[3]

The Umaiyad government controlled the distribution of booty, allotting to the rider two shares for his mount, in addition to his personal share.[4] This was done on the basis of the records in the pay-roll (*dīwān*); if a person was entered in it as a foot-soldier, he did not receive the share of a rider, even if he had acquired a horse in the meantime.[5] The Iraqians accepted this administrative practice, all the more easily as the institution of the *dīwān* was ascribed to ʿUmar. Auzāʿī, however, pointed out that the *dīwān* did not exist in the time of the Prophet and opposed to it the fictitious usage of the Prophet and of the Caliphs; for Shāfiʿī this became *sunna*. Both parties reacted in the same way to the practice of dividing the booty not on the spot but after the return of the army to Islamic territory.[6] In this case, Auzāʿī positively alleged a change from the (fictitious) old to the (real) recent practice in A.H. 126, but this change is spurious.[7] Mālik, too, referred to the fictitious practice at the beginning of Islam.[8]

The right of the killer to the spoils was recognized, but some of the ancient schools felt scruples about it.[9]

Penal Law

Byzantine and Syriac historians relate that ʿUmar b. ʿAbdalʿazīz in A.H. 100 (A.D. 717/718) fixed the weregeld for a Christian at half of that for a Muslim.[10] This does not mean that the full weregeld was paid before, which would be un-

[1] *Mud.* iii. 7 f.; Ṭabarī, 81.
[2] *Tr. III*, 28 f.; *Siyar*, i. 35.
[3] *Kharāj*, 123; Ṭabarī, 81.
[4] See above, p. 108.
[5] *Tr. IX*, 4; Ṭabarī, 72; *Siyar*, ii. 184; *Mud.* iii. 32 f.
[6] *Tr. IX*, 1; Ṭabarī, 89; *Siyar*, ii. 254; *Mud.* iii. 12.
[7] See above, p. 71.
[8] See above, p. 68.
[9] See above, p. 70 f.
[10] Caetani, *Chronographia*, year 100, § 28. This date seems preferable to A.D. 725, and there is no reason to antedate it in the reign of Walīd b. ʿAbdalmalik (A.H. 86–96). Wellhausen, *Arab. Reich*, 187, says correctly: 'under ʿUmar II'.

likely; if weregeld for a non-Muslim was paid at all, there was no fixed usage, and this regulation was the starting-point.

It is typical of the fictitious character of the frequent references to ʿUmar b. ʿAbdalʿazīz and of the lack of positive information on the part of the ancient lawyers that here where ʿUmar b. ʿAbdalʿazīz did inaugurate an important legal rule, there should be only an isolated reference to him which moreover is 'weak' by the standards of the Muhammadan critics,[1] and that the regulation should be commonly attributed to Muʿāwiya.[2] The most circumstantial version of the common story occurs in *Aghānī*, xv. 13, related by an anonymous sheikh from Hijaz on the authority of the freedman of an implicated party; and by that notorious propagator of traditions, Ibn Abī Dhi'b, on the authority of one Abū Suhail or Ibn Suhail who is no more than a name. According to it, Muʿāwiya demanded 12,000 dirham as weregeld for his Christian physician, remitted 6,000 to the public treasury and took 6,000 for himself, and this usage remained in force until ʿUmar b. ʿAbdalʿazīz cancelled the ruler's share but maintained the treasury's.

We have here a disturbed echo of a corollary to the regulation of ʿUmar b. ʿAbdalʿazīz. Half of the normal weregeld did in fact go to the next of kin of the non-Muslim victim, but the second half was demanded by the public treasury. This is explicitly stated on the authority of Zuhrī (*Tr. VIII*, 13, p. 293 *ult.*), and is another example of Umaiyad fiscal policy.

The Medinese adopted the Umaiyad regulation as far as the weregeld proper for a non-Muslim was concerned, but ignored the demand of the public treasury.[3] The Iraqians, by insisting on the full weregeld for a non-Muslim, protested against the demand of the treasury in another way.[4] The Iraqian doctrine was ascribed to the ancient authorities Ibrāhīm Nakhaʿī and Shaʿbī. It seems that the same doctrine was held by at least some Medinese in the time before Mālik, because Shaibānī quotes traditions from and through Medinese authorities to this effect.[5] On the other hand, once discrimination against the

[1] *Muw.* iv. 41; *Tr. VIII*, 13, p. 294, l. 13.

[2] *Āthār A.Y.* 972; *Āthār Shaib.* 87; *Tr. VIII*, 13. It was also projected back to the Prophet, but this too is not 'well-established' (*Tr. VIII*, 13, p. 294, l. 10).

[3] *Muw.* iv. 41; *Mud.* xvi. 195; *Tr. VIII*, 13.

[4] *Āthār A.Y.* 969; *Āthār Shaib.* 87; *Tr. VIII*, 13.

[5] *Tr. VIII*, 13. He mentions Rabīʿa (this is perhaps genuine) and Ibn Musaiyib

non-Muslim had begun, some Medinese allotted him only one-third of the weregeld for a Muslim or even less: 4,000 dirham for a Jew or Christian and 800 for a Zoroastrian. This was projected back to 'Umar and 'Uthmān on the authority of Ibn Musaiyib, and Ibn Musaiyib was made to express indignation at the doubt whether it was generally accepted.[1] But this claim is not correct nor is the protest of Ibn Musaiyib genuine, since we find a statement on the authority of Sulaimān b. Yasār to the effect that 'people used to fix the weregeld for Zoroastrians at 800 dirham, and for Jews and Christians at the amount customary between them' (*Tr. III*, 43).

The Umaiyad administration deducted the weregeld (or the fractions of it due for wounds) from the pension account of the culprit or of his tribe, if necessary in three yearly instalments, and paid it to the family of the victim (or to the victim in person).[2] Mu'āwiya is said to have instituted this procedure (Kindī, 309). This administrative practice is the basis of the common doctrine of the ancient schools of law. According to this doctrine, the *'āqila* of the culprit must pay the weregeld for accidental killing (or the fraction of it due for an accidental wounding) in three yearly instalments;[3] the *'āqila* consists in the first place not of the members of the tribe as such, as in ancient Arab tribal society from which this idea of collective responsibility derived,[4] but of those whose names are entered in the same pay-roll. The Medinese, however, made the culprit individually responsible for all fractions amounting to less than one-third of the weregeld (*Muw.* iv. 42). Shāfi'ī more or less openly reproached them with following, against analogy, the decree of some governor (*Tr. VIII*, 14), and we must conclude that they endorsed an administrative ruling which left it to the aggrieved party to collect smaller amounts from the culprit.[5]

(a fictitious authority; see below for another doctrine ascribed to him); he also quotes from Zuhrī a statement pointing out that Mu'āwiya's regulation diverged from the practice under Abū Bakr, 'Umar and 'Uthmān, and a tradition which makes 'Uthmān fix the weregeld for a non-Muslim at the full amount.

[1] *Tr. VIII*, 13, p. 294. The amount of 4,000 dirham is based on the Medinese rate of 1,000 dīnār or 12,000 dirham for the weregeld of the Muslim (see above, p. 203).

[2] See Gaudefroy-Demombynes, in *Mélanges Dussaud*, ii. 826 and n. 7.

[3] The weregeld for murder and the fractions of it due for intentional woundings are to be borne by the culprit himself.

[4] See Robertson Smith, *Kinship*, 64; Procksch, *Blutrache*, 56 ff.

[5] The Iraqians made the *'āqila* responsible for all damages for accidental wound-

The Umaiyad administration, moreover, seems to have fixed the actual fractions of the weregeld which were due for certain kinds of wounds.[1]

The Umaiyad administration did not interfere with the working of the old Arab *lex talionis*, as modified by the Koran.[2] Considerations of public policy regarding the execution of murderers, such as are found in, or rejected by, the Iraqian and Medinese schools,[3] do not necessarily reflect a corresponding administrative practice.

As regards the purely Islamic *ḥadd* punishments and similar penalties, however, there are positive traces of an Umaiyad practice from which the ancient schools of law started. This practice was in some respects irregular by later standards.[4]

The non-Muslim slave who escaped to the enemy was killed or crucified at the discretion of the government (*imām*), if he was recaptured; Auzā'ī gave his opinion (*ra'y*) endorsing this practice, the Iraqians and the Medinese rejected it.[5]

The Umaiyad administration refused to cut off the hand of a slave who had run away from his master in Islamic territory and stolen.[6] Both Medinese and Iraqians held that the slave was liable to the punishment for theft prescribed in Koran v. 38.[7] A Nāfi' tradition makes Ibn 'Umar insist on it against the Umaiyad governor Sa'īd b. 'Āṣ; another tradition makes 'Umar b. 'Abdal'azīz countermand what had hitherto been the accepted opinion.[8] The thesis of the Medinese was projected back to Qāsim b. Muḥammad, Sālim, and 'Urwa, and Mālik found it held unanimously in Medina.

Both ancient schools, however, agreed that only the government, and not the master, could cut off the hand of a slave as

ing which amounted to one-twentieth of the weregeld or more; but one-twentieth is the smallest fraction applicable. Lesser amounts, which are not assessed in fractions of the weregeld, are to be borne by the culprit himself. See *Āthār A.Y.* 979; *Āthār Shaib.* 85; *Tr. VIII*, 14. The Iraqians, therefore, whilst materially rejecting the administrative regulation, remained formally influenced by it.

[1] See above, p. 114, and below, p. 217.

[2] See *E.I.*, s.v. *Ḳiṣāṣ*; Lammens, *L'Arabie occidentale*, 233.

[3] See above, p. 111 and below, p. 274.

[4] Cf. above, p. 191 and n. 5.

[5] *Tr. IX*, 18; Ṭabarī, 97.

[6] We have seen above, loc. cit., that the usual punishment for theft under the Umaiyads was not cutting off the hand, but flogging.

[7] *Muw.* iv. 81; *Muw. Shaib.* 303; *Tr. III*, 147.

[8] 'I used to hear'; on the meaning of this formula see above, p. 101.

a punishment for theft.[1] The tradition from Ibn 'Umar, which advocates the opposite doctrine, cannot therefore be the basis of the Medinese doctrine.

Banishment as part of the punishment for fornication is known to the ancient Iraqians as a current practice,[2] but rejected by them as likely to lead to further temptation.[3] This opinion was ascribed to Ibrāhīm Nakha'ī and projected back to 'Alī, and the opinion in favour of banishment was put under the authority of Ibn Mas'ūd; all this is reported with the *isnād* Ḥammād—Ibrāhīm.[4] The Iraqian opposition put into circulation counter-traditions from 'Alī advocating banishment. Although this opinion did not prevail in Iraq, it prevailed in Medina where it found expression in traditions, among others, from Abū Bakr, 'Umar, 'Uthmān, 'Umar b. 'Abdal'azīz, and the Prophet himself.[5] For Shāfi'ī, the administrative practice had become the *sunna* of the Prophet.

It was the practice under the Umaiyads not to apply *ḥadd* punishments in the army in enemy country, for fear of desertion.[6] The information on Auzā'ī is contradictory on details; it shows, however, that he endorsed the practice whilst idealizing it. In Iraq, Abū Ḥanīfa introduced a systematic theory of the applicability of religious punishments and their territorial limits;[7] it has its basis in the old practice but goes farther in restricting *ḥadd* punishments. Abū Yūsuf and Shaibānī relate traditions from Companions, and finally from the Prophet, in favour of the practice; their *isnāds* are significantly Syrian and Iraqian.[8] The Medinese did not recognize the practice, but Mālik made at least the concession that the commander might postpone the *ḥadd* punishment if he was otherwise engaged in enemy country.

Auzā'ī considers it natural that *ḥadd* punishments in the

[1] *Mud.* xvi. 57; *Muw. Shaib.* 303.

[2] The judge Ibn Abī Lailā endorsed it: *Tr. I,* 254.

[3] *Āthār Shaib.* 90; *Tr. II,* 18 (*c*), (*z*).

[4] The person responsible for these traditions is certainly not Ibrāhīm but Ḥammād or someone who used his name.

[5] *Muw.* iv. 8, 12; *Tr. II,* 18 (*z*); *Umm,* vi. 119.

[6] *Kharāj,* 109; *Siyar,* iv. 107; *Tr. IX,* 27; Ṭabarī, 52.

[7] See below, p. 298.

[8] See also *Comm. ed. Cairo* on *Tr. IX,* 27 (p. 82, n. 1). The Iraqian *isnāds* have a common link in A'mash. In one of the later versions, with a strong anti-Umaiyad bias, Walīd b. 'Uqba, a half-brother of 'Uthmān, is involved.

army should be administered by military commanders, even those of lower rank; Abū Ḥanīfa insists, as a part of his systematic reasoning, that only the cadi is competent to do it. Shāfi'ī, with consistent and systematic reasoning, cuts across the previous divisions of doctrine. This is typical of the growth of legal doctrine out of, and away from, the old practice.

Other Branches of Law

At the same time at which the weregeld for a non-Muslim was fixed at half of that for a Muslim[1] it was decreed that Christians, and presumably non-Muslims in general, could not give evidence against Muslims. This did not imply that their evidence against Muslims had been admitted before, but it meant that their evidence was henceforth to be admitted in cases where only non-Muslims were involved. The Koran (ii. 282, v. 106, lxv. 2) had ordered the Muslims to choose their witnesses from amongst themselves;[2] but nothing was said about the evidence of non-Muslims against one another. The Iraqians endorsed the administrative practice for which they claimed the authority of Shuraiḥ (*Tr. I*, 109), and later that of the Prophet.[3] Yaḥyā b. Aktham (quoted in Sarakhsī, xvi. 133) calls this doctrine 'the consensus of the old authorities'.

The Iraqian judge Ibn Abī Lailā regarded Jews and Christians as belonging to two different religions, and therefore admitted their evidence only against their own co-religionists; this corresponded to the ancient practice.[4] Abū Ḥanīfa and Abū Yūsuf, however, opposed the unbelief of all tolerated religions to the true belief of Islam, and therefore held that all adherents of tolerated religions could give evidence against one another. In the particular case of *Tr. I*, 35, Ibn Abī Lailā by an expedient but inconsistent decision admitted the evidence of non-Muslims against one another but excluded regress against a Muslim, whereas Abū Ḥanīfa and Abū Yūsuf, with stricter systematic reasoning, rejected the evidence of non-Muslims because it would lead to regress against a Muslim.

When no Muslims were available to witness the will of a

[1] See above, p. 205.
[2] For an exception in one particular case, see what follows.
[3] See above, p. 146.
[4] See Kindī, 351, on Khair b. Nu'aim, judge of Egypt, A.H. 120–7.

Muslim who died on a journey, the Koran itself (v. 106) declared the evidence of non-Muslims valid, and Ibn Abī Lailā decided accordingly,[1] again presumably in keeping with the ancient practice. Legal doctrine from Abū Ḥanīfa onwards, however, rejected the evidence of non-Muslims in this case, and Abū Yūsuf arbitrarily declared the Koranic passage to have been repealed by lxv. 2.

The Medinese rejected the evidence of non-Muslims altogether, even against one another (*Mud.* xiii. 7), and Shāfi'ī followed this, providing systematic reasons (*Umm*, vii. 38 ff.). This doctrine represents the full victory of the tendency to religious exclusiveness over the ancient practice.

If a man disappears and is not heard of, his wife must wait four years for him before she is free to undergo the *'idda* and to remarry. The period of four years was based on an administrative regulation. Mālik and before him Rabī'a insisted that the government (*sulṭān, imām*) should fix the term of four years in every individual case (*Mud.* v. 130, 133). Rabī'a does not yet refer to any traditions, but uses the customary expressions 'we have heard' and 'it is said' for opinions that found general approval.[2] In the time of Mālik, the doctrine had found expression in a tradition from 'Umar, transmitted by Yaḥyā b. Sa'īd,[3] and Mālik regarded it as the 'practice'.

But some Medinese held that no matter when the first husband returned, he could reclaim his wife or demand the *donatio propter nuptias* back, and expressed their doctrine in two counter-traditions, one from 'Umar and the other from 'Uthmān.[4] Others went still farther in their opposition to the government regulation, as Shāfi'ī relates, and contested the time limit of four years altogether by saying: 'This does not look like a decision of 'Umar.' But their opposition, based on a religious scruple, did not prevail, and Zurqānī (iii. 57) could represent the Medinese doctrine which perpetuated the administrative regulation, as perpetuating a consensus of the Companions and the concurring opinion of a number of Successors.

[1] *Tr. I*, 111; cf. Sarakhsī, xxx. 152.

[2] See above, p. 101.

[3] *Muw.* iii. 56; *Mud.*, loc. cit.; *Tr. III*, 82.

[4] Ibn Musaiyib appears in the *isnāds* of both traditions from 'Umar; neither reference can be considered genuine.

The position of the grandfather with regard to the brothers was uncertain in the ancient agnatic Arab law of inheritance which the Koran had maintained in principle, whilst superimposing on it its new system of 'heirs by quota'.[1] The ancient doctrine of Muhammadan law makes the grandfather inherit on the same footing as the brothers, but guarantees him one-third of the combined shares if there are more than two brothers. There is no possible systematic reason for this guarantee, and a tradition (*Muw.* ii. 368) shows its origin in an administrative regulation of Umaiyad times, projected back into the period of the first Caliphs:

Mālik—Yaḥyā b. Sa'īd[2]—Mu'āwiya consulted Zaid b. Thābit by letter on the share of the grandfather; Zaid wrote back that Allah knew best, the rulers had decided it, and the two previous Caliphs ['Umar and 'Uthmān] let him share equally with one or two brothers, but if there were more brothers, guaranteed him one-third.

This was improved and transformed into the dogmatic statement that 'Umar, 'Uthmān, and Zaid b. Thābit gave the grandfather, when there were also brothers, one-third. Another version with a full, improved *isnād* acknowledges the process of backward projection by declaring ingenuously that ''Umar treated the grandfather in the same way in which he is treated nowadays'.

Two unsuccessful Iraqian opinions reject the administrative regulation.[3] One systematizes rigidly by primitive *qiyās* and makes the grandfather preclude the brothers from inheriting; this was projected back to Abū Bakr, as being senior to 'Umar and 'Uthmān, and to other Companions, and was held by Abū Ḥanīfa. The other opinion makes the grandfather inherit on the same footing as the brothers and adopts the principle of a minimum guarantee, but fixes it at one-sixth of their combined shares. The sixth is meant to replace the arbitrary third of the administrative regulation, and is derived from the sixth which is the share of the grandfather when he inherits as an 'heir by quota', on the basis of a broad interpretation of Koran

[1] See *E.I.*, s.v. *Mīrāth*.

[2] The *isnād* is interrupted (*munqaṭi'*) here; this makes it probable that the tradition originated in the generation preceding Mālik.

[3] *Muw. Shaib.* 314; *Tr. I*, 122; *Tr. II*, 16 (*a*), (*f*); *Ris.* 81.

iv. 11. This opinion was projected back to the old Iraqian authorities 'Alī and Ibn Mas'ūd, and was held by Ibn Abī Lailā. But the majority of Iraqians in the time of Shaibānī held the same opinion as the Medinese.

D. The Attitude of the Ancient Schools of Law to Umaiyad Practice

The evidence collected in this chapter makes it necessary to discard the opinion, often expressed as part of *a priori* ideas on the origins of Muhammadan jurisprudence, that the Medinese were stricter, more deeply inspired by the religious spirit of Islam, and more uncompromisingly opposed to the worldly Umaiyads than the Iraqians. There was no essential difference between the Medinese and the Iraqians, or the Syrians, in their general attitude both to Umaiyad popular practice and to Umaiyad administrative regulations, and their several reactions to each particular problem were purely fortuitous, whether they endorsed, modified, or rejected the practice which they found. We sometimes find the Iraqians stricter and more critical of Umaiyad practice than the Medinese, and the Medinese more dependent on the practice than the Iraqians.[1] The consistent reference to traditions from the Prophet as the decisive criterion was introduced only by Shāfi'ī, following the activity of the traditionists, and Shāfi'ī was bound by the fortuitous result of the growth of traditions up to his time.

The common attitude of the ancient schools of law to Umaiyad practice is anterior to the historical fiction of early 'Abbāsid times which made the Umaiyads convenient scapegoats. The following chapter will show that apart from this common attitude there existed at the earliest stage of Muhammadan jurisprudence a considerable body of common doctrine which was subsequently reduced by the increasing differences between the schools.

[1] Above, pp. 200, 207, 212. See also above, p. 73 f., on '*sunna* of the Prophet' as an Iraqian concept.

CHAPTER 2

COMMON ANCIENT DOCTRINE AND CROSS-INFLUENCES

A. The Common Ancient Doctrine

THE earliest period of Muhammadan jurisprudence is characterized by a number of features common to the several schools. We saw in the first part of this book that the ancient schools of law share the essentials of legal theory, not all of which are historically necessary and systematically self-evident. We saw in the preceding chapter that their essential attitude to Umaiyad practice, which they take as their starting-point, is the same. The present section is devoted to the considerable body of positive law which they have in common.

It will appear from the evidence collected here that this common body of doctrine is, generally speaking, not the result of a converging development from original diversity towards later unity, but that the common ancient doctrine came at the beginning and was subsequently diversified in the several schools. Not the whole of the doctrine was uniform at the beginning—we noticed in fact that the reactions of the several schools to Umaiyad practice were often different—but the existing common body of ancient doctrine certainly goes back to the earliest stage of Muhammadan jurisprudence. Because of the continual improvement on traditions and the resort to ever higher and better authorities, a process which we have considered in the second section of this book, the later variations of doctrine are often better supported by traditions than the earliest common stage. The following examples, some of which have been discussed before, are intended to illustrate the common ancient doctrine and its subsequent diversification, a process which cannot be reduced to a single formula.

Family Law

No marriage without a *walī*. See above, p. 182 f.

Privacy and presumption of intercourse. See above, p. 193 f.

Definite and triple divorce. See above, pp. 195 ff.

Offer of divorce. If the husband offers his wife a divorce by delegating to her his power of repudiation and the wife chooses to remain with her husband, the offer does not count as one of the three divorces by repudiation to which the husband is entitled. This was the common ancient doctrine in Hijaz and in Iraq.[1] By a formalistic reasoning, however, some Iraqians regarded the offer of divorce as one revocable repudiation, and projected this doctrine back to ʿAlī.[2] But this suggestion was not successful,[3] and it was countered by traditions connected with ʿĀʾisha: in Hijaz in the form of a remark additional to an anecdote on ʿĀʾisha's interference in matters of marriage,[4] in Iraq in the form of ʿĀʾisha's comment on Koran xxxiii. 28 f., a passage which orders the Prophet to offer the choice of a repudiation to his own wives.[5]

Oath of abstinence (*īlāʾ*). The ancient Arab oath of abstinence from marital intercourse was regulated by Koran ii. 226 f. The common ancient doctrine interpreted this passage as meaning that the oath of abstinence, if kept, produced a divorce automatically at the end of four months. This remained the constant doctrine of the Iraqians and was projected back to Ibn Masʿūd and other ancient authorities. In Hijaz, it was ascribed to Zuhrī, Ibn Musaiyib, Abū Bakr b. ʿAbdalraḥmān, and others.[6]

At a later stage, however, following a more literal and narrow interpretation of the Koranic passage, the doctrine prevailed in Hijaz that the husband at the end of four months was to be given the choice either of breaking the oath and expiating it, or of repudiating his wife. This was the doctrine of the Medinese in the time of Mālik; the earliest reference to it which is possibly historical, ascribes it to Abul-Zubair Makkī.[7] But the traditions to the same effect in the *Muwaṭṭaʾ*, from Ibn ʿUmar (through Nāfiʿ) and from ʿAlī, are certainly spurious.

The tradition from ʿAlī exists also with *isnāds* composed of Iraqian traditionists; this represents an unsuccessful effort by the Iraqian opposition to change the doctrine of the school.[8] Shaibānī countered the later Hijazi opinion by remarking that

[1] *Muw.* iii. 38; *Āthār A.Y.* 633; *Āthār Shaib.* 79.
[2] *Āthār A.Y.* 632; *Tr. II,* 10 (*g*).
[3] *Muw. Shaib.* 255 f.; *Tr. I,* 226.
[4] See above, p. 171.
[5] *Āthār Shaib.* 79; *Tr. II,* 10 (*g*).
[6] *Muw.* iii. 39; *Muw. Shaib.* 258; *Āthār A.Y.* 673 ff.; *Āthār Shaib.* 79.
[7] *Āthār A.Y.* 677 f.
[8] *Tr. II,* 10 (*j*). Cf. below, p. 240.

Ibn ʿAbbās, to whom the common ancient doctrine was ascribed, knew the correct interpretation of the Koran better than others.

Foster-parentship. The ancient Iraqians and Medinese were essentially agreed that a single act of breast-feeding produced foster-parentship.[1] The traditions in the *Muwaṭṭa'* and in *Tr. III*, 56, starting with one from ʿĀ'isha, were an unsuccessful effort to introduce a minimum number of feedings.[2]

Umm al-walad. See below, p. 264 f.

Contracts

Khiyār al-majlis. See above, pp. 159 ff.

Sale of the *walā'* and of the *mukātab* slave. See above, p. 173 f.

Sale of dogs. Muhammadan law at the beginning regarded dogs as *res in commercio*. According to the Iraqians, who have retained the common ancient doctrine, (*a*) the sale of dogs is valid, and (*b*) if a man destroys a dog he is responsible for its value to the owner. The idea of the ritual uncleanness of dogs was taken over from Judaism.[3] The Medinese, therefore, rejected proposition (*a*), and expressed this doctrine in a tradition from the Prophet, but inconsistently maintained proposition (*b*). Only Shāfiʿī was consistent enough to reject both propositions (*Tr. III*, 51).

Pre-emption. See below, p. 219 f.

Security. See above, p. 186 f.

Fiscal Law and Law of War

Zakāt tax of the minor. The development started with the common ancient doctrine, based perhaps on an administrative regulation of late Umaiyad times, that the property of minors was liable to *zakāt* tax.[4] This remained the Medinese doctrine, and it developed the corollary that the guardian was authorized to trade with the property of his ward, so that the *zakāt* should not eat into the capital, and to pay the tax on his behalf.

[1] *Muw*. iii. 86, 89, 93; *Muw. Shaib*. 271; *Mud*. v. 87.

[2] See also below, p. 246 f.

[3] See Lammens, *Yazîd Ier*, 461 f. and *Omayyades*, 362.

[4] *Muw*. ii. 49; *Tr. II*, 9 (*a*). We must postulate this doctrine for the earliest Iraqians not indeed from the ʿAlī tradition in *Tr. II*, 9 (*a*), but from the subsequent development of the Iraqian doctrine.

In Iraq, consideration of the ward's interest led to a progressive modification of the doctrine which became thereby inconsistent.[1] One opinion, held by Ibn Abī Lailā, was that the guardian was bound to pay *zakāt* on behalf of the ward but remained responsible for his administration. According to another opinion, the guardian had to keep a record of *zakāt* due but leave it to the ward whether to pay it or not when he came of age; this opinion was ascribed to Ibn Mas'ūd. Finally, there is the more systematic opinion of Abū Ḥanīfa, Abū Yūsuf, and Shaibānī, to the effect that the minor is not liable to *zakāt* because he is not subject to other religious duties; therefore the guardian need not pay it for his ward, but may nevertheless trade with his property; this opinion, too, was ascribed to Ibn Mas'ūd, as well as to Ibrāhīm Nakha'ī.

Shāfi'ī was the first to quote a tradition from the Prophet on the subject, endorsing the Medinese or common ancient doctrine; he pointed out the inconsistency which remained in Abū Ḥanīfa's doctrine.

Cultivation of uncultivated land. See above, p. 202 f.

Property captured by the enemy. See above, p. 158 f.

Penal Law

Criminal intent of the minor. See below, p. 316 f.

Weregeld paid by the *'āqila*. See above, p. 207.

Compensation for a molar. See above, p. 114.

Weregeld of the woman. It was the common ancient doctrine that a woman's weregeld was half that of a man in cases involving loss of life or wounds the damages for which amounted to one-third of the weregeld or more; but that it was equal to the weregeld of the man where the damages amounted to fractions less than one-third of the weregeld.[2] This remained the doctrine of the Medinese who projected it back to Ibn Musaiyib.[3] It is also well attested for Iraq, where it was pro-

[1] *Āthār A.Y.* 451 ff.; *Āthār Shaib.* 46; *Tr. I*, 130; *Tr. II*, 19 (*ee*).

[2] *Muw.* iv. 34; *Mud.* xvi. 118; *Āthār Shaib.* 85 f., 95; *Tr. II.* 13 (*k*); *Tr. VIII*, 5. This doctrine seems based on an Umaiyad regulation; see above, p. 207, for another case where fractions of more and less than one-third of the weregeld are treated differently.

[3] Zurqānī, much later, ascribes it to the Seven Scholars of Medina, to 'Umar b. 'Abdal'azīz and to other ancient authorities; he even knows a tradition from the Prophet to the same effect.

jected back into the time of ʿAbdalmalik's governor Hishām b. Ismāʿīl, and further ascribed to Shuraiḥ, Ibn Masʿūd, and Zaid b. Thābit. Within the pre-literary period, however, the Iraqians took objection to this breach in the system and taught that all fractions of the weregeld of the woman ought to be half of the corresponding fractions of the weregeld of the man. They adduced ʿUmar and ʿAlī as authorities, and made Ibrāhīm Nakhaʿī 'prefer the doctrine of ʿAlī to that of Ibn Masʿūd, Zaid b. Thābit and Shuraiḥ'. But this last, the common ancient doctrine, was in the time of Ibrāhīm only on the point of being projected back into the period of Hishām b. Ismāʿīl, on the authority of the same Ibrāhīm. Ibrāhīm's alleged statement of doctrine is therefore spurious, and the systematized and secondary stage of the Iraqian doctrine later than his time.

Weregeld of the slave. See below, p. 281 f.

Evidence

Oath of the plaintiff. See above, pp. 167 ff., 187 f.

Evidence of minors. The common ancient doctrine admitted the evidence of minors regarding wounds inflicted by minors on one another.[1] This was obviously inspired by practical necessity, but it was abandoned first in Iraq by Abū Ḥanīfa and Abū Yūsuf, and in Hijaz by some disciples of Mālik, for systematic reasons and in strict interpretation of the Koranic requirements of witnesses. Both opinions were projected back to Companions.

Occasionally, the common element consists of an abstract principle rather than of a positive doctrine, such as the principle that conversion to Islam gives a good title to all property held at the time,[2] the principle that the punishment by *taʿzīr*, at the discretion of the judge, ought to remain within the limits set by the fixed *ḥadd* punishments,[3] and the principle, referred to above, that the minor for purposes of penal law cannot act intentionally.

B. Early Cross-references and Cross-influences

There are numerous cross-references from one school of law to the doctrine of another, over the whole of the pre-literary period. These references are usually expressed in counter-

[1] *Muw.* iii. 185; *Mud.* xiii. 13; *Āthār Shaib.* 95; *Tr. I,* 115; Kindī, 351.

[2] *Tr. IX,* 46 f.; *Mud.* iii. 18 f.

[3] *Tr. II,* 18 (*y*); *Āthār Shaib.* 90.

traditions, directed against the doctrines of another school.[1] A reference to the doctrine of another school is also implied when the name of its main authority is borrowed by opponents;[2] in particular, the Iraqians use the name of the Medinese authority Ibn ʿUmar, and the Medinese that of the Iraqian authority Ibn Masʿūd.[3] Occasionally, we find explicit references to a school by its name,[4] and comments on its doctrine in the traditions of its opponents.[5] This taking cognizance of one another's doctrines and opposing one's own opinions to those of the opponents is a feature common to the ancient Iraqians and the ancient Medinese.

The following example, taken from the doctrine of pre-emption, will show how cross-references to other schools enter into the development of legal doctrine in the pre-literary period. The result of this development, as it affected pre-emption, was that two opposite doctrines prevailed in the Medinese and in the Iraqian school respectively: the Medinese restricted the right of pre-emption to the owner of a share in undivided property, and the Iraqians extended it to the neighbour.[6] The oldest Iraqian formula, however, was that 'the right of pre-emption goes by gates, and the person whose gate is nearest has the best right to pre-emption'; it was projected back to Ibrāhīm Nakhaʿī as his alleged former opinion, and on the fictitious authority of Ibrāhīm back to Shuraiḥ. This formula, which reflects the social background of the institution of pre-emption in early Muhammadan law, seems to be the common starting-point of the Medinese and of the Iraqian doctrines.[7]

The Basrians, while essentially maintaining this opinion, justified it as against the Medinese restriction of the right of pre-emption by pointing out that the lane, on which the several adjoining plots abutted, remained undivided and constituted an interest common to them all. The earlier Kufians, on the other hand, extended the right of pre-emption to all owners of plots within a single block or section not traversed by a thoroughfare, irrespective of whether

[1] See above, p. 152 ff. [2] See above, p. 155 f.

[3] See above, pp. 32, 197.

[4] See, e.g. *Āthār A.Y.* 623; *Āthār Shaib.* 76, and above, pp. 117, 153.

[5] See above, p. 203 f.

[6] *Muw.* iii. 172 ff.; *Āthār A.Y.* 766 f.; *Āthār Shaib.* 111 f.; *Muw. Shaib.* 364; *Tr. I*, 49; *Tr. III*, 107; *Ikh.* 260, 264. On legal maxims in favour of the Iraqian doctrine, see above, p. 164.

[7] A tradition in Kindī, 334 (l. 10 ff.), reflects the change in Egypt from the common ancient to the final Medinese doctrine, and the arguments adduced in favour of the latter.

the plots adjoined or opened on the same lane. Final systematic consistency was achieved in Iraq only in the time of Abū Ḥanīfa and his companions who gave the right to pre-emption to the owner of a share in undivided property in the first place,[1] then to the owner of a separate plot who had, however, retained a common interest in the lane, and finally to the owner of an adjoining plot.[2]

Besides and beyond cross-references, there exist cross-influences, cases where the doctrine of one particular school was taken over by another in the pre-literary period. In contrast to the mutual character of the formal reactions of the Iraqians and the Medinese to one another's doctrines, we notice that the material influences almost invariably start from the Iraqians and not from the Medinese. We found that Iraqian legal maxims were taken over by the Medinese, but not vice versa;[3] and we saw that an early Iraqian *qiyās* spread into Hijaz and there produced traditions from the Prophet.[4]

A further example is provided by the doctrine of *ʿumrā* and *suknā*, a kind of temporary gift.[5] Etymology and old Arabic usage show that *ʿumrā* was originally a temporary gift, to revert to the donor at the death of the donee;[6] *suknā* meant the same with regard to a dwelling house. This was indeed the doctrine of the Medinese on *ʿumrā* and *suknā*. The ancient Iraqians, however, considered *ʿumrā*, but not *suknā*, as an unconditional gift which did not return to the donor but became the full property of the donee. This doctrine is expressed in a tradition, which claims to be transmitted by Jābir from the Prophet and which exists in two versions, one with an Iraqian and the other with a Medinese *isnād*. The main transmitter in this last *isnād* is the ancient Medinese authority, Sulaimān b. Yasār. The Iraqian version reflects the change from the original concept of *ʿumrā* to the Iraqian doctrine which is secondary; the Medinese version, in an additional remark, gives the kind of rudimentary technical reasoning which caused the change of doctrine; this explanatory remark soon became fused with the main body of

1 This distinction is perhaps the result of further reference to the Medinese doctrine.

2 This opinion was also projected back to Shuraiḥ (Sarakhsī, xiv. 92).

3 Above, p. 185 f.

4 Above, p. 106 f. See also below, pp. 241, 268.

5 *Muw.* iii. 219; *Mud.* xv. 91; *Āthār A.Y.* 764; *Muw. Shaib.* 349; *Tr. III*, 41; Ṭaḥāwī, ii. 246.

6 Cf. *ʿumr* 'span of life, lifetime', and the verse of Labīd quoted in Zurqānī, iii. 219. Ibn al-Aʿrābī, quoted in *Comm. Muw. Shaib.* 349, claimed that the Arabs were unanimous on this meaning of *ʿumrā*.

the tradition, and appears as part of the words of the Prophet in the texts given by Mālik and Shāfiʿī. The Iraqian doctrine, therefore, in the form of a tradition from the Prophet, penetrated into Medina but did not succeed in changing the opinion of the Medinese school. The resistance of this school to the Iraqian doctrine is attested by Mālik, and the conflict of both opinions produced counter-traditions which were collected by Ṭaḥāwī.[1] Shāfiʿī states that all cities excepting Medina shared the doctrine of the Iraqians; this, together with the near-success of this opinion in Medina itself, shows the wide diffusion of early Iraqian legal thought.

Another example occurs in the question of damages due for wounds inflicted on a slave.[2] The original Medinese opinion was that his loss in value was to be made good; this was projected back to Marwān b. Ḥakam and other authorities. The ancient Iraqian doctrine represented a systematic refinement: the value of the slave was regarded as his weregeld, and the same fraction of his value was due as would have been due of the weregeld had the wound been inflicted on a free man; this was projected back to Ibrāhīm Nakhaʿī. The Iraqian doctrine gained a partial foothold in Medina for practical reasons; this is shown by the obviously authentic passage of Mālik's older contemporary ʿAbdalʿazīz b. Abī Salama, known as Mājashūn, quoted in the *Mudauwana*:

'If a slave is wounded, his value before and after the wounding is assessed, and the person responsible has to make good the difference. We know nothing more just than this, because if a slave loses his hand or foot, his value decreases by more than a half,[3] and he becomes almost valueless; but if he loses his ear his value decreases by less than a half if he is a weaver or another kind of artisan who commands a high price. If the damage is assessed in this way, neither the owner nor the culprit is treated too harshly; if the damage is little, little has to be paid, and if much, much—always excepting the special kinds of wounds known as *mūḍiḥa*, *munaqqila*, *ma'mūma*, and *jā'ifa* which must be assessed at something. If one considers the value here, the damage is non-existent because they cause no disability or fault or decrease in value worth speaking of; but they take place in the head and the brain, and death may result from a penetrating bone [as a consequence of these wounds]; therefore it is the doctrine (*ra'y*) to fix the damages at the fraction of the value of the slave in proportion to the weregeld of a free man.'

[1] A harmonizing doctrine, also expressed in a tradition from the Prophet (see Zurqānī, iii. 219), was pointedly rejected by Shaibānī.

[2] *Muw.* iv. 41 (see the full text in ed. Tunis, 1280, p. 350); *Mud.* xvi. 168 f.; *Āthār A.Y.* 987 f.; *Āthār Shaib.* 86; *Tr. III*, 148 (p. 247); *Tr. VIII*, 11; *Ris.* 74.

[3] For the loss of one of any pair of limbs, one half of the weregeld is to be paid.

This was in fact the doctrine of Mālik and of the other Medinese of his time. The particular decision on the *mūḍiḥa* wound was projected back, certainly fictitiously, to Ibn Musaiyib and Sulaimān b. Yasār, as Mālik states without an *isnād*. Shāfi'ī relates with the *isnāds* Ibn 'Uyaina—Zuhrī and 'a reliable man', identified as Yaḥyā b. Hassān—Laith b. Sa'd—Zuhrī, that Ibn Musaiyib followed a doctrine identical with that of the Iraqians; to this is added a remark ascribed to Zuhrī that 'some' held an opinion which corresponded with the original Medinese doctrine. All this is spurious and was abstracted from the statement as related by Mālik.

C. Later Polemics and Influences

Essentially the same conditions prevailed in the early literary period. A statement of Shāfi'ī's on the polemics between the several schools of law[1] refers roughly to this time. Examples of polemics are numerous, particularly in *Tr. VIII* and *Tr. IX*. In this period, too, the traditions which were originally particular to an individual school, began to spread to a greater extent than before and had to be harmonized with the doctrines of those schools into which they penetrated; the most conspicuous document of this process is the *Muwaṭṭa'* of Shaibānī.[2] Apart from this particular case, material influences causing changes in the doctrines of other schools continued to proceed almost exclusively from Iraq.[3] We had occasion to discuss a question on which Mālik diverged from the traditional Medinese doctrine under the influence of Iraqian thought;[4] and, on a point not decided by Mālik, Ibn Qāsim's decision seems influenced by an objection made by Shaibānī.[5]

D. Conclusions

The existence of a common body of ancient doctrine in the earliest period of Muhammadan law and its later diversification in the ancient schools of law show that Muhammadan jurisprudence started from a single centre. It does not of course imply that Muhammadan jurisprudence was cultivated exclusively in one place, but that one place was the intellectual centre of the first theorizing and systematizing activities which

[1] See the translation above, p. 7 f.

[2] See below, p. 306.

[3] For an exception, see above, p. 106, n. 5.

[4] Above, p. 108.

[5] *Muw.* iv. 32; *Mud.* xvi. 203; *Tr. VIII*, 4.

were to transform Umaiyad popular and administrative practice into Muhammadan law. The ascendancy of a single centre of Muhammadan jurisprudence must have been maintained over an appreciable period, because we find that the common ancient element sometimes comprises several successive stages of legal doctrine.

The fact that within the pre-literary period the cross-influences proceeded almost invariably from Iraq and not from Medina, shows that this centre was Iraq, and not Medina. Even when the question of influence does not arise, the doctrine of the Medinese often represents a later stage than that of the Iraqians.[1] On the other hand, we repeatedly found the doctrine of the Iraqians more highly developed than that of their Medinese contemporaries.[2] The Medinese have certainly not the monopoly of the foundation of Muhammadan jurisprudence, as has been sometimes supposed.[3] Our conclusion, that Muhammadan jurisprudence originated in Iraq, agrees with the opinion of Goldziher.[4]

[1] See e.g. above, pp. 161, 196 f.

[2] See above, p. 133 and n. 1; below, pp. 241, 275 f., 311.

[3] Cf. above, p. 213.

[4] *Principles*, 299.

CHAPTER 3

THE KORANIC ELEMENT IN EARLY MUHAMMADAN LAW

WE had occasion, in the first part of this book, to discuss the systematic place filled by the Koran in the legal theories of the ancient schools of law, of the traditionists and Shāfiʿī, and of the *ahl al-kalām*.[1] In every single case the place given to the Koran was determined by the attitude of the group concerned to the ever-mounting tide of traditions from the Prophet. The Koran taken by itself, apart from its possible bearing on the problem raised by the traditions from the Prophet, can hardly be called the first and foremost basis of early legal theory. The *ahl al-kalām*, it is true, profess to make the Koran, interpreted rationally, the only foundation of their doctrine;[2] but this conscious formula, which shows an anti-traditionist bias, is the outcome and not the starting-point of an intricate theoretical development.

The subject-matter of the present chapter is the historical influence of the Koran on Muhammadan law during its early formative period. Muhammadan law did not derive directly from the Koran but developed, as we saw, out of popular and administrative practice under the Umaiyads, and this practice often diverged from the intentions and even the explicit wording of the Koran.[3] It is true that a number of legal rules, particularly in family law and law of inheritance, not to mention cult and ritual, were based on the Koran from the beginning. But the present chapter will show that apart from the most elementary rules, norms derived from the Koran were introduced into Muhammadan law almost invariably at a secondary stage. This applies not only to those branches of law which are not covered in detail by the Koranic legislation—if we may use this term of the essentially ethical and only incidentally legal

[1] See above, pp. 15 f., 28, 40 ff., 45 ff., 53.

[2] They had a precursor in the author of the dogmatic treatise ascribed to Ḥasan Baṣrī, at a time when traditions from the Prophet hardly yet existed; see above, p. 74.

[3] This particular aspect has been pointed out before, e.g. in Bergsträsser–Schacht, *Grundzüge*, 14.

body of maxims contained in the Koran[1]—but to family law, the law of inheritance, and even cult and ritual. I have therefore chosen to speak of the Koranic element at this point of our inquiry into the transmission of legal doctrine, a point which corresponds to the zenith of the reception of Koranic norms into early Muhammadan law.

To start with problems which were based from the beginning on the Koran, we have already discussed the common ancient doctrine of divorce, and the problem of the evidence of non-Muslims.[2] Here are two more examples.

The Medinese hold that the definitely divorced wife who is not pregnant, can claim from her former husband only lodging during her period of waiting (*'idda*); the Iraqians give her also the right to board.[3] The two doctrines are based on two variants of Koran lxv. 6, the Medinese on the *textus receptus*, the Iraqian on the reading of Ibn Mas'ūd.[4] When the text of Ibn Mas'ūd was superseded in Iraq by the *textus receptus* during the reign of the Umaiyad Caliph 'Abdalmalik (A.H. 65–86), this basis of the Iraqian doctrine was forgotten, and Abū Ḥanīfa was reduced to justifying it by an arbitrary interpretation of the *textus receptus* and by a tradition from 'Umar.

Koran ii. 234 fixes the *'idda* of a widow at four months and ten days; Koran lxv. 4 makes the *'idda* of a pregnant wife who becomes divorced end with her delivery. Nothing is said explicitly about the *'idda* of a pregnant widow. The common ancient attitude was to consider her *'idda* ended and to make her available for another marriage at her delivery, even though this might happen immediately after the death of her husband and long before the completion of four months and ten days.[5] But there arose the demand, caused by the tendency to greater strictness, that she should keep the *'idda* 'until the later of the two terms'; a demand which was expressed in traditions from 'Alī and from Ibn 'Abbās.[6]

This refinement succeeded neither in Iraq nor in Medina;

[1] See ibid., 9 ff.

[2] Above, pp. 195 f., 210 f.

[3] *Muw.* iii. 62; *Muw. Shaib.* 263 and *Comm.*; *Tr. I*, 229; Sarakhsī, v. 201.

[4] 'Lodge them where you lodge [and bear their expenses] according to your circumstances'; the words in brackets do not exist in the *textus receptus*. Cf. Jeffery, *Materials*, 102.

[5] *Muw.* iii. 71; *Muw. Shaib.* 258; *Āthār A.Y.* 651 f.; *Āthār Shaib.* 72.

[6] *Muw.* loc. cit.; *Tr. II*, 10 (*m*).

the Iraqians countered it with the claim that Koran ii. 234 had been [partly] repealed by lxv. 4, a statement which they put into the mouth of Ibn Masʿūd.[1] The Medinese produced a counter-tradition according to which the Successor Abū Salama b. ʿAbdalraḥmān disagreed with Ibn ʿAbbās, and had his opinion confirmed not only by Abū Huraira but by Umm Salama, a widow of the Prophet. She quoted a precedent of the Prophet himself who allowed a widow called Subaiʿa to remarry after giving birth and before completing an *ʿidda* of four months and ten days.[2] The tradition on the Prophet and Subaiʿa was also extracted from this context, provided with the family *isnād* Hishām b. ʿUrwa—his father, and quoted as an independent *locus probans*. Finally, it was claimed against the unsuccessful refinement, that Ibn ʿAbbās himself accepted the Subaiʿa tradition as valid, or that his disciples ʿIkrima, ʿAṭā', Ṭāwūs, and others did so.[3]

As regards the problem of the effects of conversion on marriage, we shall have occasion to notice a gradual movement of doctrine away from the Koranic regulation.[4]

We now come to the numerous cases where norms derived from the Koran were introduced into legal doctrine at a secondary stage. We have already discussed the obligatory gift from husband to wife in the case of divorce, the problem of where the divorced wife ought to live, and the legal consequences of the offer of divorce; the maxim that spoils belong to the killer, and the policy of not laying waste the enemy country; the oath of the plaintiff in confirmation of the evidence of one witness, the inadmissibility of written documents as evidence, and the evidence of minors.[5] Here are two further examples.

When a man died before consummating his marriage and without fixing a *donatio propter nuptias* (*ṣadāq*) for his wife, the earliest decision, based on systematic reasoning (*ra'y*), was to give the wife the right to the average *ṣadāq* which a woman of her standing might expect; this decision is attested for Iraq

[1] *Āthār A.Y.* and *Āthār Shaib.*, loc. cit.

[2] *Muw.* and *Tr. II*, loc. cit. Comparison of the two *isnāds* shows that this tradition which appeals from a Companion to the Prophet himself, dates from the generation preceding Mālik; this is the first reference to the Prophet concerning the problem in question.

[3] Zurqānī, ad loc.

[4] Below, p. 276 f.

[5] See above, p. 101 f., 197 f., 215; 70 f., 204 f.; 73, 188, 218.

where it was put into the mouth of Ibn Mas'ūd whose opinion, it was claimed, coincided with a decision of the Prophet.[1] A literal interpretation of Koran ii. 236 and xxxiii. 49, however, seemed to imply that the wife in this case had no right to *ṣadāq*. This was indeed the opinion of an Iraqian opposition group who put their doctrine into the mouth of 'Alī, but did not succeed in changing the teaching of the Iraqian school.[2] It did prevail in Hijaz where it was projected back to Ibn 'Umar and Zaid b. Thābit; the form of the tradition shows the resistance which this doctrine had to overcome.[3]

On the problem of giving battle to unbelievers who shield themselves behind Muslim infants,[4] Auzā'ī refers to Koran xlviii. 25. But the passage is not at all relevant and is obviously an argument on second thoughts against the opposite opinion which clearly reflects the rough-and-ready practice.

Even as regards questions which presuppose the rules given in the Koran, we notice that anything which goes beyond the most perfunctory attention given to the Koranic norms and the most elementary conclusions drawn from them, belongs almost invariably to a secondary stage in the development of doctrine. Problems of this kind which have been discussed before, are *'idda* and re-marriage, the presumption of intercourse, the oath of abstinence, and—from the law of inheritance—the share of the grandfather.[5] We shall have occasion later to discuss the problems of temporary marriage, of the *mukātab* slave, and of booty taken by a private raider.[6]

[1] See above, p. 29 and n. 3.
[2] *Muw. Shaib.* 244 (and *Comm.* 245, n. 1, referred to above, p. 50); *Tr. II*, 10 (*e*).
[3] *Muw.* iii. 7.
[4] *Tr. IX*, 21; *Umm*, iv. 199; Ṭabarī, 5.
[5] See above, pp. 181 f., 193 f., 215 f.; 212 f.
[6] Below, pp. 266 f.; 279 ff.; 286.

CHAPTER 4

THE IRAQIANS

THE present and the following chapter are concerned with the outward development of the Iraqian and the Hijazi schools of law in the pre-literary period. The conventional picture of this development, as it is presented in the Arabic sources from the beginning of the third century A.H. onwards,[1] is thoroughly fictitious, as we have already had occasion to notice more than once and as we shall see in greater detail in the pages that follow. Prominent features of the conventional picture, like the pre-eminence of Medina, have no foundation in fact; important concepts current in the ancient schools, such as that of the Companions of Ibn Mas'ūd in Iraq, are neglected; essential developments, like the attack of the traditionists on the 'living tradition' of the ancient schools of law, are misinterpreted; and even the information on the doctrines of individual authorities belonging to that period is to a great extent spurious. We must therefore suspect on principle statements which refer to the pre-literary period unless they are verified; and they can be verified with the help of the method which I have endeavoured to work out and to put to the test in Part II of this book. The results of this verification, as far as I have been able to undertake it, will be found in the present chapter and in those that follow. The picture gained in this way cannot, of course, compare in completeness with that presented to us by the conventional opinion, partly on account of the character of the legal traditions which contain the only contemporary evidence on the period in question, and also because of the limitations inherent in a first effort of this kind.

A. Shuraiḥ

After Ibn Mas'ūd, whom we shall discuss in section D below, the oldest Iraqian authority is Shuraiḥ. Shuraiḥ is said to have been appointed judge of Kufa by the Caliph 'Umar, to have

[1] It exists already in Ibn Sa'd (d. 230), was taken seriously by the editor E. Sachau in his introduction to vol. iii and, lacking something better to put in its place, is presumably still more or less widely accepted among European scholars.

held this office for sixty years or more, and to have died between A.H. 76 and 99, presumably before the year 80, at a very great age. Lammens has pointed out the lack of historical information about him,[1] and Tyan has convincingly analysed his legend.[2] The opinions and traditions ascribed to him are spurious throughout and are the outcome of the general tendency to project the opinions current in the schools of law back to early authorities.[3] They often represent secondary stages in the development of legal doctrines.[4] Nor is it rare to find two contradictory opinions ascribed to Shuraih.[5]

B. Ḥasan Baṣrī

In contrast to the vague personality of Shuraiḥ, the historical Ḥasan Baṣrī is well known as one of the foremost pious men of Baṣra in the second half of the first and at the beginning of the second century A.H. But he was neither a lawyer[6] nor even a traditionist.[7] The specialists on traditions held most of the uninterrupted *isnāds* in which he appeared to be spurious.[8] The dogmatic treatise which Ḥasan wrote at the command of the Umayyad Caliph ʿAbdalmalik, and which therefore cannot be later than the year 86,[1] does not refer to any traditions from the Prophet or even from Companions.[9]

The legal opinions and traditions ascribed to Ḥasan are regularly shown, by closer investigation, not to be genuine.[10] In later times, he was considered one of the main authorities of the Basrians; but too little is known of the doctrines of this ancient Iraqian school of law, for us to ascertain the importance which they may have ascribed to him.[11]

[1] *Omayyades*, 77 ff.

[2] *Organisation*, i. 101 ff.

[3] See above, pp. 130, 218, 219.

[4] See above, pp. 160, 195. *Tr. I*, 2: the argument ascribed to Shuraiḥ is of the same character as much in the reasoning of Ibn Abī Lailā. *Tr. I*, 118, 120: the opinions ascribed to Shuraiḥ represent a rather highly developed stage of the doctrine.

[5] See above, p. 194, n. 1, 220, n. 2. Compare further *Tr. I*, 112, with *Comm. ed. Cairo*, 75, n. 3; and *Comm. ed. Cairo*, 49, n. 3 with 50, n. 1.

[6] Cf. H. Ritter, in *Islam*, xxi. 56 f.

[7] Cf. ibid. 2 f.

[8] Tirmidhī, at the end; Massignon, *Essai*, 156 f.; Ritter, ibid. 11.

[9] See above, pp. 74, 141.

[10] See above, p. 159 (highly suspect), 164 (a legal maxim expressed in a tradition from Ḥasan); below, p. 278 (the doctrine ascribed to Ḥasan in a late source reflects a secondary stage). This applies also to the doctrines collected by Massignon, ibid. 164 ff.

[11] See above, pp. 8 and n. 4; 87.

C. Sha'bī

Ḥasan's contemporary Sha'bī was one of the worthies of Kufa. He does not occupy a well-defined place in the conventional picture of the school of Kufa;[1] his name was used by the traditionists in order to discredit, by statements hostile to reasoning and analogy, the doctrine of the ancient Iraqians; these last, by equally spurious statements, tried to claim the authority of Sha'bī in favour of the doctrine of the school.

The conventional idea of Sha'bī as 'the strongest critic of *ra'y* and *qiyās* among the Iraqians' is a fiction created by the traditionists;[2] and when Sha'bī is declared, against the evidence of the Kufian texts themselves, to be the representative scholar of Kufa, this is meant to support the thesis of the traditionists.[3]

Against this, the Iraqians make Sha'bī relate traditions in favour of Iraqian *ra'y*,[4] and make him endorse the authority of the Companions of the Prophet and, by implication, the teaching of the ancient schools of law.[5] A later tradition puts into Sha'bī's mouth extravagant praise of Ibrāhīm Nakha'ī, the conventional bearer of the Kufian Iraqian doctrine.[6] This retrospective incorporation of Sha'bī into the Iraqian school was so successful that the traditionists, at a further stage of their argument, adduced Sha'bī's faithful adherence to the doctrine of Ibn Mas'ūd, or of the Companions of the Prophet in general, in confirmation of his alleged rejection of *ra'y* and *qiyās*.[7] For instance, Sha'bī is made to say: 'Is that not extraordinary? I give him information on the authority of Ibn Mas'ūd, and he asks me for my own *ra'y*.[8] . . . I would rather become a singer than give you my own *ra'y*.' Or: 'Beware of the use of *qiyās*. . . . If you take to the use of *qiyās* you will make the forbidden lawful and the lawful forbidden; but what is reported to you on the authority of men who remember it from the Companions, that act upon.'

[1] It is safe to assume that Muhammadan law hardly existed in the time of the historical Sha'bī.

[2] See above, p. 130 f.

[3] See above, p. 87.

[4] See above, p. 104.

[5] *Āthār A.Y.* 942; *Āthār Shaib.* 123.

[6] *Comm. ed. Cairo* on *Tr. IX*, 13.

[7] Dārimī, *Bāb al-tawarru' 'an al-jawāb*.

[8] This argument is typical of the traditionists; see above, p. 55 f.

Moreover, the opinions and traditions concerning details of positive law, which are ascribed to Sha'bī, cannot be regarded as authentic; they usually show indications of a later origin[1] or are otherwise suspect.[2] We cannot therefore take on trust an occasional attribution to Sha'bī of what happens to correspond to the earliest Iraqian opinion;[3] this doctrine was attributed to Sha'bī by the well-known transmitter Muṭarrif, who in another case ascribed to Sha'bī a later development of the Iraqian doctrine.[4] Accordingly, when Sha'bī appears as the common link in *isnāds* of traditions which reflect the common Iraqian doctrine and in *isnāds* of legal 'puzzles' ascribed to 'Alī,[5] we ought to consider not him but a person in the following generation responsible.

D. IBN MAS'ŪD AND HIS COMPANIONS

The cases of Shuraiḥ, Ḥasan Baṣrī, and Sha'bī are typical of the retrospective incorporation, in several ways, of ancient authorities into the tradition of a school of law. With Ibn Mas'ūd and his Companions we come to the main stream of the legal tradition of the ancient Iraqians and in particular the school of Kufa.

Ibn Mas'ūd, a Companion of the Prophet, lived in Kufa for a number of years and was later considered a main authority for the Kufian Iraqian doctrine.[6] After what we have seen in the second part of this book,[7] I need hardly elaborate the point that the legal traditions from Ibn Mas'ūd are not genuine and that his name is a label affixed to early Iraqian, and particularly Kufian teaching and reasoning.[8] In one particular case, where the Iraqian doctrine is in fact based on a variant reading in Ibn Mas'ūd's text of the Koran, the school justifies it by

[1] See above, pp. 73 f. (an 'unsuccessful' Iraqian tradition, through Sha'bī, from 'Alī), 108 (a secondary stage of the Iraqian doctrine, later than Ibrāhīm Nakha'ī; Shāfi'ī, in *Tr. III*, 54, dismisses the tradition as too badly attested to deserve notice), 161 (a late, secondary opinion).

[2] *Mud.* iii. 80 (related by Ibn Wahb, together with two pairs of contradictory statements on Ibrāhīm Nakha'ī and on Ibn 'Abbās); *Tr. IX*, 31 with *Comm. ed. Cairo*, p. 92 f. (three different types of traditions are ascribed to Sha'bī, and none of them can be considered genuine).

[3] *Tr. II*, 18 (*w*); compare this with ibid. (*o*) and with *Āthār Shaib.* 91.

[4] See above, p. 161.

[5] See below, p. 241.

[6] See above, p. 31 f.

[7] See particularly above, p. 169 f.

[8] See above, pp. 156, 217, 218, 226, 227; and below, p. 265.

reference not to him but to 'Umar.[1] The name of Ibn Mas'ūd is usually an indication of the prevailing doctrine of the school of Kufa; we find it, however, occasionally affixed to Iraqian and even Medinese counter-traditions,[2] or to mutually contradictory traditions.[3]

The formal and explicit kind of reference to Ibn Mas'ūd himself, as an authority on law, developed out of an earlier stage which consisted in a more general reference to the Companions (*aṣḥāb*) of Ibn Mas'ūd. This was the name given originally to an anonymous group of Kufians,[4] some of whom were later identified as relatives of Ibrāhīm Nakha'ī: his uncle 'Alqama b. Qais and his maternal cousins 'Alqama, Aswad and 'Abdalraḥmān the sons of Yazīd.[5] We shall discuss the position of Ibrāhīm in the Kufian Iraqian tradition of legal doctrine in section E below; these relatives of his formed the family link[6] by which the doctrine which went under the name of Ibrāhīm Nakha'ī was artificially connected with the very beginnings of Islam in Kufa in the time of Ibn Mas'ūd.[7]

The Companions of Ibn Mas'ūd are often mentioned besides Ibn Mas'ūd, for instance in *Āthār A.Y.* 49, 94, 105, 369, in the corresponding passages in *Āthār Shaib.*, in *Tr. II*, 19 (*i*) and elsewhere. They appear by themselves, without mention of Ibn Mas'ūd, for instance in *Āthār A.Y.* 110,[8] 407, in *Āthār Shaib.* 37, 91, in *Muw. Shaib.* 72 and elsewhere. Ibn 'Abdalbarr[9] says correctly that much of Abū Ḥanīfa's *ra'y* and *qiyās* was anticipated by [or, as we should say, projected back to] Ibrāhīm and the Companions of Ibn Mas'ūd. Sarakhsī (vi. 95) was well aware of their existence.

As the general reference to the Companions of Ibn Mas'ūd gave rise to an explicit reference to Ibn Mas'ūd himself, this last

[1] See above, p. 225.

[2] See above, pp. 197, 209.

[3] *Tr. II*, 10 (*p*), compared with *Āthār A.Y.* 710 and *Āthār Shaib.* 68; *Tr. II*, 19 (*e*), compared with 21 (*e*); *Tr. II*, 19 (*p*); *Tr. II*, 19 (*aa*); *Āthār A.Y.* 452 f. and *Tr. II*, 19 (*ee*), compared with *Āthār Shaib.* 46.

[4] See above, p. 39 and n. 3.

[5] Dāraquṭnī, 361; Abū Nu'aim, iv, 169 f.; and see above, p. 169.

[6] See above, p. 170.

[7] We are concerned here only with the concept of the Companions of Ibn Mas'ūd in Iraqian legal tradition, and not with their place in political history, on which see Lammens, *Omayyades*, 107, 109.

[8] Their doctrine here is identical with what Shaibānī calls the *sunna*: *Muw. Shaib.* 101. Later it was projected back to Ibn Mas'ūd and 'Alī: *Comm. Muw. Shaib.* 102, n. 8; but so was the opposite doctrine: *Tr. II*, 19 (*f*).

[9] Quoted in *Comm. Muw. Shaib.* 32.

could be taken as confirming the former, or the two attributions could be considered to contradict each other. We find, in fact, both attitudes expressed in legal traditions. For instance, ʿAlqama b. Qais is made to call Ibn Masʿūd his master (*ṣāḥib*) and to mention that Ibn Masʿūd instructed him and his companions (*Āthār A.Y.* 777). Or it is reported that ʿAlqama declared himself ignorant of the correct decision and that Ibn Masʿūd gave it (*Āthār Shaib.* 79); at the same time, Ibn Masʿūd's decision is also ascribed to Masrūq who counts as another of Ibn Masʿūd's Companions (*Āthār A.Y.* 675), and a decision on a point of detail to ʿAlqama himself (ibid. 676). On the other hand, ʿAlqama is made to reject an opinion ascribed to Ibn Masʿūd, by referring to a passage in the Koran.[1]

The authority of the Companions of Ibn Masʿūd was originally clearly distinct from that of Ibn Masʿūd himself. They also transmit traditions from ʿAlī,[2] and Ibn ʿAbbās, the usual authority of the Meccans, is claimed to have approved a decision of their representative Masrūq.[3] According to a later Ḥanafī opinion, they derived their doctrine 'from the specialists on law among the Companions of the Prophet, Ibn Masʿūd, ʿAlī, and ʿUmar'.[4] Shāfiʿī was unable to recognize a concept as informal as that of the Companions of Ibn Masʿūd, and in discussing the traditional basis of the Iraqian doctrine he omitted to mention the Companions of Ibn Masʿūd although they occurred in the Iraqian texts to which he referred.[5]

E. Ibrāhīm Nakhaʿī

Ibrāhīm Nakhaʿī who lived in the second half of the first century A.H. is the representative scholar of the Kufians.[6] In one passage, where one would expect Ibrāhīm to be mentioned, Shāfiʿī refers not to him but to Shaʿbī;[7] but this text gives an artificially simplified and systematized picture of the Iraqian doctrine.[8] The full importance of Ibrāhīm for the transmission

[1] *Āthār A.Y.* 603; *Āthār Shaib.* 66; for the opinion ascribed to Ibn Masʿūd, see *Tr. II*, 11 (*c*).

[2] Muslim, *Bāb al-nahy ʿan al-riwāya ʿan al-ḍuʿafā*; Ibn Qutaiba, 93.

[3] *Āthār Shaib.* 105.

[4] See above, p. 32.

[5] See above, p. 31, n. 1.

[6] See above, pp. 31 ff., 39 and n. 3.

[7] *Tr. IV*, 258. In *Tr. III*, 148 (p. 246), Shāfiʿī mentions him together with Shaʿbī.

[8] See above, p. 87.

of the Kufian Iraqian doctrine, in the opinion of the Iraqians themselves and that of Shāfi'ī, appears from passages such as *Tr. II*, 9 (*c*): 'The Iraqians diverge from what they themselves relate from the Prophet, Abū Bakr, and 'Umar, and from what they consider a well-authenticated tradition from 'Alī, in favour of the doctrine of Ibrāhīm and of something that is erroneously transmitted from Ibn Mas'ūd.'[1] The doctrine of the Kufian Iraqian school was based mainly on decisions ascribed to Ibrāhīm, although in the time of Shaibānī and Shāfi'ī the Iraqians had come to feel that this was not justifiable in theory.[2] Many of these opinions were projected back from Ibrāhīm to Ibn Mas'ūd, and Ibrāhīm became the main transmitter from Ibn Mas'ūd in the Iraqian school of law; but the doctrine of Ibrāhīm remained separate from the traditions going back to Ibn Mas'ūd.[3] Ibrāhīm Nakha'ī is the 'lowest authority'[4] for the ancient Iraqians of Kufa; in view of our former conclusions, we can dismiss the period before Ibrāhīm as legendary and have now to investigate how far the opinions ascribed to him can be considered authentic.

Judging from *Āthār A.Y.* and *Āthār Shaib.* which are the main sources for Ibrāhīm's doctrine, it appears that opinions of, and traditions transmitted by Ibrāhīm occur mostly in the legal chapters proper, much less in those concerning ritual, and hardly at all in those devoted to purely religious, ethical, and edifying matters. On the other hand, there are very few references to Ibrāhīm in *Tr. I* which treats of rather technical details of law on which Abū Ḥanīfa and Ibn Abī Lailā disagree. These technical legal questions, therefore, were in any case elaborated only after the time of "Ibrāhīm" or whosoever may be responsible for the opinions contained in *Āthār A.Y.* and *Āthār Shaib.*[5]

We have discussed several cases in which the opinions attributed to Ibrāhīm are presumably authentic.[6] They are all concerned with questions of ritual.

[1] The printed text has "'Alī" instead of "Ibn Mas'ūd" at the end; but I know of no erroneous tradition from 'Alī on the problem in question, and the doctrine of Ibrāhīm is in fact projected back to Ibn Mas'ūd: *Āthār A.Y.* 423; *Āthār Shaib.* 49.

[2] See above, p. 32. [3] See above, p. 33. [4] See above, p. 157.

[5] We shall see in what follows that the bulk of the opinions attributed to Ibrāhīm date in fact only from the time of Ḥammād. The technical questions of *Tr. I* can therefore be fixed more narrowly between Ḥammād on one side, and Abū Ḥanīfa and Ibn Abī Lailā on the other.

[6] See above, pp. 60, 142.

Much more numerous, however, are the cases in which the information about Ibrāhīm can be positively shown to be spurious, because the opinions attributed to him express secondary stages in the development of the Iraqian doctrines,[1] or because the reasoning ascribed to him presupposes the discussions of a later period,[2] or because the legal thought with which he is credited is too highly developed for it to be possible in the first century.

The technical legal thought, for instance, which underlies the doctrine attributed to Ibrāhīm in *Tr. I*, 140, and which is explicitly ascribed to him in the parallel passages in *Āthār A.Y.* and in *Āthār Shaib.*,[3] is so incisive and abstract that the historical Ibrāhīm cannot possibly be credited with it. It must belong either to Ḥammād himself, who comes in the *isnād* between Abū Ḥanīfa and Ibrāhīm Nakha'ī, or to his period. Further, Ibrāhīm's alleged statement on the three degrees of intention in unlawful homicide[4] is technically so well reasoned that it is not feasible in the time of Ibrāhīm, and again it must belong either to Ḥammād himself or to the period of Ḥammād.

The reasoning ascribed to Ibrāhīm by Ḥammād in *Tr. II*, 10 (*r*), is directed against, and therefore presupposes, the rhyming legal maxim 'there is no divorce and no manumission under duress'.[5] Two other legal maxims are attributed to Ibrāhīm by Ḥammād in *Tr. IX*, 15. One, 'restrict *ḥadd* punishments as much as possible', is given as a saying of 'Umar reported by Ibrāhīm, and this is one of the later forms in which this maxim appears.[6] The other maxim declares that '*ḥadd* punishment and *donatio propter nuptias* cannot go together', that is to say that an act of intercourse which creates a civil obligation of the man in favour of the woman is not punishable by *ḥadd*, and conversely that every act of intercourse either creates

[1] See above, pp. 154, 160, 198, 218, 219 (the development of the Iraqian doctrine is projected back into a change of opinion on the part of Ibrāhīm).

[2] See above, pp. 31 (a statement directed against traditions from the Prophet), 204 (this statement tries to explain the Medinese doctrine away, but overlooks the Umaiyad currency reform which happened in Ibrāhīm's lifetime).—See further *Āthār A.Y.* 421, 460; *Āthār Shaib.* 37, 41 (in the style of the discussions of the second century).

[3] Quoted in *Comm. ed. Cairo*, p. 100, n. 1.

[4] *Āthār A.Y.* 961; *Āthār Shaib.* 84. Both versions differ sensibly with regard to *shibh al-'amd*.

[5] See above, p. 180.

[6] See above, p. 184.

the civil liability to a *donatio propter nuptias* or the liability to *ḥadd* punishment.[1] This last principle, however, was not acted upon in all its implications in the early stage of the Iraqian doctrine as expressed in a tradition from Ibn Masʿūd and his Companion ʿAlqama; it was only on the point of gaining general recognition in the generation of Abū Ḥanīfa, Ibn Abī Lailā did not yet apply it consistently, and we can observe its gradual emergence in traditions from ʿUmar.[2] All this information given by Ḥammād on Ibrāhīm is certainly spurious.

Barely a century after the death of the historical Ibrāhīm, we find numerous cases of conflicting statements regarding his alleged doctrines.[3] At least one of the two contradictory versions must be spurious in each case. Even where there is no obvious contradiction, we are sometimes able to conclude that one of two versions, both of which claim to go back to Ibrāhīm, is not authentic.[4] But nothing guarantees that the other statements which have passed the first scrutiny are genuine.

On the contrary, until their authenticity is proved, we must regard the alleged opinions and traditions of Ibrāhīm as being fully as fictitious as those of his contemporaries.[5] The main transmitter from Ibrāhīm, and the only link between Ibrāhīm and Abū Ḥanīfa, with whom we enter the literary period, is Ḥammād whom we shall discuss in the following section; Ḥammād, or someone using his name, is therefore mainly[6] responsible for attributing later Iraqian opinions and traditions to Ibrāhīm. Occasionally, we can observe this process directly; for instance, what was originally an opinion of Ḥammād, was projected back through Ḥammād to Ibrāhīm, and through Ibrāhīm to Masrūq who is one of the Companions of Ibn Masʿūd, and to Ibn Masʿūd himself, then with other *isnāds* to other

[1] This second aspect is treated in *Tr. I*, 251, where Abū Yūsuf relates that Ibrāhīm decided an individual case accordingly. The corresponding abstract rule is ascribed to Ibrāhīm in *Āthār A.Y.*, quoted in *Comm. ed. Cairo*, p. 214, n. 2. Both statements are made on the authority of Ḥammād.

[2] *Tr. I*, 251, and *Comm. ed. Cairo*, p. 214, n. 1.

[3] See, e.g., *Āthār Shaib.* 63, 101; *Mud.* iii. 80; *Tr. I*, 163 (*a*); 163 (*b*) compared with *Āthār A.Y.*, quoted in *Comm. ed. Cairo*, p. 120, n. 2; and above, p. 209.

[4] See, e.g., *Muw. Shaib.* 73, compared with *Āthār A.Y.* 357. Shaibānī had his information from Muḥammad b. Abān b. Ṣāliḥ who is considered 'weak' (*Comm. Muw. Shaib.* 74, n. 9).

[5] See above, p. 159.

[6] But not exclusively: see above, n. 4.

Companions of the Prophet, partly in the form of anecdotes with circumstantial details, and finally to the Prophet himself.[1]

This necessary scepticism of opinions ascribed to Ibrāhīm, as long as they are not positively shown to be genuine, causes me to regard as insufficiently proven a number of statements which attribute to Ibrāhīm *ra'y* or systematic reasoning in general and which are not in themselves ruled out by other considerations. We have had occasion to refer to two cases of this kind, one of them concerning *donatio propter nuptias*.[2] On another question of marriage, *Āthār Shaib.* 61 ascribes to Ibrāhīm a systematic distinction introduced by *ara'aita*,[3] and simple systematic reasoning which is certainly older than Abū Ḥanīfa. On a problem of divorce, *Āthār Shaib.* 78 attributes to Ibrāhīm a rather formal and rigid interpretation of declarations.[4] Finally, on a question of *zakāt* tax, the opinion historically attested for Ibn Abī Lailā and also ascribed together with straightforward reasoning to Ibrāhīm, represents the earliest stage of doctrine.[5]

It is safe to conclude that the historical Ibrāhīm gave opinions on questions of ritual (and perhaps on kindred problems of directly religious interest) but not on law proper. This is all that we can expect of a specialist in religious law towards the end of the first century A.H.

F. Ḥammād

The *isnād* affixed most frequently to the legal doctrines of the ancient school of Kufa is Abū Ḥanīfa—Ḥammād—Ibrāhīm Nakha'ī.[6] This direct evidence confirms the consensus of other sources that Ḥammād b. Abī Sulaimān was the foremost representative of the Kufian Iraqian school in the generation preceding Abū Ḥanīfa.[7] Wakī' b. Jarrāḥ, a traditionist of the second century A.H., is reported to have remarked, disparaging the Kufians: 'Were it not for Ḥammād, there would be no jurisprudence in Kufa';[8] and in some verses in praise of Abū

[1] See *Tr. I*, 217, and the parallels collected in *Comm. ed. Cairo.*

[2] See above, pp. 105, 107 f.

[3] On this word, see above, p. 105.

[4] The attribution of this problem to older authorities in *Tr. II*, 11 (*e*) and in *Āthār A.Y.* 632 f. is secondary.

[5] See below, p. 284.

[6] See *Āthār A.Y.* and *Āthār Shaib.*, *passim.*

[7] See above, p. 32.

[8] Tirmidhī, at the end.

Ḥanīfa, ascribed to ʿAbdallāh b. Mubārak, another traditionist of the second century, we read: 'The loss of Ḥammād was grave enough, and our bereavement grievous, until he [Abū Ḥanīfa] saved us from the rejoicing of our enemies in our discomfiture, and showed great knowledge as his [Ḥammād's] successor.'[1] Ḥammād is considered to have been the first in Iraq to teach law to a circle of disciples.[2]

Ḥammād is the first Iraqian lawyer whom we can regard as fully historical. We saw in Section E that most of the opinions transmitted by Ḥammād and attributed by him to Ibrāhīm are in fact not older than the time of Ḥammād himself. Even allowing for all cases in which his name may have been used by other persons, there remains the great bulk of doctrine, preserved mainly in *Āthār A. Y.* and *Āthār Shaib.*, which must go back to Ḥammād himself and is nevertheless ascribed by him to Ibrāhīm. This retrospective involvement of a higher authority is of course a particular instance of the backward growth of *isnāds* which we have discussed before.[3] It is, moreover, part of a literary convention which found particular favour in Iraq and by which a legal scholar or author put his own doctrine or work under the aegis of his master. Shaibānī, for instance, refers at the beginning of every chapter of his *Jāmiʿ al-Ṣaghīr* and at the beginning of his *Kitāb al-Makhārij fil-Ḥiyal* to the final authority of Abū Ḥanīfa, as transmitted to him through Abū Yūsuf; this does not mean that the books in question were in any way based on works or lectures of Abū Ḥanīfa and Abū Yūsuf, but implies only the general relationship of pupil to master.[4] We must take the standing reference of Ḥammād to Ibrāhīm as meaning the same.[5]

Ḥammād had considerable freedom in formulating his own doctrine which he then put under the authority of Ibrāhīm.[6] Ibn Saʿd (vi. 232) identified Ḥammād's own doctrine with

[1] Khaṭīb Baghdādī, xiii. 350.

[2] Goldziher, *Ẓâhiriten*, 13.

[3] Above, pp. 156 f., 165.

[4] Also systematic conclusions drawn from the doctrine of a scholar were stated as if they were his own explicit decisions; see *Shaibānī, Makhārij*, introduction, p. 66.

[5] But Abū Ḥanīfa did not, as a rule, project his own opinions back to Ḥammād and, through Ḥammād, to Ibrāhīm; this appears from the considerable differences as regards technical legal thought which exist between the authentic opinions dating from the time of Abū Ḥanīfa and those introduced by the *isnād* Abū Ḥanīfa—Ḥammād—Ibrāhīm; see above, p. 234, n. 5.

[6] Compare *Āthār A. Y.* 979, with *Āthār Shaib.* 85 and with *Tr. VIII*, 14.

what Ḥammād put under the aegis of Ibrāhīm by saying: 'When he [Ḥammād] decided according to his own opinion (*ra'y*), he was generally right, but when he related traditions on the authority of others than Ibrāhīm, he made mistakes.' We find indeed opinions of Ḥammād quoted without a reference to Ibrāhīm.[1] But it is not generally possible to distinguish between the common doctrine of the Kufians in the time of Ḥammād and Ḥammād's individual opinions.

Besides the Kufian Iraqian doctrine which he put under the aegis of Ibrāhīm and which he found to some extent projected back to Ibn Mas'ūd and his Companions, Ḥammād transmitted traditions which had recently come into circulation, from the Prophet and from various Companions of the Prophet.[2] These outside traditions, which did not belong to the 'living tradition' of the school and often contradicted it and Ḥammād's own doctrine, were the result of the rising pressure of the traditionists on the ancient schools of law. We should be less critical than Ibn Sa'd if we were to suppose that Ḥammād received these traditions by oral transmission from the Successors who appear as his immediate authorities in the *isnāds*.

With Ḥammād's disciple Abū Ḥanīfa, whose opinions were collected and preserved in writing by his companions and disciples Abū Yūsuf and Shaibānī, the legal tradition in Kufa entered the literary period. The activity of Abū Yūsuf and Shaibānī transformed the school of Kufa into the school of the Ḥanafīs.[3]

Tr. I is concerned with the differences between Abū Ḥanīfa and his contemporary Ibn Abī Lailā, a judge of Kufa, regarding technical details of legal doctrine. These questions were worked out and discussed in the period between Ḥammād on one side and Abū Ḥanīfa and Ibn Abī Lailā on the other.[4] Although there is little occasion here for references to earlier authorities, it is obvious that Ibn Abī Lailā shares the 'living tradition' of the school of Kufa as symbolized by the name of Ibrāhīm Nakha'ī (and by that of Ibn Mas'ūd). Generally speaking, Ibn Abī Lailā represents an older stage of doctrine than his contem-

[1] See, e.g., *Āthār A. Y.* 740 (cf. above, p. 187, n. 4); *Āthār Shaib.* 53, 79, 80, 91.
[2] See above, p. 141.
[3] See above, pp. 6 ff.; below, pp. 306, 310.
[4] See above, pp. 234, n. 5, 238, n. 5.

porary Abū Ḥanīfa, that is to say, he is more conservative; he also pays more regard to judicial practice. All this is well in keeping with his being a judge.[1]

G. The Iraqian Opposition

Towards the end of the second century A.H., Ibn Mas'ūd and 'Alī were considered the main authorities of the Iraqians among the Companions of the Prophet.[2] We saw in Section D how the name of Ibn Mas'ūd became attached to the main stream of the legal tradition of the school of Kufa. After this had happened, and as long as the reference to Companions of the Prophet carried weight, any opinions which were to be opposed to the traditional doctrine of Kufa had to be provided with an equally high or possibly even higher authority, and for this the name of the Caliph 'Alī, who had made Kufa his headquarters, presented itself easily. It does not follow that the doctrines which go under the name of 'Alī embody the coherent teaching of any group or represent a tradition comparable to that indicated by the names of Ibn Mas'ūd, his Companions, Ibrāhīm Nakha'ī, and Ḥammād. We shall in fact be able to distinguish several separate tendencies within the body of legal traditions from 'Alī.[3] All we can say is that these traditions, generally speaking, represent opinions advanced in opposition to, and therefore later than, the 'living tradition' of the school of Kufa.[4]

This is of course a much simplified picture of the complicated development of legal doctrines and traditions in Iraq. Most of the opinions advanced under the authority of 'Alī remained unsuccessful, but some succeeded in gaining recognition.[5] The oldest stages of Iraqian doctrine are sometimes embodied in traditions from 'Alī,[6] and Iraqian unsuccessful opinions in traditions from Ibn Mas'ūd.[7] But, generally speaking, traditions from 'Alī are as typical of unsuccessful opinions of the Iraqian opposition as those from Ibn Mas'ūd are of the normal doctrine of the school of Kufa; this appears from the contents of *Tr. II*, compared with those of *Āthār A. Y.* and *Āthār Shaib.*

[1] See below, p. 292.

[2] See above, p. 31 f.

[3] Three successive stages of the doctrine on the *mukātab* slave are represented by traditions from 'Alī: see below, p. 279 f.

[4] See above, p. 66 f.

[5] See above, p. 162. There are several other examples.

[6] As in the example quoted above, n. 3.

[7] See *Tr. II*, 2 (*e*) and *Āthār Shaib.* 5; also above, p. 213.

The 'unsuccessful' ʿAlī traditions in *Tr. II* show often a rigorous and meticulous tendency, obviously inspired by religious and ethical considerations. The element of caution inherent in this[1] leads to the seemingly opposite tendency of restricting *ḥadd* punishments.[2]

We find this kind of Iraqian tradition from ʿAlī corresponding almost regularly to doctrines attested in Medina. The corresponding Medinese doctrines remained sometimes unsuccessful even there,[3] but they mostly became the common opinion of Medina.[4] It agrees with the comparatively later development of the Medinese school[5] that a body of doctrines which remained unsuccessful in Iraq, where it could not overcome the already established tradition of a school of law, succeeded in gaining recognition in Medina to a considerable extent.[6]

Another group of traditions from ʿAlī represent crude and primitive analogies, early unsuccessful efforts to systematize.[7] Occasionally, this primitive reasoning takes the form of legal 'puzzles', some of which have Shaʿbī as a common transmitter in their *isnāds*.[8] We can conclude from this that the Kufian 'living tradition', against which the ʿAlī traditions were directed, had become connected with the name of Ibn Masʿūd, or at least his Companions, at a period earlier than this primitive reasoning. Contrary to the former group of ʿAlī traditions, which anticipate the activity of the traditionists, these systematic traditions seem to reflect an early stage of Iraqian legal thought.

The Iraqians towards the end of the second century A.H. were able to say with regard to the unsuccessful ʿAlī traditions: 'No one holds this opinion',[9] and to reject them as falling outside the 'living tradition' of the school. At an earlier period, however, they did not disdain to discredit them by scurrilous and exaggerated opinions which they equally attributed to ʿAlī

[1] See above, p. 215.
[2] *Tr. II*, 18 (*f*), (*g*), (*j*), (*p*); cf. *Muw. Shaib.* 303.
[3] See above, pp. 165 (this doctrine originated certainly in Iraq), 225; further *Tr. II*, 8 (*a*) = 20 (*a*), compared with *Muw.* ii. 92, 94 and *Muw. Shaib.* 180.
[4] See above, pp. 215 (*penult.*), 227; further *Tr. II*, 2 (*c*), compared with *Mud.* I. 25.
[5] See above, p. 223; below, p. 276.
[6] See also below, p. 255.
[7] See above, pp. 106 ff., 167; further *Tr. II*, 13 (*c*).
[8] *Tr. II*, 13 (*b*) ff., (*i*), (*j*), 14 (*a*). This kind of tradition was taken over by the Zaidīs (see *Majmūʿ*, 690 ff.), but this does not make it Shiite (see below, p. 262 f.).
[9] *Tr. II*, 13 (*c*), (*e*), 16 (*a*).

and some of which are difficult to distinguish from the original doctrines ascribed to him.[1] A later echo of the disturbance created by the 'Alī traditions occurs in Muslim[2] where Ibn 'Abbās is made to object particularly to traditions from 'Alī; an anonymous companion of 'Alī is made to regret the falsifications introduced into the traditions from 'Alī; and Mughīra b. Miqsam Ḍabbī is made to say that traditions from 'Alī are reliably related only by some of the Companions of Ibn Mas'ūd. There is no trace of a bias in favour of Shiite legal doctrines in the Iraqian traditions from 'Alī.

H. Sufyān Thaurī

Sufyān Thaurī, a younger contemporary of Abū Ḥanīfa, belongs to the literary period but ought to be mentioned here as a Kufian[3] who did not join the followers of Abū Ḥanīfa but founded a school of law of his own. He was claimed by lawyers, traditionists, and ascetics as one of them;[4] Ibn Qutaiba reckons him among the systematic lawyers (*Ma'ārif*, 249), the author of the *Fihrist* (p. 225) among the lawyer-traditionists.[5] From the extensive fragments of his doctrines which have been preserved in Ṭabarī,[6] we can judge with certainty that Sufyān Thaurī was above all a lawyer and a representative of the ancient schools.[7] His opinions and reasonings, though on the whole definitely Iraqian, show that it would be a mistake to generalize, even within the circle of the Kufians, the uniformity of doctrine suggested by the *isnād* Abū Ḥanīfa—Ḥammād—Ibrāhīm.[8]

[1] *Tr. II*, 14 (*b*), 18 (*m*), and perhaps 18 (*i*), (*n*).

[2] *Bāb al-nahy 'an al-riwāya 'an al-ḍu'afā'*.

[3] He was born and lived in Kufa, and died in Basra only by accident.

[4] See Plessner in *E.I.*, s.v. Sufyān al-Thawrī.

[5] See Goldziher, *Ẓâhiriten*, 4, on these arbitrary distinctions.

[6] *Ed. Kern* and *ed. Schacht*.

[7] See above, p. 205, on his attitude to the 'living tradition'.

[8] See, e.g., Ṭabarī, 64 (cf. below, p. 286), 76 (cf. below, ibid.), 97 (cf. *Tr. IX*, 18). And see above, p. 7.

CHAPTER 5

THE MEDINESE AND MECCANS

A. The 'Seven Lawyers of Medina'

In tracing the history of the Medinese school of law, we must leave out of account 'Umar and Ibn 'Umar, its main authorities among the Companions of the Prophet.[1] We have seen that traditions from Companions cannot be regarded as genuine,[2] that the name of 'Umar, to whom many important institutions of Muhammadan law and administration were ascribed, was invoked both by the Medinese and by the Iraqians,[3] and that the traditions transmitted from Ibn 'Umar by Nāfi' in one of the best existing *isnāds* are the product of anonymous traditionists in the second century A.H.[4]

The conventional picture of Medina as the home of the *sunna* of the Prophet is artificial and late;[5] we have seen that the development of legal theory and doctrine in Medina was secondary to and dependent on that in Iraq.[6] We are therefore justified in starting our study of the Medinese school with the 'seven lawyers of Medina', a group of persons in the time of the Successors, all of whom died shortly before or shortly after the year A.H. 100. They are, according to the most widely accepted list:

Sa'īd b. Musaiyib (d. after 90)
'Urwa b. Zubair (d. 94)
Abū Bakr b. 'Abdalraḥmān (d. 94)
'Ubaidallāh b. 'Abdallāh b. 'Utba (d. 94 or 98)
Khārija b. Zaid (d. 99 or 100)
Sulaimān b. Yasār (d. about 100)
Qāsim b. Muḥammad (d. 106).

The concept of seven representative lawyers of Medina at the end of the first century has no foundation in fact. When it was a question of singling out the representative lawyers of Medina, numbers other than seven were often mentioned in the earlier

[1] See above, p. 25 f.
[2] See above, p. 169 f.
[3] See above, p. 32.
[4] See above, pp. 176 ff.
[5] For references, see above, p. 115, n. 1.
[6] See above, p. 223 and the references given there.

period. Even when seven is the number given, there are often considerable differences over the names. According to the narrator, Qabīṣa b. Dhu'aib, his circle in the mosque of Medina consisted of ʿUrwa b. Zubair, ʿUrwa's brother Muṣʿab, Abū Bakr b. ʿAbdalraḥmān, the future Caliph ʿAbdalmalik, ʿAbdalraḥmān b. Miswar, Ibrāhīm b. ʿAbdalraḥmān b. ʿAuf, and ʿUbaidallāh b. ʿAbdallāh.[1] Another list is purely adventitious and contains in addition the name of a woman traditionist: Ibn Musaiyib, Sulaimān b. Yasār, Abū Bakr b. ʿAbdalraḥmān, ʿIkrima, ʿAṭā' [who is usually counted amongst the Meccans], ʿAmra bint ʿAbdalraḥmān, ʿUrwa, and Zuhrī.[2] The earliest mentions, to my knowledge, of the conventional group occur in Ṭaḥāwī, i. 163 and, slightly later, in *Aghānī*, viii. 96; here ʿUbaidallāh b. ʿAbdallāh, in verses addressed to a lady, calls the six other lawyers as witnesses of his love; I need hardly insist that these verses are spurious.

The 'living tradition' of the school of Medina is to a great extent anonymous[3] and, where individual authorities are mentioned in the ancient legal texts, there is no trace of any fixed group. Mālik, for instance, mentions Qāsim b. Muḥammad, ʿUrwa b. Zubair, and Abū Bakr b. ʿAbdalraḥmān besides 'some [other] scholars' (*Muw.* i. 269), and the *Mudauwana*, iv. 54, refers to Mālik's authorities as 'the ancient scholars, that is Ibn Musaiyib and others'. The same is true of Shāfiʿī who makes a point of collecting spurious information on the ancient Medinese authorities and confronting with it the Medinese of his time. He says, for instance: 'How can you say that the lawyers in Medina (*al-fuqahā' bil-Madīna*) did not differ from one another?' (*Tr. III*, 85).[4]

The actual doctrine of the Medinese school often does not agree with the alleged opinions of the Medinese authorities in the time of the Successors, and the information concerning these last is to a great extent spurious.[5] This contrast between the 'living tradition' and the fictitious information on the old

[1] Balādhurī, *Ansāb*, 257.

[2] Ibn Saʿd, ii_2. 128–33. The mention of the customary group of seven lawyers, ascribed to Ibn Mubārak in *Tahdhīb*, iii. 807, is strongly suspect.

[3] See above, p. 85.

[4] On *Tr. IV*, 258, where Shāfiʿī mentions Ibn Musaiyib as the representative scholar of Medina, see above, p. 87.

[5] For references, see above, p. 151, n. 2.

authorities provided Shāfi'ī with an argument against the legal theory and positive doctrine of the school of Medina.[1]

We can sometimes observe the growth of this spurious information about the ancient authorities, for instance, in the short period between Mālik and Ibn Wahb,[2] or in the time between Mālik and Ibn 'Abdalbarr.[3] Mālik's younger contemporary Darāwardī is responsible for some of it.[4]

This makes it impossible to regard information on the Medinese lawyers in the time of the Successors as genuine unless it is positively shown to be authentic. It would be rash to exclude this possibility *a priori*, but as far as I have been able to investigate the development of the Medinese doctrine, I have not found any opinion ascribed to one of these ancient lawyers which is likely to be authentic. The general history of legal doctrine makes it improbable that the Medinese in the time of the 'seven lawyers' had progressed farther than their Iraqian contemporary Ibrāhīm Nakha'ī.[5] That the doctrine of Ibn Musaiyib showed ten essential differences from that of Mālik,[6] presupposing as it does that both doctrines are comparable, is obviously the result of later systematizing.[7]

As an example of the negative result mentioned in the preceding paragraph, it will be useful to analyse one case in which the information on the doctrine of two of the 'seven lawyers' would seem, on the face of it, most likely to be authentic. An ancient Medinese way of expressing 'practice' or consensus was to refer to what men or people used to do (*al-nās 'alaih*). This term is attested for Yaḥyā b. Sa'īd (*Mud.* i. 36), and occurs in non-legal literature in Ibn Muqaffa' (*Ṣaḥāba*, 121); it had almost fallen out of current usage in the time of Mālik, one generation later,[8] and may well go back as far as the year A.H. 100, little more than a generation earlier. The same kind of reference to the usage of men is in fact ascribed to Qāsim b. Muḥammad in his version of a legal maxim which he

[1] See above, p. 78. f.

[2] Compare *Muw.* iv. 41, *Tr. III*, 148 (p. 247) and *Tr. VIII*, 11, with *Mud.* xvi. 168 (the quotation from Mālik's contemporary Mājashūn, however, is genuine; see above, p. 221).

[3] See above, p. 64 f.

[4] See above, p. 195.

[5] See above, pp. 234 ff.

[6] Ṭabarī, *ed. Kern*, 68. Significantly enough, two contradictory opinions are attributed to Ibn Musaiyib concerning the particular problem mentioned there.

[7] This disposes of the difficulty seen by Bergsträsser in *Islam*, xiv. 81.

[8] But see *Muw.* iii. 98: *wa-dhālik al-amr alladhī kānat 'alaih al-jamā'a bi-baladinā*; for the terms normally used by Mālik, see above, p. 62 f.

adduces in favour of the common Medinese doctrine,[1] and to Sulaimān b. Yasār in a statement on the consensus of Medina;[2] this last statement certainly represents a stage of doctrine earlier than Mālik. But the same Sulaimān b. Yasār appears also as the main transmitter of a counter-tradition against the common Medinese doctrine on the problem decided by Qāsim b. Muḥammad.[3] It is apparent that the names of the ancient Medinese authorities were affixed at random to opinions which themselves may have been old.

B. Zuhrī

From Zuhrī onwards, there exists an ascertainable authentic element in the opinions ascribed to the authorities of Medina. Zuhrī died in A.H. 124, fifty-five years before the death of Mālik; their personal intercourse is therefore more likely than that between Mālik and Nāfi'.[4] Those cases in which Mālik states explicitly that he asked Zuhrī or heard Zuhrī say something, can unhesitatingly be regarded as genuine,[5] and there are other opinions ascribed to Zuhrī which are obviously authentic.[6]

But towards the end of the second century A.H., Zuhrī had already been credited with many spurious and often contradictory opinions,[7] and his name inserted in *isnāds* of traditions which did not yet exist in his time and from which fictitious statements on his supposed doctrine were abstracted. He appears as the common link in the *isnāds* of a number of traditions from the Prophet, from Companions and from Successors;[8] Zuhrī himself was hardly responsible for the greater part of these traditions. The following examples are meant to illustrate the growth of spurious information about him.

The common ancient doctrine on what constitutes legal foster-parentship was unsuccessfully attacked in Medina.[9] Counter-statements on the opinion of ancient Medinese authorities, in favour of the original doctrine, have a common link in their *isnāds* in Zuhrī

[1] See above, p. 174; for Shāfi'ī's criticism, see above, p. 65.
[2] *Muw.* ii. 338; *Muw. Shaib.* 321; *Mud.* iii. 118.
[3] See above, p. 220.
[4] See above, p. 176 f.
[5] See, e.g., *Muw.* ii. 67; iii. 36, 37, 159; iv. 12.
[6] See, e.g., *Mud.* xvi. 166; and above, p. 101.
[7] See above, p. 115.
[8] See above, p. 175.
[9] See above, p. 216.

(*Muw.* iii. 88), but he was also made the transmitter of a tradition from the Prophet in favour of the unsuccessful modification (*Muw. Shaib.* 271; *Tr. III*, 56). Ibn Wahb (*Mud.* v. 87) quotes him as stating that 'the Muslims have finally decided' in favour of what was the common ancient doctrine (*intahā amr al-Muslimīn ilā dhālik*); but this stood at the beginning and not at the end of the development.

On a question of weregeld a spurious opinion of Ibn Musaiyib, and an alleged remark of Zuhrī on it, were abstracted from a different statement, itself fictitious, on the doctrine of Ibn Musaiyib.[1]

The oldest judgment on Zuhrī of which I know is that of Shaibānī who calls him 'the greatest lawyer and scholar of the Medinese in his time, and the most knowledgeable among them with regard to traditions from the Prophet' (*Tr. VIII*, 13). This already reflects the changed standards of a later generation.

C. Rabī'a

Rabī'a b. Abī 'Abdalraḥmān, somewhat younger than Zuhrī, was according to Shaibānī (*Tr. VIII*, 13) the most prominent lawyer of the Medinese in his time. His conventional reputation as a particularly strong upholder of *ra'y*, a reputation which later earned him the nickname of *Rabī'at al-Ra'y*, is not based on facts.[2] The information which we possess on him is of the same character as that on Zuhrī: an appreciable amount of genuine doctrine, together with spurious additions. We are in many cases able to determine the authenticity or spuriousness of the opinions ascribed to him.

Certainly authentic are references such as *Muw.* ii. 229 where Mālik states that he heard Rabī'a express a certain opinion on the problem of how to expiate a particular kind of breach of the state of ritual consecration during the pilgrimage.[3]

For further examples of genuine opinions of Rabī'a see *Mud.* iv. 64, a passage which shows conscious legal thought and anticipates in its essentials Shāfi'ī's argument in *Tr. III*, 80; further, *Mud.* v. 130 and 133 which have been discussed above, p. 211; and *Mud.* xvi. 166, a reference which is connected with a genuine statement on Zuhrī. Shaibānī's reference to Rabī'a's

[1] See above, p. 222.
[2] See above, p. 114 f.
[3] See the detailed discussion in *Tr. III*, 97.

doctrine in *Tr. VIII*, 13, may also be authentic,[1] and perhaps even the quotation in Ṭaḥāwī, i. 43, which expresses the anti-traditionist attitude of the first half of the second century A.H. and contains a conclusion *a maiore ad minus*.

Examples of spurious information on Rabīʿa have been discussed above, pp. 65, 117, 151, 168 f. Apart from alleged opinions of Rabīʿa, they include traditions for which Rabīʿa was claimed as a transmitter. But Rabīʿa himself was not a traditionist.

D. Yaḥyā b. Saʿīd

Yaḥyā b. Saʿīd is still later than Rabīʿa, stands half-way between Zuhrī and Mālik, and is one of Mālik's immediate authorities. The opinions ascribed to him by Mālik and other ancient authors are certainly authentic. On the other hand, Yaḥyā is responsible for the transmission of a considerable amount of fictitious information on the ancient Medinese authorities, information which had come into existence in his time; he also transmits recently created traditions and *isnāds*.[2]

With Mālik, soon after the time of Yaḥyā, the school of Medina enters the literary period. Shāfiʿī (*Tr. IV*, 257) speaks of the struggle of opinions within the Medinese legal tradition in the time of Mālik,[3] but the details have been lost because the ancient school of the Medinese transformed itself into that of the Mālikīs and only the works of Mālik and his followers were preserved.

E. The Medinese Opposition

As we found was the case in Iraq,[4] there existed in Medina a mass of legal traditions which represented opinions advanced in opposition to the 'living tradition' of the school. By this I do not mean the unavoidable residue of ancient and later opinions which were discarded or failed to gain recognition in the normal course of the development of doctrine.[5] What concerns us here are the opinions which, in the form of traditions from the

[1] See above, p. 206, n. 5.
[2] See, e.g., above, pp. 169, 211 f.
[3] *Tr. IV*, 257, translated above, p. 7.
[4] See above, pp. 240 ff.
[5] See above, pp. 101 (on Zuhrī), 114 (l. 4 f.). Two further examples of such opinions occur in *Tr. VIII*, 9.

Prophet or from Companions, were opposed to the current doctrine of the school which they were meant to supersede.[1] This body of opposition doctrine is formally less easy to circumscribe in Medina than it is in Iraq where most of it goes under the name of ʿAlī. The most important single group of legal traditions emanating from the Medinese opposition are those with the *isnād* Nāfiʿ—Ibn ʿUmar,[2] but other Companions of the Prophet are also well represented.

Materially, the traditions and opinions of the Medinese opposition are as little uniform as are those of the opposition in Iraq, but broadly speaking they represent the doctrine of the traditionists who endeavoured to modify the 'living tradition' of the school of Medina. They were often, but by no means always, actuated by religious rigorism and scrupulousness, for instance in introducing a refinement into fasting (above, p. 152 f.), in laying down strict conditions for the creation of foster-parentship (p. 216), in making the pregnant widow keep a longer waiting period (p. 225 f.). Less rigorous, for example, is their adoption of the practice of *masḥ* (below, p. 263 f.). Neutral from the point of view of strictness is the opinion on a point of ritual which the traditionists opposed to a doctrine based on a biographical tradition on the Prophet (p. 139, n. 6).

All these doctrines proposed by the traditionists remained unsuccessful in Medina; others, however, were adopted and became part of the teaching of the Medinese school.[3] Numerous doctrines of the Medinese opposition, both successful and unsuccessful, derive from corresponding doctrines of the opposition in Iraq;[4] these connexions confirm that there existed the same kind of opposition to both ancient schools of law.

F. The Meccans

The little that we know of the school of Mecca[5] shows that it shared the main characteristics of the other ancient schools of law. The main authority of the Meccans among the Companions of the Prophet was Ibn ʿAbbās,[6] and there are traditions which

[1] See above, p. 66.
[2] See above, p. 178.
[3] See above, pp. 153, 215, 227. See further *Ikh.* 207 f.
[4] See above, p. 241.
[5] See above, p. 8, n. 6.
[6] This was known to Maqrīzī, *Khiṭaṭ*, ii. 332.

claim the sanction of the Prophet for the doctrine ascribed to him,[1] in the same way in which other traditions claim it for the doctrine ascribed to Ibn Mas'ūd in Kufa.[2] In further agreement with the procedure of the Kufians who project their doctrine back not only to Ibn Mas'ūd but to his Companions,[3] we find Meccan opinions often attributed to the Companions of Ibn 'Abbās as well as to Ibn 'Abbās himself.[4]

The representative scholar of Mecca at the beginning of the second century A.H. was 'Aṭā' b. Abī Rabāḥ.[5] He is the only Meccan lawyer whom we are able to grasp as an individual, although his companions and the Meccans in general are mentioned repeatedly and Shāfi'ī speaks of 'the majority (*'āmma*) of the muftis in Mecca' (*Tr. III*, 143).

Our information on 'Aṭā' is of the same character as that on his younger Medinese contemporary Zuhrī: an authentic core overlaid by fictitious accretions in the course of the second century. Abū Ḥanīfa states he was present at the lectures of 'Aṭā' (*Āthār A. Y.* 833; *Āthār Shaib.* 57), but himself relates little from 'Aṭā'. Abū Ḥanīfa's contemporary Ibn Abī Lailā refers to 'Aṭā' as holding the same opinions as himself (*Tr. I*, 183, 185); these references are possibly authentic. Abū Yūsuf states that he heard an opinion of 'Aṭā' related to him personally by Ḥajjāj b. Arṭāt (*Tr. I*, 181); but the opinion in question is intermediate between the two extreme opinions held by Abū Ḥanīfa and by Ibn Abī Lailā, and it presupposes both; Ḥajjāj must be suspected of putting into circulation recently forged traditions.[6]

Probably genuine are the opinions related from 'Aṭā' on the *khiyār al-majlis* (above, p. 160), on the freedom of the manumitted slave to enter a *walā'* relationship with the consent of his former master (above, p. 173, n. 3), on two questions connected with the contract of *mukātaba* (below, p. 279 f.), and on the evidence given by women (*Tr. I*, 124); this last opinion is based on a strict analogy with the Koranic rules of evidence, and its tendency is contrary to that of a spurious opinion attributed to 'Aṭā' (above, p. 167).

Other opinions, presumably genuine, which are related from

[1] *Muw.* ii. 144, discussed below; *Ris.* 61.

[2] See above, p. 29.

[3] See above, p. 232 f.

[4] *Ris.* 40; *Ikh.* 241, 365; Ibn 'Abdalbarr, quoted in Zurqānī, iii. 25. The Companions of Ibn 'Abbās were said to exist also outside Mecca, particularly in Yemen.

[5] See above, p. 7. See also *E.I.*², s.v.

[6] See above, p. 174.

the ancient Meccans but cannot be connected with 'Aṭā' personally, concern the marriage of the pilgrim (above, p. 153), the permission of the *mut'a* marriage (below, p. 266), and the definition of what constitutes the 'usury' which is forbidden in the Koran.

The current practice of Mecca, against which the relevant passages of the Koran were directed, consisted in adding the accumulated interest to the capital which was to be repaid at a fixed term, and in doubling the debt every time the debtor asked for and received an extension of the term.[1] The other ancient schools of law, by a common development of doctrine but with differences on details, extended the law of 'usury', generally speaking, to all exchanges of gold, silver, and various other commodities, and demanded not only immediate delivery of the two lots which were being exchanged, but also absolute equality in quantity if they fell under the same species.[2] The Meccans, however, kept more closely to the original circumstances of the Koranic prohibition and held that there could be no 'usury' unless there was a time-lag in the transaction (*Ikh.* 241 f.). They had therefore no objection to the exchange of one dīnār for two, or of one dirham for two, if both lots were delivered immediately, and only objected to it if the delivery of one of the lots was to be postponed. This doctrine was projected back to Ibn 'Abbās and his Companions in general.

Corresponding doctrines were also propagated, but unsuccessfully, in Iraq under the name of Ibn Mas'ūd (*Tr. II*, 12 (*g*)), and in Medina under the names of Ibn Musaiyib and 'Urwa b. Zubair (*Ikh.* 241). They represent, it is true, an earlier stage than the doctrine which prevailed in the Iraqian and Medinese schools, but the references to these authorities cannot be taken as genuine.

Some of the opinions attributed to 'Aṭā' are certainly or probably fictitious, particularly his statement against *ra'y* which is contradicted by his own use of *qiyās* and *istiḥsān* (above, p. 131); and certainly one, or possibly both, of two contradictory opinions which are ascribed to him (above, p. 186 and n. 6); for a further example, see above, p. 167.

A tradition in *Muw.* ii. 144 aims at showing that a doctrine which goes under the name of Ibn 'Abbās, the authority of the Meccans, coincides with the practice of the Prophet. Zaid b. Aslam, in the generation before Mālik, is the common link in

[1] See *E.I.*, s.v. *Ribā*.

[2] For a consequence of this sweeping rule, see above, p. 67.

the *isnāds* of this tradition,[1] and it is likely that it originated in his time. The same doctrine is ascribed to 'Umar in a tradition which has 'Aṭā' in the *isnād* (ibid.); this tradition implies the same controversy as the first, and presumably belongs to the same period; this shows the mention of 'Aṭā' in the *isnād* to be spurious.

[1] See Zurqānī, ad loc.

CHAPTER 6

THE TRADITIONISTS

WE have met with the traditionists in many parts of this book, and the present chapter is devoted to a discussion of their movement in general. Their activity is an integral part of the development of legal theory and positive legal doctrine during the first half of the second century A.H.[1] What has been known of it so far can be summarized, with Goldziher, by saying that it started in opposition to the general use of *ra'y* in the ancient schools of law and was therefore secondary to it.[2]

The traditionists[3] were distinguished from the lawyers and muftis, from the ancient schools of law and from the *ahl al-kalām*.[4] They existed 'in all countries', in Iraq, Hijaz, Egypt, and Syria,[5] and formed groups in opposition to, but nevertheless in contact with the local schools of law.[6] Shāfi'ī who, as far as law was concerned, always considered himself a member of the school of Medina,[7] nevertheless identified himself with the traditionists, adopted their essential thesis and claimed that a number of his foremost [Medinese] companions and a number of the foremost lawyers in the other countries had also accepted their tenets.[8]

The main thesis of the traditionists, as opposed to the ancient schools of law, is that formal traditions from the Prophet supersede the 'living tradition'. Their most important activity, the creation and putting into circulation of traditions from the Prophet, is of course seldom avowed openly, but its traces are unmistakable. It is openly confessed, for instance, in the traditions which make the Prophet say: '[Sayings attributed to me] which agree with the Koran, go back to me, whether I actually

[1] See above, p. 66 f.
[2] *Muh. St.* ii. 77 f.; see also *Ẓâhiriten*, 3 ff.
[3] *Aṣḥāb al-ḥadīth, ahl al-ḥadīth*; in *Tr. VIII*, 6, *ahl al-āthār*.
[4] *Ikh.* 37, 91, 338; *Tr. IV*, 256; *Tr. VIII*, 6; Ibn Qutaiba, 2.
[5] This was known to Maqrīzī, *Khiṭaṭ*, ii. 333.
[6] *Ikh.* 376 f.; *Tr. III*, 20, 47, 148 (p. 243); *Tr. IX*, 40; *Umm*, vi. 185 (this refers to *Tr. III*, 57).
[7] See above, p. 9 f.
[8] *Ris.* 38; *Ikh.* 28.

said them or not,' and: 'Whatever good sayings there are, I said them.'[1]

The traditionists are naturally specialists in the transmission and study of traditions and in the criticism of their *isnāds*; they decide which traditions are transmitted by reliable authorities, they reject traditions which are badly attested, they do not regard *mursal* traditions as reliable, and they never acknowledge *munqaṭiʿ* traditions.[2] Traditions with imperfect *isnāds*, such as *mursal* and *munqaṭiʿ*, are typical of the ancient schools of law, and the criticism of *isnāds* by the traditionists is primarily directed against the less exacting standards of the ancient schools.[3] On the other hand, the traditionists accept 'isolated' traditions,[4] whereas the ancient schools of law reject them;[5] the creation and transmission of 'isolated' traditions from the Prophet was the main weapon of the traditionists. They are of course not necessarily in favour of every individual tradition from the Prophet, and may be found to reject such traditions for reasons of their own.[6]

Notwithstanding the high qualifications which were demanded, in theory, of a transmitter of traditions,[7] the standards of reasoning of the traditionists in general were inferior to those of the ancient schools of law. Shāfiʿī complained repeatedly that their superficial and untrained adherence to traditions led them into error, and that their lack of systematic reasoning put them at a disadvantage; in particular, he disavowed those extreme traditionists who accepted all traditions indiscriminately.[8]

Shāfiʿī reports actual discussions with traditionists at some length in *Ikh.* 81 ff. and 88 ff. The traditionist gets the best of the argument in both cases, because Shāfiʿī feels obliged to adhere to the settled opinion on major points of ritual, although the evidence of traditions from the Prophet rather points to the contrary.[9]

Here and elsewhere the traditionists refer, besides traditions

[1] Goldziher, *Muh. St.* ii. 49, from Jāḥiẓ and Ibn Māja; less outspoken parallels have been discussed above, pp. 28 and 45.

[2] *Ikh.* 32, 53 f., 212, 219, 265, 271, 365 and often; also numerous cases in *Tr. I.*

[3] See above, pp. 36 ff.

[4] Ibn Qutaiba, 89.

[5] See above, pp. 50 ff.

[6] See above, p. 155.

[7] Shāfiʿī enumerates them in *Ris.* 51.

[8] *Ikh.* 100, 323, 367 f. (translated above, p. 57).

[9] Cf. above, p. 15, and below, p. 323 f.

from the Prophet, to the Koran and to traditions from Companions as auxiliary arguments. It was natural for them to avail themselves of recognized arguments whenever they happened to be in favour of their own doctrine.[1] But this did not make them any less opposed to the 'living tradition' of the ancient schools of law and to all kinds of human reasoning and personal opinion which were closely connected with it.[2] The traditions directed against the exercise of *ra'y* in law which are found in Iraq and in Hijaz, some of them attributed to Successors, were put into circulation by the traditionists.[3] The traditionists were also responsible for the arguments adduced in favour of traditions from the Prophet, and particularly the statements that Companions and other authorities revised their own decisions on hearing that the Prophet had decided differently.[4]

We have seen that the traditionists were connected with the opposition to the ancient school of Medina.[5] A group of Medinese Nāfi'—Ibn 'Umar traditions which express an effort, sometimes successful and sometimes unsuccessful, to modify the doctrine of the Medinese school, can be traced to the activity of the traditionists.[6] A close relationship exists between their opposition in Medina and an Iraqian opposition group which expressed its doctrines in a particular body of traditions from 'Alī.[7] In contrast to many Medinese Nāfi'—Ibn 'Umar traditions, however, these Iraqian traditions from 'Alī are not carried back to the Prophet and cannot be connected directly with the traditionists. As reference to Companions, which was the usual procedure in the ancient schools of law, preceded, generally speaking, consistent reference to the Prophet as practised by the traditionists, the body of traditions in question seems to represent a stage at which the opposition to the established local schools had not yet adopted the form of traditions from the Prophet.

The traditionists were presumably responsible for some of the traditions directed against Umaiyad popular and administrative practice,[8] although it is not always possible to determine whether a particular doctrine originated in traditionist circles or within the ancient schools of law. The 'Islamicizing' which

[1] Cf. above, p. 230. [2] See above, p. 128 f. [3] See above, pp. 129 ff.
[4] See above, pp. 53 ff. [5] See above, p. 248 f. [6] See above, p. 178 f.
[7] See above, p. 241. [8] See above, pp. 192 ff.

is one aspect of the process by which Muhammadan law was created out of Umaiyad practice,[1] was by no means a distinctive interest of the traditionists; they were preceded in this by the ancient schools of law themselves.

The general tendency of the traditionists is the same as that of the opposition in Iraq and in Medina: a certain inclination towards strictness and rigorism, not without exceptions, however.[2] They endeavour to subordinate the legal subject-matter to moral considerations,[3] but are also interested in purely legal issues such as the ancient Meccan custom of *khiyār al-majlis*.[4] This concern with the legal sphere is not older than the second century A.H. It is reasonable to suppose that the differences of opinion which Ibn Qutaiba (p. 103) attests for them about the middle of the third century, existed already at an earlier period. From the time of Shāfi'ī onwards, we notice the growth of extravagant 'mythological' traditions sponsored by them, such as the tradition which declares a black dog to be a devil.[5] This kind of tradition is common among those collected and defended by Ibn Qutaiba.

Shāfi'ī made the essential thesis of the traditionists prevail in legal theory, and their movement culminated in the classical collections of traditions of the third century A.H. The legal doctrine of Ibn Ḥanbal is purely traditionist. But the recognition which the traditionist principle won outside the Mu'tazila did not cause the Ḥanafīs and Mālikīs, who continued the ancient Iraqian and Medinese schools, to change their positive legal doctrine appreciably from what it had been at the beginning of the literary period.[6]

[1] See below, pp. 283 ff.

[2] They are in favour of the greater ritual ablution (*ghusl*) before the Friday service (see *Ikh.* 178), but are less exacting with regard to ritual ablution in another case (see *Ikh.* 88).

[3] See above, pp. 178, 183 f. (a legal maxim).

[4] See above, p. 160 f.

[5] See above, p. 146.

[6] For lists of traditionists, see Ibn Qutaiba, *Ma'ārif*, 251 ff. and *Fihrist*, 225 ff. Several traditionists have been discussed elsewhere in this book, e.g.:

'Abdallāh b. Dīnār: above, pp. 163, 173, 199.

'Amr b. Dīnār: above, pp. 65 f., 155, n. 2.

'Amr b. Shu'aib: below, p. 280, n. 7.

Ibn Abī Dhi'b: above, pp. 54 f., 65, 181. Shāfi'ī is uncertain whether Ibn Abī Dhi'b is reliable or not: *Ikh.* 244.

Ibn 'Uyaina: above, pp. 54, n. 2, 65 f., 131, 160, 174.

Mu'tamir b. Sulaimān: above, pp. 56, 131.

The one traditionist of whom texts of any length are easily available at present, is Ibn Qutaiba, and we have used his *Kitāb Ta'wīl Mukhtalif al-Ḥadīth* repeatedly in order to ascertain the doctrine of the traditionists on various points of legal theory.[1] Ibn Qutaiba is, however, influenced by Shāfi'ī and by the ancient schools of law:[2] he considers himself one of the Medinese, and at the same time looks back to the great scholars of the past, Iraqians, Medinese, Syrians and traditionists, with the same kind of respect; on points of detail, he is definitely eclectic, but his opinions mostly coincide with the Mālikī doctrine.[3] This attitude must not be projected back into the second century A.H. Ibn Qutaiba was a highly cultured man of letters; all the more significant is the defective character of his own legal reasoning which we are entitled, on account of Shāfi'ī's remarks to the same effect, to attribute to the traditionists. Whenever we find good legal reasoning and credible interpretations in Ibn Qutaiba, they have almost invariably been anticipated by Shāfi'ī. Ibn Qutaiba's own interpretation of traditions is arbitrary and forced, and his own legal reasoning confused and bad.[4]

[1] See above, p. 16, n. 1, on traditions from the Prophet explaining the Koran; ibid., n. 3, on the Prophet being inspired; p. 47, n. 1, on the repeal of the Koran by the *sunna*; p. 77, n. 3 on the identification of *sunna* with traditions from the Prophet; p. 94, n. 3, on the concept of consensus; p. 128 f. on the rejection of *ra'y*.

[2] See above, pp. 69, n. 2, 132.

[3] See, e.g., Ibn Qutaiba, 238 f.

[4] See, e.g., Ibn Qutaiba, 112 f., 114 f., 332 f.—Ibid. 67 (compare with *Tr. VIII*, 12), 251, 444.

CHAPTER 7

THE MUʿTAZILA

THE extreme opponents of the traditionists are the Muʿtazila who are called 'rationalists' in Shāfiʿī's writings and in other ancient sources.[1] The Muʿtazila were not a school of law proper but a political and dogmatic movement;[2] their speculative method and their insistence on the Koran as the only basis for their system of religious doctrine, however, led them to the rejection of most traditions and, by implication, of legal doctrines based on traditions, and to the consideration of questions of law in the light of their theological tenets.[3] Although they did not elaborate a system of legal doctrine of their own, their interest in problems of legal theory and of positive law found expression in numerous works on these subjects written from their particular point of view.[4]

We have had occasion to discuss their opinions on several points of legal theory.[5] References to their opinions on particular points of positive law occur occasionally.[6] As far as can be ascertained, the Muʿtazila are throughout dependent upon the development of legal doctrine in the schools of law proper and only revise the results of these last according to their own standards. In particular, their doctrine shows resemblances to that of the Iraqians in several respects;[7] the Muʿtazila did in fact originate and develop in Iraq.

Shāfiʿī takes the objections of the Muʿtazila to the traditionists seriously,[8] and devotes the first part of *Treatise IV* to the

[1] *Ahl al-kalām* in Shāfiʿī; *ahl al-naẓar* (or combined with other terms) in Ibn Qutaiba, *passim*; *ahl al-baḥth wal-naẓar* in Masʿūdī; *mutakallimūn*, as a synonym of Muʿtazila, in Ashʿarī; *mutakallimūn* and *ahl al-baḥth wal-naẓar* in Ghazālī.

[2] See Nyberg, in *E.I.*, s.v. Muʿtazila.

[3] See, e.g., Ibn Qutaiba, 15 ff., 111 f.; Khaiyāṭ, 59 f.

[4] See *Fihrist*, 172 ff.; Khaiyāṭ, 81, 88 f.; Yāqūt, *Irshād*, vi. 446; Ibn Khaldūn, *Muqaddima*, 378 f. Ibn Qutaiba, 220 ff., 241 ff., 324, 367, and elsewhere clearly copies from a book written by one of them.—Since this book was written, part xvii, concerned with religious law, of the *Mughnī fī Abwāb al-Tauḥīd wal-ʿAdl* by ʿAbdaljabbār (d. 415) has been printed (Cairo, 1963).

[5] Above, p. 40 f. on their rejection of traditions, p. 51 f. on 'widely spread' traditions, p. 88 on consensus, p. 95 on disagreement, p. 128 on systematic reasoning.

[6] *Tr. I*, 122; *Tr. IV*, 256; Ibn Qutaiba, 22 f., 56, 73, 104 f.; Khaiyāṭ, 51, 92 f.

[7] See *Ikh.* 37 and above, pp. 47, n. 5, 88.

[8] *Ikh.* 33 f., 218, and elsewhere.

refutation of their criticism of traditions.[1] According to Shāfi'ī, the Mu'tazila exist in all countries and have their own authorities in the same way as the schools of law; but his interlocutor excludes them from the orbit of those whose opinions count for establishing a consensus, because they form only a small minority (*Tr. IV*, 256 f.).

In the time of Khaiyāṭ, who wrote towards the end of the third century A.H., the essential thesis of the traditionists and of Shāfi'ī had been generally accepted in orthodox Islam, and the Mu'tazila of that time had to take this changed attitude into account. We therefore find Khaiyāṭ re-interpret or reject the opinions of the old Mu'tazila on consensus and on *ra'y*,[2] and mitigate their criticism of traditions which changes its emphasis and becomes no more negative than that of the ancient schools of law.[3] He even defends the traditionists, and when he comes to formulate in his own words the guiding principle of Ja'far b. Mubashshir (d. 234), a specialist on law among the Mu'tazila, he gives it as 'to follow the outward and obvious meaning (*ẓāhir*) of Koran, *sunna* and consensus, and not to base one's opinions on *ra'y* and *qiyās*'.[4] This formula would be unexceptionable to the traditionists, but certainly does not represent the doctrine of the ancient Mu'tazila. Ja'far's own attitude was more complex; among his writings are mentioned works directed not only against the *aṣḥāb al-ra'y wal-qiyās*, by which the Iraqians seem to be meant, but also against the *aṣḥāb al-ḥadīth*, the Traditionists.[5] Khaiyāṭ's younger contemporary, Balkhī, also called Ka'bī (d. 319), is on the defensive against the Traditionists to such a degree that he is prepared to admit even the *khabar al-wāḥid* (see above, p. 50) under certain conditions, whilst trying to show the unreliability of most Traditionists.[6]

[1] The anecdotes on the relationship between Shāfi'ī and Bishr Marīsī (Ibn Ḥajar, *Tawālī*, 73) and on Bishr's comments on Shāfi'ī's doctrine (Abū Nu'aim, *Ḥilya*, ix. 95) are, however, spurious.

[2] Khaiyāṭ, 51, 99, 160; see also above, p. 128.

[3] Khaiyāṭ, 135, 137, 158.

[4] Khaiyāṭ, 89, 143.

[5] *E.I.*[2], s.v. *Dja'far b. Mubashshir.*

[6] This is the subject of his *K. Qabūl al-Akhbār wa-Ma'rifat al-Rijāl*, a photostat copy of which exists in the Bodleian Library (MS. Facs. Or. c. 5); Brockelmann, i. 343 = 619 (needs correction).

CHAPTER 8

KHĀRIJĪ LAW

THE variants of Muhammadan law which are recognized by the ancient sects of Islam, the Khārijīs and the Shiites, do not differ from the doctrines of the orthodox or Sunni schools of law more widely than these last differ from one another. We must not, however, conclude from this well-known fact, as has been done, that the features common to Khārijī, Shiite, and orthodox law are older than the schisms which split the Islamic community within its first century. When the Khārijīs and the Shiites seceded from the orthodox community, Muhammadan law did not yet exist, as we have seen earlier in this book.[1] For a considerable period, and during the second and third centuries A.H. in particular, the ancient sects remained in a sufficiently close contact with the Sunni community, for them to adopt Muhammadan law as it was being developed in the orthodox schools of law, introducing only such superficial modifications as were required by their own political and dogmatic tenets. This point of view is not only in keeping with the main results of this book; it is confirmed by positive indications which we shall discuss in the present and the following chapters.[2]

The foundation of the legal doctrines of the Ṣufrīya and Ibāḍī branches of the Khārijīs is attributed to the two Successors 'Imrān b. Ḥiṭṭān and Jābir b. Zaid respectively;[3] both appear also among the transmitters of traditions acknowledged by the orthodox community.[4] The two historical persons in question were active though not extremist Khārijīs; their names, being those of respected members of the generation of the Successors, were used in the process of fictitious creation of *isnāds*; and this enabled the Khārijī groups to claim them as founders of their law.

The political and dogmatic principles of the Khārijīs led to certain consequences in law, particularly in the law of war.[5]

[1] See above, p. 190.

[2] My whole approach to Khārijī law is necessarily different from that of W. Thomson, in *The Macdonald Presentation Volume* (1933), 352 ff.

[3] Ancient Khārijī authorities are mentioned by Jāḥiẓ, *Bayān*, i. 131 ff., ii. 126 f.

[4] *Tahdhīb*, viii. 222, ii. 61.

[5] See *Kharāj*, 33; Ash'arī, *Maqālāt*, i. 90.

One of these consequences was that women and minors, who accompanied the army on a raid, had a right to a full share in the booty.[1] This was also the opinion held by Auzāʿī, and it was expressed in an informal tradition, without an *isnād*, on the history of the Prophet. That this doctrine was held by the ancient Khārijīs, is shown by the counter-tradition, quoted by Abū Yūsuf against Auzāʿī, in which Ibn ʿAbbās refers the Khārijī leader Najda b. ʿĀmir to the decision of the Prophet to the contrary.[2] But the official doctrine of the Ibāḍī branch of the Khārijīs, the only one on whose law there exists detailed information, reproduces the doctrine of the other orthodox schools, that women and minors receive no share but only a remuneration.[3] The legal consequence of the ancient Khārijī tenets was obviously never part of a legal system recognized by the Ibāḍīs; when these derived their law from the orthodox schools, the ancient Khārijī decision, and presumably also Auzāʿī's corresponding doctrine on the orthodox side, had been forgotten.

The doctrine of the Ibāḍīs on 5 dirham as the minimum value of stolen goods, to make the *ḥadd* punishment for theft applicable, is derived from an ancient Iraqian *qiyās*.[4] Whereas the political history of the Ibāḍīs goes back to the middle of the first century A.H., their law was derived from the orthodox schools at a much later date.

A later development of legal theory is projected back into the Khārijī movements of the sixties and seventies of the first century A.H. in the report that some Khārijīs, including the followers of Najda, acknowledged *ijtihād al-ra'y*, whereas others, the Azraqīs, rejected it and confined themselves to the outward and obvious meaning (*ẓāhir*) of the Koran. This statement presupposes a secondary Iraqian terminology.[5]

But a predilection for the interpretation of the Koran according to its *ẓāhir* meaning seems indeed to have been a feature of the ancient Khārijīs.[6]

[1] See on this question *Tr. IX*, 7, 10; *Mud.* iii. 33; Ṭabarī, 18.

[2] See *Comm. ed. Cairo* on *Tr. IX*, 7, 10.

[3] Ibrāhīm b. Qais, *Kitāb mā lā yasaʿ jahluh*, MS. Or. 3744 of the British Museum, pp. 105 b–106 a.

[4] See Ashʿarī, *Maqālāt*, i. 105 and above, p. 107.

[5] See ibid. 127 and above, p. 105.

[6] For further examples of this tendency, see *Umm*, vii. 15; Ashʿarī, *Maqālāt*, i. 95.

CHAPTER 9

SHĪ'A LAW

THE alleged origins of Shī'a literature in the Umaiyad period, and in particular the works on religious law ascribed to the Shiite imam Ja'far Ṣādiq, are apocryphal. In the second century A.H., the imam Mūsā Kāẓim and his brother 'Alī b. Ja'far are credited with fetwas and a book on lawful and unlawful things (*Kitāb fil-Ḥalāl wal-Ḥarām*) respectively, but their authenticity is doubtful. A work on law attributed to the slightly later imam 'Alī Riḍā is certainly spurious and recognized as such by Shiite scholars themselves. The authentic legal literature of the 'Twelver' (Ithnā 'Asharīya) Shiites starts only towards the end of the third century A.H., that of the Ismā'ilī branch even later.[1]

The Zaidī Shiites have a work which, if it were genuine, would be the earliest work on Muhammadan law in existence; it is the *Majmū'* attributed to their imam Zaid b. 'Alī. But Bergsträsser has shown that it derives its doctrines from the Ḥanafīs and other schools of law.[2] It presupposes the teaching of Shāfi'ī in a statement on legal theory (§ 679), where the 'words of the Prophet' are identified with *sunna*, and *ijtihād* with the use of analogy. The authentic literature of the Zaidīs starts only in the third century A.H.[3]

In its final form, from the third century A.H. onwards, Shiite law is distinguished from that of the Sunni schools by a limited number of differences, features which in themselves were not necessarily either Shiite or Sunni, but which became adventitiously distinctive for Shiite as against Sunni law. The discussion of some of these distinctive features will show that they gained their importance only in the second century A.H., and even towards its end had not yet become irrevocably fixed as Shiite as opposed to Sunni. The Iraqian traditions from 'Alī show no bias in favour of Shiite legal doctrines,[4] and an Umaiyad

[1] Cf. Brockelmann, *Suppl.* i. 104, 318 f., 323 f.
[2] In *O.L.Z.* xxv. 114 ff. See also Santillana, in *R.S.O.* viii. 745 ff.
[3] Cf. Brockelmann, ibid. 313 ff.
[4] See above, pp. 240 ff.

practice which was ascribed to members of the ruling family in Medina, was put under the aegis of 'Alī in Iraq.[1] Shiite imams appear occasionally in the *isnāds* of Medinese traditions in the *Muwaṭṭa'* and elsewhere, but these traditions do not express distinctive Shī'a doctrines.

Masḥ 'alal-khuffain. The *masḥ 'alal-khuffain*, that is the wiping of one's shoes instead of the washing of one's feet as part of the lesser ritual ablution under certain conditions, became a distinctive point of difference between the Shiites who rejected it, and the Sunnis who in opposition to them considered it as valid. This was not yet so in the second half of the second century A.H. Abū Ḥanīfa does not mention it in his creed (*Fiqh Akbar*), where he nevertheless refers to other points of difference from the Shiites.[2] Mālik, according to Ibn Qāsim, allowed it only to the traveller; he had formerly allowed it also to the resident, but changed his opinion,[3] moving towards a restriction of the *masḥ*. The Egyptian Medinese even said, in the words of Rabī': 'We do not like the *masḥ*, either for those in residence or for those travelling' (*Tr. III*, 60).

The only tradition from the Prophet, known to Mālik, in favour of the *masḥ* (*Muw.* i. 70) has a very faulty *isnād*, so much so that Zurqānī blames Mālik for two mistakes in it and the editor Yaḥyā b. Yaḥyā for another; but that was its original condition, and the improvements by which its higher part was changed almost beyond recognition, are later. Another Medinese tradition (loc. cit.) endeavours to defend the practice of *masḥ*: Mālik relates on the authority of Nāfi' and 'Abdallāh b. Dīnār that Ibn 'Umar came to Kufa and disapproved of the *masḥ* which was practised by the Governor Sa'd b. Abī Waqqāṣ, a senior Companion of the Prophet; but Sa'd referred Ibn 'Umar to his father, and 'Umar declared it valid. This can be dated by its *isnād* in the generation preceding Mālik. These and other traditions, none of which shows any trace of anti-Shī'a polemics, had not quite prevailed in Medina in the time of Mālik.

Shāfi'ī follows the tradition from the Prophet, acknowledges the *masḥ* as valid, and refutes the anti-traditionist argument that the Koran, by not mentioning the *masḥ* in the detailed

[1] See above, p. 197 f.
[2] See Wensinck, *Creed*, 103 f., 124.
[3] *Mud.* i. 41; cf. *Muw. Shaib.* 67.

instructions on the lesser ritual ablution, has repealed it.[1] This shows that the discussions about *masḥ* started between the traditionists and the adherents of the ancient Medinese school, and not between Sunnis and Shiites.

In his creed, Shāfi'ī passes over the *masḥ* although he declares the *mut'a* (see below) to be forbidden.[2] The so-called *Waṣīyat Abī Ḥanīfa*, however, a creed which can be dated in the early third century A.H., considers the *masḥ* to be *wājib*, that is an institution whose acknowledgement is obligatory and whose rejection implies danger of unbelief.[3] Only here the *masḥ* becomes one of the essential differences between Sunnis and Shiites. The so-called *Fiqh Akbar II*, a creed of the fourth century, mitigates this uncompromising formula again and declares the *masḥ* to be a normative practice (*sunna*).[4]

In the time of Ibn 'Abdalbarr, the Mālikī doctrine had definitely changed in favour of the *masḥ*, and Ibn 'Abdalbarr and others endeavoured to minimize and explain away the authentic information on Mālik, with the help of spurious statements attributed to some of Mālik's ancient companions (Zurqānī, i. 70).

Umm al-walad. Both pre-Islamic Arab custom and the Koran recognized the right of the master to take his female slaves as concubines, and a slave woman who had borne a child to her master was called *umm al-walad*.[5] The children born of these relationships, in order to become free and legitimate, had to be acknowledged by their father, the master, but this acknowledgement seems to have been regularly given. The position of the mother, however, was not privileged, and there is nothing in the Koran to show that the Prophet intended to introduce a change. Conditions in early Umaiyad times are reflected in an anecdote that Marwān b. Ḥakam ceded an *umm walad* of his own, together with her small daughter, to a freedman of his in recognition of his services (*Aghānī*, ix. 36).

Early Muhammadan law showed on one side the tendency to give the *umm al-walad* her freedom because her children were

[1] *Ris.* 33; *Tr. III*, 60; *Tr. V*, 265; *Ikh.* 48. For the anti-traditionist argument, see above, p. 46.

[2] See Kern in *M.S.O.S.* xiii. 141 ff., and below, p. 267.

[3] See Wensinck, *Creed*, 129, 187.

[4] Ibid. 192, 246.

[5] See Lammens, *Berceau*, 276 ff.; Koran iv. 3, 24 f.; xxiii. 6, 50 ff.; lxx. 30.

set free—a kind of primitive systematic reasoning—[1] and on the other, the conservative resistance to this innovation. We find both doctrines expressed in Iraqian traditions, the first, which was the ancient Kufian doctrine, ascribed to 'Umar (*Āthār A.Y.* 872), the second to 'Alī.[2]

There were, furthermore, compromises suggested between these two extreme doctrines. One, attributed to Ibn Mas'ūd but not with the standard *isnād* of the Kufian school,[3] set the *umm al-walad* free at the death of her master as a charge on the share of her child; another set her free at the death of her master as a first charge on the whole estate. This last compromise, with the provision that the *umm al-walad* could not be sold or otherwise alienated, became the common doctrine of the ancient schools of law; the Kufians interpreted the statements of their earlier doctrine accordingly,[4] and the Medinese, who entered the discussion only at this stage, expressed it in a tradition, through Nāfi', from Ibn 'Umar.[5] Later, the *isnād* of this tradition grew backwards to the Prophet.[6]

Because the ancient resistance to an improvement in the status of the *umm al-walad* happened to be expressed in a tradition from 'Alī, in pointed opposition to traditions from 'Umar and Ibn 'Umar, the Shiites, when they came to elaborate their own legal doctrines, insisted on considering the *umm al-walad* as a slave who could be sold or otherwise alienated by her master. This was not directly derived from the corresponding ancient doctrine, but introduced as a modification into existing Sunni law which the Shiites borrowed. We therefore find traces of the opposite Sunni doctrine in Shiite law: the 'Twelver' Shiites teach that the *umm al-walad* can be sold but becomes free at the death of her master provided she is still in his possession and her child is still alive;[7] and the Zaidīs allow the sale of the *umm al-walad* but forbid the sale of the *mudabbar* slave,[8]

[1] Cf. above, pp. 106 ff.

[2] *Tr. II*, 12 (*a*). This particular tradition represents 'Alī as having changed his opinion, after having originally agreed with 'Umar; it is intended to discredit the doctrine which went under the name of 'Alī, but presupposes its attribution to him.

[3] *Tr. II*, 12 (*i*): Abū Mu'āwiya—A'mash—Zaid b. Wahb—Ibn Mas'ūd.

[4] *Āthār Shaib.*, quoted in the Commentary on *Āthār A. Y.* 872.

[5] *Muw.* iii. 246; *Muw. Shaib.* 344.

[6] See *Comm. Muw. Shaib.*, loc. cit.

[7] See Querry, ii. 147 ff.

[8] *Mudabbar* is a slave to whom the master has promised freedom, to take effect on his death.

a doctrine which is based on an analogy with the *umm al-walad.*[1]

But even in the time of Dāwūd Ẓāhirī, the opinion that the *umm al-walad* could be sold, had not yet become an exclusively Shiite doctrine.[2]

Mutʿa. The *mutʿa* is a marriage concluded for a fixed term, at the end of which it is dissolved automatically. This was presumably an ancient Arab institution, and seems to have been sanctioned and regulated in Koran iv. 24. It was certainly a widespread practice in early Islam which found expression in a fuller and unequivocal version of the Koranic passage in the copies attributed to Ibn Masʿūd, Ubai, and Ibn ʿAbbās,[3] in a tradition attributed to Ibn Masʿūd for Kufa,[4] and in a doctrine attributed to Ibn ʿAbbās and his Companions for Mecca.[5] Its existence is also attested by the traditions directed against it.

The opposition to *mutʿa* prevailed among the Iraqians and the Medinese. In Iraq, the Ibn Masʿūd tradition was turned into its contrary by the assumption of a repeal of *mutʿa* in the Koran, and to this was prefixed the standard *isnād* of the school of Kufa;[6] and a more recent tradition with a Nāfiʿ—Ibn ʿUmar *isnād* affirmed the prohibition of *mutʿa* by the Prophet.[7] In Medina, a tradition with a typical family *isnād* made ʿAlī reject the doctrine ascribed to Ibn ʿAbbās by referring to the prohibition of *mutʿa* by the Prophet,[8] and another tradition, with spurious

[1] See Bergsträsser, in *O.L.Z.* xxv. 123.

[2] See *Comm. Muw. Shaib.* 344.

[3] See Jeffery, *Materials*, 36, 126, 197. The copy of Ubai is traditionally associated with Syria.

[4] *Tr. II*, 11 (*a*), and more fully *Ikh.* 254 f.

[5] I find a tradition from Ibn ʿAbbās to this effect only in the classical and other collections of the third century; but that the doctrine in question was attributed to Ibn ʿAbbās about the middle of the second century, is shown by the polemics against it in the Medinese tradition from ʿAlī (see infra). Shāfiʿī implies the existence of other authorities besides Ibn Masʿūd for this doctrine (*Ikh.* 255), and Ibn ʿAbdalbarr refers to 'the Companions of Ibn ʿAbbās in Mecca and Yemen' (quoted in Zurqānī, iii. 25).

[6] *Āthār A. Y.* 698; *Āthār Shaib.* 66. The systematic reasoning which this tradition implies at the end, anticipates essentially Shāfiʿī's argument (*Ikh.* 257), and represents a fairly developed stage.

[7] *Āthār A. Y.* 699; *Āthār Shaib.* 66. On the *isnād*, see above, p. 32.

[8] *Muw.* iii. 23; *Muw. Shaib.* 260; *Tr. II*, 11 (*a*). This counter-tradition against the doctrine ascribed to Ibn ʿAbbās, does not necessarily imply the existence of a relatively old tradition from ʿAlī in favour of *mutʿa*, a tradition which one might be tempted to expect on account of the doctrine of the 'Twelver' Shiites (see what follows).

circumstantial details, makes ʿUmar censure the practice of *mutʿa* vehemently.[1] The *isnāds* of these two traditions, and of most of the Medinese traditions directed against *mutʿa*, have a common link in Zuhrī,[2] and this shows that the explicit rejection of *mutʿa* in Medina is not older than the time of Zuhrī at the earliest. There is no reason for singling out the tradition on ʿUmar's prohibition of *mutʿa*[3] and considering it any more authentic than the other counter-traditions.

In the generation preceding Mālik, both doctrines were outwardly harmonized and the prohibition of *mutʿa* maintained by making the Prophet allow and subsequently forbid it. These harmonizing traditions or fragments taken from them, were incorporated in the biography of the Prophet, where they were difficult to reconcile with one another.[4] Nothing of this is authentic historical information.

Shāfiʿī takes the upholders of *mutʿa* seriously and discusses the problem with them in *Ikh.* 255 ff. In his creed, he declares *mutʿa* to be forbidden.[5] His opponents are not necessarily Shiites,[6] and it was only natural for him to take sides in his creed on a problem concerning the law of marriage, a subject which had gained a considerable religious importance in his time.

The Zaidīs, the first Shiite sect to secede from the Sunni community, rejected *mutʿa*, but the 'Twelver' Shiites recognized it, for no better reason than that its prohibition had been attributed to ʿUmar.

Qunūt. Ibrāhīm Nakhaʿī knew that the *qunūt*, the imprecation against political enemies during the ritual prayer, was introduced by the rivals ʿAlī and Muʿāwiya in their war against each other.[7] In the time of Mālik there had come into circulation traditions from the Prophet and from Companions, either rejecting *qunūt* altogether, or restricting it to certain prayers, or stating that the Prophet had said it only during a certain period

[1] *Muw.* iii. 23; *Muw. Shaib.* 260; *Tr. III*, 79.
[2] See above, p. 175.
[3] It was emphasized in a tradition from Jābir, in Muslim, but this is later.
[4] See Zurqānī, iii. 24, and above, p. 139, n. 6.
[5] See above, p. 264.
[6] The other article in his creed concerning a legal subject, the interpretation of the prohibition of wine, is directed against the Iraqians.
[7] See above, p. 60. To the same effect, *Majmūʿ*, 223.

and then abandoned it, which implied repeal.[1] There were also traditions from Companions in favour of *qunūt*,[2] but unambiguous traditions from the Prophet in favour of this practice appeared only in Shāfiʿī (*Ikh.* 285 f.).

One of these traditions has in its very defective *isnād* two descendants of ʿAlī, the fifth and sixth imam of the 'Twelver' Shiites. This does not make its doctrine Shiite, any more than the *isnād* of the Medinese ʿAlī tradition against *mutʿa* (see above) makes its doctrine Shiite. Other traditions from the Prophet to the same effect, quoted by Shāfiʿī, have different *isnāds*.

As a result, the ancient schools of law are divided on *qunūt*, Shāfiʿī acknowledges it on principle on account of the traditions from the Prophet, the Zaidīs and the 'Twelver' Shiites are in favour of it.[3] The history of this problem shows that a practice which was historically connected with ʿAlī failed to develop into a distinctive difference between Sunni and Shiite law.

My final example shows Khārijīs and Shiites agreeing on a doctrine which has almost disappeared from the Sunnī schools of law. The Iraqian opposition movement, at the beginning of the second century, held that unlawful intercourse constituted a permanent impediment to marriage between the guilty parties. This doctrine was inspired by the spirit of rigorism typical of that group,[4] but it did not fit well into the general background of the Muhammadan law of marriage. It was therefore rejected by the school of Kufa, and only a corollary to it, separated from its context, was adopted in Medina on the authority of a tradition attributed to ʿUmar, which was interpreted restrictively; this led to a grave inconsistency in Mālikī doctrine. The essential thesis, however, with different developments of details in each case, was taken over both by the Ibāḍīs and by the 'Twelver' Shiites; both borrowings were made in Iraq.[5]

[1] *Muw.* i. 286; *Muw. Shaib.* 140; *Tr. I*, 157 (*b*), quoting Abū Ḥanīfa.

[2] *Tr. I*, 157 (*b*), quoting Ibn Abī Lailā.

[3] *Majmūʿ*, 149 ff., 223 ff., 369; Querry, i. 81.

[4] See above, p. 241. It ultimately seems to go back, through the intermediary of Christian converts to Islam, to a doctrine of canon law.

[5] For the details, see my paper in *Archives d'Histoire du Droit Oriental et Revue Internationale des Droits de l'Antiquité*, i, 1952, 105–123.

PART IV

THE DEVELOPMENT OF TECHNICAL LEGAL THOUGHT

CHAPTER 1

THE DEVELOPMENT OF LEGAL REASONING IN GENERAL

THE development of technical legal thought is an essential aspect of the history of early Muhammadan jurisprudence. Legal theory, positive legal doctrine, and technical legal thought grew up in close connexion with one another, until legal theory and technical legal thought reached their common culminating point in Shāfiʿī. To follow the development of technical legal thought in detail would demand an historical analysis of positive legal doctrine over the whole field of law, an undertaking which falls outside the scope of our inquiry. What I propose to do, in the first two chapters of this part, is to give the broad outline and to show the significant character of the development of legal reasoning in the early period. This is to be supplemented in the final chapters by remarks on the individual reasoning of some of those ancient lawyers whom the sources available allow us to see as individuals, concluding with Shāfiʿī.[1]

Legal reasoning was inherent in Muhammadan law from its very beginnings. We have investigated in the first part of this book the appearance of systematic reasoning from the earliest period onwards and its subsequent subjection to an increasingly strict discipline.[2] The oldest stage of legal reasoning is represented by Iraqian traditions which show crude and primitive conclusions by analogy (*qiyās*).[3] The results of this reasoning were sometimes expressed in the form of legal 'puzzles',[4] or in

[1] Only genuine quotations from the ancient authorities can be used in the study of their reasoning; the statements of later authors, such as Sarakhsī, on the alleged principles underlying their doctrine, are often unreliable.

[2] See above, pp. 98 ff.

[3] See above, pp. 106 ff.

[4] See above, p. 241.

the form of legal maxims;[1] these last then became a favourite mode of expressing the results of systematic legal thought in Iraq and in Hijaz.[2] Some abstract legal principles are part of the common stock of ancient doctrine.[3] All this belongs to the first half of the second century A.H. The technical legal thought attributed to Ibrāhīm Nakhaʿī dates only, as we saw, from the time of Ḥammād,[4] and the technical details of legal doctrine which are discussed in *Tr. I* emerged in the period between Ḥammād on one side, and Abū Ḥanīfa and Ibn Abī Lailā on the other.[5] These indications provide us with a useful chronology for the development of legal reasoning.

Tr. I allows us to follow the development of legal reasoning step by step from Ibn Abī Lailā to Abū Ḥanīfa, Abū Yūsuf, and Shāfiʿī. Ibn Abī Lailā and Abū Ḥanīfa were contemporaries, but Ibn Abī Lailā's reasoning is, generally speaking, more primitive and represents an older stage than that of Abū Ḥanīfa.[6] The reasoning of Shāfiʿī is on the whole much superior to that of his Iraqian predecessors. The following examples are intended to show the general trend of the development.

Tr. I, 6: Shāfiʿī's reasoning is more detailed and articulate than that of an anonymous Iraqian.

§ 8 = *Ris.* 71 = *Ikh.* 340: The Iraqians interpret the legal maxim 'profit follows responsibility',[7] after an expedient fashion, more intuitive than logical; Shāfiʿī's reasoning is strictly systematic and superior to that of his predecessors.

§ 13: 'A man concludes a sale on condition that the seller has the right of option for one day; the buyer takes possession, and the object perishes whilst it is in his possession. Abū Ḥanīfa used to decide: "The buyer is responsible for the value, because he took it on the basis of a contract of sale", and we [Abū Yūsuf] follow this. Ibn Abī Lailā used to say: "He is a trustee and is not responsible." If the option is in favour of the buyer and the object perishes whilst it is in his possession, it is to his debit at the price for which he bought it, according to the doctrine of both [Abū Ḥanīfa and Ibn Abī Lailā]. Shāfiʿī: "If a man sells a slave, stipulating the right of option for three days or less,[8] and the buyer takes possession and the slave dies whilst he is in his possession, he [the buyer] is responsible for the value. What prevents us from making him responsible

[1] See above, p. 184 f. [2] See above, p. 188 f. [3] See above, p. 218.
[4] See above, pp. 235 ff. [5] See above, p. 239. [6] See below, pp. 290 ff.
[7] See above, p. 181.
[8] On this time limit of the right of option, see below, p 326. f.

for the price is that the sale was not completed; and what prevents us from exonerating him from responsibility, is that he took him on the basis of a sale in which he [the seller] received from the buyer an equivalent, and we must regard [the object of] the sale as covered by the responsibility [of a party]; there is no way of considering him a trustee, because one can become a trustee only of property which one does not own and from which one does not draw advantage sooner or later, and which one holds in the interest of its owner and not one's own interest. It is irrelevant whether the option is in favour of the seller or the buyer, because [in either case] the sale was not completed when the slave died." ' This shows Ibn Abī Lailā's seemingly just and reasonable solution, easily refuted by Abū Ḥanīfa's technical legal thought and Shāfiʿī's still more articulate and consistent reasoning.

§ 25: Ibn Abī Lailā, followed by Abū Yūsuf, mechanically applies the elementary rules on presumption to two contradictory claims without evidence (cf. Sarakhsī, xiii. 59); Abū Ḥanīfa, followed by Shāfiʿī in the essentials although Shāfiʿī's decision is slightly different, analyses the nature of the statements of both parties.

§ 27: Ibn Abī Lailā's decision is strictly formal; the opinion of Abū Ḥanīfa, followed by Abū Yūsuf, is more appropriate for any but the most primitive conditions of commerce; Shāfiʿī endorses it and makes it systematically more consistent.

§ 38: Abū Ḥanīfa becomes inconsistent and is reduced to a practically expedient solution (at the end), whereas Shāfiʿī remains consistent and logical.

§ 44: Ibn Abī Lailā is crudely systematic in applying the rules of pre-emption even to property given as *donatio propter nuptias*, but his solution of the problem is clumsy and inconsistent. Abū Ḥanīfa, followed by Abū Yūsuf, gives systematic reasoning against it. Shāfiʿī accepts pre-emption in the case in question, and makes this doctrine juridically acceptable for the first time. But the argument which Sarakhsī, v. 78, puts into the mouth of Shaibānī in favour of the doctrine of Abū Ḥanīfa and Abū Yūsuf is easily superior even to Shāfiʿī's reasoning; it develops Abū Ḥanīfa's argument in a masterly way and introduces a judicious distinction; this seems to be an argument that Shaibānī really did use.

§ 48: On the exercise of a minor's right of pre-emption, Abū Ḥanīfa, followed by Abū Yūsuf, holds a reasonable and defensible opinion. Shaibānī, however, with complete disregard for the stability of real property, applies purely formal reasoning (see Sarakhsī, xiv. 155; xxx. 145); in this he is followed by Shāfiʿī. Both seem to lose sight of the purpose of pre-emption and to regard it as an institution existing for its own sake. This attitude heralds the end of the formative period of Muhammadan law.

§ 52: Ibn Abī Lailā does not admit an amiable settlement which is not based on the recognition of the claim of the other party (*ṣulḥ ʿalal-inkār*); this presupposes strictly formal reasoning, of the same kind as that given by Shāfiʿī later, starting from the Koranic prohibition of 'consuming one another's property in vanity' (Sura ii. 188 and often). Abū Ḥanīfa, followed by Abū Yūsuf, admits that kind of settlement, taking a more common-sense and practical view. Shāfiʿī must, by strict *qiyās*, revert to the doctrine of Ibn Abī Lailā.

§ 55: On the validity of an acknowledgement made out of court, the decision of Ibn Abī Lailā is inconsistent but inspired by the interests of the administration of justice.[1] The decision of Abū Ḥanīfa, who is followed by Abū Yūsuf, is consistent but leaves considerations of judicial practice out of account. Shāfiʿī gives essentially the same decision as Abū Ḥanīfa on the problem in question, but raises the discussion to a higher, more juridical, plane on which he is able to provide for the need felt by Ibn Abī Lailā, whilst avoiding his inconsistency.

§ 60 f.: It is the common doctrine of the ancient Iraqians that a gift becomes fully valid only if the donee takes possession of the object. What of the gift of an undivided share in property? Ibn Abī Lailā, with a pointed reference to the common Iraqian doctrine, admits it as valid, presumably because this appeared to him as the natural solution. Abū Ḥanīfa, who gives technical reasoning of a high standard, sees a difficulty in taking possession of an undivided share, and therefore cannot admit it as the object of a valid gift; he tries to find a confirmation of this conclusion in a tradition from Companions of the Prophet and in an opinion attributed to Ibrāhīm Nakhaʿī, but neither is decisive on this particular point. Abū Yūsuf,[2] inconsistently, follows Abū Ḥanīfa in the case of § 61, but not in that of § 60. Shāfiʿī, whilst in fact returning to the doctrine of Ibn Abī Lailā, contributes an excellent systematic discussion of the concept of 'taking possession'.

§ 72: Ibn Abī Lailā gives a practicable and seemingly natural solution of a problem relating to security (*rahn*); Abū Ḥanīfa, followed by Abū Yūsuf, applies elementary legal reasoning; Shāfiʿī carries the legal analysis farther, and by excellent systematic reasoning arrives at a solution different from both opinions.

[1] Being a judge, he obviously tries to safeguard himself against false witnesses; this is suggested by Shāfiʿī's comment.

[2] Also Shaibānī; see Sarakhsī, xii. 66 f.

§ 77: Ibn Abī Lailā shows primitive legal reasoning;[1] the reasoning of Abū Ḥanīfa, whom Shāfiʿī follows, is considerably more penetrating.

§ 82: A man claims ownership of a house, and the man in occupation claims that he is only the agent of an absent owner. The ancient Iraqian doctrine was not uniform. Ibn Shubruma (Sarakhsī, xvii. 37) rejected the counterclaim and made the occupier the defendant. Ibn Abī Lailā accepted the counterclaim and dismissed the suit; but later, obviously under the necessities of the administration of justice, he demanded evidence in support of the counterclaim if he doubted the truthfulness of the occupier. Abū Ḥanīfa, more consistent, demanded evidence on principle. Abū Yūsuf followed this originally, but later, again under the necessities of the administration of justice,[2] demanded the evidence of witnesses personally known to him, if he doubted the truthfulness of the occupier. So far, this problem was treated in isolation. But Shāfiʿī put it against the background of the wider problem of the judgment against an absent party, and elaborated two sets of possible and consistent solutions, neither of which agreed with the opinions of his predecessors.[3]

§ 83: Ibn Abī Lailā saw the essential problem; Abū Ḥanīfa, followed by Abū Yūsuf, applied rigidly formal reasoning; Shāfiʿī returned to Ibn Abī Lailā's decision and gave an explicit legal argument.

§§ 92, 93, 94: The decision given by Ibn Abī Lailā in these three parallel cases is an obviously common-sense and practicable one.[4] Abū Ḥanīfa, followed by Abū Yūsuf, takes a strictly formal view. Shāfiʿī adopts essentially Abū Ḥanīfa's solution which alone is juridically acceptable to him, but he develops a more appropriate procedure which also obviates the practical difficulty which Ibn Abī Lailā had in mind. In one particular case, Shāfiʿī becomes inconsistent because he must declare a transaction which involves 'usury' null and void; there is, however, a good systematic reason for the fact that the actual results of his procedure in § 94 are different from those in §§ 92 and 93. In § 94, but not in §§ 92 and 93, Abū Yūsuf anticipates Shāfiʿī's procedure by one which is parallel to it and reconciles the guiding ideas of Ibn Abī Lailā and of Abū Ḥanīfa.[5]

[1] Sarakhsī, xxx. 147, elaborates this and adds a misplaced and faulty *qiyās* which is based on a decision of Abū Ḥanīfa.

[2] This is stated explicitly by Sarakhsī, xvii. 38.

[3] Rabīʿ adds Shāfiʿī's own choice.

[4] Sarakhsī, xii. 164 and xxx. 150, correctly considers it based on the regard for practice and therefore calls it *istiḥsān*.

[5] The argument suggested for Abū Yūsuf by Sarakhsī, loc. cit., and his statement on Abū Yūsuf's change of opinion are unreliable.

§§ 95, 228: In the case of divergencies in the evidence of two witnesses, Ibn Abī Lailā gives a seemingly practical and common-sense solution; Abū Ḥanīfa's decision is rigidly formal and in one detail even hair-splitting; Abū Yūsuf reverts to Ibn Abī Lailā; Shāfiʿī introduces a new consideration and develops a method which does justice to both points of view.

§ 96: In admitting the evidence of witnesses on the testimony of other witnesses, Ibn Abī Lailā gives a lenient and seemingly common-sense decision;[1] Abū Ḥanīfa is strict and consistent; Shāfiʿī goes one step farther and exaggerates the demand for strictness; Rabīʿ supplies the far-fetched argument for this doctrine.

§ 106: Ibn Abī Lailā, being a judge, endorses a severe and inconsistent decision, obviously on grounds of public policy;[2] Abū Ḥanīfa and Abū Yūsuf apply the general rules consistently; Shāfiʿī introduces an important distinction.

§ 108: Ibn Abī Lailā gives a seemingly obvious and formally consistent decision; Abū Ḥanīfa disagrees, on account of an important material consideration; Shāfiʿī makes a distinction, gives a straightforward and convincing argument, and proposes a well-balanced solution which does justice to both considerations.

§ 126: Ibn Abī Lailā gives a practicable interim solution; Abū Ḥanīfa, strictly systematic, does not acknowledge it; Abū Yūsuf reverts to Ibn Abī Lailā, and Shaibānī, according to Sarakhsī, xvii. 47, returns to Abū Ḥanīfa; Shāfiʿī agrees with Abū Ḥanīfa in the essentials, but shows himself still more systematic on the basis of a distinction which he introduces.

§ 141 f.: Ibn Abī Lailā pursues to its farthest consequences a formal principle which embodies crude and primitive reasoning; Abū Ḥanīfa, followed by Abū Yūsuf, gives a sound juridical decision, based on wider systematic thought; Shāfiʿī cannot but agree with Abū Ḥanīfa on principle, but on account of his different premisses he arrives in one case at the same material decision as Ibn Abī Lailā, though on different grounds.

§ 150: Ibn Abī Lailā gave a seemingly just and practicable decision, obviously inspired by material considerations; Abū Ḥanīfa's decision was more strictly formal, but not quite consistent; Abū Yūsuf followed first the opinion of Abū Ḥanīfa; later, perhaps under the necessities of the administration of justice, he came nearer to the doctrine of Ibn Abī Lailā, but remained very inconsistent; only Shāfiʿī's doctrine became fully consistent, on the basis of excellent systematic reasoning.

[1] This doctrine was projected back to Shuraiḥ and Ibrāhīm Nakhaʿī.

[2] See above, p. 111, for a similar consideration.

As we know that the doctrine of the Medinese was largely dependent on and secondary to that of the Iraqians,[1] we may assume the same of the development of technical legal thought for Medina. The sources available happen to be less abundant for this particular aspect of ancient Medinese doctrine, but we are able to see that legal reasoning in Medina in the ancient period was essentially of the same character as that found in Iraq though, on the whole, more primitive.

The ancient schools of law do not hesitate to adduce against one another arguments which they reject as inconclusive when they find them used against themselves.[2] They often interpret traditions in a more natural way, and more in keeping with their sometimes only vaguely expressed intentions, than Shāfiʿī who, having cut himself loose from the 'living tradition', can ruthlessly apply systematic reasoning which is often no more than a logical sleight-of-hand.[3] The attitude of the ancient schools of law and, after them, of Shāfiʿī to legal traditions[4] is a significant example of how a perfectly natural and reasonably consistent approach to legal problems became, by an historical process, involved in a mass of seeming inconsistencies, and how Shāfiʿī replaced it by a novel and severely consistent theory of his own. It is typical of the degree of systematic reasoning reached by the ancient schools of law, that they reject traditions or dispose of them by interpretation, for reasons of systematic consistency.[5]

Shāfiʿī has preserved long quotations which show the authentic reasoning of ancient Iraqians.[6] In *Ikh.* 383 we find rather clumsy, but straightforward systematic reasoning. *Ikh.* 385 ff. shows Iraqian legal reasoning at its best; the Iraqian opponent certainly gets the better of the systematic argument. But the primitive and rigidly formal systematic reasoning of the Iraqian in *Ikh.* 395 ff. soon breaks down and is easily refuted by Shāfiʿī. A similar kind of argument in *Ikh.* 398, inconclusive in itself, shows the desire to 'understand' as the basis of legal thought, the same desire which is voiced in Medina by Mālik in *Muw.* iii. 184.

[1] See above, pp. 220 ff.
[2] See above, pp. 26, 32, 38, 39, 74, 103.
[3] See, e.g., *Tr. VIII*, 13; *Ikh.* 75; and below, pp. 306, 323.
[4] See above, pp. 21 ff.
[5] See above, pp. 23, 30.
[6] e.g. *Ikh.* 277 ff., 339, 355 ff., &c.

The following examples will serve to show that the technical legal thought of the ancient Iraqians was, on the whole, more highly developed than that of their Medinese contemporaries.[1]

The Iraqians in *Muw. Shaib.* 230 are more consistent than the Medinese in *Muw.* iii. 10, *Mud.* v. 2 (cf. above, p. 193 f.).

In interpreting a declaration, the Medinese make a distinction based on a consideration which combines a material and a systematic element, and take the intention of the speaker into account in only one of two cases (*Muw.* iii. 36); the Iraqians, however, regard the intention as decisive in any case (*Āthār Shaib.* 74, 77; *Muw. Shaib.* 265); Shāfi'ī's reasoning is strictly formal and systematic (*Tr. III*, 142).

Tr. III, 16: The Iraqians use good systematic reasoning against the Medinese.

Tr. III, 61: The easy-going Medinese allow a relevant declaration to be made after the fact; the Iraqians are stricter and use systematic reasoning; Shāfi'ī, though he has a different opinion of his own, recognizes that the Iraqian doctrine is better.

Tr. VIII, 14: Shāfi'ī suggests that the basis of the Medinese doctrine is some material consideration of practical expediency. This is certainly the case in *Tr. VIII*, 19, and Shaibānī easily refutes their argument.

Finally, here are a few examples to illustrate the way in which the development of positive legal doctrine is connected with the development of technical legal thought.

As regards the effect of conversion to Islam on a previous marriage, the regulation of Koran lx. 10, which was enacted in a particular set of circumstances, was modified progressively, and a later stage of these modifications was expressed in traditions purporting to describe episodes from the history of the Prophet.[2] The ancient Iraqians follow the rule of the Koran, except for the one concession of offering Islam to the unconverted party before dissolving the marriage, and their doctrine is consistent as far as it goes.[3] The Medinese endorse a more far-reaching modification and arrive at a compromise the inconsistencies of which Shāfi'ī denounces. If it is the wife who adopts

[1] See also below, p. 311.

[2] *Muw.* iii. 26; *Muw. Shaib.* 266; *Mud.* iv. 147; v. 163; *Tr. III*, 44; *Tr. IX*, 36 f.

[3] Shaibānī in *Muw. Shaib.*, loc. cit., had to adduce a more recent tradition, but it did not agree with his doctrine, and he could not add his usual formula 'We follow this'.

Islam, the Medinese leave the marriage in abeyance during her waiting period (*'idda*);[1] if it is the husband, they still refer to Koran lx. 10, but maintain the concession of offering Islam to the wife, and this concession becomes another inconsistency, as Shāfi'ī points out. Only Shāfi'ī is fully consistent again in according the reprieve of the waiting period to both parties; for him, the Koranic regulation has become irrelevant.

There is the connected problem of the man who is married to more than four wives, and adopts Islam.[2] The earliest, and seemingly most natural solution, that he can choose those four wives to whom he wishes to remain married, was that adopted by Auzā'ī. It was also expressed in a tradition from the Prophet.[3] Mālik followed the same doctrine but specified that the Koranic prohibition (Sura iv. 23) of marital relationships with two sisters or with mother and daughter applied also here and limited the possible choices. The early Iraqians introduced systematic refinements. Abū Ḥanīfa declares: 'If the man was married to all his wives by one contract, and they all become Muslims, he becomes separated from all his wives.' Abū Yūsuf adduces systematic reasoning in favour of this doctrine and adds: 'But if he was married by successive contracts, the first four marriages remain valid'; this detail he also quotes from Ibrāhīm Nakha'ī. The tradition in favour of the first doctrine was still 'irregular' (*shādhdh*) in the time of Abū Yūsuf. Shaibānī, however, knew already a greater number of traditions from the Prophet and could not disregard them; but he retained the doctrine of Abū Ḥanīfa and Abū Yūsuf with regard to persons who had been members of tolerated religions; the result is very inconsistent. Shāfi'ī, under the spell of the traditions, returned completely to the oldest doctrine and supplied a good systematic argument.

It was an ancient Arab custom that the victors took the womenfolk of their conquered enemies as concubines without caring much whether they were married women or not.[4] This rough-and-ready practice continued in Islam,[5] and Auzā'ī

[1] Auzā'ī agrees with this essential feature of the Medinese doctrine.

[2] *Tr. IX*, 38; *Mud.* iv. 160; *Siyar*, iv. 87; Ṭaḥāwī, ii. 147.

[3] This tradition is missing from the text of *Tr. IX*, but identified in *Comm. ed. Cairo*.

[4] See Lammens, *Berceau*, 279, 303 f.

[5] *Tr. IX*, 16 f.; *Mud.* iv. 153.

states correctly: 'Such was the practice of the Muslims, and thus decrees the Koran' (Sura iv. 24). The Medinese accepted this practice unreservedly and simply drew the logical conclusion from it by formulating the legal principle that captivity dissolves the marriage tie. The Iraqians, however, reasoned that captivity as such did not dissolve the marriage tie, and consequently tried to introduce certain safeguards. Auzāʿī was partly influenced by Iraqian legal thought and, while endorsing the practice, regarded the marriage of captives as continuing valid after captivity, with the result that his doctrine became inconsistent. Abū Yūsuf criticizes Auzāʿī's inconsistency, and Shāfiʿī's doctrine is still more thoroughly systematic than that of Abū Yūsuf. At the same time, Auzāʿī, Abū Yūsuf, and Shāfiʿī represent three successive stages of growing formal dependence on traditions.

On the ownership of household chattels, a problem which became acute on every dissolution of a marriage, there existed a series of six more and more technically refined decisions.[1] Their relative position in this series does not necessarily imply a corresponding place in the historical development, but we notice that the first three belong essentially to the first half, and the last three to the second half of the second century A.H.

(A) First we have the old patriarchal idea that everything belongs to the husband, tempered more or less by exempting the wife's clothing; this opinion is ascribed (by Sarakhsī) to Ibn Shubruma and attested beyond doubt for Ibn Abī Lailā.

(B) Then comes the technically legal concern with ownership, and this leads to the idea of the presumption of ownership according to whose house it is, but in fact it would regularly be the house of the husband; this doctrine is projected back (in Sarakhsī) to Ḥasan Baṣrī, again excepting the wife's clothes; it is attested for 'some lawyers' by Shaibānī, and refuted by Shāfiʿī.

(C) A different idea is introduced with the presumption of ownership according to the nature of the chattels; this opinion was provided with the standard *isnād* of the Kufians, Abū Ḥanīfa—Ḥammād—Ibrāhīm Nakhaʿī; it was held by Abū Ḥanīfa himself and originally by Abū Yūsuf, and Shaibānī came near to it.

[1] *Tr. I*, 127; *Āthār Shaib.* 101; *Majmūʿ*, 706; Sarakhsī, v. 213 f.

(D) This opinion was, however, open to the objection: 'What of the husband's stock-in-trade if it consists of articles used by women?' Under the influence of this objection, Abū Yūsuf (and 'others' as Shaibānī informs us) went some way back towards opinion (A).

(E) A systematic progress was achieved with the decision to divide those chattels which do not typically belong to men or to women, equally between husband and wife, on the strength of their joint possession; this doctrine grew out of opinion (C); it is attested for Zufar and others, was also ascribed to Ibrāhīm Nakha'ī, and was taken over by the Zaidī Shiites who attributed it to 'Alī.

(F) Other Iraqians, finally, extended this consideration to all chattels, whatever their nature; they were followed by Shāfi'ī who supplied excellent systematic reasoning.

The Koran says in Sura xxiv. 33: 'And those in your possession who desire a writing, write it for them if you know any good in them, and give them of the wealth of Allah which He has given you.' The hearers were supposed to know the details of the legal transaction referred to, and a strict interpretation of the passage suggests that it was not identical with the contract of *mukātaba* which Muhammadan law, from the early second century A.H. onwards, found outlined here.[1] Under a *mukātaba* contract, the master allowed his slave to purchase his freedom by his own earnings in instalments; this slave was called *mukātab*. The ancient lawyers were concerned with embodying the commendation of the *mukātaba* contract, as they found it in the Koran, in positive legal norms.

Their earliest efforts were arbitrary, such as the decision that the *mukātab* becomes free as soon as he has paid half the stipulated amount,[2] or the decision, attributed to 'Aṭā' and probably authentic, that he becomes free as soon as he has paid three-quarters.[3] Presumably authentic, too, is the information that 'Aṭā' considered it obligatory on the master to conclude a *mukātaba* contract with his deserving slave, although 'Aṭā'

[1] The terms *mukātaba* and *mukātab* in Muhammadan law are derived from the wording of the Koranic passage, but the word *kitāb* 'writing', which seems to be a technical term in the Koran, is not so used in later legal terminology.

[2] Ascribed to 'Alī: Zurqānī, iii, 260; ascribed to Ibn 'Abbās: *Comm. Muw. Shaib.* 365.

[3] Zurqānī, loc. cit.

agreed that he had no traditional authority for this doctrine[1]—in other words, the implications of the Koranic passage began to be considered in the time of ʿAṭāʾ.

Technically more polished are the opinions that the *mukātab* becomes free as soon as he has paid off his value—this seems to have been the current doctrine of the Kufian school at one time;[2] or that he becomes free *pro rata* of his payments—this seems to have been connected with the Iraqian opposition;[3] or that he becomes free immediately, and the payments due from him are ordinary debts.[4]

Finally, the systematically most consistent doctrine that the *mukātab* remained a slave as long as part of the stipulated sum was still unpaid, prevailed in Iraq and in Medina where it was projected back to Zaid b. Thābit,[5] to Ibn ʿUmar,[6] and finally to the Prophet himself.[7] All this ante-dated documentation is later than the simple reference to the ancient Medinese authorities ʿUrwa b. Zubair and Sulaimān b. Yasār, a reference which itself dates only from the first half of the second century A.H.[8]

Even after the final doctrine on the *mukātab* had prevailed, some concessions—presupposing it—in favour of a defaulting *mukātab* were made; but they were subsequently reduced, though not completely eliminated, in the interest of stricter systematic consistency. We have discussed elsewhere[9] one of these concessions which was put into the mouth of ʿAlī and acknowledged by Ibn Abī Lailā and, to a lesser degree, by Abū Ḥanīfa and Abū Yūsuf, but rejected by Shāfiʿī. On the

[1] *Umm*, vii. 362.

[2] With the *isnād* Abū Ḥanīfa—Ḥammād—Ibrāhīm Nakhaʿī—Ibn Masʿūd: *Āthār A. Y.* 861 = *Āthār Shaib.* 99; with another *isnād* from Ibn Masʿūd: *Tr. II*, 17 (*d*); ascribed to Ibn ʿAbbās: *Comm. Muw. Shaib.*, loc. cit.

[3] Ascribed to ʿAlī: *Tr. II*, 17 (*a*), (*b*); ascribed to Ibrāhīm Nakhaʿī, on the authority of Ḥammād: *Āthār A. Y.* 860 = *Āthār Shaib.* 99.

[4] Ascribed to Ibn ʿAbbās: *Comm. Muw. Shaib.*, loc. cit.

[5] *Tr. II*, 17 (*a*); and with the Kufian standard *isnād* Ḥammād—Ibrāhīm Nakhaʿī, in *Āthār A. Y.* 862 = *Āthār Shaib.* 99.

[6] *Muw.* iii. 260 = *Muw. Shaib.* 365, through Nāfiʿ.

[7] The earliest references are those of Abū Ḥanīfa, in *Āthār Shaib.* 99, to the Barīra tradition (on which see above, p. 173), and of Shāfiʿī, in *Tr. II*, 17 (*a*), to a tradition of ʿAmr b. Shuʿaib, a prominent traditionist of doubtful authority (see *Tahdhīb*, viii. 80).

[8] *Muw.* iii. 260. A good systematic argument is put into the mouth of Zaid b. Thābit in discussion with ʿAlī: Zurqānī, loc. cit.

[9] Above, p. 111 f.

subject of another concession, Ibn Abī Lailā expresses himself in a clumsy terminology, the sign of clumsy legal thought;[1] Abū Ḥanīfa's opinion is essentially better, but at the same time he is very inconsistent as regards details, obviously on account of material considerations in favour of freedom, the same which had already influenced Ibn Abī Lailā; Shāfiʿī's opinion is again superior to that of Abū Ḥanīfa, and more consistent, but even Shāfiʿī acknowledges an accomplished fact in favour of freedom.

We have had occasion to discuss in another context the development of legal reasoning on the question of damages due for wounds inflicted on a slave.[2] The connected problem of the weregeld of a slave shows a similar development of legal thought.[3] Originally, the loss of a slave was considered merely as the loss of property, and his value was to be made good. This seems to have been the common ancient doctrine, and it found expression in the legal maxim 'the weregeld of the slave is his value'. It had the consequence that the weregeld for a valuable slave could exceed the fixed weregeld for a free man.[4] This remained the doctrine of the Medinese who ascribed it to their ancient authorities. The Kufian doctrine, however, as attributed to Ibrāhīm Nakhaʿī, while paying lip-service to the legal maxim, fixed the highest possible amount of the weregeld for a slave at the amount of the weregeld for a free man minus 10 dirham. Abū Ḥanīfa expressed the underlying reasoning by saying that there would always be found a free man who was better than any slave, and that 10 dirham represented the minimum difference in value. Shaibānī added the systematic argument that the slave was not purely property.

In the earliest *Treatises I* and *VIII*,[5] Shāfiʿī followed the Medinese doctrine and gave general reasoning in its favour. But as early as *Tr. VII* he had accepted the Iraqian principle of limiting the maximum amount of the weregeld for a slave by the weregeld for a free man, while still rejecting the reduction

[1] *Tr. I*, 134: 'the manumission is invalid until one waits and sees what he will do'; Ibn Abī Lailā wants to say that it is 'in abeyance', a concept for which the usual term *mauqūf* occurs in *Tr. I*, 140—but this may be Abū Yūsuf's wording.

[2] Above, p. 221 f.

[3] *Muw.* iv. 42; *Mud.* xvi. 196; *Āthār Shaib.* 86; *Tr. I*, 195; *Tr. VII*, 275; *Tr. VIII*, 15.

[4] On its amount, see above, p. 203.

[5] Also in *Umm*, vi. 23, which must be an early passage.

by 10 dirham, which he had very competently refuted once and for all in *Tr. VIII*. This doctrine of Shāfiʿī's is in keeping with his fully developed method of systematic analogy. He already possessed this method, it is true, when he wrote *Tr. VIII*, 11, but obviously it took him some time to work out all its implications. The Shāfiʿī school, starting with Muzanī,[1] surprisingly perpetuated Shāfiʿī's earlier doctrine.[2]

These examples serve to show the varied and interacting tendencies which contribute to the broad general development of technical legal thought.

[1] This is implied by him in *Mukhtaṣar*, v. 99 f.

[2] To suppose a further change of opinion on the part of Shāfiʿī would be unwarranted.

CHAPTER 2

SYSTEMATIZING AND ISLAMICIZING

WE saw in Part III, Chapter 1, of this book[1] that Muhammadan law came into existence through the working of Muhammadan jurisprudence on the raw material which consisted of the popular and administrative practice of late Umaiyad times and was endorsed, modified, or rejected by the earliest lawyers. These lawyers and their successors were guided by a double aim: by the effort to systematize—an effort which we have considered in the preceding chapter—and by the tendency to 'Islamicize', to impregnate the sphere of law with religious and ethical ideas, to subject it to Islamic norms, and to incorporate it into the body of duties incumbent on every Muslim. In doing this, Muhammadan law achieved on a much wider scale and in a vastly more detailed manner what the Prophet in the Koran had tried to do for the early Islamic community of Medina.[2] Those two parallel and closely connected aims underlie much of the development of Muhammadan law during its formative period, as Bergsträsser has pointed out.[3]

The tendency to Islamicize took various forms: it made the ancient lawyers criticize Umaiyad popular and administrative practice,[4] it made them pay attention to the (formerly disregarded) details and implications of Koranic rules,[5] it made them attribute the 'living tradition' of their schools of law to the Prophet and his Companions,[6] it made them take account of the rising tide of traditions ascribed to the Prophet,[7] it provided them with part of the material considerations which entered into their systematic reasoning.[8] Much as the ancient schools of law represented an Islamicizing movement of opposition—though of course not necessarily political opposition—to late Umaiyad practice, the traditionists and the opposition groups within the ancient schools formed a still more thoroughly Islamicizing minority which was partly successful and, when

[1] Above, pp. 190 ff. [2] See above, p. 224 f. [3] In *Islām*, xiv. 78 ff.
[4] See above, pp. 192 ff. [5] See above, pp. 224 ff.
[6] See above, pp. 72 f., 74 ff. [7] See above, p. 66.
[8] See above, pp. 71, 162, 213, 273, and the examples given farther on in this chapter.

this happened, became indistinguishable from the majority.[1] But the Islamicizing process by which Muhammadan law as such emerged was not a monopoly of the traditionists or, within the ancient schools of law, of the school of Medina.[2]

The process of Islamicizing was, however, not carried to its logical conclusion: the sphere of law retained a technical character of its own, and legal relationships were not completely reduced to and expressed in terms of religious and ethical duties. The traditionists, it is true, set out to do this, and tried to identify the categories 'forbidden' and 'invalid'.[3] But this did not prevail, and even Shāfi'ī who adopted the teaching of the traditionists in most other respects, distinguished between the legal and the moral aspects and maintained that Muhammadan law was concerned with the *forum externum* only.[4] This clear position was of course reached only gradually.[5]

The following examples, in addition to those which have occurred earlier in this book,[6] are meant to show the close connexion that exists between systematizing and Islamicizing, the interaction of both tendencies, and the gradual achieving of a balance between the two elements.

Tr. I, 28: Ibn Abī Lailā decides a problem of the law of contracts by a consideration of material justice and identifies the moral and the legal aspect;[7] Abū Ḥanīfa shows a higher degree of technical legal reasoning, Abū Yūsuf goes back to Ibn Abī Lailā, but Shaibānī improves on Abū Ḥanīfa and anticipates Shāfi'ī (Sarakhsī, xiii. 86); Shāfi'ī follows Shaibānī and distinguishes clearly between the moral and the legal aspect.

Tr. I, 167: According to Ibn Abī Lailā, the debtor is bound to pay *zakāt* tax on his debt. This opinion was also attributed to Ibrāhīm Nakha'ī, and so was the argument that the debtor worked with it and derived profit from it.[8] The argument is presumably not in fact Ibrāhīm's,[9] but nevertheless represents

[1] See above, p. 255 f.
[2] See above, p. 213.
[3] See above, pp. 178, 183 f.
[4] See above, p. 125.
[5] See further below, p. 317 f.
[6] See the references in the notes on this chapter. See further above, pp. 185, 279 f.: in both cases, an earlier concern with material justice and Islamic ethics was later superseded by technical legal reasoning.
[7] The argument given in Sarakhsī, xiii. 86, if authentic, would show practical reasoning and formalism.
[8] *Āthār Shaib.*, quoted in *Comm. ed. Cairo*, p. 123, n. 1.
[9] See above, p. 237.

the earliest stage of doctrine and reflects the attitude of businessmen familiar with working with other people's capital. The opinion of Abū Ḥanīfa and Abū Yūsuf, that the creditor must pay *zakāt* when he receives his credit back, is the result of a religious scruple and is expressed in a tradition from 'Alī to which Abū Ḥanīfa refers.[1] The Medinese (*Muw.* ii. 50) hold essentially the same doctrine but adduce different traditions, one from 'Uthmān and another from 'Umar b. 'Abdal'azīz who is alleged to have changed his opinion. Shāfi'ī, while maintaining this later decision in principle, makes a distinction which is already adumbrated in the 'Uthmān tradition,[2] and judiciously combines the systematic and the religious aspect.

Tr. I, 208–13, 237: Ibn Abī Lailā's decisions show the general tendency to extend the sphere of the *ḥadd* punishment for *qadhf*, a qualified kind of slander; this punishment, which was introduced by Koran xxiv. 4, is purely Islamic. It seems as if Ibn Abī Lailā's doctrine represented an early stage in which the private concern for one's reputation and the reputation of one's family caused the commandment of the Koran to be interpreted in the broadest possible way. The contrary and general Islamic tendency to restrict *ḥadd* punishments as much as possible prevailed among the Iraqians from Abū Ḥanīfa onwards.

Tr. IX, 14, and Ṭabarī, 76: Auzā'ī and the Medinese admitted the lax practice of soldiers taking back food from enemy country, without dividing it as part of the booty, and consuming it at home.[3] Under the influence of the religious scruple about dishonest conversion of booty, however, it was stipulated that this food might not be sold and might be taken only in small quantities. But if the food was acquired lawfully in the first place, the restriction on its use was inconsistent, as Abū Thaur realized. The Iraqians[4] drew the full consequences of the religious scruple, and prohibited the ancient practice altogether. Shāfi'ī, for the first time, introduced strict technical reasoning, as opposed to Abū Yūsuf's common-sense argument, superseding the material religious consideration by systematic

[1] Traditions from other Companions are attested later; see *Comm. ed. Cairo.*

[2] Shāfi'ī quotes this tradition in *Umm*, ii. 42.

[3] See above, p. 67.

[4] i.e. Abū Ḥanīfa with Abū Yūsuf and Shaibānī (*Siyar*, ii. 258 f.), and his other followers.

legal thought. The Iraqian lawyer Sufyān Thaurī almost anticipated Shāfi'ī, but not quite; he retained a trace of the religious scruple and its Iraqian common-sense solution.

Tr. IX, 25, and Ṭabarī, 64: As regards booty taken by a private raider, Auzā'ī endorses the practice by leaving to the imam, that is, the government, the final decision whether to confiscate it as unauthorized or to leave it to the raider after deducting one-fifth. This deduction is based on the general ruling concerning booty in Koran viii. 41. Mālik and Sufyān Thaurī agree with Auzā'ī that the booty of the private raider is subject to the deduction of one-fifth, but make it a hard-and-fast rule and exclude any other decision of the imam. The Iraqians (other than Sufyān Thaurī), interpreting Koran lix. 6 f. carefully, find that Koran viii. 41 does not apply to the booty of a private raider, and therefore do not subject it to the deduction of one-fifth. Shāfi'ī takes the recent traditions on the history of the Prophet into account, and arrives at the same opinion as Mālik.

Tr. IX, 33, *Tr. I*, 201, and Ṭabarī, 46: The problem is whether a *musta'min*, a non-Muslim who enters Islamic territory under a safe-conduct, is liable to *ḥadd* punishments for crimes committed in Islamic territory. Auzā'ī was influenced by the material consideration of whether the crimes, such as adultery, were committed in public or not, which made his opinion inconsistent. The Iraqians from Abū Ḥanīfa onwards showed a higher degree of technical legal reasoning, by raising the question of the competence of jurisdiction; Abū Ḥanīfa with Abū Yūsuf and his other followers answered the question in the negative, and Ibn Abī Lailā, who had formerly held the opposite opinion, joined them later. Shāfi'ī made explicit the systematic distinction between religious sanctions and civil rights (*ḥudūd Allāh* and *ḥuqūq al-ādamīyīn*), a distinction which was incipient in Auzā'ī's doctrine, and was certainly in the mind of Abū Ḥanīfa. He stands on narrower systematic ground than Abū Ḥanīfa and Abū Yūsuf, being concerned exclusively with the validity of the safe-conduct and with what is covered by it, and not with the wider issue of jurisdiction. Shāfi'ī's doctrine is therefore less technically legal than that of the Iraqians, but combines considerations of Islamic public policy with systematic consistency.

Tr. IX, 34: On the question whether a Muslim may conclude contracts involving 'usury' outside Islamic territory, Auzā'ī is moved, as he was in the preceding case, by a religious and ethical consideration, but he gives also a systematic argument of sorts. Abū Ḥanīfa uses the same technically legal reasoning as in the former case; Abū Yūsuf, however, on account of traditions to which Auzā'ī had referred but which Abū Ḥanīfa had disregarded, comes back to Auzā'ī's doctrine.[1] Shāfi'ī necessarily takes the same attitude. Nothing positive is known of Mālik's opinion. Ibn Qāsim (*Mud.* x. 103) thinks that a Muslim ought not to conclude such contracts intentionally; he is still exclusively concerned with material considerations.

From this and from the preceding chapter we can draw the general conclusion that technical legal thought, as a rule, tended to become increasingly perfected from the beginnings of Muhammadan jurisprudence up to the time of Shāfi'ī, and that material considerations of a religious and ethical kind, whether they were there from the beginning or introduced at a later stage, usually tended to become fused with systematic reasoning. In both respects, the work of Shāfi'ī represents the zenith of development, and the reader will, I hope, take it on trust that technical legal thought in Muhammadan jurisprudence hardly ever approached and never surpassed the standard he set.[2] The remaining chapters are intended to complete this general picture by remarks on the reasoning of individual lawyers, concluding with Shāfi'ī.

[1] In order to excuse Abū Ḥanīfa, Abū Yūsuf refers to a tradition which Abū Ḥanīfa himself had not adduced as an argument.

[2] This applies, for instance, to the lawyer-traditionist Ṭaḥāwī, to the learned antiquary Ibn 'Abdalbarr, and to the ruthless rationalizer Sarakhsī.

CHAPTER 3

AUZĀʿĪ'S REASONING

WE have already given an account of the extent to which Auzāʿī uses explicit systematic reasoning;[1] it is overshadowed by his reliance on the 'living tradition'.[2] This concept, as Auzāʿī understands it, is the result of scrutiny, by the scholars, of the idealized practice. We are therefore justified if, in order to gain some idea of the quality of Auzāʿī's legal thought, we not only draw on his explicit systematic reasoning, but consider the whole known body of his doctrine.[3] It remains uncertain, however, how much of it is Auzāʿī's own, and how much he took over from his predecessors. Auzāʿī (and this may include the Syrians in general) was certainly influenced by Iraqian reasoning, not only in legal theory,[4] but in the solution of at least one particular problem as well.[5]

Auzāʿī's opinions, as a rule,[6] represent the oldest solutions adopted by Muhammadan jurisprudence, whether he maintains the current practice,[7] or regulates it,[8] or Islamicizes it as is usual with him, or gives a seemingly simple and natural decision as yet untouched by systematic refinements.[9] The archaic character of Auzāʿī's doctrine makes it likely that he, who was himself a contemporary of Abū Ḥanīfa, conserved the teaching of his predecessors in the generation before him.

When the doctrine which goes under the name of Auzāʿī was formulated, the Islamicizing and systematizing tendencies of earliest Muhammadan jurisprudence had, it is true, already started to act, but they were still far from having permeated the whole of the raw material offered by the practice. The doctrine as given by Auzāʿī therefore often appears inconsistent.

This inconsistency is perhaps most immediately noticeable in the case of Islamicizing: a strong tendency to Islamicize is

[1] Above, p. 119.
[2] See above, pp. 70 ff.
[3] The references in this chapter are to *Tr. IX*, unless the contrary is stated.
[4] See above, p. 76.
[5] See above, p. 278.—In § 20 Auzāʿī counters an objection which corresponds to an Iraqian doctrine.
[6] For an exception see above, p. 277, n. 1.
[7] e.g. § 16 (see above, p. 277 f.).
[8] e.g. § 27 (see above, p. 70).
[9] e.g. § 38 (see above, p. 277).

unmistakable[1] and produces the historically false notion of an ancient practice opposed to the present, actual one;[2] but the strict observance of a religious scruple in § 2 leads to an inconsistency with the parallel case of § 14 where the current practice is followed without misgivings;[3] and in § 13 (and in the parallel in Ṭabarī, 87) the religious scruple, identical here with strict systematic reasoning, is only beginning to assert itself against an old-established practice.[4]

Auzāʿī's explicit systematic reasoning is on the whole rudimentary,[5] and the legal thought which we can postulate as underlying some of his decisions shows as a rule a rigid formalism, as in § 12, or in § 20 where he defends his unsystematic but seemingly practicable and natural decision by a rigorously literal interpretation of an *isnād*-less tradition from the Prophet. There is an appreciable amount of systematic reasoning underlying Auzāʿī's doctrine; he shows a positive interest in legal problems as opposed to the actual practice[6] and, once his doctrine is established as correct, he is prepared to accept its consequences even if they prove undesirable in practice.[7] How far systematizing went in his time may be gathered, perhaps, from the estimate that the balance between noticeable consistencies and inconsistencies, in the material we have, is just about equal.[8]

[1] See above, p. 72.
[2] e.g. § 1 (see above, p. 71).
[3] See above, p. 285.
[4] See above, p. 70 f.
[5] See above, p. 119.
[6] e.g. § 16 f. (see above, p. 277 f.).
[7] Ṭabarī, 89, parallel to § 1 (see above, p. 72).
[8] See also *E.I.*[2], s.v. *al-Awzāʿī*.

CHAPTER 4

THE REASONING OF INDIVIDUAL IRAQIANS

A. IBN ABĪ LAILĀ

WE have seen that the technical legal problems which form the subject-matter of *Tr. I*, and on which Ibn Abī Lailā and Abū Ḥanīfa differ, are later than the real or fictitious opinions ascribed to Ibrāhīm Nakha'ī in *Āthār A. Y.* and *Āthār Shaib.*, and further that these last date mainly from the time of Ḥammād.[1] The discussion of the technical legal problems must have started therefore not much earlier than the time of Ibn Abī Lailā himself. On the other hand, the doctrine of Ibn Abī Lailā is as a rule more primitive, less highly developed, and represents an earlier stage than that of his contemporary Abū Ḥanīfa.[2] In other words: Ibn Abī Lailā is more conservative, and this is well in keeping with his having been a judge (a fact of which we shall also find direct traces in his decisions), whereas Abū Ḥanīfa, a speculative lawyer, was less hampered by the necessity of paying regard to the practice.

The doctrine of Ibn Abī Lailā, taken as a whole, shows a considerable amount of technical legal thought, but it is generally of a primitive kind, somewhat clumsy and untrained, and therefore shortsighted and often unfortunate in its results. His loose and imperfect method is not incompatible with formalism and the stubborn drawing of consequences. Nevertheless, Ibn Abī Lailā's technical reasoning is far from rudimentary; the striving for systematic consistency, the action of general trends and principles, pervade his whole doctrine, and there is a considerable amount of explicit legal reasoning.[3]

In a great number of cases, Ibn Abī Lailā's doctrine represents seemingly natural and practical common-sense, and rough-and-ready decisions. The following short remarks on a few chosen examples will serve to make this clear.

§ 13: A seemingly just and reasonable, but short-sighted solution (see above, p. 270 f.).

[1] Above, pp. 234 ff.
[2] See above, pp. 270 ff.
[3] The references in this section are to *Tr. I*, unless the contrary is stated.

§ 31: A practical and 'homely' inference, combined with systematic reasoning.[1]

§ 32: An inconsistent decision, based on practical expediency.

§ 63: A decision based on a false analogy, not technically legal or logical, but practical and keeping account of the presumed intention of the party concerned.

§ 65: Ibn Abī Lailā does not see the implications of the problem and gives what must have seemed to him a practicable and materially just solution.[2]

§ 72: A practicable and seemingly natural decision (see above, p. 272).

§§ 92, 93, 94: Common-sense and practicable decisions, showing regard for the practice (see above, p. 273).

§§ 107, 110: A rough-and-ready solution, taking account of the old practice of identifying slaves and tax-payers by seals of lead attached to their necks,[3] and of the official correspondence between judges; Shāfi'ī's comment shows that this is the easiest way out of a practical difficulty, but it is against *qiyās*, legally irregular and beset with difficulties.[4]

§ 126: A practicable interim solution (see above, p. 274).

§ 190: A practical but inconsistent decision (see below, p. 295).

§ 227: Ibn Abī Lailā gives the reason for his decision; it is plausible on the face of it, but rather irrelevant.

§§ 236, 251: Makeshift method and rough-and-ready decision (see above, p. 236).

This practical, common-sense reasoning often takes material, and particularly Islamic-ethical, considerations into account.

§ 3: An inconsistent decision in favour of the liberty of a slave.

§ 17: A rough-and-ready decision in the interests of material justice.

§ 28: A decision based on material justice and on an ethical consideration (see above, p. 284).

§ 130: An inconsistent decision in favour of the orphan (see above, p. 217).

[1] The silence of the owner is treated by analogy with the silence of the virgin on her marriage. This argument, only adumbrated in *Tr. I*, is explicitly given by Sarakhsī, xxx. 140, on behalf of Ibn Abī Lailā; it is certainly authentic because Shāfi'ī refers to it.

[2] But the general theory of *tajhīl* which is attributed to Ibn Abī Lailā by Sarakhsī is spurious, as appears from a comparison of Sarakhsī, xi. 129 ff., with *Tr. I*, 67.

[3] See Becker, *Islamstudien*, i. 261.

[4] Sarakhsī, xi. 24 f., calls it 'a not very good *istiḥsān*', but states that it is in the public interest.

§§ 134, 139: Practical concessions in favour of the *mukātab* slave (see above, pp. 112, 281).

§§ 143, 235 f.: A decision based on material, non-juridical considerations.[1]

§ 150: A seemingly just and practicable decision, obviously inspired by material considerations (see above, p. 274).

Connected with these material considerations is Ibn Abī Lailā's regard for the actual practice.[2] The fact of his holding the office of judge would naturally reinforce this tendency. There are numerous traces of Ibn Abī Lailā's activity as a judge in his doctrine.[3]

We now come to a group of downright primitive features, both material and formal, in Ibn Abī Lailā's doctrine.

§§ 30, 37, 59: Traces of patriarchy in civil law.

§ 44: Ibn Abī Lailā shows himself crudely systematic, but clumsy and inconsistent (see above, p. 271).

§ 77: Primitive legal reasoning (see above, p. 273).

§ 127: A trace of patriarchy in family property rights (see above, p. 278).

§ 140: Ibn Abī Lailā gives a seemingly natural and straightforward solution, but does not see its legal difficulties which were later pointed out by Abū Ḥanīfa.

§ 189: The old Arab idea that husband and wife have no share in matters of talion; this idea was dropped from Abū Ḥanīfa onwards.

§ 245: A far-fetched specious interpretation of a statement.

The last case quoted is one example out of many of Ibn Abī Lailā's formalism. This rigid formalism is perhaps the most persistent single feature typical of his legal thought.[4]

[1] This is well pointed out by Sarakhsī, vi. 97.

[2] In common with the other Iraqians, Ibn Abī Lailā avoids the term *'amal* for practice (see above, p. 76). But the influence of the actual practice on his doctrine, to a much higher degree than in the case of Abū Ḥanīfa and his disciples, is unmistakable. See §§ 92–4 (above, p. 273), 107 and 110 (above, p. 291), 109 (above, p. 210), 111 (above, p. 211), 115 (above, p. 218), 167 (above, p. 284).

[3] See §§ 9, 49 (a change in his decision on an ancient controversial point under instructions from the 'Abbāsid Caliph Saffāḥ), 55 (above, p. 272), 82 (a change of doctrine under the needs of the administration of justice; above, p. 273), 113, 210, 211, 255 (*b*), 256 (Abū Yūsuf was present when Ibn Abī Lailā related his decision as a judge).—It can further be reasonably presumed that Ibn Abī Lailā's doctrine was influenced by the needs of judicial practice in the cases of §§ 106 (above, p. 274), 116 (above, p. 187 f.), 202, 203, 207.

[4] See § 4 (complicated reckoning instead of valuation), 10, 25 (above, p. 271), 27 (ibid.), 50 (Ibn Abī Lailā attaches formal importance to a declaration and

Such are the foundations from which rises Ibn Abī Lailā's technical legal thought. The following examples will be sufficient to show its extent and quality.

§ 16: Ibn Abī Lailā anticipates Shāfi'ī.

§ 39: Ibn Abī Lailā bases his decision on a general rule of presumption;[1] Sarakhsī shows competently that Ibn Abī Lailā misapplies the rule, but Shāfi'ī in his better attested opinion agrees with Ibn Abī Lailā.

§ 47: Ibn Abī Lailā reasons on the theoretical construction of the right of pre-emption, but his solution is practical.

§ 75: Ibn Abī Lailā reasons against contracts concerning an unknown quantity; Shāfi'ī has nothing substantial to add to his argument.

§ 83: Ibn Abī Lailā sees the essential problem, and anticipates Shāfi'ī (see above, p. 273).

§§ 123, 125, 206: Ibn Abī Lailā's decisions on two widely differing groups of problems are based on the theory of the indivisibility of acknowledgements.

§ 129: The doctrine of Ibn Abī Lailā is juridically better developed than that of Abū Ḥanīfa; it is maintained with a systematic improvement by Shāfi'ī.

§ 133: Ibn Abī Lailā enounces a sound general principle as the basis of his decision.

§§ 134, 140: Ibn Abī Lailā knows the concept of being 'in abeyance', but expresses it clumsily (see above, p. 281, n. 1).

§ 148: A common-sense and juridically sound decision, endorsed by Shāfi'ī.[2]

§ 151: A close parallel which shows, in addition, an intelligent application of a general principle and a high degree of legal thought.

§ 152: Equally good.

§ 171 (*a*), 216: Analogical reasoning, without the term *qiyās* (see above, p. 110).

§ 243: If we are to believe Sarakhsī, xxx. 165 (and this seems indeed the only possible reason for Ibn Abī Lailā's decision), Ibn

becomes systematically inconsistent), 52 (above, p. 272), 67, 68 f. (very rigid and formal, simple but consistent legal thought), 90, 97, 108 (above, p. 274), 118 (Ibn Abī Lailā's formalistic respect for the *res iudicata* is, however, not peculiar to him; see *Umm*, vii. 34), 120, 141 f. (Ibn Abī Lailā pursues to its farthest consequences a formal principle which embodies crude and primitive reasoning; above, p. 274), 174 (formalistic concern with the intention), 179, 188, 193, 205, 238.

[1] Sarakhsī, xxx. 144, mentions Ibn Abī Lailā's argument explicitly; this is confirmed by Shāfi'ī's reference to it.

[2] Sarakhsī, xi. 150, says correctly that it takes account of the outward, obvious facts (*li-'tibār al-ẓāhir*).

Abī Lailā applied the principle that a condition which cannot be ascertained is to be treated as non-existent.

The degree of systematizing achieved by Ibn Abī Lailā can be estimated by the fact that cases of remarkable systematic consistency definitely outweigh those where the inconsistency is obvious.[1]

B. Abū Ḥanīfa

The examples with which I illustrated the development of legal reasoning in general[2] show the superiority of Abū Ḥanīfa's technical legal thought over that of Ibn Abī Lailā. With respect to Ibn Abī Lailā and the Iraqian legal reasoning which Ibn Abī Lailā represents, Abū Ḥanīfa seems to have played the role of a theoretical systematizer who achieved a considerable progress in technical legal thought. Not being a judge, Abū Ḥanīfa was less restricted than Ibn Abī Lailā by considerations of practice. At the same time, he was less firmly guided by the administration of justice, and whereas Ibn Abī Lailā's doctrine is often primitive but practical, Abū Ḥanīfa's, though more highly developed, is often tentative and unsatisfactory.

In Abū Ḥanīfa's doctrine, systematic consistency has become normal. The emphasis shifts from the material aspects of legal reasoning, such as regard for the practice, Islamicizing, common-sense decisions and other material considerations which were still prevalent in Ibn Abī Lailā's doctrine, to the technical and formal qualities of legal thought. Traces of primitive reasoning and systematic inconsistencies remain but they are relatively few in number. On the other hand, there is so much explicit legal thought embodied in Abū Ḥanīfa's doctrine, that we cannot be surprised to find that an appreciable part of it was found defective and was rejected by his companions.

Regard for the practice

Kharāj, 36: Abū Ḥanīfa makes out a good case for the administrative practice (see above, p. 202).

Tr. I, 27: Abū Ḥanīfa's doctrine is more appropriate than that of Ibn Abī Lailā for somewhat more highly developed conditions of commerce (see above, p. 271).

[1] See also *E.I.*[2], s.v. *Ibn Abī Laylā.*

[2] Above, pp. 270 ff.

Islamicizing

Muw. Shaib. 249: Abū Ḥanīfa distinguishes between the legal and the moral aspect.

Tr. I, 167: Abū Ḥanīfa applies a religious consideration, as against Ibn Abī Lailā's recognition of the commercial practice (see above, p. 284 f.).

Tr. I, 246: Abū Ḥanīfa stands alone in introducing a religious scruple into a technically legal problem.

Common-sense decisions and material considerations

Tr. I, 7: Abū Ḥanīfa diverges from Ibn Abī Lailā, obviously for practical reasons, but is not followed by Abū Yūsuf, Shaibānī (Sarakhsī, xiii. 50), and Shāfiʿī.

Tr. I, 48: A reasonable and defensible opinion (see above, p. 271).

Tr. I, 52: Abū Ḥanīfa shows more common sense and is more practical than Ibn Abī Lailā (see above, p. 272).

Tr. I, 108: A very relevant material consideration, as opposed to Ibn Abī Lailā's formalism (see above, p. 274).

Tr. I, 134: Abū Ḥanīfa diverges from strict consistency in favour of the *mukātab* slave, but less so than Ibn Abī Lailā (see above, p. 280).

Tr. I, 178: An *istiḥsān*, directed against cruelty to animals (see above, p. 112).

Tr. IX, 2: An *istiḥsān*, based on common-sense (see ibid.).

Tr. IX, 19: A practical consideration, but inconclusive.

If we compare these examples with the far greater number of comparable cases which we could collect from a more restricted range of sources for Ibn Abī Lailā,[1] the regression of the material element in Abū Ḥanīfa's legal reasoning becomes obvious. The following examples show the same with regard to primitive reasoning in Abū Ḥanīfa's doctrine.

Primitive reasoning

Tr. I, 72: Elementary legal reasoning (see above, p. 272).

Tr. I, 184: Primitive analogical reasoning, leading to a systematic inconsistency.

Tr. I, 187: Abū Ḥanīfa applies an old Arab tribal idea with rigid formalism, although in *Tr. I*, 189, he is the first to discard another old Arab idea (see above, p. 292).

Tr. I, 190: Here also Abū Ḥanīfa follows the same tribal idea out to its last consequences; compared with his doctrine, Ibn Abī Lailā's decision is practically expedient but inconsistent.

[1] Above, pp. 290 ff.

Tr. I, 253: A loose and clumsy analogy, brilliantly refuted by Shāfi'ī.

Tr. IX, 3: Abū Ḥanīfa's argument reproduces a crude and primitive analogy which is obviously older than Abū Ḥanīfa himself (see above, p. 109).

More significant than these features which connect Abū Ḥanīfa's reasoning with the period of his predecessors, are those numerous cases which show Abū Ḥanīfa's legal thought not only more broadly based and more thoroughly applied than that of Auzā'ī and Ibn Abī Lailā, but technically more highly developed, more circumspect, and more refined.

Muw. Shaib. 331: in common with the other Iraqians, Abū Ḥanīfa forbids the re-sale of any object before taking possession,[1] but he is alone in exempting immovables; this distinction is legally sound, because of the exceptional character of the possession of immovables.

Tr. I, 13: Abū Ḥanīfa easily refutes Ibn Abī Lailā (above, p. 270 f.).

Tr. I, 25: Abū Ḥanīfa's analysis goes deeper than that of Ibn Abī Lailā (above, p. 271).

Tr. I, 28: Abū Ḥanīfa shows a higher degree of technical legal reasoning than Ibn Abī Lailā (above, p. 284).

Tr. I, 44: Abū Ḥanīfa refutes Ibn Abī Lailā by better systematic reasoning (above, p. 271).

Tr. I, 60 f.: Abū Ḥanīfa shows a high standard of technical legal thought (above, p. 272).

Tr. I, 65: Abū Ḥanīfa gives remarkably sharp-sighted legal reasoning: 'A man leaves a deposit with another; a third person comes forward and claims the deposit besides the [original] depositor; the depositary says: "I do not know which of you two has left this deposit", and refuses to take the oath [that it is not the deposit of either of them], and neither of them can produce evidence. Abū Ḥanīfa used to decide as follows: the depositary must return the deposit to them both, it is then their joint property, and he becomes responsible to them both for another, equal amount which is due to them in equal shares, for through his ignorance he has destroyed what was given in deposit. Consider [what would happen] if he said: "This man has left the deposit with me", and said afterwards: "I made a mistake, it was this other man"; he would then have to return the deposit to the man in whose favour he made the first acknowledgement, and would become responsible to the other for an

[1] See above, pp. 108, 200.

equal amount, because his [first] statement destroyed [what he later acknowledged to have received in deposit from the other]. The same applies to the first problem: it was the depositary who destroyed the deposit through his ignorance. We [Abū Yūsuf] follow this. Ibn Abī Lailā used to decide in the first case that the depositary is not responsible for anything and that the deposit . . . belongs to both claimants in equal shares.'

Tr. I, 77: The reasoning of Abū Ḥanīfa is more penetrating than that of Ibn Abī Lailā (above, p. 273).

Tr. I, 81: Abū Ḥanīfa introduces a sound distinction, maintained by Shāfiʿī.

Tr. I, 103: Abū Ḥanīfa, by systematic reasoning, subsumes a special case under a general decision; this, it is true, leads him into a different systematic inconsistency, as Shāfiʿī points out; Sarakhsī (xvi. 129 f.), however, gives a satisfactory and probably authentic answer to this objection and, everything considered, Abū Ḥanīfa's doctrine is more consistent than that of Shāfiʿī; it is followed by Shaibānī, but not by Abū Yūsuf and Zufar (Sarakhsī, loc. cit.).

Tr. I, 117: Abū Ḥanīfa introduces a relevant distinction.

Tr. I, 120: Abū Ḥanīfa's argument, short and to the point, shows a considerable advance on Ibn Abī Lailā.

Tr. I, 123: Abū Ḥanīfa introduces technical legal reasoning, articulate and consistent in itself, but incompatible with broader systematic consistency, as Shāfiʿī points out.

Tr. I, 126: Abū Ḥanīfa is more methodical than Ibn Abī Lailā (above, p. 274).

Tr. I, 139: Abū Ḥanīfa is more logical and consistent than Ibn Abī Lailā (above, p. 112).

Tr. I, 140: Abū Ḥanīfa shows a high degree of technical reasoning, is sharp-sighted and systematic, and anticipates Shāfiʿī's doctrine; the essential argument, was, it is true, attributed to Ibrāhīm Nakhaʿī, but this can hardly be authentic.[1]

Tr. I, 141 f.: A sound decision, based on extensive systematic reasoning, much better than that of Ibn Abī Lailā (above, p. 274).

Tr. I, 188: Abū Ḥanīfa is more concerned than Ibn Abī Lailā with the legally relevant features of a problem.

Tr. I, 196: Abū Ḥanīfa applies shrewd technical reasoning. An early Iraqian *qiyās* demanded a two-fold confession of the culprit for the *ḥadd* punishment for theft to be applicable.[2] Some Iraqians, however, held that a single confession only was required, and Abū Ḥanīfa argued in favour of this opinion which he shared, that if a two-fold confession were necessary for the *ḥadd* to be applied, a

[1] See above, p. 235.

[2] See above, p. 107.

single confession of the theft would create a civil debt, and no *hadd* could be applied after incurring a civil debt even if a second confession was made. In a broader systematic sense, this argument is hardly consistent with Abū Ḥanīfa's doctrine in § 104 (below, p. 300).

Tr. I, 227: Abū Ḥanīfa gives good systematic reasoning, besides references to Companions and to Ibrāhīm Nakhaʿī.

Tr. I, 243: The doctrine of Abū Ḥanīfa is superior to that of Ibn Abī Lailā; his decision and argument anticipate the decision and argument of Shāfiʿī.

Tr. I, 245: Abū Ḥanīfa shows deeper legal understanding than Ibn Abī Lailā; he concentrates more on essentials, and his doctrine is recognized as better by Shāfiʿī.

Tr. IX, 20 and Ṭabarī, 34: Abū Ḥanīfa shows competent systematic reasoning; he distinguishes between a declaratory and a constitutive statement.

Tr. IX, 27 and 33, *Tr. I*, 201, Ṭabarī, 46: Abū Ḥanīfa considers the territorial limits of the applicability of religious penal law;[1] his doctrine is sound and systematically consistent, and the theory in question is presumably his own achievement. Connected with this theory is Abū Ḥanīfa's reasoning on the 'difference of territory' (*tabāyun al-dārain*) in *Tr. IX*, 16, a reasoning which also underlies his doctrine in § 1 and in § 35 f. (where only Abū Ḥanīfa succeeds in being systematically quite consistent).

Tr. IX, 34: Abū Ḥanīfa makes his technical legal reasoning supersede traditions from the Prophet (above, p. 287).

Tr. IX, 41: Abū Ḥanīfa adumbrates good systematic reasoning.

Tr. IX, 45 and Ṭabarī, 120: Abū Ḥanīfa gives good reasoning and makes a sound systematic distinction; at the same time, he takes Auzāʿī's practical consideration into account.

Tr. IX, 46: Good systematic reasoning is given by Abū Yūsuf on behalf of Abū Ḥanīfa.

Abū Ḥanīfa's legal thought was, however, not final, and his companions had occasion to diverge from him on numerous points of doctrine. We are not concerned here with such material divergencies between Abū Ḥanīfa and his companions as belong to the development of positive legal doctrine in the ancient Iraqian and in the early Ḥanafī school. The following examples are intended to illustrate some of the imperfections and limitations of Abū Ḥanīfa's legal thought in general, and in particular to show how and why his companions, starting

[1] See above, pp. 209, 286.

with Abū Yūsuf, came to reject some of the explicit legal thought of their master.

Tr. I, 7: See above, p. 295.

Tr. I, 12: Neither the Iraqians nor the Medinese (*Muw.* iii. 136) originally put a time-limit to the right of option which might be stipulated in favour of one or both of the parties in certain contracts (*khiyār al-sharṭ*). Only Abū Ḥanīfa introduced a time-limit of three days; he arrived at this by analogy with a tradition from the Prophet which gives a right of option of three days in the case of a certain kind of fraud in the sale of animals (the so-called *muṣarrāt*). But Abū Ḥanīfa, in common with the other Iraqians, rejected this tradition as far as the *muṣarrāt* itself was concerned.[1] Neither Abū Yūsuf nor Shaibānī (Sarakhsī, xiii. 41) followed Abū Ḥanīfa in his self-contradictory reasoning, and both ignored the time limit. Shāfi'ī adopted it, but this time consistently, because he also recognized the tradition with regard to the *muṣarrāt*.[2]

Tr. I, 36: Abū Ḥanīfa's doctrine is on the face of it stricter and less practically expedient than that of Ibn Abī Lailā, Abū Yūsuf and Shaibānī; it represents an unsuccessful effort at greater systematic stringency. If the argument which Sarakhsī, xiv. 150 f., gives for Abū Ḥanīfa's doctrine, and which comes down to a consideration of sentimental values, is authentic, it is not surprising that this opinion was discarded.

Tr. I, 43: Abū Ḥanīfa tries to arrive at greater strictness and, if we may believe Sarakhsī, xii. 140 ff., at greater formal consistency; but Abū Yūsuf in his later opinion, followed by Shaibānī (Sarakhsī, xii. 137), returns to Ibn Abī Lailā's doctrine which is in itself sound.

Tr. I, 51: Abū Ḥanīfa rejects the customary agricultural contract of *muzāra'a* for a systematic reason, but Abū Yūsuf does not follow him in this. In the parallel case of § 55, however, Abū Yūsuf maintains Abū Ḥanīfa's doctrine (above, p. 272).

Tr. I, 76: Abū Ḥanīfa gives formal and technical reasoning against Ibn Abī Lailā, but is not followed by Abū Yūsuf nor by Shaibānī (Sarakhsī, xx. 108 f.). Also in § 83, Abū Ḥanīfa applies rigidly formal reasoning; here he is followed by Abū Yūsuf (above, p. 273). In §§ 92–4, Abū Ḥanīfa takes again a strictly formal view; Abū Yūsuf agrees substantially (ibid.). In § 95 = 228, Abū Ḥanīfa's decision is rigidly formal and even hair-splitting, and Abū Yūsuf reverts to the doctrine of Ibn Abī Lailā (above, p. 274).

Tr. I, 89: Abū Ḥanīfa's earlier doctrine is an individual effort, shared by Zufar (Sarakhsī, v. 190), to achieve material justice, but

[1] *Tr. II*, 12 (*h*); *Ikh.* 332 ff.; Ṭaḥāwī, ii. 205.

[2] Cf. above, p. 123.

it becomes systematically inconsistent. Later, Abū Ḥanīfa returns to the general Iraqian doctrine.

Tr. I, 104: Abū Ḥanīfa introduces a refinement, basing himself on the wording of a tradition which is late;[1] but this becomes systematically inconsistent with his decision in § 196 (above, p. 298).

Tr. I, 107, 110: Abū Ḥanīfa took no account of the official correspondence between judges which always played an important part in practice; by this uncompromising attitude which was systematically consistent (so that Shāfiʿī called it *qiyās*), but which merely ignored the practical problem, Abū Ḥanīfa avoided the difficulties inherent in Ibn Abī Lailā's solution (above, p. 291). Abū Yūsuf, with more regard for judicial practice, returned to Ibn Abī Lailā's decision,[2] but Shaibānī followed Abū Ḥanīfa (Sarakhsī, xi. 24).

Tr. I, 114: Ibn Abī Lailā had made the good character of witnesses a matter of public interest, so that the judge had the right to inquire into it even if it was not contested. Abū Ḥanīfa made it a private interest of the parties concerned, but this doctrine was not successful because Abū Yūsuf, Shaibānī, and others (Sarakhsī, xvi. 88; xxx. 153) reverted to Ibn Abī Lailā.

Tr. I, 121: Abū Ḥanīfa introduced a rather far-fetched reasoning which was rejected by Abū Yūsuf and by Shaibānī (Sarakhsī, xxvii. 148).

Tr. I, 133: Abū Ḥanīfa's explicit reasoning is curiously shortsighted and pseudo-rational, so that Sarakhsī, vii. 103 f., has to make an artificial distinction in order to justify it systematically. Abū Yūsuf and Shaibānī (*Muw. Shaib.* 358) disagree. Abū Yūsuf elaborates systematically the principle underlying Ibn Abī Lailā's doctrine (above, p. 293) which he follows in the essentials.

Tr. I, 137: Abū Ḥanīfa is inconsistent because he has not yet fully grasped all the implications of the problem; only Abū Yūsuf does so.

Tr. I, 148: As compared with Ibn Abī Lailā, Abū Ḥanīfa is more formalistic and in fact superficial. Abū Yūsuf and Shaibānī follow Abū Ḥanīfa (Sarakhsī, xi. 150; *Comm. ed. Cairo*, p. 105, n. 3), but Shāfiʿī endorses Ibn Abī Lailā. Also in the closely parallel case of § 151, Abū Ḥanīfa gives a sweeping and formalistic interpretation, without much regard for the consequences, of a general principle which had already been recognized by Ibn Abī Lailā. In § 152, Abū Ḥanīfa shows again rigid formalism and pseudo-logical thought;

[1] See above, p. 106, n. 5.

[2] On further details of Abū Yūsuf's doctrine, see Sarakhsī xi. 2, 24 f. If this is authentic, as it probably is, Abū Yūsuf was even less consistent than Ibn Abī Lailā.

this brings him to a systematic inconsistency which is pointed out by Shāfiʿī. In § 170, Abū Ḥanīfa applies meticulously logical reasoning which is abandoned by Abū Yūsuf. The rigid formalism of § 177 seems to be older than Abū Ḥanīfa; for it is attributed to Ibrāhīm Nakhaʿī. In § 233, Abū Ḥanīfa applies a general principle blindly, but is systematically less consistent than Ibn Abī Lailā.

Tr. I, 210: Abū Ḥanīfa's argument is irrelevant; this is shown by his own statement in § 211.

Tr. I, 246: See above, p. 295.

A rather highly developed but often somewhat ruthless and unbalanced reasoning, with little regard for the practice, such as we have found in numerous examples, is typical of Abū Ḥanīfa's legal thought.[1]

C. Abū Yūsuf

We saw in the preceding section[2] that the doctrine of Abū Yūsuf often represents a reaction against Abū Ḥanīfa's somewhat unrestrained reasoning and reverts to, or maintains, an earlier stage as exemplified by Ibn Abī Lailā. On the whole, however, Abū Yūsuf presupposes the doctrine of Abū Ḥanīfa whom he regards as his master, and the points on which Abū Yūsuf diverges from him are more relevant for appreciating Abū Yūsuf's own legal thought than those on which both are in agreement.

In the details of his doctrine, Abū Yūsuf is more dependent on traditions than his master, because there were more authoritative traditions in existence in his time.[3]

Tr. I, 51: Abū Yūsuf, deciding against Abū Ḥanīfa and reverting to Ibn Abī Lailā, finds that *qiyās*, that is to say the systematic parallel, and traditions agree.

Tr. I, 171 (*a*): Abū Yūsuf, whilst agreeing with Abū Ḥanīfa on principle, introduces a refinement of his own with explicit reference to a tradition; he is followed by Shaibānī (Sarakhsī, ii. 193).

Tr. I, 234: Abū Yūsuf, having first followed Ibn Abī Lailā, later adopted the doctrine of Abū Ḥanīfa, influenced by a tradition from the Prophet which Abū Yūsuf for the first time applied to the problem in question.

Tr. IX, 1: Abū Yūsuf draws unwarranted and unconvincing conclusions in favour of the common Iraqian doctrine from historical traditions which as often as not imply the contrary.

[1] See also *E.I.*², s.v. [2] Above, pp. 298 ff. [3] See above, pp. 139, 143.

Tr. IX, 6: Abū Yūsuf adduces traditions against Auzā'ī but does not follow them himself in all their implications, and Shāfi'ī blames him for this.

Tr. IX, 16 f.: Abū Yūsuf is bound by traditions more than Auzā'ī, though less than Shāfi'ī (above, p. 278), but he combines this with competent systematic reasoning.

Tr. IX, 34. On account of traditions which Abū Ḥanīfa had disregarded, Abū Yūsuf reverts to Auzā'ī's doctrine; he also refers to a tradition in order to excuse Abū Ḥanīfa's systematic doctrine (above, p. 287). In § 36, under the influence of historical traditions, Abū Yūsuf again falls back on the doctrine of Auzā'ī. In §§ 36 and 37, Abū Yūsuf mistakenly seeks to find a justification in traditions for the doctrine held by Abū Ḥanīfa on the basis of systematic reasoning.

Tr. IX, 38: Here, for once, Abū Yūsuf gives sound systematic reasoning which causes him to reject a tradition as irregular, applying a method which he himself set out in detail in § 5.

Kharāj, 36: Whilst himself diverging from Abū Ḥanīfa's doctrine, Abū Yūsuf defends him against the charge of disregarding traditions.

Kharāj, 126 f.: In this later parallel to the earlier passage *Tr. IX*, 22, Abū Yūsuf, though holding essentially the same doctrine, shows himself less systematic in his reasoning and more bound by traditions.

Compared with this increasing dependence on traditions, other kinds of material considerations are less prominent in Abū Yūsuf's doctrine. His legal reasoning is, generally speaking, of the same kind as that of his predecessors.

The new features which we can discern in Abū Yūsuf's legal thought are certain favourite processes of reasoning, and a habit of rather acrimonious polemics.

The *reductio ad absurdum* was used in discussions well before Abū Yūsuf, but Abū Yūsuf made it a favourite method of his.[1] It is connected with the reasoning from extreme and border-line cases, a kind of argument which had been extensively used by Abū Ḥanīfa before Abū Yūsuf adopted it.[2] An example typical of Abū Yūsuf occurs in *Tr. IX*, 33, where he tries to support Abū Ḥanīfa's excellent systematic reason with fictitious border-line cases which are not all happily chosen.

Another of Abū Yūsuf's favourite lines of attack against other opinions is to point out their inconsistency.[3] This presupposes a respectable standard of systematic reasoning on his part. He further

[1] e.g. *Tr. IX*, 2, 15, 21.

[2] See above, p. 105.

[3] e.g. *Tr. I*, 237; *Tr. IX*, 14, 16, 17, 25, 26, 27, 44, 45.

introduces strong words and vituperative expressions into the discussion with his opponents.[1]

In *Tr. IX*, 6, where Abū Yūsuf pours scorn on Auzāʿī, he is not well informed on the doctrine of his opponent, because Auzāʿī made a distinction which obviates Abū Yūsuf's objection, as appears from Ṭabarī, 57. Abū Yūsuf's attack against Auzāʿī in *Tr. IX*, 18, is equally pointless, because it appears from Ṭabarī, 97, that Auzāʿī's opinion[2] was essentially the same as that of Abū Ḥanīfa and that of Abū Yūsuf in his earlier period as represented by *Tr. IX*; it is possible, of course, that Abū Yūsuf picked out the weak point in Auzāʿī's doctrine, but then his criticism, instead of being ill-informed, would be one-sided. Comparing *Tr. IX*, 13, with Ṭabarī, 87 f., one sees indeed that Abū Yūsuf formulated Abū Ḥanīfa's opinions polemically against Auzāʿī by omitting an important distinction. In *Tr. IX*, 25, Abū Yūsuf tries artificially to establish a contradiction between Auzāʿī's doctrine and Auzāʿī's authority ʿUmar b. ʿAbdalʿazīz.

We have discussed in the preceding section[3] a number of cases in which Abū Yūsuf diverged from Abū Ḥanīfa, where it could be said in the light of the general development of technical legal thought that Abū Ḥanīfa's reasoning was unbalanced and imperfect. Abū Yūsuf, however, was by no means consistent, as can be seen, for instance, from his uncertain reactions to Abū Ḥanīfa's rigid formalism;[4] all we can say is that, generally speaking, he mitigated it. On the other hand, there are a certain number of cases in which Abū Yūsuf, again within the framework of the development of legal thought, can be regarded as having abandoned, by diverging from Abū Ḥanīfa, the sounder or more highly developed doctrine.[5]

The differences between Abū Ḥanīfa and Abū Yūsuf consist to a great extent in slight modifications and adjustments, improvements and finishing touches which Abū Yūsuf applies to the doctrine of his master, often in order to achieve a greater systematic consistency.

Tr. I, 70: Abū Yūsuf follows Abū Ḥanīfa in theory, but in practice falls back on Ibn Abī Lailā's obvious and common-sense solution.

[1] *Tr. IX*, 1, 3 (*b*), 6, 7, 8, 9, 11, 12, 23.

[2] Apart from one detail where he endorsed the administrative practice; see above, p. 208.

[3] Above, pp. 298 ff.

[4] See above, p. 299, on *Tr. I*, 76 ff., and p. 300 f. on *Tr. I*, 148 ff.

[5] e.g. *Tr. I*, 25 (above, p. 271), 28 (above, p. 284), 60 f. (above, p. 272), 103 (above, p. 297), 126 (above, p. 274).

Tr. I, 80: Abū Yūsuf abandons a distinction made by Abū Ḥanīfa, and makes his doctrine consistent. A parallel case occurs in § 81: Abū Yūsuf abandons a distinction made by Abū Ḥanīfa, and applies one of the elements of his doctrine to the whole problem.

Tr. I, 94: See above, p. 273.

Tr. I, 99: In his earlier and in his later opinion, Abū Yūsuf gradually (but not completely) reduces Abū Ḥanīfa's inconsistency.

Tr. I, 135: If the additional details given in Sarakhsī, xxx. 157, are authentic, as they seem to be, Abū Yūsuf would be more consistent than Abū Ḥanīfa, and would obviate Shāfi'ī's objection against the doctrine of his master.

Tr. I, 137: See above, p. 300.

Tr. I, 171 (*a*): See above, p. 301.

Tr. I, 181: Abū Yūsuf holds an intermediate opinion between Ibn Abī Lailā and Abū Ḥanīfa; Abū Yūsuf mentions that this opinion was also related from 'Aṭā', but this is presumably spurious (above, p. 250).

Tr. IX, 1: Abū Yūsuf introduces a distinction which he attributes to Abū Ḥanīfa, and gives sound arguments; in the result, he takes an intermediate position between Auzā'ī and Abū Ḥanīfa.

Tr. IX, 2: Abū Yūsuf seems to introduce a slight modification and distinction into Abū Ḥanīfa's general doctrine, and gives sound reasoning.

Tr. IX, 19: Abū Yūsuf gives technical legal reasoning in favour of the Iraqian doctrine; this is an advance on Abū Ḥanīfa's purely practical argument which is inconclusive.

Tr. IX, 27: See below, p. 305.

Tr. IX, 40: Abū Yūsuf is more consistent than Abū Ḥanīfa.

Tr. IX, 41: Abū Yūsuf elaborates Abū Ḥanīfa's short reasoning competently and systematically.

Tr. IX, 42: Abū Yūsuf gives the same decision as Abū Ḥanīfa, but shifts the emphasis of the problem, so as to achieve a systematic progress.

Kharāj, 11: Abū Yūsuf refutes Abū Ḥanīfa's crude analogical reasoning.

Kharāj, 108: Abū Yūsuf anticipates in essentials Shāfi'ī's relevant distinction, as against Abū Ḥanīfa.

So far we have met with a number of cases in which Abū Yūsuf shows sound and competent reasoning, and other examples could be added, such as *Tr. IX*, 50, where Abū Yūsuf argues well on a point which Shāfi'ī recognizes as controversial. These are, however, partly offset by cases where Abū Yūsuf's legal thought appears weak and superficial.

Tr. I, 60 f.: An inconsistency, see above, p. 272; other cases of inconsistency have been referred to before.

Tr. IX, 4: A weak systematic argument, easily refuted by Shāfiʿī.

Tr. IX, 13: Abū Yūsuf gives no real argument, and only assumes that 'this is too clear and obvious for any scholar to doubt it'.

Tr. IX, 20: Instead of standing by Abū Ḥanīfa's competent technical reasoning, Abū Yūsuf allows himself to be drawn into a discussion on interpretation where his own arguments are rather irrelevant.

Tr. IX, 26: Abū Yūsuf tries to refute Auzāʿī, but can do so only from his own premisses and not from those of his opponent.

Tr. IX, 27: Abū Yūsuf gives a good reply to Auzāʿī, and elaborates points of detail in Abū Ḥanīfa's reasoning, without, however, going to the root of Abū Ḥanīfa's systematic thought; the same applies to the parallel in *Kharāj*, 109, and Abū Yūsuf seems more interested than Abū Ḥanīfa in legal abstractions.

Tr. IX, 39: Abū Yūsuf gives a weak systematic reason, which is obviously beside the point, in favour of Abū Ḥanīfa's doctrine.

A remarkable feature of Abū Yūsuf's doctrine is the frequency with which he changed his opinions, not always for the better. The following are only a few typical examples.

Tr. I, 43: See above, p. 299.

Tr. I, 99: See above, p. 304.

Tr. I, 127: See above, p. 278 f.

Tr. I, 190: Abū Yūsuf followed at first the opinion of Abū Ḥanīfa, later that of Ibn Abī Lailā (above, p. 295).

Tr. I, 196: Abū Yūsuf shared at first the opinion of Ibn Abī Lailā, then adopted the result of Abū Ḥanīfa's shrewd technical reasoning (above, p. 297 f.).

Tr. I, 222: Abū Yūsuf at first held the same opinion as Ibn Abī Lailā; later he adopted a solution which, compared with that of Abū Ḥanīfa, appears as a rough-and-ready expedient.

Ikh. 121: Abū Yūsuf adopted an opinion of the Hijazis for two months, then abandoned it again.

Kharāj, 126 f.: See above, p. 302.

On another change of opinion by Abū Yūsuf see above, p. 183.

Sometimes the contemporary sources state directly, and in other cases it is probable, that Abū Yūsuf's experience as a judge caused him to change his opinion.[1] This is to his credit, as also is his occasional expression of doubt.[2] But his frequent

[1] *Tr. I*, 82 (above, p. 273), 84, 99, 112, 139 (above, p. 112), 150 (above, p. 274), 203. See also §§ 107 and 110 (above, p. 300).

[2] *Tr. I*, 170, 211.

changes of opinion show some uncertainty and immaturity in his legal thought. On the whole, Abū Yūsuf's legal thought is of a lower standard than that of Abū Ḥanīfa. It is also less original and, as we have seen, thoroughly dependent on that of his master. Abū Yūsuf represents the beginning of the process by which the ancient school of the Kufian Iraqians was replaced by that of the followers of Abū Ḥanīfa.[1]

D. Shaibānī

Shaibānī depends even more on traditions than does Abū Yūsuf. This shows itself not only in changes of doctrine under the influence of traditions, but in his habit of duplicating his systematic reasoning by arguments taken from traditions,[2] in his introducing Medinese traditions and some of the corresponding doctrines, through his edition of Mālik's *Muwaṭṭa'*, into the Iraqian and Ḥanafī school, and in the habitual formula 'We follow this' by which he almost invariably rounds off his references to traditions from the Prophet and from other authorities, even when he does not, in fact, follow them.

Muw. Shaib. 133 and *Āthār Shaib.* 23: We find here the same kind of clumsy, primitive, and unconvincing reasoning as in Mālik (*Muw.* i. 245 and *Tr. III*, 27); the Iraqians do not need this reasoning and have full traditional authority, to which Shāfi'ī refers pointedly, for their doctrine; Shaibānī presumably took the Medinese reasoning over from Mālik.

Muw. Shaib. 298: Shaibānī takes over a tradition from Mālik (*Muw.* iv. 21) and puts his own systematic reasoning beside it. Shāfi'ī (*Tr. III*, 74) adopts Shaibānī's reasoning and finds a justification for it in the very wording of Mālik's tradition; this was originally meant to express the Medinese doctrine, but Shāfi'ī succeeds in turning it into an argument in favour of his own.

Muw. Shaib. 326 (cf. *Tr. III*, 13): Shaibānī, differing from his Iraqian predecessors, adopts traditions and their interpretation from Mālik (*Muw.* iii. 102); he modifies the interpretation in order to achieve greater systematic consistency, although this goes against their outward meaning; but this doctrine did not prevail in the Ḥanafī school.

Muw. Shaib. 406: Shaibānī uses the parable of the labourers of the eleventh hour, in the form of a tradition from the Prophet, as a

[1] See above, p. 6. See also *E.I.*², s.v.

[2] He refers to traditions and analogy in pointed juxtaposition; see above, p. 27.

loose and secondary argument in favour of an old Iraqian doctrine (*Āthār A. Y.* 94; *Muw. Shaib.* 45).

Tr. VIII, 5, 21: Shaibānī first gives arguments from traditions, then adds systematic reasoning.

After Abū Yūsuf's reaction from Abū Ḥanīfa's reasoning, Shaibānī frequently returns to Abū Ḥanīfa's doctrine.[1] He also introduces technical improvements into the doctrine of his predecessors.

Āthār Shaib. 22: Shaibānī gives good systematic reasoning which represents a marked progress over the doctrine as expressed in a Kufian tradition which Abū Ḥanīfa relates with the *isnād* Ḥammād—Ibrāhīm Nakhaʿī—Ibn Masʿūd (also in *Āthār A. Y.* 607). In *Muw. Shaib.* 244 Shaibānī attributes this reasoning to Masrūq, one of the Companions of Ibn Masʿūd; this is certainly not authentic.

Āthār Shaib. 61: Shaibānī adds reasoning of a more technically legal kind to that of the ancient Iraqians which was attributed to Ibrāhīm Nakhaʿī (above, p. 237). In the rest of the section, on a parallel case, Shaibānī disagrees with the doctrine of Abū Ḥanīfa—Ḥammād—Ibrāhīm because of the same technically legal reasoning, and shows himself systematically consistent.

Siyar, i. 244: Shaibānī takes up and elaborates Abū Ḥanīfa's competent reasoning which Abū Yūsuf had neglected (*Tr. IX*, 20).

Siyar, ii. 176: Shaibānī refutes Abū Ḥanīfa's crude analogical reasoning with an argument which is better than the argument of Abū Yūsuf (*Tr. IX*, 3 (*a*)).

Siyar, ii. 260: Shaibānī's doctrine shows a shift of emphasis compared with that of Abū Yūsuf; it is also more conciliatory (*Tr. IX*, 2).

Tr. VIII, 15: Shaibānī adds a systematic argument in favour of the Kufian doctrine (above, p. 281).

On the problem of *Tr. I*, 28, Shaibānī improves on Abū Ḥanīfa and anticipates Shāfiʿī (above, p. 284).

Shaibānī used arbitrary personal opinion (*ra'y*) to the extent usual in the ancient schools of law, and in particular in order to eliminate traditions which he did not accept.[2] But most of the reasoning in Shaibānī that appears under the name of *ra'y*, is in fact *qiyās*, that is strict analogy or systematic reasoning. This systematic reasoning is the feature most typical of Shai-

[1] e.g. *Tr. I*, 103 (above, p. 297), 107 and 110 (above, p. 300), 126 (above, p. 274). On the other hand, on the problems of *Tr. I*, 32 and 133, Shaibānī follows the doctrine of Abū Yūsuf, as against the opinion of Abū Ḥanīfa (Sarakhsī xxx. 140 f. and vii. 103 f.).

[2] See above, pp. 105, 112.

bānī's technical legal thought, and the following examples are intended to show its extent and character.

Muw. Shaib. 202, 236: Shaibānī gives no argument, but his statement of doctrine is more consistent and competent than that of Shāfi'ī who argues, somewhat unfairly, from a false premiss (*Tr. III*, 35).

Muw. Shaib. 244: Shaibānī anticipates Shāfi'ī in achieving full systematic consistency (*Tr. III*, 53).[1]

Muw. Shaib. 330: Shaibānī shows himself more consistent than Mālik who is bound by the 'living tradition' (*Muw.* iii. 104), and anticipates Shāfi'ī who gives the explicit systematic argument (*Tr. III*, 102).

Muw. Shaib. 331: Shaibānī gives strict systematic reasoning, anticipating Shāfi'ī (*Tr. III*, 95); but Abū Ḥanīfa's doctrine had been legally sound (above, p. 296).

Muw. Shaib. 357: Shaibānī anticipates Shāfi'ī's reasoning, based on the strict interpretation of traditions, in all details (*Tr. III*, 58).

Siyar, i. 35 f.: Shaibānī to a great extent anticipates Shāfi'ī (*Tr. IX*, 29).

Tr. VIII, 4: Shaibānī gives impressive systematic reasoning against the Medinese: 'Abū Ḥanīfa says: "If a minor and a major kill together with *'amd* [that is, intentionally],[2] the major has to pay half the weregeld from his own property, and the minor, that is to say his *'āqila*,[3] the other half." The Medinese say: "The major is killed [in retaliation], and the minor has to pay half the weregeld." Shaibānī says: How can he be killed when he has an associate in blood-guilt who is not liable to retaliation? If a man kills himself with the help of another, does the other undergo retaliation? Those who hold that opinion must draw this consequence. If someone cuts off the hand of another and his own hand is cut off in retaliation, and then a third party cuts off his foot and he dies from both wounds, is this third party to be killed, having associated himself in blood-guilt with Allah's [penal] law? If someone is mauled by a wild beast, and another inflicts a wound upon him intentionally, and he dies in consequence of both injuries, is this other to be killed, having associated himself with an agent who is not liable to retaliation or to the payment of a fraction of the weregeld? A further consequence would be that if a major and a minor commit a theft together, the major would have his hand cut off

[1] Ṭaḥāwī, quoted in *Comm. Muw. Shaib.*, attributes this doctrine already to Abū Yūsuf in his later opinion.

[2] The intent, *'amd*, is a condition for retaliation taking place.

[3] See above, p. 207.

[as a *ḥadd* punishment] and the minor would go scot-free. Another consequence would be that if two men together steal 1,000 dirham in which one of them has a share, the latter would go scot-free and the other would be liable to *ḥadd* punishment. If a major and a minor hold a sword and together inflict a blow from which a man dies, is this blow partly intentional, involving retaliation, and partly *khaṭa'* [that is accidental],[1] and if so, what part of it is *'amd* and what *khaṭa'*? If two men lift a sword and, acting together, inflict on one of them intentionally a blow from which he dies, does this involve retaliation? There is no retaliation here if the blood-guilt is associated with another agent not liable to retaliation; the [taking of] life cannot be split up. If someone inflicts a *mūḍiḥa* wound accidentally and then inflicts another intentionally and the victim dies from these injuries, the consequence of that opinion would be that the *'āqila* has to pay half the weregeld for the accidental wound and [the culprit] is killed [by retaliation] for the intentional wounding, so that one man would become liable, [directly or through his *'āqila*,] for taking one life to a fine of half the weregeld and to the death penalty. A further consequence would be that if one has the right to retaliation for a *mūḍiḥa* wound and in carrying it out transgresses intentionally and the other dies in consequence of this, he will have to be killed for his transgression. 'Abbād b. 'Awwām—Hishām b. Ḥassān—Ḥasan Baṣrī: if several people, among them an idiot, kill a man intentionally, this is a case for weregeld. 'Abbād b. 'Awwām—'Umar b. 'Āmir—Ibrāhīm Nakha'ī: if an element of *khaṭa'* enters the *'amd*, it is a case for weregeld.' It is true that Shāfi'ī succeeds in disposing of most of Shaibānī's systematic arguments.

Tr. VIII, 6: Shaibānī gives a respectable amount of systematic reasoning which he calls *qiyās* and *ma'qūl*;[2] he tries, as Shāfi'ī was to do after him, to rationalize a traditional ruling which defies rationalizing, and gets involved in difficulties.

Tr. VIII, 8: Shaibānī gives good systematic argument, besides literal interpretation of traditions from the Prophet; he fully anticipates the reasoning of Shāfi'ī who agrees.

Tr. VIII, 11: Shaibānī gives excellent systematic reasoning, fully as good as that of Shāfi'ī; he continues Abū Yūsuf's somewhat acrimonious polemics against the Medinese and says: 'One ought to be consistent and not arbitrary, expecting people to agree with whatever one says.'

[1] *Khaṭa'*, originally 'error' or 'mistake', is used as the opposite of *'amd*. The minor cannot have a legally valid intent; therefore his voluntary act which at the beginning of the paragraph, in the words of Abū Ḥanīfa, has been loosely subsumed under *'amd*, is called here, more strictly, *khaṭa'*.

[2] Cf. above, p. 111.

Tr. VIII, 12: Shaibānī gives good systematic reasoning, though that of Shāfi'ī is more thorough; he reduces the Medinese doctrine *ad absurdum*.

Tr. VIII, 14: Shaibānī gives good systematic reasoning against the Medinese and uses an uncontroversial doctrine in order to decide a controversial point.

Tr. VIII, 16: Shaibānī gives consistent systematic reasoning.

Tr. VIII, 19: Shaibānī, by systematic reasoning, reduces the Medinese opinion *ad absurdum*, but some of the examples he adduces are surprisingly weak.

Tr. VIII, 20: Shaibānī's reasoning is inconclusive because his Medinese opponents do not share his doctrine on a parallel question which he adduces as an argument.

Tr. VIII, 21: Shāfi'ī gives systematic reasoning against the Medinese, starting from doctrines held in common.

Ikh. 186 ff., 191 ff.: Shaibānī's reasoning is much less stringent and systematic than that of Shāfi'ī, although the result is the same.

On the problem of *Tr. I*, 44, Sarakhsī reports a masterly argument of Shaibānī which is easily superior even to Shāfi'ī's reasoning (above, p. 271).

On the problem of *Tr. I*, 48, Shaibānī applies purely formal reasoning in which he is followed by Shāfi'ī; but this doctrine completely disregards the stability of real property (above, p. 271 f.).

Shaibānī's technical legal thought is by far superior to that of his predecessors in general and to that of Abū Yūsuf in particular; it is the most perfect of its kind that was to be achieved before Shāfi'ī. Shaibānī was the great systematizer of the Kufian Iraqian doctrine. He was also a prolific writer, and his voluminous works, which he put under the aegis of his master Abū Ḥanīfa,[1] became the rallying-point of the Ḥanafī school which emerged from the ancient Kufian Iraqian school.

[1] See above, p. 238.

CHAPTER 5

MĀLIK'S REASONING

THE date of Mālik's death lies almost exactly half-way between the dates of the deaths of Abū Yūsuf and of Shaibānī, but Mālik's technical legal thought is considerably less developed than that of his Iraqian contemporaries.[1] Mālik's reasoning, on the whole, is comparable to that of Auzāʿī,[2] particularly in the dependence of both on the practice, the 'living tradition', the consensus of the scholars, rather than on systematic thought. The accepted doctrine of the Medinese school itself, of course, is to a great extent founded on individual reasoning (*ra'y*), as we have seen in the first part of this book.[3] In combining extensive use of *ra'y* with dependence on the 'living tradition', Mālik seems typical of the Medinese. We shall confine ourselves in this chapter to instances of technical legal thought which can with some certainty be considered as the personal effort of Mālik himself.

Mālik's systematic reasoning appears often as the secondary, retrospective justification of the 'living tradition' which he accepts. A typical example is *Muw.* iii. 182 ff. where Mālik upholds the Medinese doctrine that evidence given by one witness and confirmed by the oath of the plaintiff constitutes legal proof.[4] Mālik establishes the *sunna* or 'living tradition' in favour of this doctrine, adds systematic reasoning because 'one wishes to understand', and concludes: 'the *sunna* is proof enough, but one also wants to know the reason, and this is it.'[5] Mālik's reasoning in detail is as follows: he first establishes that this provision applies only to lawsuits concerning property, thereby obviating possible objections; he points out other instances of apparent lack of consistency in the law of evidence; he shows that the Koranic passage (Sura ii. 282) which prescribes two male witnesses is not comprehensive; the oath of the

[1] See also above, p. 276.

[2] Compare, e.g., *Mud.* iii. 24 (for Mālik) with *Tr. IX*, 21 (for Auzāʿī), where the reasonings of both are identical.

[3] Above, pp. 113 ff.

[4] On the history of this problem, see above, pp. 167 ff.

[5] See above, p. 62.

defendant, for instance, and the refusal of the plaintiff to take the oath in support of his claim, are generally recognized as evidence although they are not mentioned in the Koran. All this anticipates the essential part of Shāfiʿī's systematic argument in *Ikh.* 345 ff.

Another significant example occurs in *Muw.* iii. 102 where Mālik does his best to justify by systematic parallels a highly irregular kind of barter, the so-called 'sale of *ʿarāyā*'. This transaction was obviously customary in ancient Arabia, but seems to have been already obsolete in the time of Mālik, because there existed at least two divergent opinions on its nature.[1] Not content with relying on the 'living tradition' or on formal traditions from the Prophet which he quoted, Mālik adduced some weak systematic parallels.[2] It is not surprising that Mālik did not succeed in systematizing it; Shāfiʿī, who blamed him for his inconsistency, was no more successful and was forced to fall back on a tradition.

The same feature appears in a long quotation from Mālik in *Mud.* iv. 54, on the question whether a man married to a free woman may conclude an additional marriage to a slave woman. Mālik defers to the opinion of earlier scholars, such as Ibn Musaiyib and others, and to traditions from Companions of the Prophet, against his own judgment which he had based on Koran iv. 25. Mālik had changed his opinion, and systematic reasoning is noticeable both in the earlier and in the later stage. He finds arguments in favour both of his earlier and of his later doctrine in the Koran, and even justifies his later decision against the upholders of his former one by a very weak and far-fetched interpretation of the same Koranic passage. The whole shows Mālik's tendency to consistent systematic reasoning secondary to and checked by his dependence on the 'living tradition'.

In the majority of cases, we find Mālik's reasoning inspired by material considerations, by practical expediency, and by the tendency to Islamicize.

Muw. i. 108: there exist two seemingly contradictory traditions; the logical distinction between the cases envisaged by both, as

[1] Mālik's own interpretation is given in *Muw. Shaib.* 327, another interpretation in *Ikh.* 327; see further Zurqānī and *Comm. Muw. Shaib.*

[2] In *Mud.* x. 91, Mālik added a material, moral consideration.

applied by Shāfiʿī (*Tr. III*, 30), is unknown to Mālik; in *Muw.*, Mālik makes an arbitrary choice between the traditions, following the practice; in *Mud.* i. 49, he blends the considerations underlying both traditions in his reasoning.

Muw. ii. 68 (and the implications of *Mud.* ii. 108): Mālik's doctrine is practical common-sense, and far less inconsistent than Shāfiʿī's strict reasoning (*Tr. III*, 52) makes it appear; Mālik himself gives sound systematic reasoning which goes a long way towards meeting Shāfiʿī's objections, and he counters a possible objection in detail.

Muw. ii. 196 and *Tr. III*, 36: The motive of Mālik's reasoning is material and practical, as opposed to that of Shāfiʿī which is formal and technical.

Muw. iii. 3 and *Ikh.* 300: Both Mālik and Shāfiʿī try to harmonize two seemingly contradictory groups of traditions and to find a legal criterion which would enable them to admit both; whereas Mālik's reasoning is superficially practical and expedient, Shāfiʿī's is formal and technical; but the way in which Mālik expresses it obviates most of Shāfiʿī's criticisms.

Muw. iii. 129: On the details of the doctrine on the re-selling of objects other than food, before taking possession[1], Mālik's reasoning is practical, concerned with the elimination of cases which seem to fall directly under the prohibition of usury, and not with pursuing this prohibition to its last systematic consequences.

Mud. iii. 118: Mālik tries to justify the inconsistent Medinese practice by a far-fetched interpretation of Koranic passages; the formalism of his reasoning recalls that of Ibn Abī Lailā (above, p. 292).

Mud. v. 2: On the problem of the presumption of intercourse if husband and wife have been left together in private, Mālik adopts the practical and rough-and-ready distinction current in Medina,[2] and Shāfiʿī blames him for his technical inconsistency (*Tr. III*, 75); Mālik indeed refers to a somewhat similar case, but this again is not strictly parallel, as Shāfiʿī points out.

Mud. v. 55: Mālik subjects a declaration to a careful philological interpretation, worthy of Shāfiʿī at his best (but Shāfiʿī ignores it: *Tr. III*, 140); in *Mud.* v. 58, Mālik adds a practical and material consideration, typical of the early period but very commendable, in favour of his doctrine; this argument is older than Mālik himself because he calls the same distinction in a parallel case 'the best that I have heard' (*Muw.* iii. 37).

This primitive reasoning leads Mālik sometimes into in-

[1] See above, p. 108. [2] See above, p. 193 f.

consistencies, as in *Muw.* ii. 299 where he gives partial expression to a religious scruple,[1] and in *Muw.* iii. 110 where he makes an inconsistent concession to the practice; Mālik states in both cases that this is his personal opinion (*ra'y*).[2] In many cases, however, Mālik's *ra'y* is nothing but strict analogy and broader systematic reasoning.[3] There are a fair number of cases where Mālik's technical legal thought shows itself sound and consistent, to a higher degree than Shāfi'ī's sustained polemics in *Tr. III* would lead one to expect.

Muw. ii. 68: See above, p. 313.

Muw. iii. 9: Mālik, in adopting the analogical reasoning of the Iraqians, starts consistently from his own, materially different, premiss (above, p. 108).

Muw. iii. 183 and *Tr. III*, 148 (p. 248): Mālik gives a strictly consistent systematic argument, basing himself, with regard to a point of detail, on the minimum of doctrine common to him and to his opponents; Shāfi'ī therefore charges him with ascribing to his opponents an opinion which they do not hold; Rabī' suggests that Mālik may have slipped, only to attract Shāfi'ī's indignant sarcasm; but Ibn 'Abdalbarr (quoted in Zurqānī, iii. 184) explains it correctly as an argument *a potiori* of Mālik.

Mud. i. 5: Mālik and Rabī' (*Tr. III*, 31) in their arguments both take the necessities of practice into account, but Mālik's argument is more consistent than that of Rabī' and less open to Shāfi'ī's objections.

On the whole, however, Mālik is distinguished not by the originality of his legal thought, but by his success in steering a middle course through the opinions of the Medinese, an average quality which made him the obvious choice for the head of the Mālikī school into which the ancient school of Medina developed.[4]

[1] See above, p. 67.

[2] See further above, p. 118 f.

[3] See above, pp. 115, 117.

[4] The average legal thought of Mālik's Medinese contemporaries should be judged by Ibn Qāsim (in *Mud.*, *passim*) rather than by Rabī' (in *Tr. III*). Whenever Rabī' gives reasoning of his own, he almost invariably shows himself incompetent.

CHAPTER 6

SHĀFIʿĪ'S REASONING

WE have seen in the first part of this book that Shāfiʿī's legal theory, and therefore also his positive legal doctrine, represent a ruthless systematic innovation, based on formal traditions from the Prophet as against the 'living tradition' of the ancient schools of law. Shāfiʿī's legal theory is much more logical and formally consistent than that of his predecessors whom he blames continually for what appears to him as a mass of inconsistencies. Explicit legal reasoning occupies a much more prominent place in Shāfiʿī's doctrine than in that of any of the earlier lawyers, even if we take differences of style and of literary form into account.[1]

The great progress in legal thought achieved by Shāfiʿī over his predecessors and contemporaries has become clear from many passages discussed in the preceding chapters; the following examples are intended to complete the picture, and also to illustrate those relatively few cases in which Shāfiʿī merely reproduces the thought of others, or those, still more exceptional, where he represents a regress in reasoning.

Tr. I, 2: Shāfiʿī shows himself strictly consistent and rejects an allowance for *vis maior* which Abū Yūsuf had made (above, p. 112); one of the two possible consistent opinions leads to a systematic difficulty, Shāfiʿī therefore eliminates it and chooses the other.

Tr. I, 32, 62, 71, 194, 237: Shāfiʿī introduces important distinctions into the discussion for the first time.

Tr. I, 44: An argument which Sarakhsī (v. 78) attributes to Shaibānī is superior to Shāfiʿī's reasoning (above, p. 271).

Tr. I, 75: Shāfiʿī has nothing substantial to add to Ibn Abī Lailā's argument, but deepens the reasoning appreciably.

Tr. I, 78, 124, 147, 152, 212, 215, 222, 226: Shāfiʿī arrives at full systematic consistency for the first time.

Tr. I, 97: Shāfiʿī agrees essentially with Abū Ḥanīfa, but introduces a relevant refinement of procedure.

Tr. I, 107=110: Shāfiʿī gives sound systematic reasoning against Ibn Abī Lailā and agrees himself, by implication, with Abū Ḥanīfa; but his reasoning is more penetrating than that of Abū Ḥanīfa.

[1] Cf. Bergsträsser's remark in *Islam*, xiv. 76.

Tr. I, 123: Shāfi'ī shows judicious appreciation of broader systematic consistency; he returns to the doctrine of Ibn Abī Lailā, but with better reasons, and gives two good parallels.

Tr. II, 11 (*b*): Shāfi'ī reproduces almost literally Shaibānī's argument from *Āthār Shaib*. 69.

Tr. III, 53: Shāfi'ī's doctrine, but not his argument, is anticipated by Shaibānī in *Muw. Shaib.* 244.

Tr. III, 57: Shāfi'ī's reasoning is anticipated in all its details by Shaibānī in *Muw. Shaib.* 357.

Tr. III, 74: See above, p. 306.

Tr. III, 102: Shāfi'ī is anticipated by Shaibānī in *Muw. Shaib.* 330 (above, p. 308).

Tr. VIII, 4: It is evident from Shaibānī's and Shāfi'ī's arguments that both the Kufians and the Medinese hold that the minor and the idiot are incapable of criminal intent (*'amd*), and their voluntary unlawful acts are therefore technically accidental (*khaṭa'*);[1] Mālik (*Mud.* xvi. 199) states in fact that the *'amd* and the *khaṭa'*, the [seemingly] intentional and unintentional acts, of the minor and the idiot are [technically] all *khaṭa'*. Compared with this sound common ancient doctrine, Shāfi'ī's distinction of real *'amd* and *khaṭa'* in the acts of the minor cannot, from the premisses of Muhammadan law, be considered an improvement; that this distinction is in fact arbitrary appears from *Mud.* xvi. 203 where Ibn Qāsim, presumably in order to escape from Shaibānī's systematic arguments, postulates a *khaṭa'* proper in the minor, but calls this doctrine his *ra'y* and *istiḥsān*.

Tr. VIII, 11: Shāfi'ī expresses his thought clumsily; Shaibānī is much clearer.

Tr. VIII, 12: Shāfi'ī's systematic reasoning is more thorough than Shaibānī's, but Shāfi'ī expresses it clumsily.

Tr. VIII, 14, 16: Shāfi'ī adopts and elaborates part of Shaibānī's systematic arguments against the Medinese, although in each case he diverges from both ancient schools.

Tr. VIII, 18: Shāfi'ī has nothing new to add to the Iraqian doctrine as ascribed to Ibrāhīm Nakha'ī and modified by Shaibānī (*Āthār Shaib.* 84), apart from a charge of inconsistency in the use of traditions, directed against Shaibānī.

Tr. VIII, 19: Shāfi'ī gives the same kind of reasoning as Shaibānī, but improves it considerably by good additional arguments; on another issue he reduces Shaibānī, and by implication Mālik, *ad absurdum*.

[1] See above, p. 308 f.

Tr. VIII, 20: Shāfi'ī's systematic reasoning is superior to that of Shaibānī.

Tr. IX, 1: Shāfi'ī points out the inconsistent and unsatisfactory character of Abū Yūsuf's doctrine; his criticisms are not always well-founded, and he too has to wind his way rather arbitrarily through a maze of conflicting traditions; but on the whole his reasoning is sound and superior to that of Abū Yūsuf.

Tr. IX, 18: Shāfi'ī shows disciplined and consistent systematic reasoning, against the solutions of his predecessors which are ruled by expediency and practical considerations. In §§ 16 and 17, too, Shāfi'ī's opinions are systematically more consistent than those of his predecessors.

Tr. IX, 20: Shāfi'ī merely borrows and repeats the reasoning of Abū Ḥanīfa (loc. cit. and Ṭabarī, 34) and Shaibānī (*Siyar*, i. 244).

Tr. IX, 23: Shāfi'ī introduces a broader systematic aspect.

Tr. IX, 26: Shāfi'ī keeps aloof both from Auzā'ī and from Abū Yūsuf, and his legal thought is superior, particularly to that of Auzā'ī.

Tr. IX, 27: Shāfi'ī is systematic and consistent and cuts across the former division of doctrines; he is less technically legal than Abū Ḥanīfa, but combines Islamicizing and systematizing; his reasoning is superior to that of his predecessors, particularly to that of Auzā'ī.

Tr. IX, 28: Shāfi'ī is anticipated partly by Mālik (Ṭabarī, 82) and to a greater extent by Shaibānī (*Siyar*, i. 35); see further below, p. 319.

Tr. IX, 39: Shāfi'ī gives better systematic reasoning than Abū Yūsuf, but exaggerates on a detail. In § 45 Shāfi'ī turns the argument, which Abū Yūsuf uses against Auzā'ī, against Abū Yūsuf himself, but neither reasoning is very convincing.

Tr. IX, 48: Compared with the ancient Iraqians (cf. Sarakhsī, x. 66), Shāfi'ī shows less of technically legal reasoning and more of Islamicizing combined with systematizing.

When Shāfi'ī wrote, the process of Islamicizing the law, of impregnating it with religious and ethical ideas, a process which we have discussed in an earlier chapter,[1] had been essentially completed. We therefore find Shāfi'ī hardly ever influenced in his conscious legal thought by material considerations of a religious and ethical kind, which played an important role in the doctrines of Auzā'ī, Ibn Abī Lailā, Abū Ḥanīfa, and Mālik.[2] We also find him more consistent than his predecessors in

[1] Above, pp. 283 ff. [2] See above, pp. 288 f., 291 f., 295, 312 f.

separating the moral and the legal aspects, whenever both arise with regard to the same problem.[1] On the other hand, Shāfiʿī's fundamental dependence on formal traditions from the Prophet implies a different formal way of Islamicizing the legal doctrine. We have seen that Shāfiʿī in his legal theory distinguishes sharply between the argument taken from traditions and the result of systematic thought.[2] In his actual reasoning, however, both aspects are closely interwoven, Shāfiʿī shows himself tradition-bound and systematic at the same time, and we may consider this new synthesis typical of his legal thought. We have already noticed cases in which Shāfiʿī's reasoning is Islamicizing, and at the same time systematizing rather than technically legal, and the following examples will give additional evidence of the intimate connexion of the two aspects.

Tr. I, 15: In Shāfiʿī's reasoning traditional and systematic considerations become blended for the first time; he makes an exception from a general rule on account of the *sunna* of the Prophet in favour of the validity of a stipulated manumission, and at the same time establishes systematically the exceptional character of manumission itself.

Tr. I, 133: Shāfiʿī's *qiyās* is better than that of Abū Yūsuf, but essentially Shāfiʿī's doctrine is based on traditions as appears from *Ikh.* 368 ff., particularly 383 ff.

Tr. I, 167: See above, p. 285.

Tr. I, 193: Shāfiʿī combines an argument drawn from a tradition with systematic reasoning.

Tr. III, 48: Shāfiʿī interprets a tradition from the Prophet strictly and consistently, and at the same time gives a general systematic argument and excellent technical reasoning against a Medinese concession to commercial practice.

Tr. VI, 266: Shāfiʿī gives technical legal reasons, besides the argument drawn from consensus, on several problems; see also below, p. 324.

Tr. IX, 19: Shāfiʿī is the first to base his doctrine on traditions; he shows the weak point in Abū Yūsuf's reasoning and introduces a distinction; he creates a consistent theoretical structure for his tradition-bound doctrine, without paying regard to the inconclusive material considerations and to the practice on which Abū Ḥanīfa and Abū Yūsuf on one side, and Auzāʿī on the other, were still dependent.

[1] See above, pp. 125, 178, 284 (on *Tr. I*, 28), 286 (on *Tr. I*, 201).
[2] See above, pp. 122 f., 135 f.

Tr. IX, 21: Shāfi'ī shows the weak point in Abū Yūsuf's argument and combines dependence on traditions with good systematic reasoning, introducing a distinction between two separate legal aspects; he himself takes a moderate, intermediate line between Auzā'ī on one side, and Abū Ḥanīfa and Abū Yūsuf on the other.

Tr. IX, 22: Shāfi'ī applies systematic reasoning to the prima-facie meaning of traditions; his argument is less formal and less technically legal than that of Abū Yūsuf; in the reasoning of Abu Yūsuf the traditional and the systematic elements were still felt to be separate and opposed to each other, but in Shāfi'ī's thought they are intimately combined.

Tr. IX, 28: Although partly anticipated by his predecessors (above, p. 317), Shāfi'ī develops a new, systematic and at the same time tradition-bound doctrine, introducing a legal distinction for the first time; he is more consistent than either the Medinese or the Iraqians, but does not himself achieve full systematic consistency either, because he remains partly influenced by a tradition from Abū Bakr;[1] the many references to the problem in Shāfi'ī's writings (cf. *Tr. III*, 65 and *Umm*, iv. 66, 161 f., 174 ff., 199) show that he must have considered this decision important.

Tr. IX, 33: See above, p. 286.

Ikh. 182 ff.: Common sense, though not very stringent reasoning by which Shāfi'ī, with considerable doubt, tries to reconcile a harmonizing interpretation of traditions with systematic tidiness.

Ikh. 219 f.: Shāfi'ī would prefer one of two contradictory traditions because it agrees with systematic analogy and with the generally held opinion, provided it were well authenticated;[2] as it is not, he is obliged to follow the well-attested tradition to the contrary, and in order to make it more acceptable he gives some systematic reasoning, though vague and unconvincing, in its favour.

Ikh. 331: Shāfi'ī does not succeed in harmonizing and rationalizing the contradictory traditions completely.

Ikh. 364: Shāfi'ī combines deference to the *sunna* of the Prophet with systematic reasoning.

Ris. 76: Shāfi'ī tries to rationalize irrational traditions but has to acknowledge that systematic reasoning sometimes breaks down over systematically irregular traditions; this shows how strong his urge to systematize is.

Umm, iv. 170: Shāfi'ī's systematic reasoning is closely interwoven with his dependence on the *sunna* as expressed in traditions from the Prophet.

[1] See above, p. 19 f., on Shāfi'ī's doctrine regarding conflicts between analogy and traditions from Companions.

[2] Cf. above, p. 14, n. 1.

Shāfi'ī's systematic reasoning has its limitations. We have noticed that it breaks down occasionally over irrational traditions which cannot be systematized and which Shāfi'ī feels himself nevertheless bound to follow. In other cases we find that the very institutions which Shāfi'ī discusses, defy rationalizing.

Tr. I, 88: Shāfi'ī, in an excellently reasoned argument, charges Abū Ḥanīfa and Abū Yūsuf with inconsistency and arbitrariness; but within the framework of Muhammadan law the doctrine of Abū Ḥanīfa and his followers on the acts of a person during his mortal illness is consistent enough, and the argument in its favour given by Sarakhsī, xviii. 26 f., is impressive; the whole idea is inconsistent in itself, and this detracts from Shāfi'ī's argument.

Tr. III, 44: Shāfi'ī shows himself strictly consistent and definitely superior to Ibn Qāsim (*Mud.* iv. 147); he only overlooks the fact that a choice is often given in Muhammadan law in comparable circumstances without the enforcement of the logical alternative which he presses home ruthlessly; his systematic reasoning is too uncompromising for the legal material as he found it.

Tr. VIII, 3: Shāfi'ī is more consistent than the Medinese, but shows himself sophistical and hair-splitting in his argument against Shaibānī; his urge towards systematic consistency breaks down over the irrational character of the traditional doctrine.

Tr. VIII, 6: See below, p. 324.

Ikh. 44: Shāfi'ī draws a specious parallel between the fact that some fornicators are not flogged [but lapidated], and the fact that some thieves do not have their hands cut off [if they steal less than the minimum value which makes the *ḥadd* punishment applicable]; his systematic reasoning breaks down.

Ikh. 356: Shāfi'ī is hard put to it to invalidate a serious systematic objection of his Iraqian opponent; he tries to rationalize the irrational.

Apart from these natural limitations of Shāfi'ī's systematic reasoning by the material to which he was bound, it is rare to find him systematically inconsistent or reasoning loosely. We have seen that he recognized, in the final stage of his doctrine, only analogy and strict systematic reasoning, to the exclusion of *ra'y* and *istiḥsān*, and regarded this even as a religious duty.[1] It is exceptional for a material consideration to interfere with Shāfi'ī's consistent legal thought.[2] It took him time, of course,

[1] See above, pp. 120 ff.

[2] e.g. in *Umm*, iv. 184, containing Shāfi'ī's own decision on the problem dis-

to realize the full implications of his principles[1] and to work out all consequences of his doctrine,[2] and there remain imperfections where he falls short of his own theoretical requirements.[3]

More serious are the faults in Shāfiʿī's reasoning which come from his polemical attitude towards the ancient schools of law, an attitude which in the case of the Medinese is mitigated by his sentimental attachment to them, but in the case of the Iraqians is allowed full scope.[4] Shāfiʿī's eagerness to prove his new legal theory and the new legal doctrine based on it as the only legitimate interpretation of Muhammadan religious law, causes him to make unjustified assumptions, to argue arbitrarily and illogically, and to misrepresent and exaggerate the opinions of his opponents.[5] A relatively harmless manifestation of this tendency is Shāfiʿī's debating device of representing his theoretical innovations as implicitly shared by his opponents, and then blaming them for not applying their own alleged principles.[6] But beyond this, there are numerous cases in which Shāfiʿī's lack of objectivity vitiates his arguments, and of which the following list contains only a few typical examples.

Tr. I, 109: Shāfiʿī's systematic reasoning is consistent and ingenious enough, but he fails to appreciate the point of the argument of the Iraqians.

Tr. II, passim: Shāfiʿī tries artificially to find contradictions between the Iraqian doctrine and the Iraqian traditional authorities ʿAlī and Ibn Masʿūd; he often misrepresents the Iraqian doctrine, for instance in § 9 (*f*), cf. *Āthār Shaib.* 105; in § 11 (*k*), cf. *Muw. Shaib.* 385; in § 19 (*k*), cf. *Āthār Shaib.* 28 ff.; in § 19 (*l*), cf. *Āthār Shaib.* 33.

Tr. III: Shāfiʿī often misrepresents the Medinese doctrine, for instance in § 35, cf. *Muw.* ii. 185; in § 40, cf. *Muw.* ii. 154; in § 52, cf. *Muw.* ii. 68; in § 56, cf. *Muw.* iii. 89; in § 82, cf. *Muw.* iii. 56; in § 86, cf. *Muw.* ii. 212; in § 103, cf. *Muw.* ii. 243; in § 113, cf. *Muw.* i. 75; in § 117, cf. *Mud.* i. 172; in § 118, cf. *Muw.* i. 269; in § 125, cf. *Muw.* i. 126, 197; in § 127, cf. *Mud.* i. 74; in § 131, cf. *Muw.* ii. 230; in § 134, cf. *Muw.* ii. 171.

cussed in *Tr. IX*, 15, where Shāfiʿī makes a concession to the practice in the style of Auzāʿī, though he is sounder than his predecessor.

[1] See above, pp. 20 f., 79 f., 88 ff., 120 ff.

[2] See above, pp. 125 f., 281 f.

[3] See above, pp. 11 f., 15, 18, 38.

[4] See above, p. 9 f.

[5] But Shāfiʿī himself says disarmingly in *Tr. IV*, 256: 'There is no one in the world who judges objectively.'

[6] See above, pp. 11, 52, 87.

Tr. III, 65: Shāfiʿī fails to understand the Medinese method of arguing; both parties talk at cross-purposes.

Tr. III, 98: Shāfiʿī gives strict systematic reasoning but does not meet the point of Mālik's argument; he seems wilfully ignorant of Mālik's reasoning as implied by *Muw.* iii. 37, which is sound and consistent as far as it goes.

Tr. III, 111: Shāfiʿī uses a specious argument which would apply equally to his own doctrine; he seems unwilling to understand the idea of 'recommended' (cf. *Mud.* ii. 159) which, though not expressed in a fixed terminology, was not unknown in his time.[1]

Tr. III, 148 (p. 248): See above, p. 314.

Tr. III, 148 (p. 249): Shāfiʿī, without regard for the context, treats a number of examples given by Mālik (*Muw.* i. 49) as if it were an exhaustive list.

Tr. VIII, 1: Shāfiʿī draws irrelevancies into his otherwise sound argument against Shaibānī.

Tr. VIII, 4: Shāfiʿī succeeds in disposing of most of Shaibānī's systematic arguments,[2] but his own arguments against Shaibānī are mostly sophistical and unconvincing, and some are mutually exclusive; Shāfiʿī's opinion represents a technical regress from the common ancient doctrine.[3]

Tr. VIII, 13: See below, p. 324.

Tr. IX, 2: Shāfiʿī exaggerates in drawing unjustified conclusions from Abū Yūsuf's doctrine.

Tr. IX, 15: Shāfiʿī shows himself prejudiced against Abū Yūsuf, and does not succeed in defending Auzāʿī which he declares to be his object; his own doctrine (*Umm*, iv. 184) agrees in the essentials and in many details with that of Abū Ḥanīfa and Abū Yūsuf; even Shāfiʿī does not arrive at complete consistency.

Tr. IX, 16: Shāfiʿī shows himself prejudiced against the Iraqian doctrine which agrees more naturally than his own with an historical tradition from the Prophet; he has to explain away the resulting difficulty in an artificial manner (*Umm*, iv. 184).

Ikh. 278 ff.: See below, p. 325.

Ikh. 329 f.: Shāfiʿī uses two mutually exclusive arguments as part of the same reasoning against the same Iraqian opponent.

Ikh. 337: Shāfiʿī tries to minimize the correct statement of his Iraqian opponent that a tradition is not followed by the scholars in Iraq and Hijaz, by asking: 'What of the other muftis in the several countries whose opinions you do not know:[4] may I presume, holding the best possible opinion of them, that they agree with the tradition

[1] See above, p. 134 f. [2] See above, p. 308 f. [3] See above, p. 316.
[4] Shāfiʿī does not know them either.

from the Prophet?' It is easy to see how helpless the opponents must have been when faced by Shāfi'ī's insidious arguments and unwarranted assumptions.

Most of the faults in Shāfi'ī's reasoning can be traced to this particular cause, or to the main thesis of his new legal theory, that is to say, to his dependence on traditions from the Prophet. This dependence which makes it impossible for Shāfi'ī to reject straightforwardly any tradition from the Prophet without the authority of another tradition from the Prophet to the contrary, and this only under strict safeguards,[1] is responsible for many bad arguments and arbitrary interpretations. Here again, I can give only a few examples which lend themselves to short comment.

Tr. III, 7: The distinction by which Shāfi'ī seeks to harmonize between two traditions goes directly against their wording; Shāfi'ī finds his distinction confirmed by the relative chronology of the two traditions, and he rules out repeal.

Tr. III, 16: Shāfi'ī draws an unwarranted conclusion from the text of a tradition, and even claims it as its obvious meaning; he has no reply to the arguments of the opponents; his unwarranted conclusion corresponds in fact to the doctrine of traditions from Companions (*Mud.* xiii. 48).

Tr. IX, 44: Shāfi'ī interprets a tradition arbitrarily, so as to make it relevant to his problem.

Ris. 33: Shāfi'ī reasons arbitrarily and unconvincingly in favour of his theory that the *sunna* never contradicts but only explains the Koran.[2]

Ikh.: A treatise of late composition but containing early passages; it has numerous examples of faulty reasoning which can be attributed to the various causes discussed so far. On pp. 166 ff., in an early passage, Shāfi'ī argues in the style of the ancient schools, acts against his own principles, and minimizes traditions that go against his doctrine in a very prejudiced and arbitrary manner; he can adduce no tradition from the Prophet in favour of his own doctrine, and gives only far-fetched conclusions; the context shows that he chose his doctrine because of the systematic difficulties of the opposite opinion, and that his technical legal thought caused him to interpret traditions arbitrarily. On pp. 244 ff., in another early passage in which Shāfi'ī uses the old idea of consensus,[3] his interpretation of traditions is equally arbitrary and unconvincing, and at variance with his own methodical requirements; in this case it is a major

[1] See above, p. 13 ff. [2] See above, p. 15 f.. [3] See above, p. 93.

point of penal law in which Shāfiʿī obviously did not wish to diverge from the majority. On p. 300, where Shāfiʿī criticizes Mālik (above, p. 313), he combines superior systematic reasoning with unwarranted and unnecessary assumptions.

Typical features of Shāfiʿī's thought are sound philological distinctions and linguistic arguments.[1]

The limitations and faults of Shāfiʿī's reasoning cannot detract from the unprecedentedly high quality of his technical legal thought which stands out beyond doubt as the highest individual achievement in Muhammadan jurisprudence. In order to convey an adequate picture of the extent and character of this achievement, I shall give a list, which could easily be extended, of passages in which Shāfiʿī's thought appears particularly brilliant, and illustrate it by the translation in full of a few selected examples.

Tr. I, 129, 138, 150, 184, 195 (cf. Sarakhsī, xxvii. 28), 196, 210, 215 (at the end of 216), 234, 245, 247, 253.

Tr. III, 31, 34, 52, 89, 141, 142, 143.

Tr. VI, 266: A beautiful piece of systematic reasoning on the interplay of religious and legal valuation.

Tr. VII, 273: Two impressive pieces of systematic reasoning in favour of *qiyās* as against *istiḥsān*.[2]

Tr. VIII, 6: Masterly systematic reasoning; already in this early treatise Shāfiʿī claims to be more consistent in his systematic thought (*qiyās*) than Shaibānī; in fact, both try to rationalize a traditional ruling which defies rationalizing.

Tr. VIII, 13: Excellent systematic arguments against the Iraqians, but combined with a cheap debating device at the end; compare the later parallel passage *Ikh.* 389 ff. (see below).

Tr. IX, 5. 25, 40.

Umm, iv. 170 ff.: This section contains at the end sound reasoning on broader systematic issues and parallels.

Umm, vii. 34: Although Shāfiʿī merely follows the Medinese doctrine (*Muw.* iii. 183), his technical legal thought is of a high standard.

Umm, vii. 394 (and, more shortly, ibid. 405): Excellently reasoned

[1] *Tr. III*, 12, 36 (above, p. 144), 91, 141; *Tr. VIII*, 20; *Tr. IX*, 3 (anticipated by Mālik), 25 (better than Abū Yūsuf); *Ikh.* 93 (a linguistic basis for a systematic argument, not necessarily inherent in the problem; Ṭaḥāwī, i. 32 ff., takes over and elaborates the rest of Shāfiʿī's argument, but does not reproduce the linguistic part).—On the other hand, Shāfiʿī in *Tr. III*, 140, ignores a sound philological interpretation given by Mālik.

[2] See above, p. 121.

against a somewhat confused distinction of Mālik (Zurqānī, iii. 256, 265).

Ikh. 73: A clear and vigorous argument, decidedly superior to Ṭaḥāwī's far-fetched counter-argument (i. 241) and to Zurqānī's scholastic reasoning (i. 264).

Ikh. 278 ff.: A masterly discussion with an Iraqian opponent; Shāfi'ī makes the best of a difficult case; he tries, in a rather forced manner, to impose on his opponents unacceptable consequences which they do not really endorse.

Ikh. 292: Excellent systematic reasoning against a Medinese opponent.

Ikh. 327 ff.: Penetrating reasoning; Shāfi'ī discusses the problem of how the contract of *salam*[1] comes to be permitted, a problem not yet envisaged by Mālik in *Muw.* iii. 117.

Ikh. 353 ff.: Shāfi'ī gives excellent systematic reasoning against the Iraqians from his own, new point of view.

Ikh. 389 ff.: Masterly and superior reasoning, more comprehensive and better than the discussion in the earlier parallel passage *Tr. VIII*, 13 (see above).

I shall now leave the last word to Shāfi'ī.

Tr. I, 6: 'If a man buys a slave girl and she has a defect which the seller has concealed from him, the case is the same in law, whether the seller did it wittingly or unwittingly, and the seller commits a sin if he does it wittingly. If, while in the buyer's possession, she acquires another defect and he discovers, too, the existence of the defect originally concealed from him, he is no longer entitled to return her [on account of the concealed defect], even though the defect which she acquired whilst in his possession be the smallest possible defect in a slave. The smallest possible defect, if it existed before the sale and was concealed, would have given him the right to return her to the seller because the existence of such a defect makes the sale binding only if the buyer so wills. So, similarly, the buyer has an equal obligation towards the seller and is not entitled to return her to the seller after the defect which developed whilst she was in his possession, just as the seller was not entitled to hold him bound by the sale of an object which had a defect whilst in the seller's possession. This is the meaning of the *sunna* of the Prophet [which is expressed in a tradition] to the effect that he decided

[1] *Salam* is a sale with postponed delivery of the merchandise but immediate payment of the price.

that a slave was to be returned on account of a defect. If a defect develops whilst she is in the possession of the buyer, he has the right of regress [against the seller] for the amount by which the defect which the seller concealed from him diminishes her [value]. This right of regress works as follows. The value of the slave girl, free of the defect, is estimated and amounts to, say, one hundred; then her value, given the defect, is estimated and amounts to, say, ninety; the relevant value is that of the day on which the buyer took delivery of her from the seller, because on that day the sale became completed. Then the buyer has the right of regress against the seller for one-tenth of her price, whatever it amounted to, be it much or little; if he bought her for two hundred, he has the right of regress for twenty, if he bought her for fifty, he has the right of regress for five. Excepting always the case where the seller is prepared to take her back, free of charge, with the defect she developed whilst in the possession of the buyer; then the buyer is given the choice either to return her or to keep her without a right of regress.'

Tr. I, 12: 'If a man buys a slave or any merchandise with the stipulation that the seller, or the buyer, or both shall have the right of option during a term which they fix, the sale is valid provided the term is three days or less; but if it is longer, even by a single moment, the sale must be rescinded.[1] If someone asks: 'How does it come about that the right of option is valid if it is for three days, but not if it is for more', the answer is: Were it not for a tradition from the Prophet, it would be inadmissible for a right of option to exist for a moment after the two parties to a sale have separated, because the Prophet granted them the right of option only until they separated.[2] For it is inadmissible for the buyer to hand his money to the seller and for the seller to hand his slave girl to the buyer, without the seller being free to use the price of his merchandise and the buyer being free to use his slave girl; if we say that [notwithstanding the right of option] both are free to use their property, [this does not obviate the objection because] we hold at the same time that both must return it if one of them chooses

[1] The gist of the following argument is that a stipulated option is systematically irregular, and thus its time-limit cannot be extended beyond the term of three days which the Prophet is reported to have allowed.

[2] See on this *khiyār al-majlis* above, pp. 159 ff.

the return. It is a fundamental part of our doctrine that it is inadmissible to sell a slave girl with the stipulation that the buyer must not re-sell her, because the seller by this stipulation withholds from the buyer part of the full rights of property, whereas it is fitting that, if he transfers the rights of property for a consideration which he receives, he should transfer the full rights of property. Equally, the stipulation of the right of option constitutes a diminution and a denial of the full rights of property. Were it not for a tradition, a sale with the right of option ought to be invalid on principle, and we consider sales invalid for less than this. But as the Prophet laid down an option of three days from the conclusion of the sale in the case of the *muṣarrāt*,[1] and as it is related that he accorded to Ḥabbān b. Munqidh an option of three days with regard to things he bought,[2] we accept the right of option as far as the Prophet laid it down but no farther, because the Prophet himself did not go farther. His recognition of the option is presumably in the nature of setting an extreme limit to it. For the fact that an animal is *muṣarrāt* is sometimes known after it has been milked for the first time within twenty-four hours, and beyond doubt within two days; if the option in this case were accorded so that one could know for certain whether the animal was a *muṣarrāt*—which is a defect—it is more likely that it would have been accorded for as long as it takes to find out, whether it were long or short, just as the option is accorded in the case of any other defect whenever the buyer discovers it without a limitation, whether the time taken to find out be long or short. And if the option had been accorded to Ḥabbān so that he could consult others, he might have consulted them on the spot or shortly afterwards, or he might have postponed the consultation for a long time. Tradition therefore shows that an option of three days is the extreme limit of an option, and we must not exceed it; whoever exceeds it makes a stipulation which in our opinion makes the sale invalid.'[3]

[1] See above, p. 123.

[2] According to this tradition, Ḥabbān b. Munqidh complained that he was being continually cheated, and the Prophet advised him to say every time he bought a thing: 'No deception!' which would secure him an option of three days. See Ibn Ḥajar, *Iṣāba*, s.v. Ḥabbān b. Munqidh.

[3] This is directed against the Medinese who do not lay down a fixed time-limit for the right of option (*Muw.* iii. 137).

Tr. VIII, 14:[1] 'Weregeld is of two kinds, that for *ʿamd* which is to be paid by the culprit, be it large or small, and that for *khaṭa'* which is to be paid by the *ʿāqila*, be it large or small, because whoever is responsible for the larger amount is also responsible for the smaller. This is, first of all, a sufficient argument in itself, because if the uncontradicted principle in the case of *ʿamd* is that the weregeld, large or small, is to be paid by the culprit, and the principle in the case of *khaṭa'* is that the larger amounts are to be paid by the *ʿāqila*, the same must apply also to the smaller amounts. Further, there is an argument taken from tradition: the Prophet made the *ʿāqila* responsible for the [whole] weregeld in the case of *khaṭa'*; if this were the only relevant tradition it would follow that the *ʿāqila* is responsible for all payments in the case of *khaṭa'*, unless one chose on principle to put the financial responsibility for all injuries on the culprit, and to consider the decision of the Prophet on the responsibility of the *ʿāqila* as [an exception] the limit of which has to be fixed; but if one fixes the limit at one-third, one may as well fix it at nine-tenths or two-thirds or one-half. . . . Abū Ḥanīfa fixes the limit at one-twentieth of the weregeld; the answer to him is the same as to those who fix it at one-third. As to the argument that the smallest amount laid on the *ʿāqila* by the Prophet is one-twentieth of the weregeld, the only consistent way of treating the responsibility of the *ʿāqila* as an exception, based on tradition, and of avoiding analogy altogether, would be to lay on the *ʿāqila* only the full weregeld and one-twentieth of the weregeld, but not the intermediate amounts, leaving them to be paid by the culprit according to the general principle. If analogy is to be used at all, only one of two things is possible: either the lack of a decision by the Prophet on amounts involving less than one-twentieth of the weregeld makes these injuries negligible, without provision for weregeld or retaliation, as strokes and blows are; or these injuries have to be decided by the exercise of systematic reasoning (*ijtihād al-ra'y*) and judged by analogy with those cases on which there is a decision of the Prophet; if this is right, the obligation of the *ʿāqila* to pay the weregeld for *khaṭa'* must also be extended by analogy.'

[1] This passage is directed against the Medinese and Iraqian doctrines on the lower limit for the payment of weregeld by the *ʿāqila*; see above, p. 207.

EPILOGUE

WE have followed the development of Muhammadan jurisprudence from its origins through its formative period to its apex which it reached in Shāfiʿī. What came after him was first a time of consolidation which produced the classical system of legal theory, and then a long period of scholasticism.

The idea we have gained of the formative period is thoroughly different from the fiction which asserted itself from the early third century A.H. onwards. After the work of Goldziher there remained no doubt that the conventional picture concealed rather than revealed the truth; and I trust that the sketch by which I have tried to replace it comes nearer to reality. Beyond the detailed evidence on which this book is based, the coherence of the picture which emerges ought to confirm its essential outlines. Furthermore, our results are in harmony with the general trends of political and intellectual development during the period. Finally, the method which we used for investigating the origins of Muhammadan jurisprudence is equally applicable to the development of positive law. But this is a subject for another book.

APPENDIX I

CHRONOLOGY OF SHĀFIʿĪ'S WRITINGS

In this diagram the uninterrupted lines represent explicit references from one book to another and indications of similar certainty, the dotted lines other probable conclusions on the relative chronology of Shāfiʿī's writings. Two absolute points of reference are the death in A.H. 198 of ʿAbdalraḥmān b. Mahdī at whose request, according to a well-attested statement (Bulqīnī in *Umm*, i. 122, n. 3), Shāfiʿī wrote his *Risāla*, and Shāfiʿī's arrival in Egypt in A.H. 198 (mentioned first in Kindī, 154), an event which accounts for the references to the Egyptian Medinese as 'the people of our country' in his later writings. The earliest reference to Shāfiʿī's death in A.H. 204 occurs in Masʿūdī, *Murūj*, vii. 49 f.

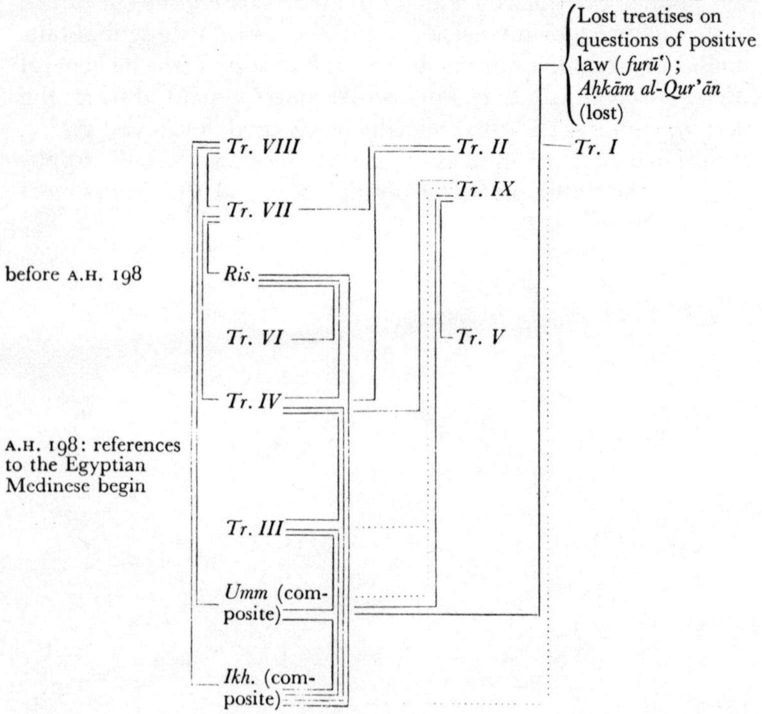

APPENDIX II

LIST OF PARAGRAPHS IN SHĀFIʿĪ'S TREATISES

SEVERAL of Shāfiʿī's Treatises divide naturally into sections or paragraphs, and I found it convenient to refer to these natural divisions of the text rather than to the pages of the printed editions. I therefore give a synopsis of the paragraphs which I have introduced, with the pages and lines on which they begin.

Treatise I

	Umm vii		*Ed. Cairo*			*Umm* vii		*Ed. Cairo*			*Umm* vii		*Ed. Cairo*	
§	*p.*	*l.*	*p.*	*l.*	§	*p.*	*l.*	*p.*	*l.*	§	*p.*	*l.*	*p.*	*l.*
1	87	21	9	2	37	97	13	29	4	73	107	25	54	14
2		23	10	1	38		17		8	74	108	1	55	4
3	88	11	11	2	39		27		16	75		4		8
4		18		6	40	98	4	30	2	76		11	56	1
5		22	12	4	41		12		9	77		15		6
6		32	13	3	42		24	33	3	78		17		8
7	89	20		11	43		30	34	1	79		22	57	2
8		26		15	44	99	2	35	2	80		27	58	1
9	90	2	15	2	45		11	36	1	81		34		7
10		19		11	46		16		6	82	109	6		13
11		30	16	1	47		23	37	1	83		16	59	5
12		34		6	48		29		5	84		23	60	3
13	91	20	17	3	49		31		10	85		30		9
14		28		8	50	101	11	38	4	86	110	1	61	1
15	92	3	18	3	51		22	41	2	87		9		5
16		13	19	1	52	102	21	43	2	88		16	62	4
17		20		5	53		29		8	89		26		11
18	93	1	20	1	54		34		12	90	111	5	63	3
19		20		9	55	103	8	44	5	91		10	64	1
20		33	21	6	56		23		9	92		18		9
21	94	4		11	57		33	45	2	93		25		12
22		15	22	6	58	104	3		7	94		33	65	1
23		22	23	6	59		15	46	3	95	112	11		8
24		33	24	6	60		22		7	96		23	66	4
25	95	7		13	61		27	47	1	97		29	67	3
26		13	25	1	62	105	4	48	6	98	113	5		9
27		20		6	63		13		12	99		20	68	9
28	96	3	26	9	64		22	50	5	100		30	69	1
29		13		14	65		27	51	3	101	114	1		5
30		17	27	3	66	106	5		12	102		7		11
31		22		6	67		8	52	1	103		11	70	2
32		26		9	68		18	53	2	104		18		7
33		32	28	3	69		23		7	105		32	71	6
34	97	1		6	70		29		12	106	115	2		9
35		5		11	71	107	1	54	3	107		10	72	3
36		10	29	1	72		10		9	108		25		12

§	*Umm* vii *p.*	*l.*	*Ed. Cairo* *p.*	*l.*
109	116	1	73	3
110		21	74	5
111		28	75	1
112		31		5
113	117	9	77	1
114		14		9
115		16	78	1
116		24		5
117		34	79	6
118	118	9	80	6
119		16	81	5
120		20	82	1
121		29	83	4
122	119	2		10
123		30	84	6
124	120	7	85	3
125		14		8
126		22	86	3
127		35		12
128	121	19	88	1
129		30	90	5
130	122	6	91	6
131		21	92	3
132		32	93	5
133	123	10		9
134	124	3	95	10
135		17	97	1
136		18		4
137		26		7
138	125	2	98	4
139		10		8
140		18	99	7
141		30	100	8
142	126	11	101	11
143		19	102	6
144		31	103	13
145	127	2	104	4
146		9		10
147		14	105	1
148		17		5
149		22		9
150		28		14
151	128	1	107	1
152		8		7
153		17	108	3
154		22		8
155		28	109	2
156		30		7
157	129	4	110	3
158		28	115	2

§	*Umm* vii *p.*	*l.*	*Ed Cairo* *p.*	*l.*
159	130	20	118	1
160		23		4
161		30		7
162		32	119	1
163		35		4
164	131	7	120	4
165		13	121	1
166		18	122	2
167		25	123	1
168		32	124	1
169	132	1		4
170		12	127	1
171		22	128	1
172	133	7	131	1
173		15		9
174		18	132	1
175		23	133	1
176		27	134	1
177		32	135	1
178	134	10	136	2
179		16		5
180		25	137	3
181		30	138	1
182	135	1	139	1
183		14	140	2
184		20	141	1
185	136	5	142	3
186		9	143	3
187		30	144	4
188	137	6	145	1
189		8		4
190		10	146	1
191		20	147	7
192		27	148	4
193	138	1	149	1
194		10	150	1
195		18	151	1
196		25	152	2
197		32		7
198	139	2	153	3
199		13	156	1
200		17		5
201		25	157	4
202		33	158	4
203	140	4	159	3
204		14	160	2
205		19		6
206		26	161	7
207		32	162	3

§	*Umm* vii *p.*	*l.*	*Ed. Cairo* *p.*	*l.*
208	141	5	163	2
209		17		9
210		21	164	3
211		31	165	1
212	142	13	168	4
213		16		7
214		21	169	2
215		26		6
216		32	170	4
217	143	13	172	1
218		22	174	3
219		26	175	1
220		33	176	4
221	144	9	178	5
222		18	180	1
223		25	181	1
224		31	183	2
225	145	5	186	2
226		16	190	4
227		23	192	1
228		30	193	6
229	146	2	195	1
230		6	196	4
231		12	198	1
232		19		7
233		25	199	1
234		31		5
235	147	12	202	1
236		15	203	3
237		20	204	1
238		26	205	3
239		31	206	4
240	148	1		8
241		3		11
242		6	207	6
243		14	208	5
244		19		9
245		21	209	1
246		28		5
247		32	210	3
248	149	6		6
249		11	212	1
250		13		4
251		18	213	1
252		26	215	3
253		31	216	2
254	150	12	218	2
255		17	220	3
256		26	223	3

Treatise II

§	*Umm* vii *p.*	*l.*
1 (*a*)	151	3
(*b*)		5
2 (*a*)		9
(*b*)		11
(*c*)		15
(*d*)		18
(*e*)		21
(*f*)		23
(*g*)		25
(*h*)		29
3 (*a*)	152	2
(*b*)		6
(*c*)		11
(*d*)		18
(*e*)		21
(*f*)		23
(*g*)		26
(*h*)		29
(*i*)		32
(*j*)	153	1
(*k*)		5
(*l*)		7
(*m*)		9
(*n*)		11
(*o*)		21
(*p*)		29
(*q*)		31
(*r*)		34
(*s*)	154	1
(*t*)		3
4 (*a*)		13
(*b*)		15
(*c*)		18
(*d*)		22
(*e*)		24
(*f*)		30
(*g*)	155	7
5 (*a*)		11
(*b*)		15
(*c*)		17
(*d*)		23
(*e*)		27
(*f*)		30
(*g*)		34
6 (*a*)	156	10
(*b*)		16
7 (*a*)		24
(*b*)		26
(*c*)		29
8 (*a*)	157	2
(*b*)		4
9 (*a*)		9
(*b*)		11
(*c*)		20
(*d*)		30
(*e*)	158	1
(*f*)		4
(*g*)		8
(*h*)		12
10 (*a*)		18
(*b*)		23
(*c*)		26
(*d*)		29
(*e*)		31
(*f*)	159	2
(*g*)		5
(*h*)		9
(*i*)		14
(*j*)		16
(*k*)		23
(*l*)		30
(*m*)		32
(*n*)	160	5
(*o*)		8
(*p*)		20
(*q*)		24
(*r*)		27
(*s*)		29
(*t*)		31
11 (*a*)	161	2
(*b*)		11
(*c*)		17
(*d*)		20
(*e*)		33
(*f*)	162	5
(*g*)		7
(*h*)		10
12 (*a*)		14
(*b*)		16
(*c*)		21
(*d*)		25
(*e*)		28
(*f*)		30
(*g*)		33
(*h*)	163	3
(*i*)		6
(*j*)		9
(*k*)		11
13 (*a*)	163	16
(*b*)		22
(*c*)		26
(*d*)		29
(*e*)		30
(*f*)		34
(*g*)	164	3
(*h*)		5
(*i*)		9
(*j*)		14
(*k*)		21
(*l*)		23
14 (*a*)		27
(*b*)	165	3
(*c*)		7
(*d*)		13
(*e*)		16
15		19
16 (*a*)		28
(*b*)		31
(*c*)	166	4
(*d*)		6
(*e*)		9
(*f*)		13
(*g*)		16
(*h*)		20
(*i*)		21
(*j*)		24
(*k*)		26
(*l*)		27
17 (*a*)		32
(*b*)	167	3
(*c*)		5
(*d*)		7
18 (*a*)		12
(*b*)		16
(*c*)		18
(*d*)		23
(*e*)		27
(*f*)	168	5
(*g*)		10
(*h*)		14
(*i*)		21
(*j*)		24
(*k*)		28
(*l*)		35
(*m*)	169	8
(*n*)		10
(*o*)		15
18 (*p*)	169	19
(*q*)		20
(*r*)		25
(*s*)		32
(*t*)	170	4
(*u*)		7
(*v*)		8
(*w*)		12
(*x*)		16
(*y*)		19
(*z*)		23
19 (*a*)		26
(*b*)		29
(*c*)	171	1
(*d*)		6
(*e*)		14
(*f*)		31
(*g*)		33
(*h*)	172	5
(*i*)		12
(*j*)		14
(*k*)		23
(*l*)		26
(*m*)		35
(*n*)	173	4
(*o*)		10
(*p*)		16
(*q*)		31
(*r*)		34
(*s*)	174	7
(*t*)		12
(*u*)		14
(*v*)		19
(*w*)		22
(*x*)		26
(*y*)		31
(*z*)	175	4
(*aa*)		6
(*bb*)		11
(*cc*)		12
(*dd*)		16
(*ee*)		19
20 (*a*)		29
(*b*)		30
(*c*)		33
(*d*)	176	2
(*e*)		4
(*f*)		6

	Umm vii			*Umm* vii			*Umm* vii			*Umm* vii	
§	*p.*	*l.*	§	*p.*	*l.*	§	*p.*	*l.*	§	*p.*	*l.*
21 (*a*)	176	15	21 (*c*)	176	27	21 (*e*)	176	34	21 (*g*)	177	6
(*b*)		20	(*d*)		31	(*f*)	177	4			

Treatise III

	Umm vii			*Umm* vii			*Umm* vii			*Umm* vii	
§	*p.*	*l.*	§	*p.*	*l.*	§	*p.*	*l.*	§	*p.*	*l.*
Introd.	177	12	37	198	18	76	217	26	113	229	30
1		29	38		26	77	218	9	114	230	3
2	178	3	39	199	9	78		33	115		9
3		12	40		33	79	219	4	116		18
4		18	41	201	2	80		10	117		25
5		29	42	202	8	81		20	118		32
6	179	13	43		10	82		29	119	231	4
7		28	44		17	83	220	14	120		17
8	180	4	45	203	25	84		28	121		25
9		10	46	204	2	85	221	8	122		32
10		25	47		13	86		18	123	232	7
11	181	7	48		24	87		28	124		15
12		21	49	205	2	88	224	12	125		21
13		33	50		15	89 (*a*)		22	126		32
14	182	13	51		25	(*b*)	225	13	127	233	17
15		23	52	206	12	90		30	128		25
16	183	2	53		26	91		33	129		32
17		15	54	207	13	92	226	7	130	234	20
18		31	55	208	5	93		9	131		28
19	184	20	56		12	94		12	132		31
20	186	9	57		31	95		20	133		33
21	187	4	58	209	17	96		30	134	235	5
22		20	59		29	97	227	1	135		18
23	188	31	60	210	10	98		17	136		27
24	189	15	61		28	99		30	137	236	1
25	190	6	62	211	25	100		32	138		8
26		23	63	212	2	101		33	139		13
27	191	15	64		19	102	228	1	140		21
28		34	65		27	103		10	141	237	2
29 (*a*)	192	10	66	213	9	104		14	142		19
(*b*)		22	67		34	105		18	143	238	2
(*c*)		26	68	214	19	106 (*a*)		30	144		20
30	193	15	69	215	4	(*b*)		32	145 (*a*)		33
31	194	27	70		20	107		34	(*b*)	239	8
32	195	26	71		27	108	229	6	146		29
33	196	4	72	216	17	109		10	147	240	7
34		14	73		25	110		13	148		18
35	197	17	74		32	111		20			
36		33	75	217	6	112		26			

Treatise VIII

	Umm vii			*Umm* vii			*Umm* vii			*Umm* vii	
§	*p.*	*l.*	§	*p.*	*l.*	§	*p.*	*l.*	§	*p.*	*l.*
1	277	6	7	284	26	12	289	2	17	299	6
2	279	28	8	285	16	13	290	31	18		21
3		31	9	286	6	14	295	25	19	300	20
4	280	28	10	287	11	15	297	24	20	301	28
5	282	12	11		30	16	298	22	21	302	17
6	283	7									

Treatise IX

	Umm vii		*Ed. Cairo*			*Umm* vii		*Ed. Cairo*			*Umm* vii		*Ed. Cairo*	
§	*p.*	*l.*	*p.*	*l.*	§	*p.*	*l.*	*p.*	*l.*	§	*p.*	*l.*	*p.*	*l.*
1	303	7	1	3	18	316	2	56	6	35	326	27	98	6
2	305	11	13	2	19		24	61	10	36		31	99	6
3	306	7	17	2	20	317	15	63	1	37	327	30	103	2
4		33	22	1	21	318	4	65	3	38	328	5		10
5	307	23	23	6	22	319	2	68	5	39	329	5	107	5
6	310	4	34	7	23		30	70	7	40	330	12	111	2
7		35	37	6	24	320	28	75	4	41	331	15	115	2
8	311	14	39	1	25	321	5	76	10	42		26	117	2
9		24	40	6	26	322	5	79	3	43	332	8	121	2
10	312	6	42	5	27		16	80	7	44		16		12
11		19	43	8	28	323	9	83	4	45		33	124	3
12	313	1	44	9	29	324	5	85	9	46	333	21	126	2
13		11	45	5	30		27	89	9	47	334	8		10
14		26	47	6	31	325	10	90	9	48		25	129	5
15	314	11	49	3	32		23	94	4	49	335	4	130	4
16	315	9	53	6	33		28		10	50		10	131	3
17		25	55	6	34	326	16	96	4					

BIBLIOGRAPHY AND LIST OF ABBREVIATIONS

THE following bibliography contains only works which have been quoted in this book, and does not aim at being complete. I have referred, wherever possible, to paragraphs and not to pages. In quoting *Muw.*, *Muw. Shaib.*, and *Mud.*, I often found it convenient to give only the first page of the whole section in which the reference is to be found.

ARABIC

Abū Dāwūd (d. 275), *al-Sunan* (quoted by chapters).

Abū Ḥanīfa (d. 150), *al-Fiqh al-Akbar*, see *Fiqh Akbar*.

——, *Musnad Abī Ḥanīfa, see* Khwārizmī.

Abū Nu'aim (d. 430), *Ḥilyat al-Auliyā'*, 10 vols., Cairo, 1932–8.

Abū Yūsuf (d. 182), *Ikhtilāf Abī Ḥanīfa wa-bn Abī Lailā*, see Shāfi'ī, *Treatise I*.

——, *K. al-Āthār*, with a commentary by the editor Sheikh Abul-Wafā, Cairo, 1355 (*Āthār A.Y.*).

——, *K. al-Kharāj*, Bulaq, 1302 (*Kharāj*).

——, *al-Radd 'alā Siyar al-Auzā'ī, see* Shāfi'ī, *Treatise IX*.

Aghānī: Abul-Faraj Iṣbahānī (d. 356), *K. al-Aghānī*, 20 vols., Bulaq, 1285.

Ash'arī (d. 324), *Maqālāt al-Islāmīyīn*, ed. Ritter, 2 parts, Istanbul and Leipzig, 1929–30.

Āthār A.Y., *see* Abū Yūsuf, *K. al-Āthār*.

Āthār Shaib., *see* Shaibānī, *K. al-Āthār*.

b. = *ibn*, 'the son of'.

Baihaqī (d. 458), *al-Sunan al-Kubrā*, 10 vols., Hyderabad, 1344–55.

Balādhurī (d. 279), *K. Ansāb al-Ashrāf*, vol. xi, ed. Ahlwardt, Leipzig, 1883.

——, *Liber Expugnationis Regionum*, ed. de Goeje, Leiden, 1866 (*Futūḥ*).

bint = 'the daughter of'.

Bukhārī (d. 256), *al-Jāmi' al-Ṣaḥīḥ* (quoted by chapters).

Comm. ed. Cairo, *see* Shāfi'ī, *Treatises I* and *IX*.

Comm. Muw. Shaib., *see* Shaibānī, *al-Muwaṭṭa'*.

Dāraquṭnī (d. 385), *al-Sunan*, Delhi, 1310.

Dārimī (d. 255), *al-Musnad al-Jāmi'*, or *al-Sunan* (quoted by chapters).

Dhahabī (d. 748), *Tadhkirat al-Ḥuffāẓ*, 4 vols., Hyderabad, 1333–4.

Fihrist: Ibn al-Nadīm (wrote 377), *K. al-Fihrist*, ed. Flügel, Leipzig, 1871.

Fiqh Akbar: al-Fiqh al-Akbar, based on the opinions of Abū Ḥanīfa, with a commentary wrongly ascribed to Māturīdī (d. 333), Hyderabad, 1321.

Ḥamāsa: Abū Tammām (d. 231), *al-Ḥamāsa*, with the commentary of Tibrīzī (d. 502), 4 vols., Bulaq, 1296.

Ibn 'Abdalbarr (d. 463), *al-Istidhkār*, a commentary on Mālik's *Muwaṭṭa'*, MS. Or. 5954, British Museum (used mostly in the quotations given by Zurqānī).

Ibn Ḥajar 'Asqalānī (d. 852), *al-Iṣāba*, 4 vols., Cairo, 1328.

Ibn Ḥajar 'Asqalānī (d. 852), *Tahdhīb al-Tahdhīb*, 12 vols., Hyderabad, 1325–7 (quoted by the numbers of biographies within each volume).
——, *Tawāli l-Ta'sīs*, Bulaq, 1301.
Ibn Ḥanbal (d. 241), *al-Musnad*, 6 vols., Cairo, 1313.
Ibn Hazm (d. 456), *al-Iḥkām fī Uṣūl al-Aḥkām*, 8 vols., Cairo, 1345–8.
Ibn Hishām (d. 218), *al-Sīra*, ed. Wüstenfeld, 2 parts, Göttingen, 1858–9.
Ibn Khaldūn (d. 808), *al-Muqaddima*, vol. i of his *History*, Bulaq, 1284.
Ibn Māja (d. 273), *al-Sunan* (quoted by chapters).
Ibn Muqaffa' (d. about 140), *Risāla fil-Ṣaḥāba*, in *Rasā'il al-Bulaghā'*, ed. Muḥammad Kurd 'Alī, Cairo, 1913, pp. 120–31.
Ibn Qutaiba (d. 276), *K. al-Ma'ārif*, ed. Wüstenfeld, Göttingen, 1850.
——, *Ta'wīl Mukhtalif al-Ḥadīth*, Cairo, 1326 (quoted as Ibn Qutaiba).
Ibn Sa'd (d. 230), *K. al-Ṭabaqāt al-Kabīr*, ed. Sachau and others, 8 vols., Leiden, 1904–17.
Ikh., *see* Shāfi'ī, *K. Ikhtilāf al-Ḥadīth.*
Jāḥiẓ (d. 255), *K. al-Bayān wal-Tabyīn*, 2 vols., Cairo, 1313.
——, *K. al-Ḥayawān*, 7 vols., Cairo, 1323–5.
K. = *Kitāb*, 'The Book of'.
Khaiyāṭ (wrote before 300), *K. al-Intiṣār*, ed. Nyberg, Cairo, 1925.
Kharāj, *see* Abū Yūsuf, *K. al-Kharāj.*
Khaṭīb Baghdādī (d. 463), *Tārīkh Baghdād*, 14 vols., Cairo, 1931 (quoted by the numbers of biographies).
Khwārizmī (d. 665), *Jāmi' Masānīd al-Imām al-A'ẓam*, a collection of 15 versions of the *Musnad Abī Ḥanīfa*, 2 vols., Hyderabad, 1332.
Kindī (d. 350), *The Governors and Judges of Egypt*, ed. Guest, Leyden and London, 1912 (Gibb Memorial Series XIX).
Koran: in the numbering of the verses, I have followed the Egyptian official edition.
Majmū' al-Fiqh, wrongly ascribed to Zaid b. 'Alī (d. 122): *'Corpus Iuris' di Zaid ibn 'Alī*, ed. Griffini, Milan, 1919.
Mālik (d. 179), *al-Muwaṭṭa'*, version of Yaḥyā b. Yaḥyā (d. 234), with the commentary of Zurqānī (d. 1122), 4 vols., Cairo, 1310 (*Muw.*).
——, ——, version of Shaibānī, *see* Shaibānī, *al-Muwaṭṭa'*.
Maqrīzī (d. 845), *al-Khiṭaṭ*, 2 vols., Bulaq, 1270.
Mas'ūdī (d. 345), *Murūj al-Dhahab*, ed. Barbier de Meynard and Pavet de Courteille, 9 vols., Paris, 1861–77.
Mud.: *al-Mudauwana al-Kubrā*, edited by Saḥnūn (d. 240), a collection of opinions and traditions of Mālik, Ibn Qāsim (d. 191), Ibn Wahb (d. 197) and others, 16 vols., Cairo, 1323–4.
Muslim (d. 261), *al-Ṣaḥīḥ* (quoted by chapters).
Muw., *see* Mālik, *al-Muwaṭṭa'*.
Muw. Shaib., *see* Shaibānī, *al-Muwaṭṭa'*.
Muzanī (d. 264), *al-Mukhtaṣar*, on the margin of *Umm*, vols. i–v.
——, *K. al-Amr wal-Nahy*, ed. and transl. Brunschvig, in *Bulletin d'Études Orientales*, Institut Français de Damas, vol. xi, pp. 145 ff.
Nasā'ī (d. 303), *al-Sunan* (quoted by chapters).
Naubakhtī (wrote before 300), *K. Firaq al-Shī'a*, ed. Ritter, Istanbul and Leipzig, 1931.

Ris., *see* Shāfi'ī, *al-Risāla.*

Sarakhsī (d. 483), *al-Mabsūṭ*, 30 vols., Cairo, 1324–31 (quoted as Sarakhsī).

——, Commentary on Shaibānī's *Siyar*, *see* Shaibānī, *K. al-Siyar al-Kabīr.*

Shāfi'ī (d. 204), *K. Ikhtilāf al-Ḥadīth*, on the margin of his *K. al-Umm*, vol. vii (*Ikh.*).

——, *al-Risāla*, Bulaq, 1321 (*Ris.*); ed. Sheikh Aḥmad Muḥammad Shākir, Cairo, 1940 (*ed. Shākir*).

——, *Treatise I* = *K. Ikhtilāf al-'Irāqīyīn*, Shāfi'ī's comments on a work of Abū Yūsuf, comparing the opinions of Abū Ḥanīfa and Ibn Abī Lailā, in Shāfi'ī's *K. al-Umm*, vol. vii, pp. 87–150 (*Tr. I*); separate edition of the work of Abū Yūsuf, *Ikhtilāf Abī Ḥanīfa wa-bn Abī Lailā*, Cairo, 1357 (*ed. Cairo*), with a commentary by the editor Sheikh Abul-Wafā (*Comm. ed. Cairo*).

——, *Treatise II* = *Ikhtilāf 'Alī wa-'Abdallāh b. Mas'ūd*, in Shāfi'ī's *K. al-Umm*, vol. vii, pp. 151–77 (*Tr. II*).

——, *Treatise III* = *K. Ikhtilāf Mālik wal-Shāfi'ī*, ibid., pp. 177–249 (*Tr. III*).

——, *Treatise IV* = *K. Jimā' al-'Ilm*, ibid., pp. 250–62 (*Tr. IV*).

——, *Treatise V* = *Bayān Farā'iḍ Allāh*, ibid., pp. 262–5 (*Tr. V*).

——, *Treatise VI* = *K. Ṣifat Nahy Rasūl Allāh*, ibid., pp. 265–7 (*Tr. VI*).

——, *Treatise VII* = *K. Ibṭāl al-Istiḥsān*, ibid., pp. 267–77 (*Tr. VII*).

——, *Treatise VIII* = *K. al-Radd 'alā Muḥammad b. al-Ḥasan*, Shāfi'ī's comments on a work of Shaibānī, perhaps part of Shaibānī's *K. al-Ḥujaj*, ibid., pp. 277–303 (*Tr. VIII*).

——, *Treatise IX* = *K. Siyar al-Auzā'ī*, Shāfi'ī's comments on a work of Abū Yūsuf, arguing in favour of the opinions of Abū Ḥanīfa against those of Auzā'ī, ibid., pp. 303–36 (*Tr. IX*); separate edition of the work of Abū Yūsuf, *al-Radd 'alā Siyar al-Auzā'ī*, Cairo, n.d. (*ed. Cairo*), with a commentary by the editor Sheikh Abul-Wafā (*Comm. ed. Cairo*).

——, *K. al-Umm*, 7 vols., Bulaq, 1321–5 (*Umm*).

Shaibānī (d. 189), *K. al-Āthār*, Lahore, 1329 (*Āthār Shaib.*).

——, *K. al-Ḥujaj* (?), *see* Shāfi'ī, *Treatise VIII.*

——, *al-Jāmi' al-Ṣaghīr*, on the margin of Abū Yūsuf, *K. al-Kharāj.*

——, *K. al-Makhārij fil-Ḥiyal*, ed. Schacht, Leipzig, 1930.

——, *al-Muwaṭṭa'*, version of Malik's *Muwaṭṭa'*, Lucknow, 1297 and 1306 (*Muw. Shaib.*), with a commentary by 'Abdalḥai Laknawī (d. 1304) (*Comm. Muw. Shaib.*).

——, *K. al-Siyar al-Kabīr*, with the commentary of Sarakhsī (d. 483), 4 vols., Hyderabad, 1335–6 (*Siyar*).

Siyar, *see* Shaibānī, *K. al-Siyar al-Kabīr.*

Ṭabarī (d. 310), *Annales*, ed. de Goeje and others, 13 vols., Leiden, 1879–98.

——, *Ikhtilāf al-Fuqahā'*: the Cairo fragment, ed. Kern, Cairo, 1902 (quoted as Ṭabarī, *ed. Kern*); the Istanbul fragment, ed. Schacht, *Das Konstantinopler Fragment*, Leiden, 1933 (quoted as Ṭabarī, or as Ṭabarī, *ed. Schacht*).

Ṭaḥāwī (d. 321), *Sharḥ Ma'ānī l-Āthār*, 2 vols., Lucknow, 1301–2.

Tahdhīb, *see* Ibn Ḥajar 'Asqalānī, *Tahdhīb al-Tahdhīb.*

Tibrīzī (d. 502), *see Ḥamāsa.*

Tirmidhī (d. 279), *al-Jāmi' al-Ṣaḥīḥ* (quoted by chapters).

Tr. I–IX, *see* Shāfi'ī, *Treatises I–IX.*

Umm, *see* Shāfi'ī, *K. al-Umm*.

Wāqidī (d. 207), *K. al-Maghāzī*, translated by Wellhausen, *Muhammed in Medina*, Berlin, 1882.

Yāqūt (d. 626), *Dictionary of Learned Men*, ed. Margoliouth, 2nd ed., 7 vols., London, 1923–31 (Gibb Memorial Series VI, 1–7) (*Irshād*).

Zurqānī (d. 1122), Commentary on Mālik's *Muwaṭṭa'*, 4 vols., Cairo, 1310.

EUROPEAN

Aghnides, N. P., *Mohammedan Theories of Finance with an Introduction to Mohammedan Law*, 1916.

A.H. = *anno hegirae*; dates are normally given according to the Muslim era.

Becker, C. H., *Islamstudien*, vol. i, 1924.

Bell, R., *The Qur'ān Translated*, 2 vols., 1937–9.

Bergsträsser–Schacht: *G. Bergsträsser's Grundzüge des Islamischen Rechts*, bearbeitet und herausgegeben von J. Schacht, 1935.

Brockelmann, C., *Geschichte der Arabischen Litteratur, Supplementband I–III*, 1937–42.

Caetani, L., *Annali dell' Islām*, 10 vols. in 11 parts, 1905–26.

——, *Chronographia Islamica*, 5 parts [1912–18].

E.I. = *Encyclopaedia of Islam*, 1913–1938; *E.I.*² = new edition, 1960 –.

Goldziher, I., *Muhammedanische Studien*, 2 vols., 1889–90 (*Muh. St.*).

——, *The Principles of Law in Islam*, in *The Historians' History of the World*, vol. viii, 1904, pp. 294–304.

——, *Die Richtungen der Islamischen Koranauslegung*, 1920.

——, *Die Ẓâhiriten*, 1884.

Graf, L. I., *Al-Shāfi'ī's Verhandeling over de 'Wortelen' van den Fikh*, 1934.

Guidi–Santillana: *Sommario del Diritto Malechita di Ḫalīl ibn Isḥāq*, translated by I. Guidi and D. Santillana, 2 vols., 1919.

Islam = *Der Islam*.

J.A. = *Journal Asiatique*.

J.A.O.S. = *Journal of the American Oriental Society*.

Jeffery, A., *Materials for the History of the Text of the Qur'ān*, 1937.

J.R.A.S. = *Journal of the Royal Asiatic Society*.

Lammens, H., *L'Arabie occidentale avant l'hégire*, 1928.

——, *Le Berceau de l'Islam*, 1914.

——, *Études sur le siècle des Omayyades*, 1930.

——, *Fāṭima et les filles de Mahomet*, 1912.

——, *Islām, Beliefs and Institutions*, translated by Sir E. Denison Ross, 1929.

——, *La Cité arabe de Ṭāif à la veille de l'hégire*, 1922.

——, *Le Califat de Yazîd Ier*, 1921.

Marçais, W., *Le Taqrīb de en-Nawawi*, in *J.A.*, 9th series, vols. xvi–xviii, 1900–1.

Margoliouth, D. S., *The Early Development of Mohammedanism*, 1914.

Massignon, L., *Essai sur les origines du lexique technique de la mystique musulmane*, 1922.

Mélanges Dussaud: Mélanges Syriens offerts à M. René Dussaud, vol. ii, 1939, pp. 819–28: Gaudefroy-Demombynes, *Sur les origines de la justice musulmane*.

Migne, *Patrologiae Cursus Completus, Series Graeca* (*Patr. Gr.*).

M.S.O.S. = *Mitteilungen des Seminars für Orientalische Sprachen, Zweite Abteilung.*

Nachr.Ges.Wiss.Gött. = *Nachrichten von der Königlichen Gesellschaft der Wissenschaften . . . zu Göttingen.*

O.L.Z. = *Orientalistische Literaturzeitung.*

Procksch, O., *Über die Blutrache bei den vorislamischen Arabern*, 1899.

Querry, A., *Droit musulman, recueil de lois concernant les musulmans schyites*, 2 vols., 1871–2.

R.S.O. = *Rivista degli Studi Orientali.*

de Sacy, A. I. Silvestre, *Traité des monnaies musulmanes, traduit de l'Arabe de Makrizi*, 1797.

Santillana, D., *Istituzioni di Diritto Musulmano Malichita*, 2 vols., 1926–38.

Sitzungsber. Wien = *Sitzungsberichte der Kaiserlichen Akademie der Wissenschaften in Wien, Phil.-hist. Classe.*

Smith, W. Robertson, *Kinship and Marriage in Early Arabia*, new ed. by S. A. Cook, 1903.

Snouck Hurgronje, C., *Mohammedanism*, 1916.

——, *Verspreide Geschriften* (*Gesammelte Schriften*), 6 vols., 1923–7 (*Verspr. Geschr.*).

Tyan, E., *Le Notariat et le régime de la preuve par écrit dans la pratique du droit musulman*, 1945.

——, *Histoire de l'organisation judiciaire en pays d'Islam*, 2 vols., 1938–43.

Wellhausen, J., *Das Arabische Reich und sein Sturz*, 1902.

Wensinck, A. J., *A Handbook of Early Muhammadan Tradition*, 1927.

——, *The Muslim Creed*, 1932.

Z.D.M.G. = *Zeitschrift der Deutschen Morgenländischen Gesellschaft.*

INDEXES

INDEX OF LEGAL PROBLEMS

Cult, Ritual, Dietary Laws

Major ritual ablution before the Friday prayer, 145.
Masḥ ʿalal-khuffain, 263 f.
Prayer without recitation of the Koran, 154 f., 181.
Time of morning prayer, 142.
Imprecations (*qunūt*) in ritual prayers, 60, 267 f.
Witr prayer, 134.
Funeral prayer, 152.
Prayer over the tomb, 165.
Starting fast in a state of major ritual impurity, 153.
Breaking the fast inadvertently, 157.
Fasting during pregnancy, 113.
Fasting in expiation of breaking the fast of Ramadan by intercourse, 142.
Use of perfume before assuming the status of a pilgrim, 155.
Breach of state of ritual consecration during pilgrimage, 247.
Marriage concluded by a pilgrim, 153.
Ishʿār of sacrificial animals, 112.
'Sacrifices cannot be shared', 180.
Eating lizards, 146.

Fiscal Law

Zakāt tax, 73, 167.
  on property of orphans, 143, and of minors, 216 f.
  on horses, 199.
  deducted from government pensions, 199 f.
  on debts, 284 f.
Assignments on government stores, 200.
Tolls, 201.
Minting fees, 67.

Obligations in general

'Muslims must abide by their stipulations', 174, 181.
'No damage and no mutual infliction of damage', 183 f.
Duress, 180, 235.
Vis maior, 112, 315.
'Profit follows responsibility', 123, 181, 270.
Declaratory and constitutive statements, 298.
Contracts concerning an unknown quantity, 293.
Conditions which cannot be ascertained, 294.
'Who joins a people belongs to them', 180.

Sale

Earnest money, 186. [256.
Khiyār al-majlis, 64, 159 ff., 167, 184,
Stipulated option, 299, 326 f.
Sale of bales by specification, 64.
Defects in merchandise sold, 325 f.
Sale of a *muṣarrāt* animal, 123, 327.
Responsibility for object sold with right of option, 270 f.
Usury, defined, 251.
  transactions involving it considered invalid, 273. [67.
  increasing strictness of prohibition, Mālik's attitude, 67, 313.
  outside Islamic territory, 287.
  exchange of precious metals, 67.
Sale of meat for meat, &c., 67.
Sale of animals for animals, 108.
Sale of animals with anticipated payment and deferred delivery, 146.
Re-selling before taking possession, 108, 200 f., 296, 313.
Sale of fruit before it is ripe, 104.
Uncertainty (*gharar*), 64.
Mulāmasa and *munābadha* contracts, 144.
Muzābana contracts, 153 f.
Sale of *ʿarāyā,* 153 f., 312.
Sale of dogs, 216.

Other Contracts and Obligations

Salam contract, 145 f., 325.
Mukhābara contract, 54.
Muzāraʿa contract, 299.
Loan of slaves with restitution in kind, 118.

Negligence of the depository, 296 f.
Security (*rahn*), 186 f., 272. [272.
Gift of an undivided share in property,
ʿ*Umrā* and *suknā*, 220 f.
Amiable settlement, 272.
Pre-emption, 61, 155, 164 f., 219 f., 271 f. (twice), 293.
Foundlings, 161.
Manumission, right of *walāʾ*, *muwālāt*, 161 f., 173.
Mukātab slave, 111 f., 173 f., 279 ff.
Mudabbar slave, 265 n. 8.
Umm al-walad, 264 ff.

Family Law

Donatio propter nuptias, 107 f.
Marriage without a *walī*, 182 f.
Marriage of a free man to a slave woman, 312.
Presumption of intercourse, 313.
Ownership of household chattels, 278 f.
Divorce before consummation of marriage, 193 f.
Death of husband before consummation of marriage, no *donatio propter nuptias* having been fixed, 226 f.
'Definite' divorce, 195 ff.
Triple divorce pronounced in one session, 146, 196 f.
Gift to wife in case of divorce, 101 f.
Offer of divorce, 215.
Oath of abstinence (*īlāʾ*), 215 f. [211.
Effect of disappearance on marriage,
Waiting period of divorced wife or widow, 181 f.
of a pregnant widow, 225 f.
domicile of divorced wife or widow during waiting period, 197 f.
rights of divorced wife during waiting period, 225.
Mutʿa marriage, 266 f.
Paternity, 181 f.
in case of *liʿān*, 94.
Foster-parentship, 48, 194 f., 216, 246 f.
Illegal intercourse as impediment to marriage, 268.

Inheritance and Legacies

Right of the killer to inherit, 159.
Share of the grandfather, 66, 212 f.
Slave in law of inheritance, 184 f.
Legacies restricted to one-third of estate, 201 f.
Acts of a person during mortal illness, 320.

Penal Law

Lex talionis and execution of murderers, 208.
Murder by guile, 154.
Choice between weregeld and retaliation, 55.
Retaliation, conditions for its application, 308 f.
Criminal intent (ʿ*amd*), defined, 308 n. 2.
of the minor, 218, 308 f., 316.
'Talion depends on the weapon', 185 f.
Retaliation for broken fingers, 68.
Lex talionis, whether applied to several culprits for one victim, 111.
Husband and wife have no share in matters of talion, 292.
Amount of weregeld in gold and silver, 145.
Weregeld of a woman, 217 f.
of a slave, 281 f.
of non-Muslims, 148, 205 ff.
Responsibility of the ʿ*āqila* for weregeld, 207, 328.
Method of payment of weregeld, 207.
Compensation for fingers of a woman, 79 f., 117.
for a molar, 114.
for teeth, 117.
for lips, 117 f., 125.
Damages for wounds inflicted on a slave, 221 f.
Injury caused by an animal, 185.
Ḥadd punishments, 208 ff.
in the army, 209 f.
territorial limits of their applicability, 209, 286, 298.
to be restricted as much as possible, 184, 235, 285.
prescription and repentance, 126.
whether to be applied in the mosque, 162.
Adultery and fornication, 53 n. 4, 73 f., 106, 191 n. 5, 209.
'*Ḥadd* punishment and *donatio propter nuptias* cannot go together', 235 f.
Slander (*qadhf*), 285.
Wine-drinking, 75, 126, 191 n. 5.
Theft, 107, 191, 261, 297 f.
by a fugitive slave, 208 f.

Conversion as theft, 149.
Non-Muslim slave who escapes to the enemy, 208.
Punishment of witches, 164.
Ta'zīr punishment, 104.
its limits, 218.

Procedure and Evidence

Procedure, 73, 187.
Evidence of witnesses, 188.
Good character of witnesses, 300.
Divergencies in evidence of witnesses, 274.
Evidence of witnesses on testimony of other witnesses, 274.
Evidence of one witness together with oath of plaintiff, 167 ff., 187 f., 311 f.
of one woman on feminine matters, 51.
of minors, 218.
of non-Muslims, 147, 210 f.
Acknowledgment made out of court, 272.
Indivisibility of acknowledgments, 293.
Presumptions, 271, 293.
Written documents, 188.
Judgement against an absent party, 273.
Official correspondence between judges, 291.
Res iudicata, 292 n. 4.

Law of War, Conversion to Islam

Unbelievers shielding themselves behind Muslim infants, 227.
'The spoils belong to the killer', 70 f., 180.
Booty, 108 f., 113, 205.
taken by a private raider, 286.
Remuneration of women and minors, 261.
Laying waste enemy country, 144 f., 204 f.
Taking food from enemy country, 67, 285 f.
Concubinage with captive women, 277 f.
Slaves and other property captured by the enemy and recaptured from them, 158 f.
Musta'min, whether liable to *ḥadd* punishments, 286.
Conversion to Islam gives title to property, 218.
its effect on previous marriages, 276 f. (twice).

Administration

Dīwān, the state register or pay-roll, 60 n. 5, 205, 207.
Currency, 203 f.
Grants of uncultivated land, 202 f.
Seals of lead for identifying slaves and tax-payers, 291.

GENERAL INDEX

'Abdallāh b. Dīnār (d. 127), traditionist, 256. Alternates with Nāfi' in *isnāds*, 163.
'Abdalmalik, Umaiyad Caliph (65–86), 168, 194, 203 f., 218, 225, 244.
Abū Ḥanīfa (d. 150), Kufian, 6, 239. His interest in traditions, 33. His legal reasoning, 270 ff., 284 ff., 294 ff. Disciple of Hammād, 238 f. Heard 'Aṭā', 250.
Abū Yūsuf (d. 182), Kufian, 7. His attitude to traditions from the Prophet, 28. His interest in traditions, 33. His legal reasoning, 270 ff., 284 ff., 301 ff. His alleged books on the theory of law, 133.
Administrative practice as a source of law, 58 f., 60 n. 5, 63, 68, 70, 72, 74, 76, 78, 114, 191, 193, 198 ff., 205, 207, 209 f., 211 f., 216 f.
Ahl al-kalām, *see* Mu'tazila.
'Alī, Caliph (35–40), authority of the Iraqians, 31. Traditions from him typical of the Iraqian opposition, 240 ff. Lack of Shiite bias in Iraqian traditions from 'Alī, 242, or in Medinese traditions with Shiite imams in their *isnāds*, 263, 268.
Ancient schools of law, 6 ff. Their doctrine essentially the same, 21, 27, 75 f., 82, 87. Bases of their doctrine, 42. Apparent inconsistency of their doctrine, 21, 26, 32, 38 f., 60, 67, 74, 103 f. Their attitude to *mursal* traditions, 38 f. Consensus of the scholars their final argument, 42 f. On the defensive against traditions from the Prophet, 43, 47 f., 57, 63 n. 2, 80, 96. Put their doctrines under the aegis of individual Companions, 25, 31 f., 43 f., 66. Take their knowledge from the 'lowest source', 69, 77, 157. Their legal reasoning, 275 ff., 283 ff.
'Aṭā' b. Abī Rabāḥ (d. 114 or 115), Meccan, 7, 87, 160, 167, 173 n. 3, 185 n. 2, 250 f., 279 f.
Auzā'ī (d. 157), Syrian, 34 f., 48, 70 ff., 119, 277 f., 285 ff., 288 f.

Balkhī (Ka'bī) (d. 319), Mu'tazilite, 259.
Basrians, 8, 83, 85 f., 104, 219, 229.

Caliph, his authority in law according to Ibn Muqaffa', 59, 95, 102 f. His *ijtihād*, according to Mālik and Rabī', 116. His personal opinion, according to 'Umar b. 'Abdal'azīz, 119. Caliphs and 'living tradition', according to Auzā'ī, 34, 70 ff. His decisions irrelevant in law, according to Shāfi'ī, 59.
Caliphs, the first, 18, 24 f., 30, 62, 70, 167, 193.
Civil war, the end of the 'good old time', 36 f., 71 f.
Classical theory of Muhammadan law, 1, 11, 43, 77, 94, 132, 133 ff., 137.
Codification, 59, 95.
Common transmitters of traditions, 171 ff.
Companions (of the Prophet), traditions from them, according to Shāfi'ī, 16 ff. According to the Medinese, 23 f., 26. According to the Iraqians, 29 f. Statistics, 22. Earlier than traditions from the Prophet, 20, 30. Later than traditions from Successors, 33. Later than 'practice', 63. Not authentic as a rule, 66, 150, 169. Their doctrine cannot be reconstructed, 169 f.
of Ibn 'Abbās, 250, 266 n. 5; of Ibn Mas'ūd, 232 f.
Consensus, in the classical theory, 2, 94 f. In the ancient schools and in Shāfi'ī, 82 ff. Small minorities not taken into account, 259.
Custom and practice as a source of law, 64 f., 67, 70 f., 75, 147, 192 ff., 219 f., 277, 285 f., 288 f., 292, 294, 312, 314, 318.

Darāwardī (d. 187 or 189), Medinese, 7, 168, 174, 195, 245.

Egyptians, Egyptian Medinese, 9, 69, 100 ff.

First century, authentic doctrines dating from it, 60, 100, 142, 234, 245.
'Five legal categories', 133 f., 136 n. 5, 284.
Foreign influences, 83, 95, 99 f., 182, 186, 187 n. 2, 216, 268 n. 4.

Ḥammād b. Abī Sulaimān (d. 120), Kufian, 187 n. 4, 236 ff.
Ḥanafī school, 6, 29 n. 4, 85, 239, 306, 310.
Ḥasan Baṣrī (d. 110), authority of the Basrians, 87, 229. His dogmatic treatise, 74, 141.

Ibn 'Abbās (d. 68), Companion of the Prophet, authority of the Meccans, 249 ff.
Ibn Abī Dhi'b (d. 158), traditionist, 54 f., 65, 181, 206, 256.
Ibn Abī Lailā (d. 148), judge in Kufa, 7, 161 f., 209 n. 2, 210 f., 239 f., 270 ff., 284 f., 290 ff., 300.
Ibn Mas'ūd (d. 32 or 33), Companion of the Prophet, authority of the Kufians, 31, 231 ff. His doctrine coincides with that of the Prophet, 29.
Ibn Muqaffa' (d. about 140), secretary of state, 58 f., 95, 102 f., 129 n. 3, 137.
Ibn Musaiyib (d. 93 or 94), authority of the Medinese, 7, 27, 87, 114, 243 ff.
Ibn Qāsim (d. 191), Medinese, 314 n. 4. Edits Mālik's opinions, 118. Influenced by Shāfi'ī, 115 f., and by Shaibānī, 222.
Ibn Qutaiba (d. 276), traditionist, 257. Misrepresents Naẓẓām, 128. His attitude to human reasoning in law, 129.
Ibn 'Umar, son of the Caliph 'Umar (d. 73 or 74), authority of the Medinese, 25, and of the Iraqians by imitation, 32. Spurious nature of traditions transmitted from him by Nāfi', 176 ff.
Ibn 'Uyaina (d. 198), traditionist, 256. Practises *tadlīs*, 37. Tradition in praise of the 'scholar of Medina' put forward in his name, 174.
Ibn Wahb (d. 197), Egyptian Medinese, 85.
Ibrāhīm Nakha'ī (d. 95 or 96), authority of the Kufians, 7, 33, 86 f., 105, 233 ff. His traditions from Ibn Mas'ūd, 31, 39, 234. Authentic opinions, 60, 142.
***Ijtihād*, originally = discretion, estimate, 48, 105, 116. Use of individual reasoning (*ijtihād al-ra'y*), 99, 105 f., 115, 130. Use of analogy, 127 f. Later meanings, 132.**
Iraq, first centre of Muhammadan jurisprudence, 223.
Iraqians, theoretical bases of their doctrine, 27, 109 f. Their interest in traditions, 27. Their method of interpreting traditions, 28, 30, 47 f. Recognize traditions from the Prophet as authoritative, 28. Put their doctrine under the aegis of the Prophet, 75 f.; see also *Sunna* of the Prophet. Their inconsistency with regard to *mursal* traditions, 39. Their arguments against traditions from the Prophet, 46 ff. Their authorities among Companions, 31 f., and among Successors, 32 f. Their inconsistency in polemics, 74. Their inconsistency with regard to consensus, 85, 87. Their inconsistency with regard to individual reasoning, 103 f. Their legal theory more highly developed than that of other schools, 29, 76, 87, 105, 133. Their legal reasoning, 275, more highly developed than that of the Medinese, 276 ff.
Isnād, defined, 3. Its origin, 36 f. Technical terms concerning *isnāds*, 36, 38. Interference with *isnāds* by *tadlīs*, 37. *Isnāds* put together carelessly and arbitrarily, 54, 163 ff. The most perfect *isnāds* the latest, 39, 165. Analysis of the *isnād* Mālik–Nāfi'–Ibn 'Umar, 176 ff.

Ja'far b. Mubashshir (d. 234), Mu'tazilite, 259.
Judges and judgements, 54 f., 64 f., 68 f., 78, 100 ff., 103 f., 105 f., 121, 127, 131, 161 f., 168, 187, 191, 193, 209 n. 2, 210 f., 228, 239 f., 272 ff., 290, 292, 294, 300, 305.

Khabar, khabar lāzim (*yalzam*), 27, 110, 122, 129 n. 3, 136.

Khabar al-khāṣṣa, khabar al-wāḥid, defined, 41.
Khaiyāṭ (d. about 300), Muʿtazilite, misrepresents Naẓẓām, 128. Expresses the later attitude of the Muʿtazila, 259.
Koran, subordinate to traditions, 15 f. A criterion for traditions, 28, 30, 45 f. Koran and *sunna*, 46 f. Its study without traditions dangerous, 53. Its rules often disregarded at the beginning, 181, 188, 191, 224 ff.
Kufians, 32 f. List of representatives, 7. Their main *isnād*, 231 f., 234, 237, 239. Authorities and scholars outside their main *isnād*, 228 f., 230 f., 242. *See also* Iraqians.

Mālik (d. 179), Medinese, 6 f. His imperfect knowledge of the biography of the Prophet, 23 n. 5. Practises *tadlīs*, 37. His inconsistency with regard to *mursal* traditions, 39. His slender link with Nāfiʿ, 176 f. His legal reasoning, 312 ff. His *Muwaṭṭa'*, 6 f., 69. His personal contacts with Zuhrī, 246.
Mālikī school, 6 f., 25, 48, 69, 85, 248, 314.
Marwān b. Ḥakam, Umaiyad governor and Caliph (64–5), often mentioned in traditions concerning Umaiyad practice, 114, 192 f., 195, 197, 200, 221.
Meccans, 8, 161, 173 n. 3, 186, 249 ff. List of representatives, 7.
Medina, fictitiously considered home of true *sunna*, 8, 53, 76, 84. Its local consensus a provincialism, 83 f., 93. Hereditary transmission of knowledge in Medina denied, 69, 84. Tradition in praise of the 'scholar of Medina', 174. Medina not the starting-point of Muhammadan jurisprudence, 223. 'Seven lawyers of Medina', 243 ff.
Medinese, list of representatives, 7. Their interest in traditions, 22 f., 26. Their method of interpreting traditions, 23. '*Sunna* of the Prophet' originally not a Medinese concept, 62, 76. Their arguments against traditions from the Prophet, 46, 48. Their attitude to them not more favourable than that of the Iraqians, 57. Their authorities among Companions, 25, and among Successors, 243 ff. Charged with inconsistency by Shāfiʿī, 79. Not less given to individual reasoning than the Iraqians, 114 f. 'Islamicizing' the law not their monopoly, 213, 284. Influenced by the Iraqians, 76, 106, 185 f., 220 ff., 241, 249, 275. Their legal reasoning, 276 ff., 285 ff. *See also* Egyptians.
Muʿāwiya, Umaiyad Caliph (40–60), often mentioned in traditions concerning Umaiyad practice, 55, 114, 155, 192, 196 n. 2, 199, 206 f., 212.
Muhammad, *see* Prophet.
Muhammadan law and jurisprudence, defined, v. Development outlined, 57, 66 f., 80, 94 f., 98, 188 f., 190 f., 213 f., 222 f., 228, 237, 240 f., 256, 260, 269 f., 275, 283 f., 287 ff., 290, 294, 306, 310, 314, 317 f., 329.
Mujāhid (d. after 100), authority of the Meccans, 114 n. 8. Main transmitter from Ibn ʿAbbās, 162.
Mujtahid, defined, 99. His reward, 96 f. Whether right or wrong, 96, 128. Later restricted meaning of term, 132.
Mursal traditions, 36, 38 f. Older than traditions with full *isnāds*, 39.
Muʿtamir b. Sulaimān (d. 187), traditionist, 56, 131.
Muʿtazila, called *ahl al-kalām* by Shāfiʿī, 41, 128. Their hostility to traditions, 40 f., 44 ff. They demand that traditions be 'widely spread', 51 f., 88. Agree with Iraqians in particular, 46, 47 n. 5 and 7, 88. Hostile to disagreement, 95. Their interest in legal theory and positive law, 258 f. Their later attitude, 259. Not taken into account for establishing a consensus, 259.
Muzanī (d. 264), disciple of Shāfiʿī, 6, 282.

Nāfiʿ (d. about 117), freedman of Ibn ʿUmar, 177. Authority of Mālik, 176 f. Alternates with Sālim, ʿAbdallāh b. Dīnār, and Zuhrī in *isnāds*, 163. Character

of traditions that go under his name, 177 f. Traditions ascribed to him not uniform and spurious, 178 f. Not a representative of school of Medina, 179.
Naẓẓām (d. after 220), Mu'tazilite, 88, 128.

Projecting doctrines back into the early period, 66, 70, 156 f., 165, 232, 236 f., 238.
Prophet Muhammad (d. 11), imitating his personal tastes, 49. Knows best how to interpret the Koran, 53. Traditions from him, *see* Traditions.

Qāsim b. Muhammad (d. 106), authority of the Medinese, 113, 117, 243 ff.

Rabī' (d. 270), originally an Egyptian Medinese, then converted by Shāfi'ī, 13. His reasoning incompetent, 314.
Rabī'a b. Abī 'Abdalraḥmān (d. 136), Medinese, 54 f., 114 f., 247 f. Alternates with Yaḥyā b. Sa'īd in *isnāds*, 164.
Repeal, according to Shāfi'ī, 15. According to the ancient schools, 46, 48. According to the traditionists, 46 f.

Sālim, son of Ibn 'Umar (d. about 106), authority of the Medinese, 113, 117. Alternates with Nāfi' in *isnāds*, 163. Traditions under his name transmitted in written form, 177 n. 4.
Scholars whose opinions count, 82, 84, 89, 94, 97, 113, 120, 127. Specialized scholars, 93. Their doctrine expresses the 'living tradition' of the school, 68 f., 70, 75. Their consensus, 42, 82 f., 85 f., 88 ff., 94, 96. It is mostly anonymous, 84, 86.
Sha'bī (d. 110), worthy of Kufa, 87, 230 f. Several groups of traditions put under his name, 131, 203 n. 4, 231, 241.
Shāfi'ī (d. 204), considers himself a member of the school of Medina, 9 f. His prejudice against the Iraqians, 10. Development of his doctrine, 10, 12, 20, 79 f., 88 ff., 120, 282. His inconsistencies, 14 f., 18 f., 38 f., 111, 122, 126, 134, 323 f. His debating devices, 11, 17, 21, 43 n. 1, 44, 52, 83 n. 1, 87 f., 93 n. 5, 109, 117, 324 f. His lack of objectivity, 321 ff. Accepts the thesis of the traditionists, 55, 253, 256, but not of their extremists, 57, 254. Argues against traditionists, 254. His method of interpreting Koran and traditions, 13 ff., 20, 56, 323 f. His lenient standards with regard to traditions, 37. His carelessness about *isnāds*, 38. His personal achievements in legal theory, 56, 77, 134. His doctrine an innovation, 59, 79, 93 n. 4, 97, 122. His prejudice against personal opinion, 113, 121. His main assumptions, 136. General characteristic of his doctrine, 137. His legal reasoning, 270 ff., 284 ff., 315 ff. Represents the zenith of Islamic legal thought, 287, 315 ff., 324 ff.
Shāfi'ite school, 6. Differs occasionally from Shāfi'ī's final doctrine, 282.
Shaibānī (d. 189), Kufian, 6, 10. His interest in traditions, 34. His inconsistency with regard to traditions, 32, 38. His legal reasoning, 270 ff., 284 ff., 306 ff.
Shuraiḥ, legendary judge of the first century, 228 f.
Sources of law, according to the ancient schools, 42. According to Shāfi'ī, 134 ff. According to Tabarī, 136 n. 1. According to the classical theory, 1 f., 135.
Spurious information on ancient authorities, 65, 69, 78, 85, 93, 113 f., 117, 130 f., 151, 159, 194 n. 1, 195, 222, 229 ff., 235 f., 244 ff., 264.
Successors (of the Companions), traditions from them according to Shāfi'ī, 20, 123. According to the Medinese, 26 f. According to the Iraqians, 32 f., 109. Statistics, 22, 33. Earlier than traditions from Companions, 33. Mostly fictitious, *see* Spurious information.
Sufyān Thaurī (d. 161), Kufian, 7, 205, 242, 286.
Sunna, the old concept, defined, 58. Called an innovation by Shāfi'ī, 60. Survival of the old concept, 80. Expressed in a tradition, 151.

according to Shāfi'ī, 77. Synonymous with traditions from the Prophet, 77 f. *Sunna* and Koran, 46 f. Traces of the old concept in Shāfi'ī, 79 ff.
in the classical theory, defined, 2 f. The equivalent of the Koran, 148.
of the Prophet, rare in ancient Medinese texts, 62. In Auzā'ī, 70. Originally an Iraqian concept, 73 f., 75 f.
a term for 'recommended', and its ambiguous use, 133 f.
Syrians, 9. Influenced by Iraqians, 76, 119. *See also* Auzā'ī.

Ṭaḥāwī (d. 321), a Ḥanafī, his method of interpreting traditions, 30, 48.
Taqlīd, 6, 18.
Traditionists, 253 ff. Their criticism of traditions, 36. Not embarrassed by spurious traditions, 37. Their polemics in favour of traditions from the Prophet, 46 ff., 54 ff. Ignorant of law, 54, 129, 257, and inferior to members of ancient schools, 254. Their extremists, 57, 254. They try to change doctrines of ancient schools, 66, 144, 178, 184. Disparage human reasoning in law, 130 ff. Connected with Medinese opposition, 255. 'Islamicizing' the law not their monopoly, 255 f., 283 f.
Traditions, defined, 3. Their classical corpus, 3. Their character, 4. Current opinion regarding them, 57, 138. 'Isolated' traditions, 28, 50 ff. Science of traditions, 36 n. 1. Criticism of traditions on material grounds, 37 f., 45. Traditions from the Prophet an innovation, 20, 30, 40, 57, 59, 61, 63, and later than the 'living tradition', 80. Their gradual introduction into the ancient schools, 43. Recognized as authoritative by the Iraqians, 28. Regarded as co-extensive with the Koran, 53. Opposed to *sunna* by the Medinese, 61 f., and by the Iraqians, 73, 75. Opposed to 'practice' by the Medinese, 63 ff., and by the Iraqians, 75. Opposed to the 'living tradition' of the Medinese, 68. Their growth parallel with the development of doctrine, 66 f., 79, 159. A means of influencing the doctrine of a school, 66, 178, 215 f., 225 ff., 240 ff., 246 f., 249, 255, 263 f. Identified by Shāfi'ī with the *sunna* of the Prophet, 77. Traditions concerning the biography of the Prophet, 139, 153, 204, 267, 276, 301, 322. 'Mythological' traditions, 45 n. 3, 146, 256. Legal traditions from the Prophet not authentic, 149. Traditions from Companions of the Prophet, *see* Companions. From their Successors, *see* Successors.

Umaiyad period, part of the 'good old time', 71 f.
'Umar, Caliph (13–23), an authority of the Medinese, 25, and of the Iraqians, 32. His instructions to judges, 104.
'Umar b. 'Abdal'azīz, Umaiyad Caliph (99–101), often mentioned in traditions concerning Umaiyad practice, 62, 71 n. 3, 101, 119, 131, 144, 161, 167 f., 183, 192, 195, 199, 201, 205 f., 208 f., 217 n. 3, 285. Representative of the fictitious 'good old' practice, 34, 70, 192. His orders for recording traditions and *sunnas*, 62. His instructions against uniformity, 96. Consulted by a judge, 101. Restricts the right of the Caliph to personal decisions, 119. Disclaims legislative initiative, and follows traditions from the Prophet, 131, 144. References to him fictitious, 206.
'Uthmān, Caliph (23–35), often mentioned in traditions concerning Umaiyad practice, 153, 192, 196 n. 2, 198, 200, 204, 206 n. 5, 207, 211 f., 285.

Yaḥyā b. Sa'īd (d. 143), Medinese, 248. Alternates with Rabī'a in *isnāds*, 164.

Zuhrī (d. 124), Medinese, 24, 115, 244, 246 f. Alternates with Nāfi' in *isnāds*, 163. Traditions attributed to him, 175, 246. Credited with spurious opinions, 246.

ADDENDA

P. 8: The earliest reference to Medina as the 'true home of the *sunna*' of which I know occurs in a non-legal work, the *Sīrat Rasūl Allāh* of Ibn Hishām (d. 218), p. 1014 (ed. Wüstenfeld), in a tradition which Ibn Hishām attributes to the work of his predecessor Ibn Isḥāq (d. 150 or 151) as edited by Ziyād b. ʿAbdallāh Bakkāʾī (d. 183). The attribution to Ibn Isḥāq ought not to be accepted without reserve, and Caetani has already pointed out the difference in style between the tradition in question, which in any case is not authentic, and the fragment of a genuine quotation from Ibn Isḥāq, concerning the same events, which precedes it immediately in the text of Ibn Hishām (*Annali*, ii/1, year 11, § 36). The context shows that *sunna* in the passage in question has a meaning sensibly different from *sunna* as understood in the ancient schools of law, let alone the '*sunna* of the Prophet'. The parallel tradition in Ṭabarī (d. 310), *Annales*, i, 1820, the *isnād* of which by-passes Ibn Isḥāq, represents a re-formulation in the light of the then prevailing ideas. Even if the tradition should have originated in the first half of the second century A.H. (because the lowest common transmitter in the two versions is Zuhrī), the time-lag before the concept of Medina as being the 'true home of the *sunna* of the Prophet' entered legal discussion is significant.

P. 29, n. 4: Even Ibn Taimīya (d. 728) uses the argument that the Companions of the Prophet would have known best the intentions of their master (see, for example, G. Hourani, in *Studia Islamica*, xxi (1964), 36); this represents a return to the position of the ancient schools from that of the Traditionists, and shows how deeply ingrained that idea was.

P. 37: Criticism of traditions on material grounds. It was said of Abū Muṣʿab al-Anṣārī: 'If he were a Companion that (particular) tradition would be sound because its *isnād* going back to him is sound; now the authorities on *ḥadīth* have judged that this text is unsound; therefore we must conclude that he is not a Companion.' (Ibn Ḥajar al-ʿAsqalāni, *Lisān al-Mīzān*, Hyderabad 1331, vi, No. 1143.)

P. 58: On the whole of this and of the following chapter, cf. R. Brunschvig, 'Polémiques médiévales autour du rite de Mālik', *Al-Andalus*, xv (1950), 377–435.

P. 67, n. 3: On the question of minting fees, see further Qurṭubī (d. 671), *al-Jāmiʿ li-Aḥkām al-Qurʾān*, on Koran ii, 275 (Cairo 1933 ff., iii, 351 f.); ʿAlī b. Yūsuf al-Ḥakīm (wrote 749–59), *Regimen de la Casa de la Moneda*, ed. H. Monés, Madrid 1960, 100.

P. 70: The legal maxim 'the spoils belong to the killer' appears in the form of a tradition from the Prophet, with two imperfect *isnāds*, in the work of Ibn Isḥāq, as quoted by Ibn Hishām (p. 848), but both Abū Ḥanīfa and Abū Yūsuf disregarded it, and Abū Yūsuf disdainfully upbraided Auzā'ī for accepting it as evidence of a 'valid *sunna* going back to the Prophet'. It appears with a full *isnād* for the first time in Mālik.

P. 74: The term '*sunna* of the Prophet' occurs also in the statement which 'Abdallāh b. Ibāḍ sent to the Umayyad Caliph 'Abdalmalik, at his command, about the year 76, and which has been preserved in the *Kitāb al-Jawāhir* of Barrādī (lithogr. Cairo 1302, 156–67). The term is used always in conjunction with a reference to the Koran, and it does not refer to authoritative acts of the Prophet, and hence definitely not to traditions. The *sunna*, the norm to be followed, comes directly from Allah, and the '*sunna* of the Prophet' consists in following the Koran. Cf. J. Schacht, 'Sur l'expression "*Sunna* du Prophète" ', in *Mélanges Henri Massé*, Teheran 1963, 361–5.

P. 143: Another tradition originating between Abū Ḥanīfa and the classical collections is the saying: 'Prayer behind every man, be he of good or bad behaviour, is valid.' This originally controversial principle of orthodox Islam, which goes back to the Umayyad period, is pronounced by Abū Ḥanīfa as his own statement, in answer to a question, in the *Fiqh al-Absaṭ* (*al-'Alim wal-Muta'allim*, followed by two other treatises, ed. Muḥammad Zāhid al-Kautharī, Cairo 1368, 52); it appears as a tradition from the Prophet for the first time in Abū Dāwūd (*ṣalāt* 63; Wensinck, *Creed*, 221). A similar statement with regard to the holy war occurs in Bukhārī (*jihād* 44) not as a tradition but only as part of Bukhārī's comments. The putting into circulation of traditions concerned in the first place with defining the community of Muslims and with other points of dogma (traditions which were, on the whole, earlier than those concerned directly with religious law), continued well into the second century A.H.; cf. J. Schacht, in *Oriens*, xvii (1964), 116; see also A. Guillaume, in *J.R.A.S.*, Centenary Supplement, 1924, 234; F. Nau, in *J.A.* ccxi (1927), 313 and n. 2.

P. 176: On the fictitious character of the *isnād* Mālik—Nāfi'—Ibn 'Umar, see J. Schacht, in *Acta Orientalia*, xxi (1953), 292 f.

P. 177, n. 2: Darāwardī used not only his own notes but *cahiers* of the collected traditions of others (*kutub al-nās*), and he made mistakes in reading from these (Ibn Ḥajar al-'Asqalānī, *Tahdhīb*, vi. 677).

P. 194: Opposition against the extension of the effects of foster-relationship by the doctrine of the *laban al-faḥl* was voiced not only in Medīna but in Iraq, where it was attributed to Ibrāhīm Nakha'ī

(*Āthār A.Y.* 669). It is difficult to say whether this attribution is genuine; if it is, the opinion of the school of Kufa must have changed between Ibrāhīm and Abū Ḥanīfa (cf. *Muw. Shaib.* 275).

P. 244: The 'Seven Lawyers of Medina'. Ibn al-Nadīm (wrote 377) attributes to Ibn Abil-Zinād (d. 174; cf. above, p. 7) a 'Book on the *ra'y* of the seven lawyers of Medina and their points of difference' (*Fihrist*, p. 225, ll. 28 f.). According to Ibn Ḥajar (*Tahdhīb*, vi. 353), Ibn Abil-Zinād derived his 'Book of the seven (lawyers)' from his father. But according to the same Ibn Ḥajar (iii. 807, on the authority of Aṣma'ī), Ibn Abil-Zinād singled out three persons as the prominent scholars of Medina, according to Dhahabī (A. Fischer, *Biographien von Gewährsmännern*, 46) he singled out four, and both short lists contain names outside the group of Seven. I therefore regard the reference in the *Fihrist* as Ibn al-Nadīm's description, in the terms of his own time, of the work, and not an exact quotation of its title as formulated by the author. R. Brunschvig, in *Al-Andalus*, xv (1950), 399, refers to 'Abd al-Raḥmān b. Zaid b. Aslam (d. 182; *Tahdhīb*, s.v.) who, according to Ibn Ḥazm (*Iḥkām*, ii. 113), composed a book in which he collected the opinions 'on which the seven lawyers of Medina, to the exclusion of others, agreed, but this only amounted to a few pages'. As the person in question is known only as an exceedingly unreliable traditionist and not as a Mālikī scholar (he occurs neither in the *Dībāj* of Ibn Farḥūn nor in the *Shajarat al-Nūr* of Muḥammad Makhlūf), I am not prepared to accept this statement as authoritative. The *Mudawwana*, iv. 8, refers to the opinion of 'the seven' and enumerates them painstakingly one by one 'together with other authorities among their equals' (*ma'a mashyakha siwāhum min nuẓarā'ihim*); it is possible that the idea of the group of the 'seven lawyers' started from this passage.

P. 246, n. 4: Ibrāhīm b. Sa'd was born in A.H. 108 and died between 182 and 185, and doubt was thrown on the traditions which he related from Zuhrī because he was too young when he heard them from him (Ibn Ḥajar al-'Asqalānī, *Tahdhīb*, i. 216).